Parenting in a Multicultural Society

Parenting in a Multicultural Society

Edited by
Mario D. Fantini
René Cárdenas

*This study was made possible through a grant
from the Lilly Endowment to BCTV*

New York and London

PARENTING IN A MULTICULTURAL SOCIETY

Longman Inc., New York
Associated companies, branches, and representatives
throughout the world.

Developmental Editor: Lane Akers
Production Editor: Joan Matthews
Cover Design: Dan Serrano
Manufacturing and Production Supervisor: Robin B. Besofsky
Composition: Southern Graphic Arts, Inc.
Printing and Binding: BookCrafters Inc.

Library of Congress Cataloging in Publication Data
  Main entry under title:

Parenting in a multicultural society.

  Bibliography: p.
  Includes index.
  1. Parenting–United States–Addresses, essays, lectures. 2. Parenting–
Study and teaching–United States–Addresses, essays, lectures. 3. Pluralism
(Social sciences)–Addresses, essays, lectures. 4. Minority youth–United
States–Addresses, essays, lectures. I. Fantini, Mario D. II. Cárdenas, René.
HQ755.8.P38   649'.1   79-24658
ISBN 0-582-28144-X

Manufactured in the United States of America
9 8 7 6 5 4 3 2 1

Acknowledgments

Figure 1.1 on p. 5 adapted from "Macrostructural Influences on Child Development and the Need for Childhood Social Indicators" by Orville Brim and Urie Bronfenbrenner. Copyright © by the American Journal of Orthopsychiatry. Reprinted by permission of the publisher.

Quotation on p. 6 from *Pluralism in a Democratic Society,* ed. by M. Tumin and W. Plotch. Copyright © 1977 by M. Tumin and W. Plotch. Reprinted by permission of Holt, Rinehart and Winston.

Quotation on p. 6 from "What Do We Know About Parents and Teachers" from *Theory Into Practice* by I. J. Gordon. Copyright © 1972 by Ohio State University College of Education. Reprinted by permission of the publisher.

Quotations on p. 7–8 from *The Status of Children* by K. Snapper et al. Copyright © 1975 by George Washington University Social Research Group. Reprinted by permission of the publisher.

Figures 1.2 on p. 8, 1.3 on p. 9, 1.4 on p. 12, and 1.5 on p. 13 from *America's Children,* pp. 32 and 55, published by the Coalition for Children & Youth, 815 15th St. NW, Washington, DC 20005. Reprinted by permission of the publisher.

Quotation on p. 10 from E. Ferri, *Growing up in a One Parent Family.* Copyright © 1976 by NFER Publishing Company.

Quotation on p. 29 from *Child Development and Personality* by Paul Henry Mussen, John Jay Conger, and Jerome Kagan. Copyright © 1969 by Harper & Row, Publishers, Inc. Reprinted by permission of the publisher.

Quotation on p. 47 from *The Family and Human Adaptation* by Theodore Lidz. Copyright © 1963 by International Universities Press, Inc. Reprinted by permission of the publisher.

Quotation on p. 50 from *Lay My Burden Down: A Folk History of Slavery* by Benjamin Botkin. Copyright © 1958 by The University of Chicago Press. Reprinted by permission of the publisher.

Quotation on p. 61 from *Deficit, Difference, and Bicultural Models of Afro-American Behavior* by Charles A. Valentine. Copyright © 1971 by Harvard Educational Review. Reprinted by permission of the publisher.

Quotation on p. 67 from *Young Native Americans and Their Families: Educational*

Needs and Assessment by Harriet K. Curffaro, Susan Ginsberg, Gordon Mack, Winona Sample, Edna Shapiro, Doris Wallace, and Herbert Zimiles. Copyright © 1976 by Bank Street College of Education. Reprinted by permission of the publisher.

Quotations on pp. 68 and 73 from *The Hopi Child* by Wayne Dennis. Copyright © 1940 by Hawthorn Books. Reprinted by permission of the publisher.

Quotation on page 68 from a court transcript cited in *The Law of the People: A Bicultural Approach to Legal Education for Navajo Students,* Volume 3, published by the Ramah Navajo School Board. Quoted in Unger, Steven, Editor. *The Destruction of American Indian Families.* New York: Association on American Indian Affairs, 1977.

Quotation on p. 128 from "Racial Outlook: Lack of Change Disturbs Blacks," by Roger Wilkin, September 28, 1979. Copyright © 1979 by The New York Times Company. Reprinted by permission.

Quotation on pp. 133–134 from *Intelligence, the University and Society* by Kenneth B. Clark. Copyright © 1966 by Kenneth B. Clark. Reprinted by permission of the author.

Table 10.1 on p. 154 and Table 10.2 on p. 155 from Yankelovich, Skelly, and White, Inc., *The General Mills American Family Report 1976–77.* Reprinted by permission of the publisher.

Quotation on p. 157 from *Family in Transition,* ed. by A. S. Skolnick and J. H. Skolnick. Copyright © 1971 by Little, Brown and Company. Reprinted by permission of the publisher.

Quotation on p. 191 from *Psychology Applied to Teaching* by Robert F. Biehler. Copyright © 1978 by Houghton Mifflin Company. Reprinted by permission of the publisher.

Figure 13.1 on p. 196 based on Hierarchy of Needs in "A Theory of Human Motivation" in *Motivation and Personality,* 2nd edition by Abraham H. Maslow. Copyright © 1970 by Abraham H. Maslow. Reprinted by permission of Harper & Row, Publishers Inc.

Summaries/interpretations on pp. 242–243 from *All Our Children: The American Family under Pressure* by Kenneth Keniston and the Carnegie Council on Children. Copyright © 1977 by Harcourt Brace Jovanovich, Inc. Printed by permission of the publisher.

Quotations on pp. 215–216 from "The Origins of Alienation" by Urie Bronfenbrenner. Copyright © by *Scientific American,* August 1974. Reprinted by permission of W. H. Freeman & Company Publishers.

Contents

Foreword

René Cárdenas

Some eighty years ago, dramatist and social critic Bernard Shaw very smartly observed that the most arduous of normal human activities is the bearing of children; the most important, he argued, is the rearing of them. Shaw spent the larger portion of his next thirty years attempting to dissuade women from doing either, unless handsomely paid for their services. The remaining time and energy he spent attempting to persuade society to pay up.

Shaw's plays, it is obvious today, were generally better attended than were his political critiques. Americans, at any rate, appear unshakable in their conviction that outright remuneration necessarily dishonors *any* relation between man and woman, but especially the marriage relation. Payment, we apparently believe, implicitly cheapens motherhood as well as its product, though nowhere in either the Protestant ethic or the spirit of capitalism do we find reason for withholding our dollars from lawyers, doctors, or the clergy.

Consequently, women have, until now, shown the utmost perseverance (and occasional enthusiasm) in assuming the role of wife and mother, despite all the hazards of the job and personal restrictions such a constant occupation has traditionally entailed. Until now, that is, women have accepted motherhood as the natural, if not inescapable, conclusion to womanhood—a correlation which the nonprofessional status of motherhood has meant all the while to imply. Had housewifery been historically a salaried position, it would presently share the status and character of other salaried positions: It would be a situation of choice, assumed according to individual inclination and talent rather than ascribed (self-evidently, God-givenly) by gender. But, as persistently as women have married, men have doggedly married them, at the same time recruiting into the female marriage force a surplus—and, therefore, the cheapest—of laborers. They have done so by quite cunningly maintaining the opposite of fact: by referring to their feminine helpmates as "priceless," "precious," or simply "dear," and by sophistically equating housewifery with the idle, and the idle, as sophistically, with the Good.

Still, women have come to see through it all that to be a mother is not always to be a housewife, to be a housewife is seldom to be idle, and that to be treated as precious is most often to be penniless, immobilized, and weak. In ever-increasing numbers, they have taken the choice to be ministers, truckers, shopkeepers, lawyers and/or wives; to be wives and/or mothers. Of those who have chosen to bear children, more than 45 percent are working; their children will be reared substantially by other women, the children's fathers, or other men. Of those women who have chosen to become wives, 30 percent will become single again through divorce; over 11 million of their children will be reared in one-parent (mother- *or* father-headed) homes.

As women's self-image has expanded and altered, so too has the supporting framework of their children's development. As mothers go out further into the professions, more and more professionals enter the family home: Where once there was mother, Dr. Spock, and an occasionally visiting pediatrician to bring up baby, there are now social scientists, social workers, psychologists, and counselors, too. What once was named "mothering" is the less restricted phenomenon less restrictively known as "parenting" today.

Yet an elementary question persists: Has our attitude toward the actual process of child-bearing and rearing in any way changed to reflect the change in its participants and terms? It seems not. As reluctant as we have been either to pay mothers for their motherly service or to admit them into regularly paying jobs, we shrink from guaranteeing support—even self-supporting work—to parents. Such guarantees would, of course, mean insurance not after, but against unemployment, underemployment, and the general counter-employment practices currently threatening minority parents, single parents, and every other "special" parent except the exceptionally rich.

We do not, in short, make it easy for parents—both parents or the one single parent—to work. Part-time jobs seldom if ever carry proportionately partial wages and almost never carry any real job security or benefits. Flexible work schedules, even within a forty-hour work week, are rare; pregnancy leaves are brief, taken often at the expense of seniority, and sometimes costing mother or father the job.

On the other hand, if we make it difficult for parents to work, we make it quite impossible for them not to. Day-care centers, without question a growing business, are far from a fully effective, even adequate public service. To many families—particularly to those "special" families—they are geographically as well as financially out of reach. So, too, health care. Federal, state, and community agencies have neither the time nor the personnel to provide satisfactory *and affordable* preventive or remedial services to the average family—nor certainly, once again, to the "special" family with children of special needs.

This anthology is intended to ask why we have refused to support our nation's families, and is designed to suggest ways we might someday accede. Before we even venture our primary question, however, let us answer one we are bound to meet. No: those social scientists, social workers, educators, psychologists, and counselors mentioned above may well administer to very real needs, but they are not the support services contemporary families still lack. They are to true support, true maintenance systems, what remedy is to prevention or adult compensatory schooling is to Head Start. They dress the wounds a family suffers when its own inner strengths—its own parenting functions—have failed.

What we consistently withhold and our lawmakers, with apparent insistence, leave unplanned are state and federal policies empowering families to sustain themselves. Why, for example, do we institute free breakfast programs in our schools, while never thinking to assure each child an adequate diet at home? Why do we provide the few clinics we can, but balk at educating parents to the nutritional needs of their young or to a few medicinal procedures such as any layperson might perform? Why, that is, do we close our fists on an ounce of prevention, while spending billions each year—in the courts, hospitals, and police houses—on pounds and pounds of often too late, too little cures?

For some reason, our nation (one of the wealthiest and, in respect to the basic care of its citizens, *the* stingiest in the West) will not pay for its most integral parts and products, that is, its children. Nor will it finance the implementation of policies ensuring against the collapse of its most essential institution of parenthood.

The reason cannot be that we simply haven't the funds. We do have the revenue, but quite evidently see fit to spend the bulk of our monies elsewhere, despite the obvious fact that there cannot be in any society an investment (by definition) more generative than parenting. Indeed, when we speak of "parenting," we speak politely of the very intimate act of producing children. But, we speak also more broadly of rearing them into adulthood, of reproducing our future citizens as well as the society they will populate. Clearly, then, the act of parenting may well be an intimate one, but, inasmuch as the state of the family is the state of the nation today and to come, its effects must be of national concern.

Therefore, research into the health and hygiene issues of parenting, for instance, may bring us to a maternal act as private as breast feeding. However, it will bring us further, too: among such factors as the *custom* of breast feeding, cultural dietary habits, national food production and distribution, and finally the interfunction of them all.

Thus family issues become public matters—potential matters of policy and eventual political issues. And, thus we are brought to a second common argument against public support for parenting, which in itself seems to involve one or both of two common myths—wives' tales, if you will. The first myth presents the home as sort of shrine to the Madonna of Housewifery and sanctuary to the ruling *Pater Noster Familias*; the second, more courtly than sacred but to similar effect, identifies the family home as its eldest male inhabitant's castle. Each myth, in the name of individual freedom, protects against federal, state, or local officials intruding upon the familial domain. Each myth, in short; pretends that political actions taken outside the home have no consequence within it. The notion is, of course, patently absurd. It demonstrates the badly false logic of a rugged individualist—read "white, patriarchal"—ideology that simultaneously endows and emasculates men. Every "castle," in fact, is a fief within a larger fiefdom; every "king," the pawn of a more powerful king—that is, a knave of higher class, status, and political pull.

So: what is felt in the home—in every home but the whitest and richest—may appear to be sourceless and senseless frustration, but its origin is really out there: in an imbalance of wealth and the tax system that promotes it; in inflation and the dollar's decay; in bigotry of every sort, violence of every type, and a growing population of battered children and wives.

Those of us who fear government encroachment are not foolish in our fear, but we are foolish in our naive surety that to keep big government out of our homes is to keep them free from all the politics of power. We are daily touched, and touched hard, by forces beyond our control. And we recoil with the impotent yet savage anger roused by political hegemony, by a rudimentary imbalance of power and the basic, indispensable rewards it brings.

It is a common theory that recognizes insensible control. It is a practice of the strong, the white, the male, and the rich, however, to keep that theory only and to keep their own strength unchallenged. The anger floods downward. Those who must bear it are the weakest among the weak: wives and children—and, increasingly, children's victims, too. This a brutal age of brutalized and brutalizing children. According to multicited statistics, over 28 million wives last year were battered by their husbands, and 2 million youngsters were battered by their parents. Last year, American school children responded in kind: they committed 100 murders, 9,000 rapes, 204,000 aggravated assaults, and 12,000 armed robberies. The National Institute for Education, following a three-year study, has reported that each month 5,200 secondary school teachers are physically attacked and 6,000 are robbed by threat or force. In addition, 282,000 junior and senior high school students are attacked at school each month and 112,000 are robbed.

Chances are, those 2 million battered children will batter their children, and those children will multiply in murderers, rapists, and robbers—legatees of unjust parenting in an uncaring world.

We appear to spend far more on our own surplus defenses against but speculative alien threats than we are willing to spend protecting our young against such real and imminent dangers as poverty, hunger, disease, ignorance, and parental incompetence or outright abuse. That the United States is the only technologically advanced country in the world today without a national child-care program for working parents or health-care program from families with young children has brought charges from more than one critic that it is not the family that is destroying itself, but the indifference of the rest of society. And even these critics may be too circumspect to strike their target dead-center.

At present, there is no benign neglect nor is there withholding without colossal cost. With determination, indifference, or misguided goodwill, American society seems resolved to preserve its traditionally hierarchical structure at the expense of its families, its children, and (eventually) itself.

Let us be more precise: To preserve our most powerful "patriots"—here read, politicoes and patriarchs—we will act our own victims. We will sacrifice ourselves—all lesser fathers, mothers, and off-spring—to the false image of each man as his own god and separate king. We will sacrifice, too, the ideals of democracy to the idols of autocracy and notions of hereditary right.

This anthology begins to address the concerns of millions of parents across the country who want to care for their children and who are genuinely asking assistance, but from a society apparently as uncaring of its young as it is without child care or health care for its families. American society, that is, withholds from its parents the policies, laws, and funds supportive of them for the same apparent reason it has always withheld payment from mothers and wives. We want the total parenting process to seem as natural and instinctual as the act by which it began. We want parents, that is, to be nonprofessionals. Moreover, we want *every* family characteristic to appear biological—not social, artificial, or, in effect, eradicable. Thus, down through the generations pass ignorance, unemployment, and poverty: each inherited trait as "natural," "typical," "inborn" as black skin, almond eyes, jet hair.

Now, let us be honest. For all America's worrisome talk of becoming a "welfare state," do we really love our poor only enough to keep them that way? Do we want to keep our "special" families—like our "precious" women—penniless, immobile, and weak? Or, can we support them with money? Do we recognize their well-being as a right, instead of doling out welfare as a begrudging gift? Would we make every parent a professional parent, and every exercise in parenting a success?

Do we do any of these things? Do we establish parent-training programs in communities nation-wide? Do we assure that the right of each new generation of parents to learn from their elders is a matter of choice, not chance or necessity? No, not as yet. As a result, parenting skills do indeed appear inadequate to the daily demands of advanced industrialization. Instead of adapting familial situations to the contemporary conditions outside, or enriching the environment of childhood growth to enhance future states of maturity, these parents cannot but perpetuate the conditions in which they grew up, nurturing or not. Nor can this society but perpetuate (and ultimately ossify amid) its own outmoded ways, so long as it continues to identify the "natural" with the "normal," and the "normal" with the white, middle- and upper-class, male-dominated clan.

In the mid-1950's, the Supreme Court of Chief Justice Earl Warren confronted school administrators with a simple yet near-revolutionary pronouncement: Separate is *not* equal in a truly democratic system. Today we must presume a similarly radical courage to extend the Warren Court's vision, and not only examine the familial superstructure, but perhaps even challenge the entire social infrastructure upon which it rests. We must be prepared, in short, to admit that if separation disallows equality, assimilation does not make for equality either.

Those writing for this anthology do have the courage it takes to be honest. They do not write "nontraditional" and imply "grotesque." These investigators do not variously examine Asian-American, black American, and Mexican-American parenting processes to diagnose them indifferently "nonwhite" and, therefore, inherently dispossessed. Nor do they perceive the single father as "surrogate," "substitute mother," or the single-parent family, in general, as the mutant consequent of death or divorce. These researchers know the variety of paternal and maternal roles played throughout the world as well as this nation. And so, they know there is no single set, assigned by sex, but a plethora of *parenting* roles undetermined by any gender: "mothering" fathers here are freed to be the true parenting figures they are, and mothers are freed from the scapegoat guilt for all their children's ills.

However varied their perspectives, methods, and personal opinions, the writers for this anthology concur on one critical fact: A truly pluralistic society such as our own can have no single model, type, or even ideal. Aware that "tradition"–like any standard or rule–suggests an arbitrary dominance and power, they look beyond tradition's norm to study families in themselves and in vital relation with each other. They look beyond the "nonwhite" to see a black family as black in itself, and as it negotiates its social course through the particular straits constraining blacks today. They look, too, beyond the accidentally matrifocal family, beyond the patriarchy-gone-awry. These writers can conceive of a single-mother unit, an unmarried-mother family, a lesbian home: They can conceive, that is, of a family fatherless yet fully intact.

As well as radical courage, the contributors to this anthology demonstrate the radical generosity of true researchers. Willing to prepare for policies of real power sharing, they will *not* advocate the "giving" of power to the people, the families, the groups under study. For these men and women know that the ability to *give* implies a power of its own: To "give power" is a logical impossibility–unless the gift is made outright, once and for all.

This anthology prepares to challenge not only the patriarchy, but also its national character, the unbounded paternalism that doles power to citizen and foreign country alike in the way a father doles out his child's weekly allowance. The writers here represented look toward policies that will *empower* individuals as well as individual families to sustain for themselves quality life, and to preserve for others the equality and integrity necessary to it. Paternalism will thus be proven as outmoded as the patriarchal system that fosters it; with traditionalism will fall predominance, domination, and the privileged position of the "typical" white, middle-class *familia americana*. For, these writers will show that the distribution of power, its wealth, and the social peace they can together bring begins in respect: in, that is, absolute–not relative–respect. It begins in the respect every person, family, and group is granted–not for its approximation of the American family image or its assimilation of the American dream–but for the very distinction and diversity that identify one United States of vastly different ethnic kind.

The articles collected in these pages are, in short, as open-ended, their view-points as varied as the pluralistic society they address. No one here points to a disintegrating family unit, announcing: "This is the origin of social decay," or, "This is the innocent victim of decadence." In fact, no one here points and claims, "This is *the* American family," at all. Each recognizes instead as many types of American family as there are races, nations, and religions comprising one United States; each recognizes, too, common problems all families share and special problems particular ethnic groups are made to confront on their own.

To deny the virtue of the model American family, or to withhold judgment on its social role, is not to underestimate the part actual families play in the structure and style of American life. True, when these commentators prove brash enough to ask, at the really critical moment in contemporary history, just what "family" is in crisis, we become suddenly aware that *there is no typical American family to rule the typical American dream*. And, in a minute, like the dapper emperor laid bare by a little girl, the American ideal must itself be scrutinized without familial trappings.

Still, if reality has exposed a basic weakness in our ideal—as well as in the ideal family, church, and school—we cannot hope to diagnose the ailment without removing the old dressings that now enwrap it mummy-wise. And if this anthology seems to disavow the one and model family, it is because those actual American families—currently living through their own and the nation's crises—are, in truth, as varied as their members who comprise one manifold culture called the United States. To these diverse families—in all their ethnic distinctions, customs, and traditions—this anthology addresses itself, not with tolerance but with the true reverence they individually deserve.

There is no "American family." There was, however, a *mythical* American family, just as there was a mythical American state, identified as a "melting pot." Just real enough to be affected by this country's newest phase of constantly accelerating progress, its molecules have correspondently accelerated, until the "melting pot" of national unity has become a potential cauldron of intestinal ferment and broil—in which the myth that produced it itself has dissolved. Having failed to spill forth "Americans"—identically treated *and* individually empty of all ancestral memory but that of a unified history, heritage, and language of one United States—it continues to wear away nonetheless all ethnic claim, all the special properties and traditional qualities once celebrated by its diverse inhabitants.

Social inequality still exists, supported by the racial discrimination and ethnocentricity that attend it. The majority of American families live in a state of constant confusion, within an evanescent world of perpetual uncertainty. "Home Sweet Home" has been razed and replaced by high-rise apartments or high-cost condominiums, serving only as temporary resting places for "highly mobile"—rootless—Americans. The social changes taking place since the days of the Depression have nearly obliterated the extended-family concept, once the basis of social unity in this country. The nuclear family, stripped by industrial capitalism of its productive value, has taken on the awesome responsibility of providing a sole locale of psychic recuperation and retreat from the anxious marketplace—from the center of commercial life that simultaneously determines and denies the family's worth. Father no longer knows best; the Lawrence family weekly survives crises that would have left Anderson or Nelson family in shards. But, how do those allowed only to visit these "typical" homes in "typical" white, middle-class neighborhoods manage to survive at all? How can those without equal representation, education, or rights hope to win a niche in society presently closed to them, or preserve the familial home as traditionally defined? In a torrent of societal changes, the common future eludes their grasp, as a private heritage falls away beneath their feet.

The Asian-Americans, black Americans, Mexican-Americans, native Americans, and Puerto Rican-Americans of today—like the Irish, Italians, and Jews before them—are caught in a cultural drift, more rightly termed a cross-fire. Subject to all the explosive influences bombarding the family, they are subject also to all the family's own corrosive influence upon the communal values and customs that lend ethnic kinship's systems their integrity and life. And they are subject, too, to all the demoralizing stigmata marking those excluded from "the family album."

Anxious to advance, today's poor ethnic family often finds itself only "rootless"; upward mobility, in a life of economic and educational handicap, is a vision as unreal as the model to which all are urged to conform. Anxious to provide retreat from the business world that refuses its members profit or partnership, today's ethnic family is attacked as "counterproductive," "dysfunctional," if not "pathological."

The essays in this anthology are not attacks; their authors understand that the matrifocal black family, for instance, is not "pathologically" emasculating. It is not "pathological," at all. To the contrary, it may well provide the single means of maintaining a black family unit in the midst of an overtly unsupportive, covertly hostile, and fundamentally pathogenic white society. The matrifocal black family, in short, is one American family established to meet real crises and currently suffering a crisis of its own. It is only one type of family represented here: one among the many types of family observed in themselves as well as in relation to other family structures and the social system at large.

If any attack is here made, it is made against "the family" in order to save families. If one idea does constitute the common denominator of this varied collection, it is the highly complex realization that the American family is fast disappearing because it does not exist: To preserve American families will require us first to dispel "the family" myth. This is not to say that the authors of these essays want the American family structure to die. Quite the opposite: They want a vital social system, nurturing all its members equally, to thrive. Yet, they know that no such system survives in changing times by remaining rigid; they know the family, always an abstract entity, must be newly perceived, not as the static model it was made, but as the living mode it really is: as an arrangement of kindred elements, as manifold as the society outside and various as the individual members within. These writers do have an ideal vision of a vigorous and truly humane state. And, they are determined to see it finally coincide with a realistic image of the American nation, as it exists in contemporary circumstances.

There is no question that a link does exist between societal and family crises, however that link is formed. Nor, is there any question that the converse is equally true: The survival of American society will be intimately involved in the survival of its family unit—whatever form that unit may take. Whether or not the nuclear family remains the dominant family structure, the family system will most likely remain the determinant transmitter of social values, morals, ethics, and allegiances. And the state of tomorrow's family will undoubtedly reflect the state of society at large. It will not, however, reflect the family of yesterday, or the one we see presented on commercial television and in the popular press today.

Even at this moment, the National Center for Education informs us, approximately 28 million persons in the United States, including about 5 million school-age children, have mother tongues other than English or live in households in which languages other than English are spoken. About two-thirds of all these persons and more than four-fifths of the school-age children are native born. The number is still growing.

The current overall population of the United States (218 million people) will double in the next 116 years. The population of Latin America (344 million), on the other hand, will double in just 26 years—and for *every* 26 years after that. Consequently the almost zero population growth among white Americans is expected to be offset by an unprecedented birth rate within and equally unprecedented influx from the Latin community.

As a result, the population of New York City is expected to double within the next twenty years. By the year 2000 it will have reached 22.2 million. Detroit, by then, will have a population of 8 million; Chicago, 12 million. The population explosion in American cities, and rural districts as well, is foreseen as unparalleled since the World War II "baby boom." Its effects will be without parallel absolutely. For this "boom" will not simply enlarge the most common American family units; it will radically transform their ethnic makeup, traditional orientation, economic condition, and racial hue. The dominant family trait will be the character of servitude and submission —of poverty, ignorance, crime, addiction, and disease—unless planned changes make today's institutions answerable to the minority groups of yesterday, to the American majority of tomorrow.

The authors of this anthology are prepared for tomorrow: they are prepared to redefine the family continually and according to its true composition, knowing that the family fit to be so named will be the families that truly survive. The focus of this anthology is, therefore, upon the one universal and indispensable family factor: parenting. As the biological basis of every family unit, parenting takes no special talent: as the production of children, it is an originally instinctive act and natural process. But, as the sociological foundation of the American nation, as the nurturing of wholly productive future adults, parenting is an art and a skill, which like every talent, must be itself nurtured, exercised, and trained. That is what ultimately makes this anthology the really invaluable contribution to us all that it is: It provides the very necessary background and prepares for the very vital development of a public policy designed to make parenting the reasoned, caring, and rewarding performance it can be—a performance to be played out within a family of actors, well cast in their roles and equipped with a script well adapted to the contemporary stage of their world.

About the Authors

Terrel H. Bell, Commissioner of Higher Education for the State of Utah, has served as United States Commissioner of Education, Utah State Superintendent of Public Instruction, and as a Superintendent of Schools in Idaho, Wyoming, and Utah. He is the author of *Active Parent Concern* (Prentice-Hall) and *Your Child's Intellect* (Olympus Publishing Co.).

Elizabeth L. Bowen serves on the staff of the Gesell Institute of Human Development in New Haven, Connecticut. She is a consultant in Nutrition and Preventive Health.

Tobias Brocher, M.D., originally Ordinarious at the Justus Liebig University in West Germany, is now Distinguished Professor of Applied Behavioral Sciences at the Menninger School of Psychiatry. He founded and developed the "School for Parents" movement in West Germany in 1954 which expanded to various European countries. He is the author of "Eine kleine Elternschule" and numerous articles, books, and TV series on child development and parent education.

Bill J. Burgess, President of Native American Research Associates, Inc., has worked exclusively within the Native American community since 1963. He has served as a consultant, teacher, administrator, lecturer, and writer. In his research efforts, he has participated in numerous projects, including a 1975–1976 national study to determine the educational and health needs of native-American children ages zero to eight. Native American Research Associates has as its mission providing assistance to native Americans, native Alaskans, and native Hawaiians in their quest for self-determination. Recent publications include "Native American Learning Styles" (1978).

Dr. José A. Cárdenas is currently executive director of Intercultural Development Research Association in San Antonio, Texas. He has published numerous articles and monographs on bilingual education, segregation, school finance, planning for desegregation, migrant education, parental involvement, and the utilization of teacher aides. In addition to providing expert testimony at various desegregation hearings and litigation proceedings, he has also given technical assistance to the National Urban Coalition; the Hearst, Rockefeller, Carnegie and Ford Foundations; the Department of Health, Education, and Welfare and U.S. Office of Education.

Dr. René Cárdenas is the president of Bilingual Children's Television (BCTV) in Oakland, California. He earned his Ph.D. at the University of California, Berkeley, in anthropology and has been involved in the development of national programs in the areas of educational television and parenting/family, and in the development of career lattice programs at Stanford and other leading United States educational institutions. He was formerly Vice President of the Kingston Trio during the folk era and worked in the International Market for both AMPEX and MGM. His work experience ranges over a broad variety of activities which include involvement with Stanford Research Institute and as a film/television writer in major television production areas.

Jean V. Carew is a Senior Research Associate and Lecturer at the Harvard Graduate School of Education now on leave at the Center for Research on Women, Stanford University. She is the author of *Observing Intelligence in Young Children: Eight Case Studies* (Prentice-Hall) and of many professional articles. Dr. Carew has directed several pioneering research projects on the development of very young children.

Magdalene M. Carney has been in public school education for over twenty years and has served as consultant for staff development and teacher education for many school systems throughout the United States.

James P. Comer is the Maurice Falk Professor of Child Psychiatry at the Yale Child Study Center. He is the director of a mental health team in urban school system, lecturer and a consultant to numerous programs serving children and families. He is author of *Beyond Black and White*, Quadrangle Books, and co-author of *Black Child Care*, Simon and Schuster and Pocketbooks, and of many popular and professional articles.

Barbara Goffigon Cox is co-director of the Bilingual Bicultural Preschool Research and Development Project and associate director of the Follow-Through Model at the University of California at Santa Cruz. She is co-author of *Spanish/English Bilinguism in the United States* (CAL) and has conducted training workshops in bilingual, multicultural education throughout the west and southwest.

Mario D. Fantini, one of the nation's best-known educational reformers, is a leading spokesman for increasing educational options for students, parents, and teachers within our educational system. Presently Dean of the School of Education at the University of Massachusetts, Amherst, he was architect of the controversial school decentralization plan for New York City. As a Ford Foundation officer, Dr. Fantini helped initiate some of the most innovative programs now being implemented throughout the country. He is an active speaker, author and co-author of many books, including *Community Control and the Urban School* (with Marilyn Gittell and Richard Magat): *Toward Humanistic Education* (with Gerald Weinstein); *Decentralization: Achieving Reform* (with Marilyn Gittell); *Disadvantaged: Challenge to Education* (with Gerald Weinstein); *Public Schools of Choice: A Plan for the Reform of Ameri-*

can Education; *Alternative Education: A Source Book for Parents, Teachers, Students, and Administrators;* and *What's Best for the Children? Resolving the Power Struggle between Parents and Teachers.*

Joseph Fitzpatrick is Professor of Sociology at Fordham University. Father Fitzpatrick is well known for his studies of the Puerto Rican Community, such as *Puerto Rican-Americans: The Meaning of Migration to the Mainland* (Englewood Cliffs, N.J.: Prentice-Hall, 1971), and for his activities with the community. He is vice president of the Puerto Rican Family Institute and a member of the Board of the Puerto Rican Legal and Education Defense Fund. He also is a member of the Consortium for Research on the Puerto Rican Migration.

Ira J. Gordon, the late Kenan Professor and Dean of the School of Education at the University of North Carolina at Chapel Hill, died in the autumn of 1978 at the age of 55. He had been Director of the Institute for Development of Human Resources at the University of Florida, and served as a consultant to federal and state governments as well as school systems on issues of parent education and parent involvement. Author of fourteen books and numerous articles, he had established a reputation in the fields of parent-child relationships and family-school relationships. Dr. Gordon's last book is *Baby to Parent-Parent to Baby, A Guide to Loving and Learning in the Child's First Year* (St. Martin's Press).

Robert D. Hess has a long-time interest in the relationship of culture and social institutions upon learning in children. His research includes analysis of the family interaction and transmission of behavior patterns in families, effects of divorce on the social and school performance of children, and family influences upon school readiness in both United States and cross-national settings. Since 1967 he has held the Lee L. Jacks Professorship in Child Education at Stanford. He came to Stanford from the University of Chicago by way of the Center for Advanced Study in the Behavioral Sciences.

Daniel C. Jordan, Director of the Center for the Study of Human Potential at the University of Massachusetts, has a background in both the arts and the sciences. He holds an M.A. in Music from Oxford University where he studied for three years as a Rhodes Scholar and an M.A. and Ph.D. in Human Development from the University of Chicago. His dominant professional interest is long-range educational planning based on human development science.

Michael E. Lamb is Assistant Professor of Psychology and Assistant Research Scientist at the Center for Human Growth and Development at the

University of Michigan. His research is concerned with social and personality development (especially in infancy and early childhood) and with the determinants and consequences of different parenting styles. He has published widely in professional journals and has authored or edited several books: *The Role of the Father in Child Development; Social and Personality Development; Social Interaction Analysis: Methodological Issues; Psychological Development in Infancy*; and *Infant Social Conditioning*. In 1975 he was named Prize Fellow in the Social Sciences at Yale University. In the next year he received a Young Psychologist Award from the American Psychological Association and he was honored by the same organization in 1978 when he received the Boyd R. McCandless Young Scientist Award for distinguished contributions to developmental psychology.

James A. Levine, Research Associate at the Wellesley College Center for Research on Women, is a consultant on child care and social policy for the Ford Foundation and many other organizations. He is the author of *Who Will Raise the Children? New Options for Fathers (and Mothers)* (Bantam Paperback), *Day Care and the Public Schools: Profiles of Five Communities* (EDC), and of many popular and professional articles.

Robert A. LeVine, Roy E. Larsen Professor of Education and Human Development and Director of the Laboratory of Human Development at the Harvard Graduate School of Education, is an anthropologist who has worked in Kenya and Nigeria. He is the author of *Nyansongo: A Gusii Community in Kenya* (1966, John Wiley & Sons), *Culture, Behavior and Personality* (1973, Aldine) and other professional books and articles.

Manuel Ramirez III, Professor of Psychology at Oakes College of the University of California at Santa Cruz, directs two research and development bilingual, bicultural early-education programs. He also directs several research programs addressing various aspects of the development of multiculturalism in Mexican-Americans. He is co-author of *Cultural Democracy, Bicognitive Development and Education* and author of various professional articles in psychology and education.

John Russo recently completed post-doctoral research at the Labor Relations and Research Center at the University of Massachusetts at Amherst and is currently an Assistant Professor of Labor and Industrial Relations at St. Francis College, Loretto, Pennsylvania. Dr. Russo has written extensively in the areas of educational policy and public sector labor relations.

Bob H. Suzuki is Professor of Education at the University of Massachusetts in Amherst. He has authored many articles on Asian-Americans and education, and is a specialist in the field of multicultural education. In addition to his scholarly pursuits, he has been actively involved for more than a decade in the areas of civil rights and community organizing, and in 1976, received the National Education Association's Human Rights Award for Leadership in Asian and Pacific Island Affairs.

Lourdes Travieso is Director of the Bilingual Teacher Corps Project of the City College of New York and the Center for Bilingual Education of the New York City Board of Education. She has been a National Urban Fellow at Yale University, Assistant Director of Title I Programs for Community School District 7 of New York City, and Director of the Educational Leadership Development Program of the Center for Urban Education in New York. She is the author of several articles on Puerto Ricans in the *Journal of Teacher Education* and in the *Philadelphia Daily News.*

David P. Weikart, President of the High/Scope Educational Research Foundation, has been active in early childhood research since the early 1960's. He and his colleagues at the Foundation have developed the High/Scope Cognitively Oriented Curriculum which is updated and outlined in a new book, *Young Children in Action* (High/Scope Foundation). The Foundation has also released several monographs on the longitudinal outcomes of early intervention.

Gloria Zamora's performance as a teacher, lecturer, workshop presenter, consultant, and author of many publications has gained her national recognition for her expertise in bilingual and early childhood education, curriculum and instruction, staff development, and curriculum development. Prior to becoming director of the center, she was director of IDRA's AMANECER Project which is developing a bilingual, preschool curriculum model. She has directed Edgewood I.S.D.'s Title VII Bilingual Education Program and was Acting Associated Superintendent for the Experimental Schools Project. She has served on the faculties of Our Lady of the Lake University and the University of Texas at San Antonio. In 1974–1975 she was named as one of the Outstanding Educators of America and has been nominated to the Directory of Significant 20th Century American Minority Women.

For her critical acumen and editorial skill, a debt of gratitude is owed to Marcia S. Curtis. To Irma Castillo, Nancy A. Kaminski, Vanessa Mas, Nancy Powling, and Juan Rosario goes the recognition that without the aid they consistently offered and the editors consistently accepted, this anthology would have remained unfinished.

Mario Fantini extends his profound thanks to his parents, Caroline and Mario, and to his wife, Temmy, and their children, Brianne, Marc, Steffan, and Todd, for the support they always lend him and upon which he relies.

René Cárdenas extends his sincere thanks and appreciation to his wife, Doris, and their sons, Kevin and Gregory, for their continued encouragement and support in this and all his other efforts.

The editors want to specially recognize the contributions of the following individuals:

Richard Foster, *former superintendent of schools, Berkeley, California, and a nationally known consultant to various school systems in the country, for his instrumental efforts in designing the conference that led to this anthology.*

Susan Perschetz Machala, *for her overall editorial contributions.*

John Russo, *for his careful design and critique of the sequence of this anthology.*

Benjamin Soria, *of BCTV, for his leadership in the various phases of the production of this anthology.*

Introduction
Parenting in Contemporary Society

MARIO D. FANTINI
University of Massachusetts
Amherst, Massachusetts

JOHN B. RUSSO
St. Francis College
Loretto, Pennsylvania

The protection, nurture, and education of children by adults is fundamental to human life. In a way that seems entirely natural to most people, the primary responsibility for providing these essential aids to the child falls to its parents. It is the biological parent or the adult acting in his or her place who must assume the central task of overseeing the physical, intellectual, and emotional development of the child into adulthood.

The experience of this role—parenting as it is now frequently called—is neither simple nor predominantly natural, however, as it inevitably involves both the child and the parent in highly variable social and economic contexts. The physical, psychological, and economic requirements for acceptance as an adult simply are not the same in all societies, as contributors to this anthology are cautious to point out. Even within the same society, a vast range of differing expectations may be faced by the parent and child. This is particularly true in a highly complex, pluralistic society like our own which encompasses great cultural diversity. Furthermore, the entire process of parenting is constantly exposed to the same pressures of rapid historical change as the society at large and these pressures are especially evident in the prolonged "crisis" of the institutional context of parenting, namely the modern family. Given the many ways that society mediates the relationship between parent and child, this volume has been organized to provide a framework for understanding what effective parenting involves for the parents, professionals, and researchers who deal directly with what is now a recognized field of inquiry, and further, to suggest ways in which this understanding might contribute to the development of criteria for establishing public policy which will affect the greater society. Parenting, as it is understood here, involves us all since, ultimately, it represents not only the expression of a society's concern for its children, but also that society's concern for its own future well-being.

THE SOCIAL CONTEXT

Before even introductory remarks are made regarding the possibilities of public policy in this area, or regarding the state of research at this time, some attention must be paid to *how* the questions concerning what constitutes effective parenting in our society arise, and *why* they seem relevant at this point in our history.

The family, of course, has been the focus of extensive scholarly research and popular debate during the last ten years. The intense interest in this topic usually is associated with contemporary social disintegration and deviance: the problems of crime and particularly juvenile crime, child abuse, teenage pregnancies, alcoholism, run-away children, infant mortality, drugs, youth alienation, and other symptoms of social malfunction are linked to the weaknesses of the modern family structure, which, in turn, are evidenced by their own symptoms: rising divorce rates, desertion or financial irresponsibility, neglect of the elderly, and so forth. In other words, the "crisis" of the family is the source of the "crisis of society" in the minds of many people.

This theme has been greatly elaborated upon by the mass media which routinely features articles and reports on "saving the family" with little or no precision as to *which* family or ideology of the family is being resuscitated. Is it the middle-class nuclear family which is threatened? Is it the matriarchal (or matrilocal) black family which is responsible for untrained and unemployable black youth and which must therefore be reconstructed to reflect the norms of the dominant society? Is it the single-parent family a family at all? Are families only legal when blood relatives live together, or are divorced and/or remarried parents still families in relation to their children? Although these questions and others like them are not always asked in popular treatment of the family, they are brought up again and again in the actual conditions of our daily life and in the scholarly research which seeks to clarify effects not only of the changes in the structure of the family on society, but in the effects of demographic, economic, and historical changes in society on the family.

The question of which family is the model of that normative or ideal family which we have lost or are in danger of losing is a confusing one not only with regard to our present day society, but also with regard to our past. Until quite recently, the history of the modern family was outlined as a gradual withdrawal of the small unit known as the nuclear family from the more inclusive kinship structure of the extended patriarchal family which had provided services and protection to family members of all generations. The economic and educational functions of that family were slowly usurped by the new organization of industrial society which emphasized work and schooling outside the larger family structure. More and more, the authority and responsibility belonging to the patriarchal head of the family were surrendered to the state, with the nuclear family left to provide those emotional and domestic needs which were left unfulfilled by these changes.

This traditional account of the development of the family still dominates social theories of family history, but recently, serious historians of the family have challenged its assumptions and offered evidence which suggests that the nuclear family predated industrialization and was, in fact, a feature of the life of the Middle Ages rather than a creation of the nineteenth century. If this is the case, it suggests that the nuclear family is neither "modern" nor a product of industrial society but rather a more complicated development which exists sometimes as a response to social and economic change, and sometimes as a precondition of it. Such a view of the historical status of the family, while still very much open to question, suggests the exercise of intellectual restraint in our assessments of the contemporary family as being in a near-terminal state: It may well be that our lament for the dying family is premature, and as inappropriate, in fact, as our nostalgia for the family which may never have existed historically in the way that we had previously conceived it.

This is not to suggest that the problems of the family are present only in the consciousnesses of scholars and writers. In some ways, the questions which surround the current debates over the family were raised implicitly by the social movements of the 1960's. The civil rights movement was accompanied by a reemergence of pride in ethnic difference which served to remind the nation that the white middle-class family which had dominated our national image was by no means the only family structure in the United States. The experience of immigrant minorities, blacks, and native Americans in their family life has been at variance in important ways with the media image of the American family. The present status of these family structures, as analyzed in the papers included in this collection, reflects both the traditional cultural differences of these groups and their often painful history as minorities in the United States. One result of this renewed awareness of ethnic and cultural difference is the recognition that, in the crisis of the family as it exists in the popular imagination, there are features which may not apply at all to the structures of some ethnic groups in the United States. These groups may, in fact, have separate problems or alternative models of the family and parenting which should be considered.

As the reemergence of ethnic consciousness challenged some aspects of our traditional notion of the American family, so the reappearance of feminism challenged other aspects of that model. Apart from the specific phenomenon referred to as the women's movement, it is clear that changes in the perception and function of women's roles have had great influence on the current sense of alternatives in styles of family life and parenting. Apart from its more polemical aspects, the women's movement has indisputably focused attention on the existing economic and social realities which have governed how women carry out their roles as wives, mothers, and increasingly, as partial or sole economic providers for themselves and their children. The current statistics which show a rising divorce rate and an increased number of children being raised in single-parent homes have certainly contributed to the urgency of the demand that women be paid fairly and have fair access to jobs and to job advancement. As this is not yet a reality, particularly for lower-class women, the welfare system has intervened in the maintenance of the many families now headed by women. It is not yet clear what effects being raised by a single parent or being influenced by the welfare system from childhood may have on a child or on the concept of the family.

For those women in functioning marriages there is the increased expectation of personal fulfillment as well as participation in family life. Whether or not both parents in a family work outside the home, there is now at least a certain number of men willing to take on responsibilities traditionally assigned to women, including the primary care of the physical and emotional needs of children. Additionally, there is a greater dependence on services outside the home to provide the supervision and guidance which the children of working parents may require. It is difficult to assess the effects of changing sex roles and reliance on institutional support on the child, but these changes have focused attention on existing family situations and the possible alternatives to the patterns of responsibility and authority within families which may emerge in the future.

The role of children in the family has shifted perhaps more gradually than the role of women but there is little doubt that significant changes have taken place even in the very recent past. The "youth culture" is an expression of the separateness of childhood, both as a developmental stage (children were once seen as merely "little adults") and as a distinctive and occasionally contradictory style of being in the world with youth-oriented clothes, music, language, attitudes, and values. The youth culture has been linked primarily with the loss of a socioeconomic place for American youth over the past century. In the last century, most children past a reasonable age were valued as economic assets in the family, sharing in the work which maintained the family within the home, in the fields, or in the newly developing industries of the towns and cities. While the exclusion of exploitative child labor from the marketplace has been a humane development, the fact that no other economic or social contributions have been required of children except as consumers, has made childhood a period of great financial and emotional investment for the parent, and a period of freedom or alienation (depending on the circumstances of the family) for the child.

Again, it is not only the family which registers the effects of these changes. For the children as well, whose experience of childhood is one of deprivation and alienation, for those many young people who have neither an emotionally strong environment at home nor a respected place in the community, the state has tried to provide the services and institutions to support (or even in some cases, to salvage) their lives. The failure of society and of the family to reach large numbers of youth is a matter of public record: The schools, the juvenile court system, the narcotics trade, the police records, the maternity wards, and psychiatric service facilities all have their separate evidence to present.

Children are not the only group to be set apart from the socioeconomic functions of the "adult world" and the family. Another group is even more severely isolated from the marketplace and from the traditional familial roles. Much less disruptive, often silent, with less to spend commercially and less to contribute to the family economy, the elderly are increasingly dependent upon the institutions—the nursing homes, the welfare system, the social service agencies—which take over (however inadequately) the supportive function of family members.

Often as forgotten in discussions of the family as they are in life, the gradual removal of the elderly from the active community and from contact with the young is significant on many levels. Perhaps most relevant to our outline of how the question of parenting arises within the changes in family structure are two rather simple points. First, we are once again relying more and more on the intervention of professionals and state financial support to care for dependent family members, whether children, the disabled, or the elderly. Second, yet another traditional expectation is being removed from the heavy investment of parenting, namely, that parents can look forward to being cared for in their old age by their children. In our society this expectation has been submerged in the rhetoric of independence for some time, but in many cultures the number of children, the care of children by adults of all ages, and the resulting allocation of resources within the family are all predicated upon the assumption that parenting is one step in a cyclical process of mutual support which will come back to the parents in their old age.

Given these tendencies, it seems reasonable to ask whether the institutionalization of the elderly is related to the "professionalism" of child care. The fact that these and other aspects of family life are changing does not mean, of course, that the alternatives which may emerge are necessarily signs of social deterioration or crisis. Focus on parenting as an element of social and family life which has, at least, the stability of being a constant process (however interpreted) in all societies may very well clarify the priorities of other confusing aspects of family and community life: Children *must* be cared for and be given access to the information about their future lives as adults, so that they may take their places in the community. This process which is basic to cultural and social continuity has emerged as a separate field of inquiry, partly in response to the confusions which surround it in more complex discussions of the family and society.

The recent focus on "parenting" as a necessary social art and as a new field of inquiry is a recognition of the reality of our time: The questions, the problems, and the alternatives presented in this volume are all reflections of social and historical realities which govern our lives. The attempt to systematically organize this experience with the possibility of formulating public policy does not suggest, however, that trends such as the institutional intervention in our lives are irreversible, but rather, it affords us an opportunity to review those factors which have contributed to our present situation and to understand the full range of possibilities which may be rejected or planned for in the future.

PARENTS, PROFESSIONALS, AND RESEARCHERS

Although the greater society is implicated in all aspects of parenting, three groups who deal most directly with the problems of child-rearing and parent education are represented prominently in this volume: the parents themselves, the professionals, and the researchers who study the interactions of these former groups with children. Of these, the most heavily scrutinized are, of course, the parents; but the roles which professionals and researchers play must be subjected to the same critical analysis as that of parents since they, too, are extremely influential in shaping our perceptions of how well or badly parents are performing their functions.

The problems of parents have been touched upon in the above description of changes in family structure though not necessarily from their point of view. Parents themselves must face more immediate questions in their practical experience of their relationship with their children. It may be that parents have always asked, however unconsciously, whether it was worth it to have children and to care for them. However, today the calculations in terms of psychological and financial investment, and expectations of return on such investments in the form of love, identity, or financial support in old age may be viewed somewhat differently. The rapidly rising cost of seeing a child through adolescence or paying for his higher education has certainly influenced the number of children that parents choose to support. In India, where an adult's security is directly proportional to the number of children who potentially can care for him, a high family birth rate still seems worth the price of national poverty to many. If this motivation of future security is completely removed from the lives of American parents, some nonetheless do question the extent to which they may want to jeopardize their own interests for the sake of more children who may feel at liberty to desert them.

Once committed to the life of the child, the parent must continuously ask at what point his own individual needs as an adult must be sacrificed for the good of the child. Other crucial questions follow: Can a parent know *what* the good of a child is?

Can he rely on his own judgment and experience to decide what is good for children? Is he a good parent? Must there be *two* good parents with separate roles for parenting to be totally successful? Do professionals really know better than parents whether parents are being effective? Finally, is there a scientific basis for an understanding of their performance, or is it an art which is best left to instinct and common sense?

Both professionals and researchers are dedicated to answering these questions for parents, but frequently from quite different perspectives. The professionals— teachers, social workers, family counselors, clergy, psychologists, and psychiatrists— are all members of what are called the "helping professions." This label alone goes a certain distance in answering the question of whether parents are best left to raise their children alone; from the point of view of professions which very often only see children who are in need of special diagnostic or therapeutic services, parents clearly do need assistance. For teachers of basic education, this question has long been put to rest, for few adults are capable of educating their children for the complexities of the modern world. The nature of the activities of professionals is now tending to shift away from that of merely reparative involvement with families, however, and toward a more comprehensive supportive and preventative role.

Many members of this professional community have become involved in educational endeavors focused on teaching adults how to become parents. Conferences, study groups, and written material are newly available to these "parent educators" on the subject of adult-child interaction, discipline, and cognitive and physical development. These professionals would seem to have expanded their roles from helping parents to teaching them. The assumption of a scientific basis for this teaching does not conceal the obvious moral and ethical aspects of implying standards of effective parenting.

In fact, the prospect of further intrusions into family life has not been accepted entirely by either the public or the research community. Critics of continued professional involvement in the child-parent relationship often maintain that the dependency on external sources has greatly inhibited parental authority and confidence. A prominent spokesman for this viewpoint, social historian Christopher Lasch, has described this influx of professionals as the systematic expropriation of parental prerogatives and the commodification of value systems, the result of which may be a society of individuals who are unable to make moral and ethical distinctions by themselves and who, having depended on professional guidance throughout their lives, are unable to deal independently with the uncertainties and contradictions which inevitably accompany family relationships.

Researchers deal with parenting with more distance than the parents and professionals who are called upon to practice the art rather than to study it. Nonetheless, as the social sciences have become more self-conscious about their influence and responsibility in affecting and being affected by social policy, the distinction between the "science" of social behavior and its uses has become somewhat less certain and new questions have arisen.

Some of these problems relate to the nature of research itself. For one thing, the research process is often slow and after the fact. The society in which such research may occur, on the other hand, is dynamic and may demand more rapid accomodations to change than the research is prepared to indicate. As serious researchers often point out, this is especially problematic with regard to research on the dynamic interaction which constitutes the family in society. In addition, researchers often have little control over the uses made of their work in the social policy decision-making process, except to urge caution in applying research results without a critical appraisal of whether results are tentative, outdated, or premature with regard to the formation of public policy. With this in mind, discussions of the state of research on parenting are included in this volume to indicate the limitations of our present knowledge and, in turn, to suggest those areas in need of further study.

OVERVIEW

The anthology itself is largely composed of selected papers developed from those presented at the Conference on Effective Parenting sponsored by Bilingual Children's Television and the Lilly Endowment in New Orleans in 1977. Overall, the articles reflect the many facets of the current debate over parenting. Leading researchers and other professionals in the fields of parent education, child psychology, human development, and public education are represented among the contributors to this anthology.

Regardless of their professional backgrounds or perspectives, the authors have been asked to include any policy recommendations that follow from their discussions. The recommendations represent a broad range of policy issues dealing not only with the family, but with American society in general. Some articles will seem extremely tentative and will emphasize the complexity of the problems involved in understanding effective parenting. Given the preliminary nature of the research in this area, their policy recommendations may seem overly cautious. Other authors, in perceiving an urgent crisis in the nature of parenting and family life, will advocate more ambitious policy recommendations. Although reflecting a willingness for action, these formulations may appear at once both hopeful and yet hopelessly optimistic, given the present resources and attitudes which exist in our society.

If the anthology has a unifying theme, apart from reviewing the broad scope of material associated with parenting, it can be found in the concept of cultural pluralism. That is, in examining parenting, there must be a recognition of the community values, the dignity inherent in local cultural customs, and the need for tolerance in relating to cultural diversity.

The selections in the anthology have been organized into six sections, each focusing on a different aspect of parenting. In many respects, the categorizations seem somewhat arbitrary in that it is possible that some articles could have been placed in several different sections. These categories are deliberately broad in order to encompass the literature while providing a useful framework for studying parenting and parenting policy.

The first section, "Cultural and Universal Issues in Parenting," provides a general structure within which other features of parenting can be discussed. It is composed of three subsections: one dealing with sociocultural factors in parenting, one outlining cross-cultural perspectives on parenting, and one concerned with defining universal goals in the parenting process. These articles express the richness and diversity which surround the process as well as simultaneously indicating what are shared concerns in the child-rearing procedure.

"Parenting in a Multicultural Society" is the title of the second section of the anthology. This section investigates the pluralistic nature of American communities. Viewing ethnic communities in the American cultural context, these articles display the wide variation in parenting styles and family life which exist in our society. While illustrating cultural diversity, however, the articles demonstrate the influence of larger socioeconomic factors that cross ethnic lines and are related to social class. Represented in the anthology are ethnic groups which are most often ignored in the debate over parenting policy, but which will nonetheless be affected drastically by any such policy decisions which are made. Included among those groups are black Americans, Asian-Americans, Mexican-Americans, Puerto Rican-Americans and native Americans.

The third section, "Is There a Scientific Base for Child-rearing," contains information about the current status of research on parenting. The articles evaluate contemporary research in terms of both methodology and content. The presentations indicate the extent of our knowledge and understanding of parenting and suggest those areas where more study is necessary. This analysis is of obvious importance insofar as future research will provide the basis for prospective family policy.

The fourth section in the anthology is entitled "Improving Parenting at Home and in the School." This segment explores the two most powerful influences in a child's development—namely, the home environment and that of the school—and how they can be utilized to improve parenting. Specifically, the articles examine the task of the parent as teacher, the role of schools in bettering parent education, and the relationship between home and family in improving the early education of minority children.

The fifth section, "Support Systems in Parenting," considers new programs outside the home and school which are intended for the development of parent education. These articles examine the use of television, books, self-help groups, and various experts in facilitating the growth of both the parent and child while improving the quality of their relationship. At the same time, the dangers inherent in "professional parenthood education" are outlined. Especially important is the discussion of how parent education can quite innocuously ignore parenting styles, show little respect for cultural diversity, and create the impression of parental inadequacy in order to accomodate the needs of professionals.

The final section discusses the policy recommendations that have been suggested earlier in the anthology. In addition to the summary, this concluding segment provides guidelines for both the planning and the implementation of the recommendations themselves. Lastly, it proposes a schematic outline by which the policy recommendations may be systematically evaluated.

In sum, we make no claim at definitiveness in this anthology; as with most complex subjects, there are gaps. Nonetheless, we believe that this collection does provide a useful framework for approaching the subject of parenting, in particular, parenting from a multicultural perspective. Our suggestions for public policy are just that—suggestions. Our intent is not to foreclose any future discussion, but rather to stimulate further the national debate on the family and parenting.

Parenting in a Multicultural Society

Part One
Cultural and Universal Issues in Parenting

Parenting encompasses a diverse pattern of emotions, beliefs, values, and behaviors. These patterns form a cultural setting in which the human personality and experience are organized, developed, and given meaning. While there are many cross-cultural similarities in the parenting process, it is important to remember that variations exist not only among national and cultural settings but within the same society.

This section explores the relationship between the universal exigencies of parenting and cultural and societal variables. Among the central issues addressed by the authors represented here are: What are the social forces that impinge on the family? What effect are these forces having on the family? What are the basic needs of all families? What happens when these needs are not met? What effect does a particular culture have on family needs, on how these needs are pursued, and on the consequences of child-rearing? Are there ways of identifying the "universal" features of human growth and development? Can these common principles of development be applied cross-culturally? What are the policy implications of a culturally based family system? Of a universally conceived family system?

In the first selection, Ira J. Gordon provides a framework for the analysis of societal influences on parenting. Broadly defining parenting in terms of physical and psychological survival, Gordon sees child development as the result of interactions involving macro-systems, exo-systems, meso-systems, and micro-systems. Based on this systems analysis he recommends that parent-education programs of the future be comprehensive in scope in order to influence each system simultaneously.

In the second selection, Robert A. Levine discusses both the universal and culturally variable aspects of parenting. Levine sees three universals: the physical survival and health of the child, the development of the child's behavior capacities for economic self-maintenance, and the development of behaviors related to cultural values (morality, ethics, and so forth). According to Levine, there also exists in each society a set of variables (parent-investment strategies) which are a manifestation of a compromise between what parents want for their children and what they may ultimately expect from them. Given the inherent tension between the universals and cultural variables, Levine warns parents and policy makers about didactic parent-education programs that are insensitive to cultural and societal diversity and that fail to respect the traditional "folk wisdom" associated with parenting.

The final selection by Daniel C. Jordan is a philosophical exploration of human growth and development. Basing his analysis on the organismic philosophy of Alfred North Whitehead, Jordan suggests that human potential and development are expressed in both positive (social adjustment) and negative (social malfunction) ways. To be an effective parent, Jordan argues, one must promote the "actualization" of a

1

child's potential by developing his or her biological, educational, economic, moral, and religious potentials in the positive direction. Lastly, Jordon suggests that by developing each child's potential to its fullest, the society will better itself, and perhaps, lay a better foundation for world peace.

1

Significant Sociocultural Factors in Effective Parenting

IRA J. GORDON
Late Kenan Professor and Dean
School of Education
University of North Carolina
Chapel Hill, North Carolina

When one is asked to define the most significant factors in effective parenting, it is obvious that the first question that might be raised is how to define "effective" in a cultural context. Does effective parenting depend on the society in which one lives? The anthropologists, for example, have shown us the hundreds of ways of child-rearing in societies ranging from the most simple to the most complex. In Africa, for example, the Bagand society considers smiling and sitting as important landmarks of development at six months of life. The infant, therefore, is conscientiously trained to sit. Mothers place the children in appropriate positions, wrap cloths around the infants to support the waist, and sit them in small basins so the babies' hands are able to hold on to the side. These behaviors are appropriate in this culture because the women are engaged in agricultural pursuits which require digging, and it is important that children sit rather than be strapped or held. Tests of infant motor development show these infants to be precocious in their sitting behavior (Kilbride and Kilbride, 1975). Several decades ago Margaret Mead's pictures illustrated the tremendous fluidity of movement of Balinese children when compared to the body movements of Gesell's New Englanders. Studies of parent-infant interactions of Japanese and Japanese-American children indicate that distance between the pair and the use of language relate to culture. For example, Japanese parents in the first three months hold their children more and communicate more through direct body contact than first generation Japanese-Americans. The latter more closely resemble American mothers who maintain some distance and establish relationships by means of voice (Caudill and Weinstein, 1969).

Given this diversity, one may question whether there are some universals which, in spite of particular techniques, seem to override and apply to all of us as humans. The first step would be to define the term effective and then to move on to particulars.

To define an effective parent requires some notion of the goals of parenting. What is it parents and their society would like children to be when they grow up? As one of those who spent the whole week watching *Roots*, I believe it contained a demonstration of goals. One might assume that the goals for effective parenting in that situation were to instill in children self-respect, a sense of group pride, and the ability to overcome the terrible circumstances of daily life. One vehicle was the use of the oral tradition. The goals were not simply physical survival, but psychological survival as intact human beings with a sense of belonging, cohesion, and indeed, roots.

In my culture, faced with various forms of abuse and deprivation throughout the last three thousand years, one can detect the same goals. Originally there was the reliance on oral tradition, but a major survival technique was the utilization of the written word. In this culture the family is the center of life in which there is the continued effort to instill a sense of pride, of tradition, of belief, of "groupness" which enables not only physical but cultural survival. No doubt these two examples could be reproduced many times in the culturally pluralistic American society. Each group has its cultural goals and traditions, from which its patterns of child-rearing flow, and which determine its original definition of effectiveness. But all these cultures now live in a broader social context, with the inevitable cultural borrowing and merging as well as conflict and confusion over values.

In today's modern world, are these goals mentioned above important? Are they sufficient for either the child's or the culture's survival?

Effective parenting, although there may be universal elements which will be discussed below, has to be understood in a cultural context. It has to be related to the societal goals as well as to the families' goals and makeup. Figure 1.1, developed from articles by Brim (1975) and Bronfenbrenner (1976), presents a visual means of examining the system network which influences the family. It can be seen immediately that different systems in the outer square (economic, social, political, legal), which has been labelled the macro-system, will make completely different sets of demands on all the people and agencies in the squares going toward the center. It is noteworthy that neither Brim nor Bronfenbrenner included the religious system in their descriptions. I believe this to be a significant omission, since much of cultural identity, for many millions, is closely tied to religious identity.

If we turn back to the African illustration, an economic system dependent upon a certain means of agriculture influences the way work is carried out, which in turn influences the arrangements of people in the neighborhood or tribe for caring for infants, which in turn influences the activities and roles of mother and infant. Such a view places the family, and the individual within the family, in a position of being influenced by, but not influencing, the larger systems.

However, another way to look at this is to recognize that influences can flow from the center out. As a family seeks to change, or as members of a family change their activities and roles and concepts, they influence the reactions of the meso-system in their immediate face-to-face environment and the reverberations extend all the way out. Much of parent education, at least in the United States, makes that assumption.

In our society, which places such a theoretical importance on the individual as a decision maker, changes in the culture are assumed possible through the behavior of the individuals in the center. For example, the Head Start program focused heavily on parent involvement based on the view that if parents became involved in the education of their young children, this would have an impact on the learning of the child. But it also included the notion that as parents learned about and became involved in the education of their young children they would influence the neighborhood, the

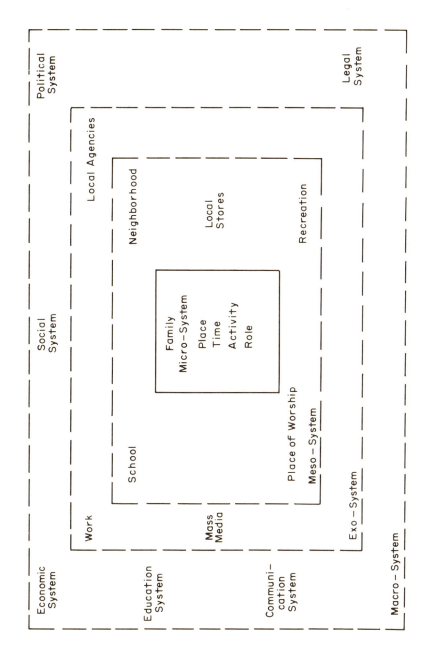

Figure 1.1 *The system network influencing a child's development.* [Source: *Developed from O. Brim (1975) and U. Bronfenbrenner (1976)*].

school, and the larger setting. This, indeed, proved to be true to some extent (Kirschner and Associates, 1970). Indeed, the evidence is clear that parent involvement led to political action in some ways which were not predicted by the originators (Moynihan, 1969).

▬▬ From an American perspective, the goals of belonging and cohesion and psychological survival rest as much on the behavior of the people within the family micro-system as they do on the systems which surround it. It is influenced by the family arrangements for space, the amount of time members spend with each other, what they do and the quality of these transactions, and the roles they play. In a Marxist framework the behavior within that family is completely subject to and influenced by the arrangements at the outer rim. One's overall view of the relative influences of systems on each other will play a significant role in the decisions and policy judgments as to modes of attack and places of attack for improving a child's well-being. From a social science viewpoint, the most reasonable interpretation may be a transactional one, that is, that all systems impinge on each other. Influences go both out from the center and in from the outer rim. This means that policy decisions do not have to be strictly ideological. We can develop strategies for influencing each subsystem directly as well as influencing the relationships between and among them.

We are concerned with improving the relationships between home and school. States are legislating community school acts and various forms of parent involvement; federal legislation in compensatory education and education for the handicapped requires parental involvement. Involvement reflects the very often unstated assumption of both the American political and the social science position. This view is that by bringing home and school into a close relationship two things will happen. First, the school will be able to influence the internal environment of the home in ways which are predicted to enhance the child's learning. Second, the parents will be able to influence the school to be more understanding of not only the issues and problems that face that individual family, but also of the family's culture, particularly if it differs from that of the milieu in which the family lives.

Pluralism in a Democratic Society (Tumin and Plotch, 1977) includes a chapter by Nathan Glazer describing the social aspects of cultural pluralism. In his discussion of implications for education, he indicates that we all have as common goals in the American society such things as basic skills (reading, writing, calculating), a sense of history and socialization, that is teaching students "to work on their own and in groups, to respect the common rules in any social order, to regard achievement through their own efforts as possible and rewarding" (p. 17). Finally, the schools are still attempting to make a nation. I have previously defined the common goals that cover both life goals and educational goals as follows: Effective parenting is providing "the opportunities and climate that start the child toward becoming a person who is (1) competent in his relationships with others; (2) an inquiring, thinking, perceptive adult; (3) comfortable with himself; (4) open to the world around him; (5) able to adapt yet with a sense of balance; (6) with a sense of responsibility to others and for his own behavior" (Gordon, 1975, p. 124). Such goals, of course, are broad. Obviously, the broader you make them, the easier it is for varying groups to accept them.

The key question in our attempt to define effectiveness in the American culture is: What do we know about parental behaviors which enhance or retard the chances that children will attain those goals? This is to some degree the heart of the matter. If we wish to engage in programs for parents, what is it specifically we can suggest or recommend or call to their attention that, if their goals are similar or identical with the ones above, would either encourage them to continue with what they are already doing, or suggest to them alternative parenting strategies or behavior?

We can attempt to answer this question in two ways. First, we can examine the general literature as it was reviewed by Robert Hess (1969) and in my own summary (Gordon, 1969), adding to it the British longitudinal work over the last two decades (Davie et al., 1972; Douglas et al., 1971; Kellmer Pringle et al., 1966; Miller, 1971), the reports from the International Educational Achievement Studies (Coffman and Lee, 1974; Coleman, 1975; Comber and Keeves, 1973; Keeves, 1972; Keeves, 1975; Purvis, 1973; Thorndike, 1973) and the reanalyses of the Coleman work (Coleman, 1966; Berger and Simon, 1974; Mayeske, 1975). The problem here, in addition to various methodological ones, is that family process and family structural variables have been correlated with academic achievement goals, and these academic achievement goals are much narrower than our general goals for children. The goals used in most of these research projects were primarily those of educational (academic) achievement. Nevertheless, since these studies were conducted in a number of countries it is important to note the common threads. If a major goal of parents is to enable the child to make it in the school system in which he or she will spend about twelve years, then we can say that: (1) engaging in direct face-to-face instruction with the child; (2) modeling by reading and discussing materials; (3) engaging in dinner conversations which move beyond description to planning; (4) providing the child with a consistent set of expectations for behavior, both as they apply to a single adult dealing with the child or to many adults, so that the child does not get different messages from different people; (5) utilizing not only the home but the neighborhood and the community as a resource; (6) spending time with the child; and (7) providing a secure and orderly home, all seem to be important variables. The amount of independence training may also be a factor. It seems that homes where thinking and freedom of discussion are valued and occur and where curiosity is encouraged, provide the background for success in school. It is clear that parental attitudes and ambitions are important and that the home must provide for stimulation.

One might suggest that these are not universals, but somewhat culture bound. At least they seem to apply in Western-oriented industrialized societies of which we, of course, are a major example. But given these answers, with what reasonable expectation can we assume that information to parents alone might influence the family micro-system? Here we need to examine what is happening to families. Although the statistics are American, similar data most likely can be organized in most of the Western industrialized world. Two reports, *The Status of Children, 1975* (Snapper et al., 1975) developed by the Social Research Group from George Washington University, and *America's Children, 1976*, a fact book developed by the National Council for Organizations for Children and Youth, contain the data.

We can examine the realities of the American family versus the mythology of the typical American family. If the family micro-system consists of time people spend with each other, the activities they perform and the roles played, it is obvious that the demographic trends in the 1970's show that the amount of time parents, particularly mothers, spend in the home, the activities in which they engage, and their role relationship with partners and their children are going through dramatic and dynamic change. "Changes in the size of families have been accompanied by changes in the structure of families and the roles of parents. For example, there was an 18 percent increase in the number of female family heads between 1970 and 1973, compared with a 24 percent increase in the entire preceding decade. . . . Overall, 12.4 percent of

American families were headed by females. . . . Overall, 60 percent of female-headed families have children under 18 and about 24 percent of the female-headed families had children under 6" (Snapper et al., 1975, p. 5–7). Contrast this with the fact that only 26 percent of husband and wife families in March 1974 had children under six. Today, about half the families rearing children under six are single-parent families. Further, there is a sharp rise in the number of divorces involving children. We have had fundamental changes in the relationship between the family micro-system and the world of work. "In March 1974, 43 percent of all married women were in the labor force . . . about 34 percent of women with children under 6 were in the labor force . . . labor force participation for women with preschool children (under 6) rose between 1970 and 1974 with the sharpest rise (26 percent to 31 percent) for mothers with children under 3" (Snapper et al., 1975, p. 8). The data are portrayed graphically in *America's Children* (Figures 1.2 and 1.3).

The number of teen-age pregnancies in the United States is also on the rise and represents a significant problem not only for the teen-agers but also for their families, their children, and society at large. Similarly, the number of births to unwed mothers is increasing. For example, in 1976 in the city of Washington, D.C., there were more abortions than live births and more illegitimate births than legitimate ones. Such statistics make it difficult to preserve an image of the American family to which our children, not many years ago, were exposed to when they learned to read with books such as *Fun with Dick and Jane.* Here the family was portrayed as suburban, two parents, two children, two pets, and two cars.

Any examination of policy development for strengthening the American family must include some redefinitions as to what constitutes the family, as well as what consitutes effective parenting within the family. To assume that many of the parents now bringing children into the world can be easily reached, have the attitudes, or the time, or the wherewithal to provide the above seven patterns of effectiveness is to presume, indeed, more than reality permits.

A long-term study of the effects of growing up in one-parent families was recently completed in Great Britain (Ferri, 1976). The conclusions indicate that the

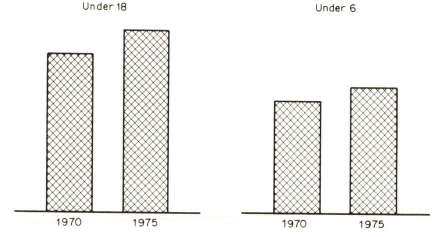

Figure 1.2 *Children with mothers in the labor force, 1970 and 1975.* (Source: America's Children, *p. 54*).

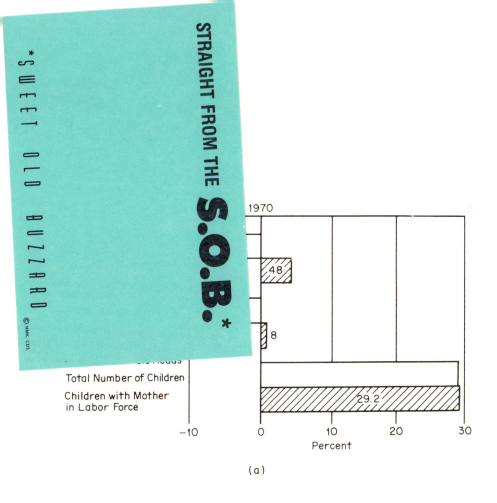

SWEET OLD BUZZARD

STRAIGHT FROM THE **S.O.B.***

© HMK. CDS.

1970

48

8

Total Number of Children

Children with Mother
in Labor Force

29.2

−10   0   10   20   30

Percent

(a)

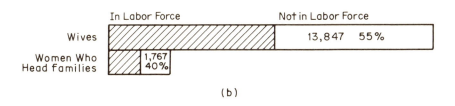

	In Labor Force	Not in Labor Force
Wives		13,847 55%
Women Who Head families	1,767 40%	

(b)

Figure 1.3 (a) *Percent changes in children and labor-force status of others, 1970 and 1974;* (b) *women in the labor force, 1975 (in thousands).* (Source: America's Children, *p. 55*).

child growing up in a one-parent home is at risk. Some of the risk, however, or a major portion of the risk, may be due to social class and family size factors, as well as limited parental aspirations. But Ferri concludes that "the attitudes which the family meets, and the treatment it receives in the wider social context will play a crucial role in its ability to recover from the unhappy experience of losing a parent, and to come to terms with its changed circumstances" (Ferri, 1976, p. 148). She indicates that it is the societal attitudes which isolate the family and increase its difficulties. The final paragraph is worth reporting:

> Bringing up children single-handedly is an arduous task, both physically and mentally. Help is needed, not only in providing for the family's material welfare which is so gravely threatened by the loss of a parent, but also in offering guidance, assurance, and moral support to unsupported parents in their lonely role of bringing up children without another adult to share the responsibility. If such help is not forthcoming, the strains and pressures on some lone parents may become so intolerable that they are finally forced to relinquish their burden, resulting in perhaps the worst of all possible outcomes—a no-parent family [p. 149].

The English study does not deal with the problems faced in the United States of the high rate of illegitimacy and the high number of teenage mothers. Her study is a part of the British longitudinal studies and concerns children who were born into two-parent families, but who by the age of seven or eleven were living in one-parent families.

A second way to develop an empirical definition of effective which can be used for policy determination is to examine the variety of studies which have been and are being done with infants and their relationships with their parents. Again, unfortunately, the usual dependent variable is some measure of intellectual performance. We lack the tools for measuring those very important variables indicated in the first paragraphs of this paper, especially for measuring them in the early years of the child's life.

Here the intervention studies yield a number of clues from studies in which homes were observed and then relationships drawn between what was seen and the performance of children on various intellectual measures. Gordon and Jester (1972) and Gordon (1974) used videotapes and recorded the behavior of the mother, the infant, and the home visitor in a somewhat structured teaching situation, beginning when the baby was thirteen weeks old and every six weeks thereafter until the baby was forty-nine weeks old. This taping was embedded inside a home-intervention project in which the parent educator or home visitor spent an hour a week in the parent's home demonstrating ideas about activities, using materials that could be found in the home. Analysis of those tapes, using as a standard the child's performance on the Bayley Mental Development Index and various types of Piagetian activities at age one, clearly indicated four patterns of infant-adult interactions which were related to child performance. The first of these we labeled "Ping-Pong" because it is a fairly rapid interchange of parent doing something followed by child doing something followed by parent doing something, focused around some particular task. It has a gamelike quality and may not last very long at any one time. Indeed, it occurred less than 10 percent of the time, on the average, for the taped episodes over the nine-month period of the program. It is similar to what Escalona (1973; 1974) found in her studies in natural observations in the homes and also to Jean Carew Watts's

(1973) findings in the Harvard preschool project. The pattern begins early. There was variability in the amount of the pattern displayed by families as early as our earliest tapes (thirteen weeks of age). It probably begins before that. We know also that by as early as nineteen weeks of age, the amount of Ping-Pong is predictive of cognitive development by age one as measured by Piagetian activities. We believe that this is not culture bound. A little phamphet by Haimen (1972) called "Soul Mother" states that Soul is playing with your child, singing or talking to your child, baby is smiling and cooing at the sound of his mother's voice. Our thirteen-week activity was the encouragement of baby cooing and sounding followed by the mother cooing and sounding back.

A second pattern was mutual gaze. This was an item we developed from Escalona's work. There is a power in looking into each other's eyes. Adult lovers know it, but it is also very potent at very early ages. We found it seemed to be particularly relevant for boy babies. The amount of mutual gazing as early as nineteen weeks of age is predictive of language and Piagetian performance at age one. Beckwith et al. (1971) found that there was a relationship between caregiver-infant gazing at one month and sensory motor scores at nine months for a group of premature babies observed at home. We labeled that pattern "passion."

A third pattern is persistence. This is shown when a parent begins an activity with a child, or engages with a child in an activity and then steps back so that the child himself or herself carries on and plays and explores the activity on his/her own. The amount of child sustained behavior, like the other two patterns, related positively to performance at age one. In addition, we found one pattern that was strongly related in a negative way. This was the pattern of an adult talking away at a child without attending to or being responsive to the cues the child may be giving. It was a one-way street. Because we are academicians very familiar with this pattern, we labeled it "professor."

None of these are uncommon behaviors. It is quite clear from our research that parents, even within a subculture, differ sufficiently in their use of these four patterns to make reliable differences in their babies' performances on intellectual measures at age one. We are currently replicating this study with middle-class families and attempting to examine the behavior of the father especially. As I look at both sets of tapes, I realize our coding inadequacies, because there are qualitative parenting behaviors we are not capturing.

I would add that a most important parenting pattern is responsiveness to the individuality of the child. If I can turn back again to a cultural example, in my tradition we read the Hagadah at Passover. We are instructed as a part of the ritual, and you will remember my point about the written word as our survival technique, to read how to handle the behavior of different children as they sit around the Passover dinner table. The parent is instructed as to how to respond to the questions of the wise child, the wicked child, the simple child, and the child who doesn't have the wits to ask. We are again becoming aware of the tremendous individuality in the child at birth. Effective parenting requires an understanding by the parent of the child's own activity rate, sensitivity to the environment, moods, biorhythms, alertness, and the like so that expectations are matched and communicated in ways which are not stereotypic.

A problem with using the survey and observational research is that it might give parents the idea that if they behave in a specific way they will get a specific result. Nothing could be more dangerous. Effective parenting is an art form. We can provide clues and ideas: we can suggest and demonstrate that one should talk with his child; that if you read and talk about books or magazines, your child will get the idea this is good, that if you promote consistency, your child will get a sense of security. Many of the particulars as to how to do this, and what "dosages" to use rest upon the particular individual biological make-up of the child and the parents. For example, given a highly active baby and a tired, energy-drained mother, it does little good to suggest that she should play with her baby. We may have to embed such suggestions in both the realities of individual biology and the social context.

This raises a broader question. Can effective parenting only be sustained well in a society which provides a structure for encouraging the family to be effective? What does it take in the systems which surround the family, and in the family's transactions with those systems, so that the patterns of effectiveness found thus far in the research can occur in the home? If there are problems of income, jobs, time, food, housing, then we may be asking more of a parent than a parent can provide. For example, a worn-out parent may only be effective if we can provide temporary parental substitutes. In a multiadult home we may have to encourage all to share so that no one is worn out, and the load is distributed, especially as far as the infant is concerned. This would then create time and emotional quality for playful interaction.

It is a common belief that the family is the first and major learning environment and parents are the child's first and most important teachers. We have seen above that there are some patterns of interaction within the family micro-system which relate to the performance of the child in the next system, the school. We have also seen, however, that the relationships between the family and the world of work and the social system are undergoing rapid change. Using the systems viewpoint and the emerging social data on demographic changes in our society, suggests that any defini-

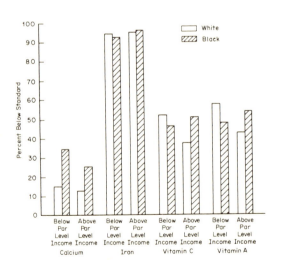

Figure 1.4 *Percent population aged 1–5 years below nutritional standard: 1971–1972.* (Source: *K. Snapper et al.,* The Status of Children, *1975, Figure 2-7, p.25*).

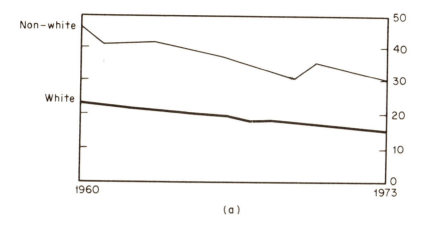

(a)

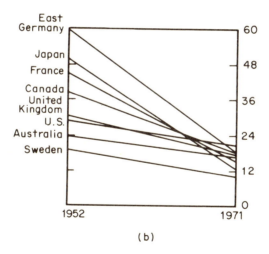

(b)

Figure 1.5 (a) *U.S.infant mortality rates by race, 1960–1973;* (b) *infant mortality rates of industrialized countries, 1952–1971.* (Source: America's Children, *p. 32.*)

tion of effective parenting requires changes in the nonfamilial system which will enable a family, however constituted and defined, to provide the simple survival basics of life before it can be expected that the family can make a major effort to deal with the psychological processes.

The demographic statistics are again revealing. For example, American children of all races and classes suffer major nutritional deficits (see Figure 1.4). Infant mortality in the United States is higher than that in other industrial societies regardless of their social system (Figure 1.5). This means that the medical system, which is at the outer fringe and is part of the economic and social system, has to be modified in some fashion and function in the neighborhood (the meso-system) in ways which enable a family to provide adequate nutrition and adequate health care.

With the changing picture of the world of work, the increasing flow of parents with young children into the work force, and the lack of adequate caring facilities, part of the definition of an effective parent is being able to locate and place one's child in a developmental situation for those hours when one is at work. This requires adjustments between the family and the school and local agencies so that spots exist for children which are not simply garage locations for parking the baby for the day. They must be places in which the caretakers function in the psychological ways that parents formerly functioned, and which match the list of interpersonal variables found to be important in development.

Housing too becomes part of the picture. If one has to work away from the neighborhood in which one lives, or if housing is available in such fashion that extended family networks which used to provide support systems (particularly for the single-parent family and the teenage parent) are destroyed because of small units or project rules, then although a "decent" place to live may be achieved, the social and psychological costs may be more destructive than the attainment of the housing goal.

We cannot examine programs for creating or enabling parents to be effective without dealing with all of the other factors involved. We require a comprehensive approach. We can attack each variable or each agency, to some degree, in isolation. But when we do, we have to be aware and measure and provide for the effects that such narrow programs will have on all of the other variables in the system.

I began on a cultural note and end on the same. There are those who will be effective parents enabling their children to survive physically and psychologically under the most adverse conditions. But it would be far better for the society as well as for the child if we found ways to provide that family with what it needs, in addition to parent education via television, home visitors, or group meetings. The family needs the social necessities for the effective physical and psychological survival of the parent and of the family structure. In the long run, the location of the family at the center of Figure 1.1 is symbolic of its real place in society.

BIBLIOGRAPHY

Beckwith, L. Relationship between attributes to mothers and their infants' IQ scores. *Child Development*, 1971, *42*, 1083–1097.

Berger, A., and Simon, W. Black families and the Moynihan report: A research evaluation. *Social Problems*, 1974, *22*, (2).

Brim, O. Macro-structural influences on child development and the need for childhood social indicators. *American Journal of Orthopsychiatry*, 1975, *45*, 516–524.

Bronfenbrenner, U. The experimental ecology of education. *Educational Research*, 1976, *5*, 5–15.

Caudill, W., and Weinstein, H. Maternal care and infant behavior in Japan and in America. *Psychiatry*, 1969, *32*, 12–43.

Coffman, W., and Lee, L. Cross-national assessment of educational achievement: A review. *Educational Researcher*, 1974, *3* (6), 13–16.

Coleman, J. *Equality of educational opportunity.* Washington, D.C.: United States Government Printing Office, 1966.

———. Methods and results in the IEA studies of effects of school on learning. *Review of Educational Research*, 1975, *45* (3), 335–386.

Comber, L., and Keeves, J. Science education in nineteen countries. In *International studies in evaluation*. Stockholm: Almqvist and Wiksell, 1973, *1*.

Davie, R.; Butler, N.; and Goldstein, H. *From birth to seven.* London: Longman, 1972.

Douglas, J.; Ross, J.; and Simpson, H. *All our future.* London: Panther Books, 1971.

Escalona, S. Basic modes of social interaction: Their emergence and patterning during the first two years of life. *Merrill-Palmer Quarterly*, 1973, *19*, 205–232.

Escalona, S., and Corman, H. Early life experience and the development of competence. *International Review of Psycho-Analysis*, 1974, 151–168.

Ferri, E. *Growing up in a one parent family.* London: NFER Publishing Company, 1976.

Glazer, N. Cultural pluralism: The social aspect. In M. Tumin and W. Plotch (Eds.), *Pluralism in a democratic society.* New York: Praeger, 1977.

Gordon, I. J. Developing parent power. In *Critical issues in research related to disadvantaged children.* Princeton, N.J.: Educational Testing Service, Seminar #5, September 1969, pp. 1–24.

———. *An investigation into the social roots of competence.* Gainesville, Florida: Institute for Development of Human Resources, University of Florida. Final Report on Project No. 1 RO1 MH 22724, to NIMH, November, 1974.

———. *The infant experience.* Columbus, Ohio: Charles E. Merrill, 1975.

———. Parenting, teaching, and child development. *Young Children*, 1976, *31* (3), 173–183.

———. What are effective home learning environments for school age children? In I. J. Gordon, M. Hanes, and W. Breivogel (Eds.), *Update: The first ten years of life.* Gainesville, Florida: Division of Continuing Education, University of Florida, 1977.

Gordon, I. J.; Beller, E.; Lally, J.; Yarrow, L. et al. Studies in socio-emotional development in infancy. JSAS *Catalog of Selected Documents in Psychology,* 1975, *4*, 120.

Gordon, I. J. and Jester, R. Instructional strategies in infant stimulation. *JSAS Catalog of Selected Documents in Psychology,* 1972, *2*, 122.

Haimen, P. *Soul mother.* Cleveland, Ohio: Case Western Reserve University Press, 1972.

Hess, R. Parental behavior and children's school achievement implications for Head Start. In *Critical issues in research related to disadvantaged children.* Princeton, N.J.: Educational Testing Service, Seminar #5, September 1969.

Keeves, J. *Educational environment and student achievement.* Stockholm: Almqvist and Wiksell, 1972.

———. The home, the school and achievement in mathematics and science. *Science Education*, 1975, *59* (4), 439–460.

Kellmer Pringle, M. L.; Butler, N.; and Davie, R. *11,000 seven-year-olds.* London: Longman, 1966.

Kilbride, J., and Kilbride, P. Sitting and smiling behavior of Baganda infants. *Journal of Cross-Cultural Psychology*, 1975, *6* (1), 88–104.

Kirschner Associates, Inc. (Ed.). *A national survey of the impacts of Head Start centers on community institutions.* May 1970, pp. 119, 121, 125.

Mayeske, G., and Beaton, A. *Special studies of our nation's students.* Washington, D.C.: United States Department of Health, Education and Welfare, 1975.

Miller, G. *Educational opportunity and the home.* London: Longman, 1971.

Moynihan, D. P. *Maximum feasible misunderstanding.* New York: Free Press, 1969.

National Council of Organizations for Children and Youth. *America's children, 1976; a bicentennial assessment.* Washington, D.C.: NCOCY, 1976.

Purves, A. Literature education in ten countries. *International studies in evaluation* Stockholm: Almqvist and Wiksell, 1973, *2*.

Snapper, K.; Barriga, H.; Baringarner, F.; and Wagner, C. *The status of children 1975.* Washington, D.C.: The George Washington University, 1975.

Thorndike, R. Reading comprehension education in fifteen countries. *International studies in evaluation* Stockholm: Almqvist and Wiksell, 1973, *3.*

Tumin, M., and Plotch, W. (Eds.). *Pluralism in a democratic society.* New York: Praeger, 1977.

Wachs, T.; Uzgiris, J.; and Hunt, J. McV. Cognitive development of different age levels and from different environmental background: An explanatory investigation. *Merrill-Palmer Quarterly*, 1971, *17*, 282–318.

Watts, J.; Barnett, I.; and Halfer, L. Environment. *Experience and development in early childhood.* Final Report to OEO, Head Start Division, 1973.

Wedge, P., and Prosser, H. *Born to fail?* London: Arrow Books, 1973.

2

A Cross-Cultural Perspective on Parenting

ROBERT A. LEVINE
Roy E. Larsen Professor of Education and Human Development
Graduate School of Education
Harvard University
Cambridge, Massachusetts

An intelligent consideration of "effective parenting" in our own society requires an understanding of cultural diversity in parental goals, values, and behavior among human societies past and present. Parenthood is at once a universal and highly variable aspect of human behavior. In all human societies, as in infrahuman populations, sexually mature adults protect, nurture, and educate the young, but among humans the patterns of child-rearing are not uniform. In the last forty years, anthropoligists have shown, with increasingly convincing evidence, that the environments of infancy and early childhood are shaped by cultural values. These values vary widely among ethnic groups and become firmly established in the personal preferences and inner regulations of individuals who seek to reestablish them in the next generation. Some of the best studies in this area have been conducted by Caudill, comparing middle-class Japanese and Americans (Caudill and Plath, 1966; Caudill and Weinstein, 1969) and by Whiting et al. (1966), comparing Zuni, Texans, and Mormons in New Mexico. It is clear from these studies that parents of different cultural backgrounds define the universal situation of child-rearing differently and attempt to organize the lives of their children accordingly from birth onward. In this chapter, I try to identify and illustrate both universal and culturally variable aspects of parenting and bring that cross-cultural perspective to bear on issues of parental effectiveness in contemporary American society.

Human parents everywhere can be seen as sharing a common set of goals in their role as parents:

1. The physical survival and health of the child, including (implicitly) the normal development of his reproductive capacity during puberty.
2. The development of the child's behavioral capacity for economic self-maintenance in maturity.
3. The development of the child's behavioral capacities for maximizing other cultural values—for example, morality, prestige, wealth, religious piety, intellectual achievement, personal satisfaction, self-realization—as formulated and symbolically elaborated in culturally distinctive beliefs, norms, and idealogies.

If one asks the question, "What do parents want for their children?" the answers from all human societies would include and be exhausted by these categories. There is a natural hierarchy among these goals because the physical survival of the child is a prerequisite of the other two and economic self-maintenance is usually prerequisite to the realization of other cultural values. Thus, if the child's physical survival is threatened, it is likely to become the foremost concern of parents, and if his future economic self-maintenance is considered to be jeopardized, it is likely to assume a high priority among parental goals. There is also a natural developmental sequence in this set of parental goals, in that physical survival and health are normally of greater concern in the first years of life, while the others take precedence after the child's survival seems assured and his capacities for learning are more conspicuous.

Parents do not face the problems of attaining these goals entirely on their own. Each culture contains an adaptive formula for parenthood, a set of customs evolved historically in response to the most prominent hazards in the locally experienced environment of parents that jeopardize attainment of these goals. Thus, in areas where the incidence of disease or danger causes high infant mortality rates, customary patterns of infant care will not only be organized by health and survival goals, but will also embody avoidance of specific local hazards as conceptualized in the folk belief system; in areas of precarious subsistence, the cultural formula for parents will be designed around the priority of enabling the child to make a living in adulthood, particularly after his physical survival is assured. The parents as conforming members of their society can act in accordance with the customary formula without having to make their own encounter with the environmental hazards or devise their own adaptive solutions. It is only in migration or rapid social change, where the environment of child-rearing changes drastically from one generation to the next, that parents are deprived of this comfort, and even then many parents fall back on it, despite the inadequacy of traditional adaptations.

Cultural norms of parenthood are more than hazard-avoidance formulas; they are also designed to maximize positive cultural ideas in the next generation, as indicated in the third set of goals. But for most societies, historical and contemporary, the pressures of disease, physical danger (for example, from cooking fires), and economic uncertainty have contributed more heavily to the design of child-rearing customs than one might conclude from the anthropological literature. (See LeVine, 1974, for some examples of this contribution.) In this context, modern Western societies generally, especially their middle- and upper-class segments, constitute a special case in which parents are uniquely free of the worst hazards of infant mortality and subsistence risk that have been the common human condition for millennia. In comparing our situation and standards with those of Africans, we are in a limited sense examining our own past. This comparison, however, is primarily intended to illustrate how diverse are the human standards of parental behavior and to develop a culturally sophisticated approach to the assessment of parental effectiveness in our own and other societies.

I take the societies of tropical Africa as representing one type of cultural adaptation among non-Western populations because I am best acquainted with them; they share many child-rearing customs with peoples of the Pacific, Latin America, and Asia (as noted below). In making the comparison with the West, I use the concept of parental-investment strategies. This refers to the allocation parents make of their valued resources, including time and attention, in the pursuit of their goals as they perceive them. The goals pursued are usually compromises between what the parents want *for* their children (the three sets of goals outlined above) and what they want *from* their children (sooner or later); the strategies represent culturally acceptable pathways toward the compromise goals. For societies on both sides of the comparison, we shall inquire into the outcomes of their investment strategies, attempting to identify costs as well as benefits.

Among the agricultural populations of tropical Africa, infant mortality has long been high and subsistence precarious, and in many rural places these hard facts have not significantly changed; the child's physical survival and economic future remain in jeopardy and must be salient goals for parental behavior. At the same time, African parents expect their progeny to contribute to the family labor force during childhood and to become filial adults who will support their elderly parents; these goals must also be represented in child-rearing practices. As African parents see it, the investment strategy that best meets these goals is to maximize fertility, giving each one of many children highly attentive physical care in infancy, followed by training in obedience, responsibility, and sharing, much of which is delegated to older siblings. Maximizing fertility increases the probability of having some children who survive infancy to become agricultural workers on the family land and providers of support to parents in their old age. If many survive, more hands and help can always be used, in the extended kin network if not in the immediate family.

In the African context, however, maximizing fertility does not mean giving birth annually, but as often as is consistent with child health, usually every two or three years, permitting the baby to be breast-fed for eighteen to twenty-four months. During that period the lactating mother sleeps with her baby, feeds him on demand, makes sure he is carried most of the time (by herself or a child nurse), and responds rapidly to his cry (usually with feeding, sometimes with shaking). This pattern, which is also found in many non-African tropical areas of high infant mortality, can be seen as folk pediatrics, an attempt to react to the most frequent precipitant of infant death, dehydration from diarrhea, by constant close monitoring for acute discomfort and rapid administration of liquid when the baby cries. It can also be seen as aimed at minimizing the infant's disturbance of the African mother's work in the fields or market, for the baby managed this way is remarkably quiet by Western standards and easily lulled by carrying, shaking, and breast-feeding. Thus, the rural African mother pursuing the goal of the quiescent infant may be serving his health needs as best she can while keeping her primary attention focused on her work.

Once the child is weaned, the mother is ready to give birth again and devote the same attention to the new baby. The weaned child, often as compliant a toddler as he was a quiet infant, learns interdependence by sharing sleeping space, food, and eating bowl with other children, obedience by carrying small items at the command of his elders, and respect by greeting adults appropriately. The customary parental goal for childhood after weaning is formulated by the vernacular term for obedience, a phenomenon found in many agricultural societies in other continents as well as Africa. As Harkness and Super (1977) found among the Kipsigis of Kenya, mothers shape their small children's behavior toward comprehension of speech without speech production, that is, following maternal orders rather than conversing with mother. Such a child is soon ready to perform useful tasks at home, in the fields, and in the market. Parents see the pursuit of obedience in child-rearing as preparing the child to be a filial son or daughter, a respectful member of the local community, and (potentially) a willing client or apprentice to a powerful patron. This emphasis is on obedience, so salient in the child's relationship with his parents, is mitigated by more playful, relaxed, and emotionally nurturing interaction with other children of all ages and with grandparents and other adult kin.

Rural parents of tropical Africa look upon children as an investment; this is by no means an alien perspective to them. They expect themselves to be united with their children in a long-run relationship of "serial reciprocity" in which parents nurture the child physically when he or she is young, providing food and medical care; in return, the children help their parents in cultivation, in bridewealth payments (brought in by the daughter who obediently weds a man of substance), and in material support in old age. They are aware that such expectations are not uniformly met by adult children, and this is a source of much concern, but it serves only to reinforce their conviction that they must have more children to increase their chances of raising some who are as filial, obedient, and grateful as they ought to be. The role of the parent in his or her own investment strategy is as the provider of a nurturing environment; the actual care and training of children is often delegated to others in the family, particularly older children, so that as the child leaves infancy behind, his care may be supervised by parents (closely by mother, remotely by father) but his primary interaction will be with other caretakers and peers. There is much individual variation in this, but the point is that parents are normatively expected to invest most of their time in work and in interaction with other adults; they are not expected to devote much interactive attention to each postinfancy child, and no one will criticize them for not doing so as long as the child is supervised by someone older than himself. By the same token, while parents are expected to feed, house, and clothe each child, they need not provide him or her with separate living space or special possessions until maturity. Thus, parents do not feel unable to afford the cost of having another child; they experience the small cost as outweighed by the potential gain. Once the mother is past the risk of giving birth to a child and the task of carrying him through infancy, the greatest part of the parental investment, in terms of attention and special resources, has been made. (Where schooling and school fees have been introduced, this has begun to change.)

To summarize, rural parents in the agricultural societies of tropical Africa pursue an investment strategy aimed at goals which link the child's welfare to that of the parents and family, in both the long and short run. Since the economic welfare of the family as an agricultural production team and that of the parents as potential dependents in old age are seen as benefited by raising as many children to maturity as possible, maximizing fertility while minimizing infant mortality is central to this strategy. This is conceived primarily in material terms, beginning with the man's investment through bridewealth in the reproductive capacity of his wife, and continuing in her investment in the physical nurturance of the infant and small child. Once husband and wife are together, the cost of each additional child is seen as minimal, at least in comparison with the anticipated benefits, and this is reflected in the minimal allocation of individual resources to each child and the expectation that the older children will give more attention to their post-infancy juniors than the parents themselves. In infancy the goal of the quiescent child represents the mother's effort to maximize her child's chances of survival while minimizing his disturbance of her work routine. In childhood, the goal of obedience represents the formula for maximizing child labor on the family land, filial support for parents in their later years, and the child's capacity for economic adaptation to an institutional order that demands subordination. The success of this parental investment strategy in terms of benefits and costs will be assessed in comparison with the parental investment strategies of Americans.

It is obvious that Americans have different parental investment strategies. We have a low infant mortality rate, no child labor, and bureaucratically organized sources of care for the elderly; in our largely urban and suburban society, the family is a domestic economic unit sharing income and consumption rather than production. We see children as economic costs with no benefit to the economic welfare of parents and family; benefits tend to be conceptualized in terms of the emotional comfort or moral satisfaction a parent can derive from devoting personal resources to the raising of a new generation and maintaining long-term relationshps when he or she would otherwise be lonely. Parents frequently deny any expectation of material return or other calculated reciprocation from their children, and the emotional or moral benefits they hope for are often seen as attainable through having only a few children, sometimes only one, sometimes at least one of each sex. Concerning what parents want *for* their children, the survival problem is not paramount and most parents focus on the child's attainment of a position in life that is equivalent to or an improvement upon that of the parents. The maintenance or improvement of socioeconomic status is perhaps the one widespread parental goal specific enough for rational evaluation of investment strategies directed toward it. Parents tend to experience this goal, however, as part of a cultural ideology requiring the development of character traits such as independence which confer moral as well as practical advantages. In middle-class America, the nurturing of character traits sufficient for socioeconomic success and moral autonomy is assumed to be so costly of human time, effort, and attention as to require a full-time maternal role in which mothers are replaceable only by expensive arrangements simulating the personalized care of the mother herself. This conception of child-rearing virtually guarantees that the preferred parental investment strategy will involve a large investment in each of a small number of children.

A pervasive theme of American child-rearing ideology is independence, which can be considered under three headings: (a) separateness, (b) self-sufficiency, and (c) self-confidence. The emphasis on separateness begins at birth among middle-class Americans, with the allocation of a separate room to the neonate, requiring him to sleep in his own bed removed from others in the family. Compared with Africans, American infants experience a particularly sharp distinction between situations in which they are alone and those in which they are with others—for African infants are never alone and are often present as nonparticipants in situations dominated by adult interaction, while the American infant is often kept in solitary confinement when he is not at the center of adult attention. This creates (for the American) a bifurcation between extremes of isolation and interpersonal excitement that is unknown in Africa and may underly some of the striking differences in interactive style between peoples of the two continents. The American infant, unlike his African counterpart, has numerous possessions earmarked as belonging to him alone; their number and variety increase as he grows older, permitting him to experience the boundaries of his developing sense of self represented in his physical environment. American parents begin to emphasize sharing only after the child has become habituated to eating, sleeping, and being comforted alone, on his own terms, and with his own properties—which he has become reluctant to give up.

Self-sufficiency is at first closely associated with separateness, for the baby whose separate sleeping arrangements involve crying himself to sleep, even if only occasionally, acquires a primitive capacity for self-comforting not required by infants who always have mother's body available for this purpose. As the American baby gets older, self-sufficiency may be an ideal more than a reality, but it becomes a salient ideal. That is, the American child may not be able to do more for himself than his African counterpart—in practical terms he may be able to do less—but those things he does do receive so much praise and other positive forms of parental attention that he comes to see them as a valued part of himself, a source of pride. The African parents I have worked with generally believe that praise is bad for children because it will make them conceited and potentially disobedient (see LeVine and LeVine, 1966, p. 147), and African children acquire a wide range of skills without receiving (or expecting) praise for their performance. As adults, they take these skills, including the capacity to weave a fine basket or build a strong house, for granted rather than as a badge of honor or a type of invidious distinction the way Americans do. In this perspective, the American child grows up with an excessive but strongly motivating sense of pride in what he can do for himself; it provides a permanent source of striving for an idealized self-sufficiency in which others are not needed and dependence is a mark of failure.

If self-sufficiency represents an ideal for American parents and their children, "self-confidence" is the American folk concept of the psychological process by which the goal is achieved. This concept helps make sense of the lavish praise and enthusiastic attention that American parents give their infants and small children; they believe it gives the child confidence in his own capacity to deal with the world and master unfamiliar situations, a confidence he will need in growing up as an adult. A child who does not receive such attention from his parents is seen as emotionally impoverished, likely to become too fearful and insecure to adapt successfully to the challenges of life, or to adopt an active position (to take initiative) with respect to its opportunities. Americans are continually demonstrating to each other that self-confidence is the key factor in worldly success and even inner contentment, and no parent wants his child to grow up without this powerful kind of positive self-regard.

The American emphasis on the independent individual is so intense one might wonder what standards bear on the small child's social relationships. In contrast with the African parent's concept of serial reciprocity, here we might speak of "concurrent reciprocity" as the American emphasis. From early infancy the child is seen as a separate individual capable of exchange in face-to-face interaction with others, and parents attempt to elicit reactions that can become interactively elaborated in what Brazelton et al. (1975) call "play dialogues." Conversational exchange is the preferred medium for the maintenance of the parent-child relationship. In the long view that African parents take, their children are permanently bound to them, and the physical nurturance they give unilaterally in infancy will be reciprocated in filial support (equally unilateral but reversed) later in the course of the parent-child relationship. In the long view of American parents, their children will be independent and apart from them, and they, therefore, focus on the immediate reciprocity of conversational exchange as the symbol of the positive affect that binds them now and might continue to do so after the period of physical and economic dependence is over. In both the serial reciprocity of material exchange for Africans and the concurrent reciprocity of affective dialogue for Americans, the parent-child relationship can be seen as a normative prototype for other intimate social relationships.

To produce a self-confident, independent adult, love is not considered enough; Americans spend an enormous amount of money on their children, providing the personal space and individual possessions that contribute to their separateness and sense of worth as distinctive individuals. It is estimated that it took an average of $27,578 to raise a child from birth to age eighteen in New York City, starting in 1958, and that it took $84,777 to do so in 1976 (*New York Times*, September 20, 1976). These figures presume a modest standard of living; the allocation per child in the middle and upper classes would be much greater. And they do not include the costs of keeping women out of the labor market to serve as full-time mothers or the costs of day-care arrangements when mothers work. For the present purpose, the figures should be seen as indicating what a large material investment American parents in general, including those of modest means, make in the individual child before maturity. From infancy onwards, the child is encouraged to characterize himself in terms of his favorite toys and foods and those he dislikes; his tastes, aversions, and consumer preferences are viewed as not only legitimate but essential aspects of his growing individuality—a prized quality of the independent person.

The parental investment strategies of Americans, then, involve a large allocation of material and human resources (including maternal attention) to a small number of children, with the goals of producing an independent person who is able to cope with a changing environment, maintain or enhance in his own life the parents' social position, and continue in later child-parent relations the positive affect of early dialogues. There are unconscious meanings involved that make the pursuit and attainment of these goals satisfying for American parents, but they are not the concern of the present discussion, which is centered on whether the parental investment strategies work at a more superficial level. My first answer is that they do work remarkably well in both Africa and America, within limits set by the environment. It is not possible for Africans to solve the infant mortality problem by good mothering nor for Americans to ensure that no child will lose socioeconomic status, but each parental investment strategy that has evolved as a cultural pattern in a changing society represents a compromise formula providing a tested solution for each problem parents face. These solutions are at least effective enough in their milieu to warrant close examination before they are swept away by the advice of experts.

While I cannot provide a complete example of such a close examination in this chapter, I shall illustrate it in the context of the African-American comparison. The first question we might ask concerns the effectiveness of parents as child psychologists: are they able to shape the social behavior of their children in the directions they desire? One bit of comparative data from the Six Cultures Study sheds some light on this question. In that study, Whiting and Whiting (1975, p. 64) distinguish twelve categories of acts and give their frequencies in the naturalistically observed social behaviors of children aged three to ten years old from six culturally diverse communities. For the American children observed, the category "seeks attention" represents 14.6 percent of their (self-initiated) acts; for the African children (from "Nyamsongo" community of the Gusii people of Kenya), the proportion of attention-seeking is only 4.6 percent, less than one-third as much. This can be understood as reflecting outcomes of the divergent parental investment strategies described above. The Gusii do seek the quiescent infant, giving close physical care without a great deal of interpersonal excitement; they omit praise and emphasize obedience as the child gets older. Gusii children do not become exhibitionistic, but tend to avoid "public" attention, particularly that of their elders. This is because in the delegated command system of the family, obedience attracts no attention, but disobedience or other misbehavior does. The child comes to feel safest when not noticed; hence attention-seeking is infrequent. The other non-Western samples in the Six Cultures Study, all drawn from agricultural communities in which obedient children are needed and valued, show proportions of attention-seeking ranging from 3.3 percent to 6.6 percent, much closer to the Gusii than to the Americans.

The relatively high proportion of attention-seeking of the American children can also be seen as shaped by their infant experience—isolated much of the time and lavished with positive attention the rest, with praise and emotionally exciting conversation as basic elements in early social life. The early experience of American children leads them to expect attention to be intrinsically rewarding; hence the peculiar tendency they have to misbehave in order to attract attention, even at the risk of being punished. This tendency in itself, along with the larger pattern of attention-seeking, shows American parents are successful in producing the self-confident children they want, at least in a comparison with a culture of drastically different values, for seeking attention does involve risk, and the American children are less inhibited by it.

The divergent patterns of development indicated here can be analyzed for their costs and benefits as outcomes of parental investment. The data are impressionistic and the analyses speculative, but as illustrations they may prove instructive. On the side of the tropical African agriculturalists, the benefits are clear. The quiescent infants become obedient children who contribute agricultural labor; their support for elderly parents is not as reliable as it used to be, but many children continue to grow up filial. The costs are observable primarily in relation to environmental change. Compliant children used to close supervision are likely to take less initiative and show a less active attitude in coping with the tasks introduced by Western schools; but even this is a judgment of Western observers and not necessarily relevant to the adaptation of the African child. Another cost is experienced in the area of social control. As the community discipline imposed by the mutual supervision of village life decays, it becomes clear that children who are used to close and censorious supervision both need and want to have it continue in adult life. When it is absent, they suffer an anxious anomie and resort to litigation, alcoholism, and crime. In other words, they are not prepare psychologically to fill the void left by social-structural decay.

As for middle-class Americans, the outcomes of their parental investment strategies can also be seen to involve costs as well as benefits. On the benefit side, the evidence as I read it leaves little doubt that the parenting pattern described above produces children with the social competence to perform well in school. Compared with their rural African counterparts and children in many other parts of the world, American middle-class children are relatively uninhibited in the presence of adults and hence freer to act curious, responsive, and competitive in the classroom. They are verbally fluent, accustomed to conversing with adults, and predisposed to seek adult attention and approval through displays of self-sufficient accomplishment. Their strong sense of separateness makes them able to compete with other children without fear of the interpersonal consequences. Having been encouraged earlier to enjoy themselves in artificial problem-solving situations defined by toys and games, many become able to derive pleasure from school work and other utilitarian tasks; for some, this initiates the harnessing of hedonic strivings to work in a pattern that energizes learning and later occupational performance. This type of social competence, so taken for granted in middle-class America that only a comparative perspective brings it into focus, sets the child on an academic pathway toward the higher-ranking occupations and justifies pragmatically the investment parents may be making on moral/emotional/ideological grounds. However, the return on this enormous investment might be measured objectively, most middle-class parents regard not only the growing social competence of their children in school and other settings but also their growing capacities for independent judgment and choice, as the unquestionably beneficial results of parental devotion.

Without questioning the benefits, it is possible to begin assessing the costs. The child who receives a great deal of positive and exciting attention at one developmental level brings a high expectation for attention and excitement to the next levels. If it is not forthcoming, he actively seeks it, as in the American sample of the Six Cultures Study mentioned above, and if seeking in a quiet way does not work, he demands it or becomes disruptive enough to co-opt it. In a family with several small children, the demands for parental attention escalate through the simultaneous quest for an exhaustible resource. Parents often report considerable dissatisfaction with this phase in their lives. Aware that they have created in their children the expectation that now burdens them, they are unable or unwilling to deny its fulfillment, and they find themselves allocating more time than anticipated to parenting, while seeking relief in television, peer activities, and anything else that might distract the preschool child. At every stage from birth to puberty, the American middle-class child presents his parents with major demands for attention that are virtually unknown in Africa. From the sleepless weeks for parents before the newborn "sleeps through the night" to the restlessness of rainy weekends and lengthy school holidays, the autonomous centers of activity nurtured by American parents impinge upon adult family life to a degree that rural Africans can not imagine.

The real cost involved here, however, seems to reside in the psychological vulnerability of children with high expectations for attention, stimulation, and exchange. Once their expectations have been elevated in early experience, what happens if their subsequent environment falls short or fails to provide age-appropriate organization for the energy and curiosity that is brought forward? Many of the psychiatric disorders of childhood, from hyperactivity to neurotic symptoms and psychotic conditions, seem to have their origins in a matrix of disrupted or inconsistent patterns of parental attention that presume a child whose expectations for such atention is already high. It is beyond the scope of this paper to do more than speculate briefly about childhood psychopathology and its causes. But I have often wondered if the lower level of interactional excitement to which African infants become habituated does not protect them from a range of emotional disturbances found among middle-class American children, whose exposure to more concentrated attention from fewer persons might entail a higher level of risk. In other words, it might be that the pursuit of American values such as separateness and self-confidence in infant and child care, while resulting in a highly valued social competence in the next generation, also fosters vulnerabilities to emotional problems that mental health practitioners are called upon to treat. This is no more than a hypothesis, but it is one that deserves serious investigation before we advocate the spread of middle-class American styles of child-rearing to other groups in our own and other societies.

SUMMARY AND POLICY RECOMMENDATIONS

In this chapter I have examined the problem of whether cultural patterns of parenting make sense in adaptive terms, whether customary formulae for parental behavior embody such "folk wisdom" that they must be preserved or such fallacious concepts that they must be changed. To consider the problem comparatively I outlined the goals all human parents share in terms of protecting the young from survival threats and maximizing their future economic and social adjustment. The natural and institutional environments of human societies are so diverse that these goals must be realized differently in different places, with concomitantly varying criteria of parental effectiveness. There is no single yardstick for all human parents, but their adaptive responses can be comparably conceptualized as parental investment strategies, in which resources are allocated among immature offspring in such a way as to realize certain culturally formulated goals representing compromises between what parents want *for* their children and what they want *from* them. To illustrate the considerations that belong to future comparative analyses of parental investment strategies, a crude comparison of tropical African agriculturalists with middle-class Americans was attempted. Parents of both groups were seen to be pursuing strategies that work (or at least *have* worked) in the sense of realizing values and benefits the parents want, but at costs they might not be aware of.

There is nothing in this trial comparison that gives encouragement to those who would provide "expert" guidance for American parents. The closer one examines the subject calculus of parental behavior in a given culture, the more respect one has for its elements of "folk wisdom," no matter how outdated it has become or how much its failures are disguised. Parents everywhere need (a) information about the environments their children are likely to face, (b) contact and communication with other parents old and young, and (c) confidence in organizing an appropriate environment for their children. Policies that help American parents, who suffer particularly from social isolation, on these terms are timely and should be welcomed. Programs of didactic parent education should be viewed with suspicion if (a) they fail to assess the possible emotional costs in child-rearing practices designed to foster cognitive development and school achievement, (b) they make parents feel excessively responsible for the successes and failures of their children, adding to an already unwieldy burden of guilt, and (c) they tend to be insensitive to the cultural implications of spreading middle-class American child-rearing customs to other groups.

BIBLIOGRAPHY

Brazelton, T. B.; Tronick, E.; Adomson, L.; Als, H.; and Wise, S. "Early Mother-Infant Reciprocity." London: *CIBA Symposium* 33: 137, 1975.

Caudill, W., and Plath, D. "Who Sleeps by Whom? Parent-Child Involvement in Urban Japanese Families." *Psychiatry*, Vol. 29, 1966, pp. 344–366.

Caudill, W., and Weinstein, H. "Maternal Care and Infant Behavior in Japan and America." *Psychiatry*, Vol. 32, 1969, 12–43.

Harkness, S., and Super, C. "Why African Children Are So Hard to Test." In L. Adler (Ed.), *Issues in Cross-Cultural Research, Annals of the New York Academy of Sciences*, 1977, Vol. 285, pp. 326–331.

LeVine, R. "Parental Goals: A Cross-Cultural View." *Teachers College Record*, December 1974, Vol. 76, No. 2, pp. 226–239.

LeVine, R., and LeVine B. *Nyansongo: A Gusii Community in Kenya.* New York: Wiley, 1966.

Whiting, B., and Whiting, J. *Children of Six Cultures.* Cambridge: Harvard University Press, 1975.

Whiting, J. W. M.; Chasdi, E. H.; Antonovsky, H. R.; and Ayres, B. C. "The Learning of Values." In E. Z. Voget and E. M. Albert (Eds.), *People of Rimrock.* Cambridge: Harvard University Press, 1966.

3

Developmental Universals and Their Implications for Parental Competence

DANIEL C. JORDAN
School of Education
University of Massachusetts/Amherst
Amherst, Massachusetts

One of the most disturbing symptoms of modern Western society is the low priority given to the prevention of pathology and tragedy. When there is clear evidence of pathology, our society eventually comes around to investing resources in some remedial effort to deal with it. Unfortunately, such an effort is inevitably more costly and less effective than a preventive approach. Ultimately, the lack of concern for prevention decreases the quality of life and threatens survival itself.

It is my thesis that a society determined to guarantee its own survival and perpetually improve the quality of life for its people must give the highest priority to the prevention of pathology by generating and using whatever resources are required to meet the developmental needs of each new generation. Knowledge about human development is therefore a prerequisite to the effective use of resources to achieve those ends. These two elements, knowledge and resources, must be combined with a third essential factor to have a successful program. This factor is a structure or agency capable of carrying out the program. Since parents and families are in the most powerful position to influence each generation, they are the agencies that can apply human development knowledge to the greatest social advantage. Taken together they are the most logical point of leverage by which society can elevate the quality of life for its people. (For a full discussion of this thesis, see Daniel C. Jordan, 1978).

What might we expect if all parents could increase their competence by understanding the nature of universal development needs and applying their knowledge to meet them for all members of the family, particularly the very young ones? Such a massive preventive approach would surely bring about a transformation of society to the benefit of everyone.

But do we have enough knowledge about developmental processes at the present time to significantly improve the competence of parents and other social service institutions or agencies? How would such knowledge increase the effectiveness of parents? The purpose of this chapter is to suggest definitive answers to these questions and to provide the broad interpretive framework necessary to appreciate their full meaning.

Trying to understand the nature of human development is one of the most important undertakings of modern man.* It was also a concern of primitive man. Since the dawn of civilization man has wondered about his own nature and why he behaves the way he does. Before the birth of the scientific method, attempts to understand human nature depended primarily on philosophical speculation, religious tradition, and folklore. Today, these are insufficient for effective program planning. To them must be added the knowledge gained from careful empirical investigation.

Thus, behind every effective program is a significant empirical investigation. But this is only part of the study. Behind every significant investigation there is an implicit or explicit theory. During the past fifteen years, my colleagues and I, at the Center for the Study of Human Potential at the University of Massachusetts, have engaged in an investigation of the nature of human beings and how they grow, learn and develop. We have integrated into this inquiry the construction of a comprehensive theory of human development that, in conjunction with empirical work, has resulted in the identification of several developmental universals which have rich implications for the formation of social policy. In particular, they have significance for the kinds of policies required to strengthen the family and increase the effectiveness of parents.

Up to the present time, no single unifying theory of human development has existed. This is not surprising, since the human organism is extraordinarily complex and human behavior is even more varied and changes over time and under varying circumstances. Mussen, Conger, and Kagan (1969) state:

> There is no single comprehensive theory encompassing the vast body of accumulated data in the field of develomental psychology. A complete theory would have to include explanatory concepts accounting for the origins, as well as the mechanisms of development and change, of all aspects of psychological functioning–motor, cognitive, emotional, and social. It may be impossible to construct such an ideal theory; certainly no one has accomplished it yet [p. 16].

While the theory we have constructed may not turn out to be the "ideal" theory mentioned above, we believe it is a significant step in that direction and over time the theory can be tested, modified, retested, and continually refined. Such an undertaking is of extreme importance because in the absence of a comprehensive theory of development, the formation of social policies will be without a unifying framework. They will have no preventive effects because actions resulting from them will be at cross-purposes and undermine one another. Educational practices will be without a secure foundation, and any planning of programs designed to increase parental competence and strengthen the family will be fragmented and ineffective.

PHILOSOPHICAL AND THEORETICAL CONSIDERATIONS OF DEVELOPMENTAL UNIVERSALS

The great mathematician, logician, and philosopher, Alfred North Whitehead, stated in the opening section of his own philosophy of organism that it is the purpose of philosophy to create a scheme of thought within which every item of experience

---

*"Man" and "he" are used in the generic sense. "Humankind" and "it," "one," or other alternatives may be substituted.

can be interpreted. Since this is also the function of a good theory, we used his philosophy to test the comprehensiveness, logical consistency, and adequacy of our theory of development. While it is beyond the scope of this article to discuss organismic philosophy at any length, it is nonetheless important to explain several of its most general ideas, since without them it will be difficult to appreciate the comprehensive nature of the theory of human development we are proposing and the developmental universals that it sets forth.

In simple terms, a philosophy specifies assumptions or beliefs about life and creation, and the grounds justifying them. We studied the works of the great philosophers and thinkers, both past and present, to find out what they believed about the nature of man and the universe, and why they believed what they did. We found that most philosophers could be placed into one of two basic groups: those that believe man is no more than a machine, albeit a very complex one, and those that believe he is a soul or spiritual being "housed" in a body. Beliefs are important because they determine action. For instance, if you believe that man is a machine, you will treat him like one. If he gets sick, you will tend to think that he is ill because one of his parts has worn out or because he put the wrong fuel in his tank. If you regard children as machines, you will expect them to behave exactly as you want them to, for machines are not supposed to have minds of their own. You will tend to believe that you can manipulate and control them and that their feelings, intentions, and aspirations are illusions. This approach to medicine and child-rearing is largely based on a mechanistic view of life and creation. This view reached its peak in the work of the great physicist, Sir Isaac Newton. By the end of the eighteenth century, Newtonian mechanics dominated all scientific thought. When the human sciences such a psychology and sociology began to evolve, they borrowed heavily from the physical sciences. For this reason, many theories of human development reflect a mechanistic view of man.

Around the turn of the century, however, many physicists began to find that the philosophical view of the universe as mechanism had serious shortcomings and that as long as that philosophical outlook prevailed, it was impossible to generate new theories that would more adequately explain certain physical phenomena that could not be explained by Newtonian mechanics. In the Western world, we are now experiencing a shift away from the mechanistic view of man and the universe to an organismic one. The view of man as mechanism now seems no longer intellectually tenable.

Essentially, organismic philosophers regard the universe in dynamic rather than in static terms. They believe that everything is connected to everything else and that you cannot understand any one thing apart from the connections it has with everything around it. In other words, there is no way to understand the part until you see how it fits into the whole and a whole is more than the sum of its parts. (From this point of view, a family can be regarded as a whole, and no one member can be understood apart from his connections to that whole, which is far more than just the individual members or parts "added up.")

Because organismic philosophers are interested in process, time is an important variable. Time is irreversible because process is not reversible. Everything has a past, a present, and a future, all of which are interdependent. What takes place in the present not only becomes the past but influences the future. Thus, prevention is a better investment than remediation, for prevention means guiding the process of development in the right way the first time around. Organismic philosophers do not believe that whatever changes occur in something are always caused by events external to it but that in fact every entity in the universe has some say over its own destiny. This is particularly true of the higher forms of life. (Human beings are largely self-determining; volition is a developmental reality.) Finally, because of the central role of process in their thinking—how something changes from a former condition to its present condition—these philosophers are interested in the nature of potentiality and how it is actualized. Whitehead proposed that the translation of potentiality into actuality is the fundamental process of the universe characterizing its ultimate reality and that this process is what is meant by creativity, the "universal of universals" (Whitehead, 1960). Mechanistic philosophy does not give an adequate•explanation of creativity and therefore fails to account for the emergence of the new forms in the universe that are evident in evolution and human development.

For these and other reasons, we chose organismic philosophy as the interpretive framework within which to understand the nature of man. From this framework we generated the following propositions descriptive of the nature of man: that because we have no evidence to suggest limitations on man's ability to learn, we may assume that he is a creature of unlimited potential; that his ability to symbolize bestows upon him an extraordinary memory that connects past with present and endows him with a consciousness that creates awareness of the future and enables him to know that he knows and to know when he doesn't know; that when he knows he doesn't know he experiences a tension we call curiosity that motivates him to search and to learn; that because he is relatively free from instincts and dependent for so many years during the early part of his life, until he learns how to survive on his own, he has a capacity for love and trust that attracts the support he needs and inevitably makes him a social and moral being naturally equipped to assume, when his time comes, responsibility for socializing and caring for his own offspring; that his need to love and be loved and his awareness of knowing and not knowing make him yearn to find his place in the cosmos and set him on a search that gives rise to his art, religion, philosophy, and science; that his knowing and loving capacities, when used to create communities in service to man, are the most effective instruments of human and cultural evolution; and, finally, that he is a purposeful being whose perpetual becoming depends upon the formulation of ideals, plans, hypotheses that he consciously pursues. All of these qualities place man at the forefront of evolutionary forces and enable him to assume considerable control over them.

There will no doubt be many among those who determine social policy, administer parent-effectiveness training programs, or work as community and educational planners, who may object to this conception of man and assert that it has no real place in a scheme for practical action to strengthen families and increase parental effectiveness. But since this conception of man is reflected in the noblest visions and passions that have animated philosophy, religion, art, and sciences throughout history, it seems reasonable that any view of man that ignores these expressions of his highest aspirations will, in fact, be out of touch with the reality of man. I submit that any program that is supposed to serve man and is out of touch with this reality will certainly be rendered ineffective in the long run if not right from its beginning. It is simply not possible to be practical in service to man and at the same time ignore his distinctive characteristics and ultimate concerns—value and emotion, purpose and intention, consciousness, faith and trust, beauty and art, aspiration and love, meaning and knowledge, morality and self-sacrifice, and his cosmic yearning to find out how he fits into the universe.

These distinctive characteristics of man have to be developed. They each represent complex potentialities that become actualized through maturation and learning. A theory is needed to explain how their actualization takes place. From these philosophical perspectives on the nature of man, we deductively derived a comprehensive theory of human development that accounts for every developmental needs at any point in the life cycle, whether biological, psychological, sociological, technological, moral, aesthetic, religious, or philosophical. The theory is useful and practical because it enables anyone who understands it to generate ways to identify and meet basic developmental needs of human beings in any setting at any age level.

In accordance with organismic philosophy, our theory defines development as the translation of potentiality into actuality. Since we have already affirmed the infinitude of man's potentialities, it would be impossible to make a list of them. It is possible, however, to classify them, and once types of potentialities are clarified, it is possible to discover what promotes the actualization of each type. The theory also explains the nature and treatment of two major social pathologies—crime and mental illness—and all the varieties of their expression that come in the wake of the suppression of human potential.

From this statement of philosophy and theory, we can now suggest a broad definition of parental effectiveness. *To be an effective parent is to promote the actualization of one's children's potentialities at an optimum rate in positive directions.* As we shall see, in order to do this, parents must promote the actualization of each other's potentialities. In the case of single-parent families, children must be able to see their parent interacting with at least one other adult such that the interaction draws out the potentialities of both. There is no substitute for this kind of modeling as one of the most effective means of promoting the actualization of a child's potentialities.

One of the main purposes of the theory of human development is to make the general definition of parental effectiveness more specific. The theory helps answer such critical questions as: What are the potentialities to be developed? How do parents facilitate the actualization of these potentialities? How can they do so at an optimum rate? What is meant by "positive directions?"

Every child begins with the union of a sperm from his father and an egg from his mother. Each parent contributes twenty-three chromosomes that contain the basic genetic blueprint that guides the development of the fertilized egg into a little human being inside the womb. After the child is born, he gradually turns into an adult over a fifteen- to seventeen-year period of time. Whatever qualities this adult has must have existed as potentialities in the sperm and the egg, which constituted his beginning. Development refers to the sum total of the changes that take place from the point of conception on. Each change represents a potentiality being actualized. But as everyone knows there are millions upon millions of changes, far too numerous to list and describe in detail. No parent would be able to memorize the names of so many changes, let alone the sequence of their occurrence. We have therefore found it more useful to think of development in terms of basic patterns of change associated with the actualization of fundamental types of human potentialities.

Of course, parents cannot do anything about altering the genetic endowment of their offspring to achieve a predetermined developmental objective, but they can learn to understand the basic nature of human potentialities—the developmental universals—with which all children are endowed and learn how they can promote their actualization at an optimum rate. According to the theory of human development briefly outlined above, there are several kinds of potentialities. Each one of them constitutes a developmental universal. To be effective, parents need to know what they are and how to promote their actualization.

THE ROLE OF PARENTS IN ACTUALIZING BIOLOGICAL POTENTIALITIES

Since the basic structural design of each human being is contained in the genetic code, the first task of a parent is to insure the fullest translation of the genetic code into a living, spirited, human being. To do this, specific building materials are needed, particularly during the nine months of gestation and in the formative years of the child after birth. These building materials come initially from the nutrients carried by the sperm and the egg that fuse to form the conceptus. Secondly, the nutrients come from the food that the mother eats. Finally, the building continues with nutrients from the food that the child consumes after birth. Nutrition therefore plays a critical role in the actualization of biological potentialities–the translation of the genetic code into the bones, hair, nails, vessels, nerves, muscles, organs, and bodily fluids that make up the living physical body of the child. If the genetic blueprint calls for certain nutrients and they are unavailable, or not available in adequate quantities at the time required, the physical development of the child can be impaired. During certain periods, particularly during the pre-natal months and during the months right after birth, nutritional deficiency may result in irreversible damage. If the proper ingredients are not in the child's diet his growth can be impaired, or he may get sick, develop learning disability, become the victim of chronic ailments, and have any number of other physical problems.

There are factors other than nutrition that also have a direct bearing on the actualization of biological potentialities. For instance, every child needs rest. He needs protection from extreme temperatures. Pure water to drink and clean air to breathe are essential. Finally, accidents can retard growth or cause permanent damage to the physical body or lead to chronic problems, handicaps, or death. A properly nourished and cared for child will have fewer diseases and accidents, but when children do become sick or have serious accidents they need medical attention.

Thus, to be competent and effective parents requires that potential parents insure that they themselves are in the best health, looking after themselves nutritionally, before conception, and that the mother in particular will eat properly during the gestation period. They will provide the best food possible and help the child to develop eating habits that will insure the best of health. Effective parents will also provide adequate shelter, make certain that the child sleeps sufficiently, drinks pure water, has clean air to breathe, is supervised so that accidents are prevented, and provide medical attention when sickness or accidents occur. Unfortunately, many parents do not see the importance of their own physical health in the promotion of the actualization of their children's potentialities. This is particulary true in the case of pregnant women who do not realize that they place their unborn babies at risk by an inadequate diet, smoking, drinking, taking drugs, and not getting enough fresh air, rest, and exercise.

In other words, the effective parent is one who insures the actualization of biological potentialities by preventing unnecessary physical ailments, diseases, handicaps, and accidents through proper nutrition and medical care when necessary. Nutritional needs and the physical requirements of rest and shelter are the most basic developmental universals. If these are neglected or ignored, the actualization of psychological potentialities, to which we now turn our attention, will be impaired.

THE ROLE OF PARENTS IN ACTUALIZING PSYCHOLOGICAL POTENTIALITIES

Just as nutrition is the key factor in the actualization of biological potentialities, learning is the means by which psychological potentialities are developed. Thus, it is necessary for parents to understand these potentialities and acquire a basic knowledge of the nature of learning.

Our theory identifies five basic universal dimensions of psychological development, each one of which will be fostered by parents if they are to be considered effective:

1. perceptual
2. psychomotor
3. cognitive
4. affective
5. volitional

Perceptual development depends on learning how to process and interpret information that comes into the child's mind through the senses. Experience has shown that vision, hearing, and the sense of touch are the predominant means by which children learn about and understand their world. In part, developing perceptually comes about through maturation, but developing efficiency or acuity in perception also depends on learning. It is therefore important that parents provide the right kinds of stimulation to promote the development of perceptual abilities. The primary means of doing this is to create for the child a rich environment that contains many different kinds of sounds, different textures, wide varieties of shapes, colors, and variations in light and shadow, as well as many opportunities for manipulating objects.

Psychomotor development refers to gaining control over the voluntary muscles so that the child can handle his own body with efficiency and poise. Proper psychomotor development has an influence on other kinds of development and it should therefore be given a high priority by parents. Again, much of psychomotor development occurs naturally through maturation, but the refinements come about through learning. Children need opportunities for strengthening their muscles through climbing, jumping, swimming, running, and playing games that require coordination. Sitting passively watching television for long hours is not a good idea for young children since they should be up and moving about. Each day the child wakes up in the morning with several hundred thousand new muscle cells that need exercising.

Cognitive development means learning how to think and reason. Although thinking and reasoning depend largely upon language development, they have their roots in both perceptual and psychomotor development. Parents can stimulate cognitive development by providing experiences that enable a child to develop a variety of thought patterns such as seriation, classification, induction, and deduction, by involving them in speaking and listening, constantly showing them how things are related, and by giving explanations for everything. Parents who make opportunities for the children to solve problems, ask many questions, listen to answers and so forth, and who encourage their children to pose questions are promoting the actualization of cognitive potentialities. If a proper foundation of cognitive development is laid during the first few years of life, children will find that learning to think and reason in school will be greatly facilitated.

Affective development refers to the progressive organization of emotions and feelings by associating them appropriately with given environments, events, and ideas. For instance, fear appropriately associated with the right things makes a child properly cautious and serves a protective function. On the other hand, if a child associates fear inappropriately with certain places or things, such as bed or nutritious food, emotional development can be impaired. In essence, ensuring the proper emotional development of a child means associating the pleasing or hope-related emotions with those things he needs to do in order to continue growing and developing while associating the painful or fear-related emotions with those things that are likely to impair development. Parents can help their children grow emotionally by being reasonably consistent in rewarding and punishing them. The primary emphasis should be on rewarding them rather than on punishment because rewards indicate what the child should do, thereby providing a clear indication of appropriate action, whereas punishment by itself only indicates what he should not do. Rewards pave the way for action; punishment primarily inhibits action. A child is best guided if he knows what to do as well as what not to do. In other words, both reward and punishment are needed in order to promote the actualization of affective potentialities. However, a note of caution is warranted. Excessive rewarding leads to spoiling and excessive punishment leads to withdrawal and emotional disturbance. Both extremes should be avoided.

By *volitional development* we mean the emerging capacity to make choices about what to do, focusing attention on whatever is required to accomplish self-selected goals. In other words, volitional development is at the heart of gaining independence and self-reliance. Parents can facilitate volitional development by encouraging children to make decisions. Children, in their turn, have a natural inclination to become independent. They like to do things "all by themselves." While volitional development requires careful supervision, the child should have ample periods of time during which there is little or no interference except to ensure safety. If volitional capacity is impaired, lack of initiative, clinging dependency, and lack of self-confidence will result.

ROLE OF PARENTS IN HELPING THEIR CHILDREN TO BECOME COMPETENT LEARNERS

Because the actualization of five types of potentialities briefly discussed above are all largely dependent on learning, it is extremely useful for parents to understand as much as they can about the nature of learning and what promotes it.

We arrived at a very general definition of learning after analyzing all the basic learning theories developed by psychologists over the past seventy-five years. At first, our definition may seem difficult to grasp because it is necessarily general and abstract, but once understood, it has the virtue of enabling parents and teachers to generate many approaches to help the child when he is having difficulty learning. According to our theory of development, to learn is to *differentiate* experience (whether perceptual, psychomotor, cognitive, affective, or volitional) by breaking it down into contrastible elements, to *integrate* these elements into new patterns, and to *generalize* the pattern to new situations. In other words, any time parents can help a child to experience, understand, or see the difference between things or ideas (differentiation), grasp new connections among these different things (integration), and apply the integration to similar situations (generalization), they will be facilitating learning. Just grasping the full implications of this one statement would enable parents to develop a highly effective child-rearing/teaching style that fosters the growth of learning competence in their children.

It follows from our theory of development and its definition of learning that if the child is having trouble learning, it will be because:

1. he suffers from biological impairments due to poor nutrition;
2. he does not grasp the difference between two things or two ideas (that is, is confused);
3. he can see that things are different, but cannot see how they are connected or integrated (that is, sees only the trees but not the forest);
4. he can't generalize or transfer his learning to similar situations (that is, can't see how turning a faucet generalizes to driving a screw);
5. or some combination of any or all of the above.

Parents can facilitate learning by providing their children with a rich environment in which they can manipulate objects and discuss their actions, so that they see differences and relationships, and are able to generalize something learned in one situation by applying it to a different but related one. Consolidation of learning experiences for most children requires a certain amount of repetition that they usually enjoy. On the other hand, the rate of learning will be slowed down if there is too much repetition and no new experiences that require differentiation, integration, and generalization. New experiences may come from new ways of interacting with old environments or the introduction of new things into the environment (such as new toys, games, or activities).

Eventually, children come to understand that learning tasks require them to differentiate, integrate, and generalize and as they become conscious of this requirement, they can analyze problems and direct and guide their own learning most effectively. When that occurs, they have learned how to learn. This is one of the greatest gifts parents can bestow upon their children, for it places them in charge of their own destiny and liberates them to become the best that they can become.

PARENTS' ROLE IN PROVIDING FOUNDATION IN LANGUAGE, MATH, AND THE ARTS

One of the chief characteristics that sets human beings apart from all other animals is the capacity for symbolization—the ability to allow one thing to stand for something else. This ability not only makes communication possible but bestows the gift of a practically infinite memory. It enables us to record events, ideas, and plans for future reference. It also appears that symbolization is a critical factor in consciousness itself. Our sense of the past, our awareness of the present, and our anticipation of the future all depend upon consciousness. A proper integration of these three types of awareness enables us to plan our lives sensibly, thereby avoiding certain pitfalls, and to improve the quality of our lives. Language, mathematics, and the arts are the basic symbol systems through which culture becomes cumulative and is transmitted from one generation to the next. Thus, gaining a foundation in these symbol systems is a primary means of both cultural advancement and personal achievement. Symbolization is a critical developmental universal. If it is neglected, the general rate of the development of psychological potentiality will be slowed down.

I have already made reference to language development in connection with cognitive development. Given the central role of language in human development, no parents would be considered effective if they ignored this aspect of their children's development. Without adequate foundations in language, children enter school at a serious disadvantage that may plague them throughout their lives, but particularly during the school years. School failure is practically guaranteed for children whose facility with language is limited, especially if reading is never mastered and the capacity for oral or written expression remains undeveloped. There are many ways to promote language development, but two stand out as especially effective: (1) conversing freely and frequently with children, engaging them in discussions that describe events, deal with abstract ideas, and center around problem solving, and (2) reading to them from the very earliest ages and infusing within them a love of books and reading.

Children whose capacity for quantitative thinking is limited will also be at a disadvantage. Since everything that exists, exists in some amount, and because so much of the understanding of science depends upon mathematics, developing the foundations for quantitative thinking is extremely important. Again, the effective parent builds a foundation by exposing children to quantitative concepts and engaging them in activities that emphasize amounts, measurement, comparisons, and the cardinal and ordinal use of numbers.

Exposure to the arts—music, dance, theater, and mime, painting, and sculpture— is important because it develops the expressive and creative capacities of the child. The arts are a natural means through which language and mathematical abilities are also developed. Furthermore, the capacity to create and appreciate beauty is one of the most distinctive characteristics of man. Parents who rear their children devoid of experiences in the arts will be depriving them of one of the richest sources of meaning and pleasure in life. No civilization or society in which art was absent has ever existed. It is one of the cultural universals of all time and we should therefore not be surprised to find its counterpart as a developmental universal in children.

PARENTAL RESPONSIBILITY FOR THE DEVELOPMENT OF HIGHER ORDER COMPETENCIES: TECHNOLOGICAL, MORAL, AND RELIGIOUS/PHILOSOPHICAL

Mankind's capacity to survive depends in large measure on understanding the physical environment and being able to modify it for productive purposes. One of the outstanding features of man throughout his long history has been the capacity to invent and use tools. Those who understand how things work and who are able to use tools are at an advantage compared to those who can't. We are in a technological age. Adaptability and employability in the future will more and more depend upon technological competence. Effective parents will therefore want their children to develop some measure of *technological competence.* This can be done by engaging children in activities that depend on learning how things work—understanding cause and effect relationships. The average home is well equipped with materials and appliances suitable for such activities. They are the natural means for developing a demeanor of inquiry based on the scientific method. Without a grasp of these fundamentals, technological competence is not possible.

While competence in this area is important, it has to be recognized that our great technological advancements have had many deleterious side effects: energy wastage; pollution of air, land, and water supplies; ruthless depletion of natural resources; production of weapons capable of destroying mankind; and the marketing of large numbers of products that impair health. It is therefore clear that technology must be controlled by moral principles, otherwise technology will control us and dehumanize our lives. At the foundation of *moral competence* is a commitment to protect the right of every human being to a life filled with opportunities for the actualization of his own potentialies. This commitment inevitably entails controlling and directing technology so that it not only does not threaten survival, but rather is used to improve the quality of life for everyone. In addition, moral competence determines the way one individual relates to all others. In this age, when the planet has shrunk to the size of one country—a global village, as some have said—it is essential that children grow up sensing the oneness of mankind; committed to justice, and free from those prejudices that underlie discrimination on the basis of language, race, creed, national origin, sex, or economic status. In other words, in this day and age, parents cannot be effective if they do not lay the foundations for the establishment of world peace in the character of their children.

Because of consciousness, man has an acute awareness that he is distinct and separate from all other entities in the universe. This has impelled him to wonder how he is related to all other things, including the unfathomable mysteries underlying creation. His curiosity about the splendors of the universe and the ultimate unknowns confronting him have given rise to religious beliefs or philosophical orientations to life. It appears that no adult is fully mature if he has avoided coming to grips with such ultimate concerns and issues. At the heart of these concerns is the capacity to trust or to have faith. Children who grow up devoid of the capacity to trust or to have faith in others and in themselves will be afraid to approach any unknown. They are likely to be maladjusted, disturbed in their relationships with others, and will probably discover that they are their own worst enemy. Effective parents will therefore make efforts to lay a firm foundation for trust and faith that will enable their children to deal with the ultimate issues and concerns. This may take the form of a particular religious orientation or some philosophical view of life and its significance. Having developed such an orientation or view that is free from superstition is what we mean by *religious or philosophical competence.* The sanctions of moral convictions that, in turn, can control technology and make it serve mankind are derived from such a religious or philosophical overview.

Each of these higher-order competencies rests on a related set of values and each set of values is organized around an ideal. Technological competence rests on material values organized around the ideals of scientific inquiry. Moral competence is determined by social values organized around the ideals of justice, human rights, cooperation, and service. Religious or philosophical competence depends on spiritual values ordered by the ideal of reverence for life and its relationship to ultimate unknowns in the universe- a relationship that must be taken on faith. When these material, social, and spiritual values are integrated, they define the Self—the character of the self-actualizing child and the maturing adult.

The importance of the parents' role in assisting children to form positive values and attitudes of these three types is so great that it is almost impossible to overestimate it; what humanity values determines the social priorties that have the heaviest claim on resources. If these priorities do not reflect a high regard for the developmental universals we have outlined, the social order will be suppressive of human potential and will eventually be weakened to the point of collapse—even if the collapse is preceded by a show of totalitarian strength on the part of the ruling few. If, on the other hand, what parents value draw out the potentialities of their children, they will very likely adopt and further refine the values of their parents.

As children mature, it is essential that they see their parents performing more roles than just parental roles. After all, parents do other things than raising children and these other things have a bearing on how effective they are as parents. Parents are also neighbors, inhabitants of a city, town, or civil jurisdiction, citizens of a state or country, and most importantly, members of the family of man—a family of remarkable diversity spread over the face of the earth. The evolution of humanity is unthinkable apart from the progressive development of wider spheres of social and cultural unity through the effective coordination of human diversity. This principle is an evolutionary universal that is expressed in the developmental universals reflected in material, social, and spiritual values and their respective higher-order competencies: technological, moral, and philosophical/religious. The individual personalities of growing children must contain within them the seeds of values that foster trust and guarantee social security through an abiding commitment to human rights—rights that in turn guarantee the opportunity for everyone to develop his potentialities to the fullest. Such a commitment, unlikely to survive severe tests if it is not grounded in religious and phillosophic sanctions, is a prerequisite to the actualization of potentialities in "positive directions." Parents who transmit prejudices to their offspring are guiding the actualization of their potentialities in negative directions. The opposers of human rights espouse values that are not universalizable. Eventually they become the tragic victims of the values they model.

Civilization must have some basis in order, and that order ultimately inheres in the value systems shared by the individuals comprising it. Commitment to human rights is an indispensable element of social order and the ground of human rights is the provision of and protection of opportunities for the actualization of human potential for everyone. When these rights are guaranteed, goodwill flourishes and parents and families will be at peace because developmental universals are being universally met. If families and parents are at peace, the world will be at peace.

Thus, the attainment of world peace is only possible if people in their capacity as responsible and effective parents and community members are prepared to adopt and to educate their children in the universal ideals that can create a stable and progressive social order.

Parents cannot raise children without a community and a community at war with other communities is no place to model the values of human rights. Hence, parent effectiveness includes participation in community building. The great task here is to keep alive the vision of the developmental universals, for it will nudge the human species forward and enable us to invest our resources in helping each other, as parents and community members, to overcome every obstacle in the path of our individual and collective becoming.

SUMMARY

A working definition of parental competence must be clear, comprehensive, and universal. Without such a definition, parent education programs and the formation of social policies related to strengthening families will lack coherence and effectiveness. To achieve such a definition requires a philosophical perspective and theoretical treatment coupled with the findings of empirical research concerning human growth and development. In this chapter, we presented organismic or process philosophy as the most useful perspective, and a comprehensive theory of human development derived from it as a highly promising interpretive framework for understanding all of the issues concerning effective parenthood. The distinguishing feature of the theory is the identification of developmental universals—universal needs and developmental processes related to them that, if supported and facilitated, will ensure maximum actualization of human potential. From this theory, we generated a broad definition of parental effectiveness. *In essence, it means meeting the developmental needs of children in a timely manner so that the actualization of their potentialities is promoted at an optimum rate in positive directions.*

We specified two universal types of potentialities that effective parents would help to actualize: the biological and psychological; explained how their actualization has to be structured, thereby forming three universal types of values: material, social, and spiritual, on which three higher-order competencies rest: technological, moral, and religious or philosophical; discussed the role of ideals in the organization of value sytems; and, showed how participating in building a community that recognizes the moral ideal of the oneness of the human species and operates on the principle of human rights is an indispensable element in parental effectiveness. Injustice, violence, and prejudice all suppress human potential and lead to costly social pathologies. Thus, effective parents are necessarily committed to human rights and to the building of communities based on them, for they are the guarantors that the developmental universals we have presented will not be suppressed, but encouraged and actively promoted.

BIBLIOGRAPHY

Anshen, Ruth Nanda (Ed.). *The Family: Its Function and Destiny.* New York: Harper Bros., Publishers, 1949.

Asimov, Issac. *Asimov's Guide to Science.* New York: Basic Books, Inc., 1972.

Bronfenbrenner, Urie. *Influences on Human Development.* Hinsdale, IL: The Dryden Press, Inc., 1972.

Bronowski, Jacob. *The Ascent of Man.* Boston: Little Brown & Co., 1973.

Cohen, Stewart and Komiskey, Thomas J. (Eds.) *Child Development: Contemporary Perspectives.* Itasca, IL: S.E. Peacock Publishers, Inc., 1977.

deRivera, Joseph. *A Structural Theory of the Emotions.* New York: International University's Press, Inc., 1977.

Dobzhansky, Theodosius. *Mankind Evolving.* New Haven: Yale University Press, 1962.

Dubos, Rene. *A God Within: A Positive Philosophy for a More Complete Fulfillment of Human Potentials.* New York: Charles Scribner's Sons, 1972.

Firkiss, Victor. *Technological Man: The Myth and the Reality.* New York: New American Library, Mentor ed., 1970.

Gibson, Eleanor J. *Principles of Perceptual Learning and Development.* New York: Appleton-Century-Crofts, 1967.

Hesburgh, Theodore M.; Miller, Paul A.; and Hort, Clifton R. *Patterns for Lifelong Learning.* San Francisco: Jossey-Bass, 1973.

Huxley, Julian. *Science in Synthesis.* New York: Spring Lerlag, 1971.

Jordan, Daniel C. "The Process Approach." Chapter 11 in Seefeldt, Carol (Ed.) *Curriculum for the preschool-primary child: a review of the research.* Columbus, OH: Charles E. Merrill Publishing Co., 1976.

Jordon, Daniel C. "Applying Knowledge of Human Development: New Dimensions in Parent and Teacher Education." In book by S.P. Raman, *Nutrition in Human Development.* Stamford, CT: Greylock, Inc., 1978.

Jordan, Daniel C., and Streets, Donald T. "The Anisa Model: A New Basis for Educational Planning." *Young Children*, Vol. 28, #5, June 1973, 289–307.

Laszlo, Ervin. *A Strategy for the Future.* New York: George Braziller, 1974.

May, Rollo. *Love and Will.* New York: W. W. Norton, 1969.

Mussen, Paul Henry; Conger, John Jay; and Kagen, Jerome. *Child Development and Personality.* 3rd edition. New York: Harper & Row, 1969.

Ornstein, Robert E. (Ed.) *The Nature of Human Consciousness.* New York: Viking Press, 1974.

Phenix, Philip H. *Man and His Becoming.* New Brunswick, NJ: Rutgers University Press, 1964.

Polanyi, Michael. *Science, Faith and Society.* Chicago: University of Chicago Press/Phoenix Books, 1964.

Rokeach, Milton. *The Nature of Human Values.* New York: Free Press, 1973.

Ryan, Thomas Arthur. *Intentional Behavior: An Approach to Human Motivation.* New York: Ronald Press, 1970.

Tagore, Rabindranath. *University Man.* New York: Asia Publishing House, 1961.

Wallace, Helen M., et. al. (Eds.) *Maternal and Child Health Practices.* Springfield, IL: Charles C. Thomas, 1973.

Whitehead, Alfred North. *Process and Reality*, New York: The Macmillan Co., 1960.

Wilson, John; Williams, Norman; and Sugarman, Barry. *An Introduction to Moral Education.* Baltimore, MD: Penguin Books, 1967.

Young, John Zachary. *An Introduction to the Study of Man.* New York: Oxford University Press, 1971.

Part Two
Parenting in a Multicultural Society

Parenting styles are derived from the enculturation process. In our multicultural and class-stratified society, the experiences that compose enculturation vary widely for both the adult and child; this fact has been largely ignored throughout American history. Despite the richness and diversity on its ethnic enclaves, American society has been seen in terms of white, middle-class, Anglo-Saxon values and beliefs. This ethnocentrism is reflected both in the images of the family that dominate our national consciousness and in our social programs. Often this has resulted in a mistaken sense of embarassment, guilt, and feelings of inadequacy on the part of members of minorities and the poor.

The second section of the anthology explores the family life of five minority groups. Some of the keen issues tackled in this section are the following: Have minority-group families dealt with the pressures of the larger society? What have been some of the the results of the interface? What are the unique cultural values of the black American, Mexican-American, Puerto Rican-American, native-American, and Asian-American? What is the relationship between those subcultural values and those of the dominant society? Which values should prevail? Why? What are the policy implications for a multicultural society such as that of the United States?

In the first selection, James P. Comer discusses the adaptive behavior of black families necessitated by a social history of descrimination and exploitation. In response to the treatment they have received in a racist society, the black family is seen to have developed institutions (namely, the church) and coping skills that have enabled black parents to fulfill their basic responsibilities to their children and the society. Comer warns that any future family policy that is based on comparisons of the black family to the white family which does not take into account the diverse experiences of the two groups will ultimately confuse the issues and undermine supportive and restorative intervention.

In the second selection, Manuel Ramirez and Barbara G. Cox question the validity of the traditional conflict/replacement model of enculturation and suggest that a multicultural model may be better suited for American society. The conflict/replacement model implies that ethnic diversity creates problems for the dominant culture and the individual, and that only through assimilation (Americanization) can these difficulties be overcome. Ramirez and Cox feel that this model is both narrow and degrading, and instead, suggest a model based on the Mexican-American parenting experience in which biculturalism leads to multisocial identities, tolerance, and the personal and intellectual flexibility necessary to function successfully in a multicultural society.

The third selection by Bill J. Burgess explores the differences between child-rearing in native-American communities and the dominant society. The author describes parenting in native-American communities as stressing social values (cooperation, collective organization, extended family, and respect for the aged) which are in direct conflict with the values associated with the dominant culture. Burgess suggests that any future policy recommendations concerning native Americans respect these values, while providing adequate means to overcome basic economic, educational, and health handicaps.

The fourth selection by Bob H. Suzuki discusses Asian-American parenting. As exemplified by their economic and educational accomplishments, Asian-Americans have been, perhaps, more successfully acculturated than any other ethnic group. Yet, Suzuki suggests that this has been accomplished while the Asian-American family has retained its cultural identity. In this family structure, parents teach egalitarian values and respect for age, while at the same time enforcing discipline through non-physical means. The author recommends that any family policy decisions should respect cultural diversity while providing for basic physical and economic needs.

The fifth selection by Joseph Fitzpatrick and Lourdes Travieso examines the Puerto Rican family. The family structure is studied in terms of kinship patterns, sexual dynamics, marriage, and parenting as experienced on the island. Using the island experience, they then discuss the degree to which these values and relationships are exhibited by the Puerto Ricans living in the United States.

In the final selection, Magdalene Carney and Elizabeth Bowen, writing from the perspective of the black family, in effect summarize the concerns of all minority community members. They suggest a range of policy recommendations concerning parenting that include health, housing, educational, and economic issues, as well as the basic organization of future policy research and development.

4

The Black Family: An Adaptive Perspective

JAMES P. COMER, M.D., M.P.H.

Yale Child Study Center
Yale University
New Haven, Connecticut

In recent years the black family has received more study and elicited more controversy than most American institutions. The contested issues have been many: Is the black family matriarchal or patriarchal? If it is matriarchal, don't we really mean matrifocal or maternal? Is there a role reversal in the black family? But if so, in what area of family function and in relationship to what—a white family standard? Is that an indication of pathology? Is the mother-headed family necessarily pathological? Is pathology largely a product of black family interaction or largely a product of environmental conditions? Is there a deterioration of the black family or is it becoming a stronger and more effective institution?

These questions, implicit and explicit, are raised in response to a white American, middle-income model or normality. This is not a very helpful approach. The black family has not had the same experience as the white. The criteria of success cannot be the same. A black and white family comparison is like trying to determine which of two ditchdiggers did the most work by examining the earth removed when one is digging in sand and the other in clay.

A more fruitful approach is to simply ask how well the black family performs its adaptive task under given social circumstances. A full description of the task of the black family and its adaptive efforts should suggest a perspective and assessment approach which goes beyond issues of illegitimacy, welfare dependency, crime, and the questions raised above. In addition, black family practices, from strict child-rearing approaches to the absent father, might represent adaptive rather than pathological efforts when viewed from this different perspective. A review of the universal function of the family is needed.

FAMILY FUNCTIONS AND RESPONSIBILITIES

Theodore Lidz (1963), a student of the family, wrote:

Each society has a vital interest in the indoctrination of the infants who form its new recruits. It lives only through its members, and its culture is its heart

43

which they must keep pulsating. Without it, its members are rootless and lost . . . they must be so raised that the culture exists in them and they can transmit it to the next generation. It is a task that every society largely delegates, even though unwittingly, to an agent—the family [p. 19].

In addition to transmitting the culture, adult partners meet most of their sexual and relationship needs in this unit. This protects the society from emotional stress and strains which would result from a more competitive and uncertain arrangement. The family is an economic unit. Adults meet their own food, clothing, and shelter needs and those of their children. In the United States, families must take the responsibility for meeting the health care and some of the educational and training needs of their children. The same is true for recreation and expression needs. Through child-rearing efforts, parents or caretakers attempt to meet the psychological, social, emotional, and intellectual growth and development needs of their children. This includes helping the children acquire a sense of belonging, adequacy, and worth. Through the child-rearing process they transmit attitudes, values, ways, and skills which permit their children to move from a state of complete dependency to a more or less independent adulthood status. As adults they must be able to function well in the society they are in and, hopefully, to which they belong.

To achieve these ends, parents or caretakers must promote the psychological, social, and intellectual development of their children. They must teach and model the required behavior of the society. They do this best when they can earn a living and provide for their basic needs.

Several examples will convey the way in which social skills and expectations are taught and modeled. When Mary, the two-year-old, wants a glass of milk but the caretaker is busy feeding John, the new baby, the caretaker tells Mary that she must wait just a little while and then he or she will get her the milk. The two-year-old's frustration tolerance is low. Children of this age want what they want right *now*, even yesterday. They will try to intimidate the caretaker with a temper tantrum. But because the parent or caretaker is so important to them, they will generally wait. When the caretaker praises the waiting, a child will feel that it is worthwhile to display such ability in the future. In this process a child increases his or her capacity to tolerate frustration, wait, understand the needs of others, understand the behavior which will meet his or her needs, and bring him or her approval. Such success is addictive.

Billy wants Betty's ball. Because he is two years older he may just walk over and try to take it. The caretaker forbids such a response and teaches the appropriate response expected in the larger society. In a similar fashion the caretaker teaches appropriate religious practices, customs, attitudes, values, and ways.

Adults are best able to do this in a positive way when they themselves have had their own needs met, when they are an accepted and valued part of the society with a resultant high sense of self-esteem, belonging, and security. Persons who are employed feel that they are making a contribution to themselves, their family, and the society. They are able to participate in and trust the institutions of the society and are therefore most likely to feel a high sense of self-esteem, belonging, and security (Comer and Poussaint, 1975).

These family conditions do not develop by chance. Specific political and economic policies and practices create them. For example, economic policies which promote jobs permit people to work, take care of their families, feel good about themselves, and promote a sense of value and worth among individuals. Being able to vote for government leaders permits people to feel that they have a sense of control over their destiny, that the leaders must be responsive to their needs. This promotes a sense of trust in the vital societal institutions.

Although they did pertain to the African family, most of these conditions did not pertain to the slave family. What follows is a discussion of the social conditions of these families.

THE AFRICAN FAMILY

Most Afro-Americans are decendents of the people of the west African gold and ivory coast, around the Niger Delta and Dahomey. While conditions varied between groups, certain structural and functional elements were common or similar to all of them (Comer, 1972).

A close-knit family or kinship was at the core of all political, economic, and social organization. Weaving, blacksmithing, woodcarving and other traditional crafts were usually hereditary within a lineage (a group of people numbering from 12 to 500 who can trace their descent to a known ancester or lineage founder). Each lineage had its own ancestral shrine, history, taboos, and rituals. Art, music, and literature (story-telling or folklore) were not reserved for professionals. They were an integral part of life, present and utilized in every aspect of life from birth to death. Every African was literally his own musician, bard, and artist, although some were better than others and there was some degree of specialization.

Lineage members generally lived together in one section of town and had a special responsibility to each other. Each lineage was usually composed of a number of extended families. The relationship of adults to children and of children to adults was well defined and was transmitted from generation to generation. In general, there was a reverence for age in African societies that was more marked and institutionalized than in European societies. For example, government decision-making was often in the hands of older men; and deference was given to age even in the expression of an opinion.

While children were to show respect to adults, adults in return were expected to be supportive of and helpful to children. Thus, a child in need could call upon any adult within his lineage and tribe and expect concerned attention. Parents expected others to be concerned about the conduct of their children. They welcomed the help of others in setting limits for their children and even in punishing them for misbehavior. Kinship arrangements were formerly established for counselling, care and disposition of wives, children, and property during the life of a man and after his death. For example, in the Afikpo Ibo tribe, the oldest brother in a family was the counselor and advisor to the son of his sisters, even while their father lived.

Among the Yoruba, a group significantly represented among present day Afro-Americans, each lineage had its own farmland. The land belonged to all members of the lineage; no man had to work for hire. All helped to provide or secure basic needs such as food, clothing, and shelter. The reverence of land, animals, and/or nature was more marked than in European societies.

Among the Ewi, three grades of chiefs constituted the government and there were chiefs representing each lineage. The opinions of people within a lineage were expressed through the junior chiefs to the senior chiefs, who made the decisions. When possible, a dispute between two members of the lineage was settled within the lineage. Where it was not possible, disputes were settled by the elders at the village and town levels. In cases of irreconcilable disputes between the lineages, the king's decision was final. Thus, government was not only by the people, for the people, and of the people, but government by the kinspeople, for the kinspeople, and of the kinspeople.

An important element of social organization in west Africa was the age-set and age-grade system. Among the Afikpo Ibo an age-set comprised all the people of the town or village born within approximately three years of one another. Membership was automatic and crossed lineage line. Several age-sets combined to form a larger body, an age-grade, with specific village functions or services to perform. The young adult was responsible for maintaining law and order. The next older grade formed the executive arm of government. The older men made up the legislative and judicial bodies. Young men learned their future rolls while working as apprentices to older men. Parallel age-grades existed for women, and the male and female supported each other in social and ceremonial activities. Age-set members were very supportive of each other and had strong feelings of loyalty. They often participated in village and tribal ceremonies in a group and they usually attended the personal ritual and ceremonial events of fellow members.

Child-rearing among the west African societies from which many black Americans are descended range from the informal and noncoercive to the strict and authoritarian. Specific attention was given to the narration of folklore and of important events in the history of a tribe. Through such stories, the youngsters learned what was expected of them in the present and in the future.

West African family conditions were not utopian. But meaningful mechanisms from kinship ties to courts encouraged acceptable behavior; meaningful ritual and ceremony shared with members of one special age-set gave the African an intense sense of belonging and being a part of things. These elements guaranteed a sense of security that is in marked contrast to the anomie and alienation of modern "advanced" societies.

By contrast, the black family in American was cut off from the organization and management or executive function of the old culture. Only the dance and song aspects of religion—all modified—were permitted to remain. These African remnants did not threaten the master; in fact, they sustained the slave and minimized depression and were therefore useful to the master. Where expressive or stylistic remnants were threatening, such as the drum, they were eliminated. The slave family was required to operate in a way antithetical to meeting with needs of its own members as it did in Africa. The slave family was expected to prepare its children to accept exploitation and abuse. Its entire purpose was to be a productive unit for the master and to rear children to be the same.

An examination of the black family under the three major conditions which have existed in America—slavery, overt suppression, and emergence—should make the unique nature of the black family task more apparent.

THE SLAVE FAMILY

Slaves had no self-serving economic function. The purpose of a family, when it existed, was to serve the master. The slave had no other value. To maintain psychological health and social survival, the slave family had to develop a social system in which physical survival, organization, and purpose were possible under degrading conditions. It had to be able to create a sense of worth and value for its members while they experienced rejection and abuse, or acceptance as inferior or less deserving persons, from the master and other whites. To do this, the slaves took a foreign institution—the white church—molded it in their own image and created a substitute society—the black church (Frazier, 1963).

The concept of a hereafter provided by a Christian religion gave blacks some sense of freedom from the white master control. It gave blacks some sense of belonging and worth. The Lord cared when the white master and the white American society did not. Thus, the words of the spiritual:

> If you cannot preach like Peter,
> If you cannot pray like Paul,
> You can tell the love of Jesus,
> And say, "He died for all."

Restraint and responsible conduct, one to another, as the price of entrance to heaven provided a basis for humane interpersonal conduct and social organization independent of master-imposed control. Again, the verse of the spiritual is revealing:

> I'm work-in' on the build-in' for my Lord,
> If I were a sinner, I tell you what I would do,
> I'd throw away my sinful ways and work on the build-in' too.
> I'd throw away my dancin' shoes and work on the build-in' too.
> I'd throw away my gamblin' dice and work on the build-in' too.

The church provided an outlet for individual talents, self-realization and self-expression in a slave culture which had no opportunities for blacks other than meeting the needs of their masters. Religion in general, and church services in particular, provided an outlet for a discharge of tension which might have been psychologically damaging for many more had it not existed. The practice of "shouting," verbal response to the sermons and other distinctly black church styles served (and still serve) this function. It was the black church—often maligned and misunderstood by blacks and whites alike—which was the major adaptive mechanism for black families during slavery. Thus, black families psychologically and socially oriented and organized around religion, and the church maintained a relatively positive individual and black group concept in spite of the conditions of slavery.

A second major adaptive effort was organization around the white master. From this relationship emerged a black family that was often a carbon copy of the white. It embraced religion, but for this group, church and religion was less important, not a substitute society. Respect and dignity came primarily from acceptance or approval by the white master. This came from being a good slave or accepting an inferior life status. Individuals and families within this psychological and social organization framework developed coping skills and adjusted to the slave role, but could not develop a healthy sense of themselves as blacks. These families met the task expected of them by the slave society better than they met their responsibility to their own membership. The slave society prepared the young to accept exploitation and abuse, to ignore the absence of dignity and respect for themselves as blacks. The social, emotional, and psychological price of this adjustment is well known.

This is the group commonly referred to as having an Uncle Tom personality or character. Obsequious, acquiescent, passive, ingratiating relationships with the master and with other whites is the mark of "Tom." Sometimes passive-aggressive behavior was displayed where possible—leaving farm equipment to rust, working as slowly as possible, undermining the more powerful master of whites wherever possible. Having low esteem for themselves as blacks, and for other blacks as well, is part and parcel of this system.

"Bad nigger" was another adaptive response. The literature and folklore of slavery is full of "bad nigger" stories. This was the defiant African- or American-born slave who would not submit partially or fully to the indignities of slavery. Some ran away. Some actively terrorized the master and some partially submitted and actively sabotaged the master wherever possible.

Large numbers of slaves could not make adequate adaptive responses. Some were infantilized, or rendered dependent to the point of not being able to function as family heads when slavery was over. Some lived under such degrading slave conditions that they were not able to mobilize significant or healthy organizational forces. This group was not able to meet the slave society's or its own membership's needs. Benjamin Botkin (1958) told of the problem in his collection of slave narratives:

> He (the slavemaster) went on to my grandpa's house and says, Toby, you are free! He raised up and says, You brought me here from Africa and North Carolina, and I going to stay with you long as ever I get something to eat. You got to look after me.

The repression of the small percentage of pre-Civil War black families was severe. By and large they experienced exclusion and a marginal existence in the mainstream of American life. These factors plus their small number meant that they were not able to make an adaptive effort which was significantly different from that of slaves. To cite Botkin (1958) again:

> With the free niggers it was just the same as it was with them that was in bondage. . . . The slaveowners, they just despised them free niggers and made it just as hard on them as they can. They couldn't get no work. . . . So because they was up against it and never had any money or nothing, the white folks make these free niggers 'sess [pay] taxes, and 'cause they never had money for to pay the taxes with, they was put up on the block by the court man . . . and sold out to somebody for enough to pay the tax what they say they owe.

Thus, slavery was antithetical to the creation of healthy family life. Large numbers of black families and children were adversely affected over the 250-year span that slavery existed in America. Obviously, many used the church and other mechanisms to obtain a sense of purpose, dignity, and direction and to rear their children in a healthy fashion. But under these overwhelming circumstances, too many could not succeed in this goal.

THE PERIOD OF SUPRESSION

From the end of slavery until the 1940's more than 90 percent of the black population worked as sharecroppers, tenant farmers, low paid laborers, and domestics—

the lowest level of the job market. Black participation in politics in the South—where 90 percent of the black population lived—was held to a minimum through blatantly illegal registration and voting procedures, economic and physical intimidation, and violence. Thus, a disproportionate number of black adults were unable to earn a living wage, take care of themselves and their families, control the environment around them, and experience the sense of adequacy, control, and belonging relating to being able to do these things.

With the end of slavery, the white master was no longer the link to the larger society. The black family had to relate to the larger system and compete directly with antagonistic whites.

The tasks facing the black family remained conflicting and complex. The society continued to require black families to transmit a value system which included negative attitudes about themselves and to teach ways which were demeaning, limiting, and harmful. At the same time, the society expected the black families to meet the biological, social, and emotional needs of its members, young and old. Again, the black family managed to do both. In addition, it established its own healthy task: to change the attitudes and ways of the total society so that meeting the human dignity of its members would not be in conflict with the expectations of the society.

In other words, the adaptive task of black families and the black community was to force the society to drop its racist and demeaning expectations for blacks. This task has been responsible for a new phase in the black experience, the Civil Rights and Opportunity Movement, which eventually spawned the period of the emergence of the black family.

For three quarters of a century after slavery, many black families did the suppressive society's dirty work first and best (Comer, 1969). They prepared their children to accept a degraded position in the society. Parents crushed aggression in children, especially boys. A black father in Texas scolded his teenage son who was beaten for entering a bus before whites, "You know you ain't got no business 'gittin' on the bus before the white folks." A youngster watched his father, a college professor, stand in "the black line" at a store and receive insults from a white teenage clerk. A black woman, fearful of her husband's life, pleaded with him not to argue with an arrogant white policeman even though he had cause.

Harsh discipline observed in excess in many black families today is directly related to the black parents' need to "beet the badness out of the boy" . . . lest it cause him to forget his place with the white policeman. Given the level of overt suppression possible and practiced, such preparation and reaction was adaptive and necessary for black survival. It was harmful to black self-esteem and group esteem and social development, however.

Even with such rejection and marginality, many black families turned toward the mainstream and took a total culture orientation. The black subculture or substitute society, the black church, was not their social or psychological frame of reference. Other black families maintained the very strong church involvement even while developing a total society orientation. A third group found their frame of reference in the black church or black subculture almost exclusively and operated beyond it only to earn a living. Also in this group was a non-church-going subculture too complex to describe in detail here. Its organizing forces were "the black world"—style, support system, social and economic organizations—which had their origin in the black church but were no longer intimately involved in it. The fourth group which persisted was a rootless, referenceless, traumatized group with inadequate adaptive capacities; these were the overwhelmed.

Adults in the first three groups, each in their own way, managed through their particular reference groups to secure a reasonable level of organization, purpose, and self-esteem. As a valued member of a meaningful social network or subsystem, they had the motivation and desire to try to meet their own needs and those of their children in a way which met with approval from members of their own reference group. Many mechanisms, tendencies, habits, styles, and so forth, emerged to make this possible in spite of degrading social conditions and limited political and economic opportunities. These were more or less unique adaptive efforts. The man behind the door was one of the most successful. In many black families the male took no agressive or leadership role out in public. A society determined to suppress blacks would not tolerate this. Many outside observers who did not appreciate the survival strategy involved here described black males as ineffectual and ineffective. Hence, the notion of the matriarchal black family. Behind the door, the black male was often planner, organizer, protector, and provider. This was most often the case where males were able to earn a living wage. Mothers often taught their children to honor and respect their fathers even when they were not able to provide for the needs of the family.

In *Tally's Corner,* (1966) Elliot Liebow pointed out that even the absent father is an adaptive effort in many respects. Many black males can meet the affectual and relationship needs of the family, but must rely on public aid to meet the economic needs. Some black men either consciously or unconsciously arrange to leave their families to make them eligible for support.

Camille Jeffers (National Institute of Mental Health), who studied life syles in a predominantly black housing project, demonstrated that many low-income blacks developed patterns of shared services—babysitting, cars, errands, housekeeping, loans, and so forth—which were unique and necessary to maintain family stability in the face of severe poverty. Extended family relationships, rent parties, shared homes for travelers who were denied rooms in hotels, and a host of other arrangements made stable family life possible in spite of discrimination and economic hardship. Sleeping on a cot on the floor and socializing with strangers attending the local church convention who were barred from hotels because they were black, provided rich and warm contacts for many black families.

Some observers feel that slavery and then social and economic hardship resulted in a disproportionate number of blacks being involved in relationships which fostered the development of interpersonal skills rather than those which promoted "executive" skills. Planning and management skills are less necessary where social and economic advancement are not probable. Frustration and denial training to help children prepare for long-range goals is not necessary when such goals are minimally available.

It has been suggested that the rich affectual relationships in many black families are responsible for the large number of creative people in the group. Verbal bantering, mental combat, defensive and adaptive humor made tolerance of great stress possible and added to the richness of black community relationships. These heightened interactions produced a warm cabaret-church culture in which many black families could survive and thrive in spite of social oppression and economic hardship.

None of these mechanisms were as effective as reasonable black access to political and economic power and education would have been. Thus, while many black families survived and thrived psychologically in the black social system, most remained marginal to the political and economic mainstream. A disproportionate number of blacks were denied the experiences available to most European immigrants (Comer, 1972).

In the 1860's, families could gain stability simply because the "breadwinner" had a strong back. Education and skill were not necessary for the vast majority of heads-of-households to earn a living. In the generation between 1900 and 1940, moderate education and skill were needed to be secure on the job market. Since the mid-1940's, and increasingly so in the 1970's, a high level of education and training has been required to ensure security on the job market. A living wage and family stability give children in one generation the best chance to develop well and to gain the education needed to ensure their security on the job market in the next generation.

Industrial development in this country, and the related job market, paralleled the coming and evolution of the immigrant family. A three-generational movement from unskilled to moderately skilled to highly skilled and educated people was possible for large numbers of immigrant families. Because blacks lived largely in the socially oppressive and regressive South, because they were not recruited for jobs in the industrial North in the same fashion as whites and were often violently excluded when they did attempt to enter the industrial job market, black family evolution and development lagged one to two generations behind industrial development.

We can recall that the majority of blacks worked as share croppers, tenant farmers, or at the lowest level of the job market until the 1940's. Blacks came north seeking job opportunities as uneducated and unskilled workers at a time when the job market was already beginning to require a high level of education and skill. Even blacks with a high level of education and skill were excluded because of the high level of racism during this period.

As a result, a disproportionately large number of black children grew up in families where economic security was not adequate; therefore, social and psychological development could not be optimal. Today, the level of job exclusion on the basis of race remains high. Educational underdevelopment is still a great problem in the black community. Blacks are now in competition with large numbers of white women who have entered the job market in recent years. All of these factors jeopardize black family functioning.

In addition, some of the former adaptive efforts of blacks are now detrimental to that goal. Social and economic hardship necessitated an understanding of and an effort to beat the man—the white man. Such passive-aggressive acts as leaving tools in the field to rust and working as slowly as possible, permitted the discharge of anger during slavery and during the period of extreme economic exploitation, but are harmful work traits in the job market today. Anger and alienation from the master or a white employer—subsequently from the entire white authority system—made it difficult for too many to identify with some of the universally desirable values of the society. For example, some black students have called mathematics "white stuff." Some black workers have taunted efficient and competent black workers, accusing them of not being black. Such blacks are often said to have lost the warmth and spontaneity of the black culture. Teasing, deceiving, rejecting "the man," was understandable and even adaptive in the slave and suppressive society. Such activities today are not only a waste of energy, but are detrimental in an environment of reasonable political and economic opportunity. Fortunately, only a minority of blacks are caught up in such self-defeating behavior. Most have adequate "executive skills" and have adopted universally desirable values and goals. But the decline in overt societal racism and increased opportunity may be too late for a good many black families.

THE PERIOD OF EMERGENCE

The black family and the community—with help from others—has forced the institutions of American society to drop overt racist practices and even to establish affirmative action approaches with respect to education, government, and economic opportunities. While there is societal resistance, few black families continue to feel any need to prepare their children for abuse and denial. The role of the black family is now the same as that of other American families—to provide for basic food, clothing, and shelter needs and to promote health, psychological, social, and intellectual development. Helping to bring about this end is a remarkable black family accomplishment.

But critical years were lost (Comer, 1977). As mentioned, blacks did not undergo three generations of family and community development as did European immigrants. During that period, 1900 to the present, there has been more technological and scientific change than ever before in the history of the world. This requires more social development than ever before. Marginal families—economic, social, psychological—from all groups have difficulty functioning in this complex modern age. Out-of-wedlock pregnancies among young girls have increased at a greater rate among whites than among blacks, the latter already being high. Single-parent families, welfare dependency, and every other indicator of social problems have increased among these families. Such families are more often marginal. Because of historical conditions, a disproportionate number of them are black.

Since the 1940's, a large family has become an economic liability and not the asset it was when we were an agricultural society. Families with long-range goals and obligations have had fewer children. Dependent families and those with a social and psychological carryover or tradition of large families still continue to have them. As the training and educational demand of the society grow and the opportunities to meet them decrease, out-of-wedlock pregnancies increase, particularly among younger girls. This, in turn, decreases the probability that children of such pregnancies will be reared well. Blacks, as a result of past conditions, are vulnerable on all scores. In addition, because the black middle class is at the lowest middle-income level and less economically secure, it tends to have fewer children than its white counterpart. All of these factors account for an apparent paradox in the black community.

The educational level and employment status of black families that were able to make reasonably good adaptations prior to this period of emergence is rising while the social condition of those who were not able to make reasonably good adaptations (a sizable group) is worse than a decade ago. Unless there are improved opportunities for large numbers in this group, these circumstances bode ill for the black family of the future. But just as slavery and suppression did not spell doom, neither do the present circumstances.

Skills of the technological age are necessary and this will become apparent as blacks take greater responsibility for black community development. The conflicts of identity—what and who is black—will be resolved in the process of black family and community development. Skills needed in this technological age are really not in conflict with the warmth and spontaneity of the black folk cultural style. In fact, the latter could reduce some of the relationship problems associated with the former. Black civil rights groups, religious, political, educational, and economic leaders are beginning to promote the idea of blacks taking greater responsibility for black community development.

Several community development corporations, church-led economic development groups, school program successes, and so forth, in different communities have indicated that even the most troubled black communities and families can be revitalized. Expansion of these efforts will require the large predominantly white society to support favorable educational, economic, and political policies. Such policies are necessary to promote black community development, family stability, and successful child-rearing. There is and will be resistance to the formulation of such policies, but there is little choice. Either the black family will continue to survive and thrive or deteriorate. Efforts to crush the symptoms of deterioration—crime, dependency, and so forth—will bring an end to the American social system as we now know it. The same ends can be achieved without the loss of our relatively free and humane system through black community and family development.

In summary, the black family has permitted large numbers of its members to survive and thrive in the face of potentially overwhelming negative social conditions. Whether it can continue to do so in the future will depend greatly on the behavior of the larger society. Comparing the black family with the white family without considering the differences in the experiences of the two groups confuses the issue and delays supportive and restorative intervention.

BIBLIOGRAPHY

Botkin, Benjamin. *Lay My Burden Down.* Chicago: Phoenix Books, The University of Chicago Press, 1958, pp. 73–74, 230–234.

Comer, James P. "The Dynamics of Black and White Violence." In Hugh D. Graham and Ted R. Gorr (eds.), *The History of Violence in America.* New York: Praeger Publishers, 1969, pp. 444–464.

———. *Beyond Black and White.* New York: Quandrangle/New York Times Books, 1972.

———. "The Case for Affirmative Action." *Boston Sunday Globe,* September 11, 1977, pp. 22–30.

Comer, James and Poussaint, Alvin F. *Black Child Care.* New York: Simon and Schuster, 1975.

Frazier, E. Franklin. *The Negro Church in America.* New York: Schocken Books, 1963.

Jeffers, Camile. "Child Rearing Among Low Income Families in the District of Columbia," a project sponsored by the HEW Council of the National Capital Area, National Institute of Mental Health Grant 5–R–11–Mh278–5.

Liebow, Elliot. *Tally's Corner, A Study of Negro Streetcorner Men.* Boston: Little Brown and Co., 1966.

Lidz, Theodore. *The Family and Human Adaptation.* New York: International Universities Press, Inc., 1963, p. 19.

5

Parenting For Multiculturalism: A Mexican-American Model

MANUEL RAMIREZ III AND BARBARA G. COX
University of California
Santa Cruz, California

Child-rearing under the best of economic and social circumstances is a difficult and demanding task. The complexities of parenting are dramatically greater for minority parents who have historically faced not only worse economic and social conditions than other Americans, but also critical choices and decision-making with regard to their children's participation and identity in an ethnic or cultural context. Latino parents must deal with processes of identifying or deciding how best to prepare a child to survive and cope in a society that is not primarily Latino. American institutions, particularly the educational system, have strongly encouraged minority parents to help their children become as much like middle-class American mainstream children as possible. In the past, part of the responsibility for this posture resided in the belief that minority individuals would suffer conflict and pathology by attempting to maintain a strong ethnic identity while attempting to achieve "success" in the dominant culture of American society. More current views of minority experiences, identity, and competencies, however, emphasize the increased positive potentials of flexibility and adaptability in multicultural persons, as well as the importance of developing inter-ethnic competencies. Given the nature of American society, it would seem important that encouraging multicultural experience—diversity in belief systems and life styles—in order to help children achieve the potentials of multicultural functioning should be among the goals of effective parenting. In achieving the goal of multicultural parenting many Mexican-American families can serve as models.

Throughout much of our history, active identification with an ethnic group has been viewed by social scientists, educators, and politicians as dangerous. Individuals' ethnic identification and ethnic group solidarity were viewed as obstacles to the development and establishment of an "American national character," to national unity, and were thought to be a basis for a loose collection of diverse, separate ethnic, racial, and religious groups. One was either foreigner or American—and to become an American the "foreigner" was required to deny his cultural identity. In an analysis of the immigrant experience in America, Wheeler (1971) described an American rite of passage: "The sole sacrifice which America has asked of its immigrant sons has been denial of origin, and the consequences of that denial, though often invisible, are real.

The research on Mexican-American biculturalism reported in this paper was supported by Office of Naval Research grant N00014-76-C-0223.

Changed names, altered faces, dropped religions are but the conspicuous signs of the identity crisis in America" (p. 10).

In addition to the supposed threats of separatist movements, maintenance of an ethnic identity was seen as potentially pathological: How could a person comfortably belong to two or more ethnic groups? Such a dual identity would result in conflicts and confused loyalties.

CONFLICT/REPLACEMENT MODELS

Personality development of minority-group members was often previously conceptualized according to a model of personality conflict and cultural replacement. If two sociocultural systems were incompatible, it would follow that conflict would result for the individuals participating as members of the two systems and eventually the values, belief systems, and coping behaviors of one culture would be replaced with those of another. The models implied that as an individual becomes more identified with one of the cultures, he moves away from the other culture, replacing the values and life styles of one with those of the other. At the simplest level, the models describe a linear process of cultural identity change.

One early conceptualization based on the conflict replacement model was proposed by Stonequist (1937) who referred to members of minority groups as "marginal." Stonequist conceived the marginal man as "poised in psychological uncertainty between two (or more) social worlds, reflecting in his soul the discords and harmonies, repulsions and attractions of those worlds."

According to Stonequist (1964), the "life-cycle" of marginal man follows three stages: (1) positive feelings toward the host culture; (2) conscious experience of conflict; and (3) responses to the conflict, which may be prolonged and more or less successful in terms of adjustment. Furthermore, the third stage may encourage the individual to adopt one of three roles: (1) nationalism—a collective movement to raise the groups' status; (2) intermediation—promoting cultural accommodation; and (3) assimilation. Stonequist noted the possibility that some of these conditions might result in creativity, citing the case of the Jewish people, but for the most part his model focused on conflict and implied that the only "healthy" resolution is assimilation into the dominant culture.

Another conceptual framework of the conflict genre was proposed by psychologist Irving Child (1943), who focused on young adult male second-generation Italian Americans in New Haven. Child suggested a framework based on three types of conflict reaction: (1) the rebel reaction—desire to achieve complete acceptance by the American majority group and reject Italian associations; (2) the in-group reaction—desire to actively participate in and identify with the Italian group; and (3) the apathetic reaction—a retreat from conflict situations and avoidance of strong "rebel" and "in-group" identity. This apathetic reaction, according to Child, could be observed in the individual making a partial approach toward both cultures in an effort to find a compromise as solution to the conflict.

Somewhat more recently, Madsen (1964) subscribed to the conflict/replacement model when interpreting observations he made of young adult Mexican-Americans in south Texas. "The Alcoholic Agringado" describes traumas of cultural transfer in acculturating Mexican-American males. Madsen depicts the Mexican-American as standing alone between two conflicting cultural worlds and resorting to alcohol for anxiety relief.

Models such as these convinced many Americans, minority and majority alike, that diversity creates problems and that assimilation assistance policies and programs would help solve or avoid those problems.

PARENTING DECISION: ASSIMILATION, ISOLATION, OR MULTICULTURALISM?

Parents who are members of ethnic groups have been keenly aware of the social scientists' grim picture of dual cultural membership. Many of these parents experienced prejudice and discrimination themselves because their life styles or belief systems were different or because their primary language was not English; they were, and often still are, denied opportunities because of such differences. To spare them similar experiences, some Latino parents have encouraged their children to assimilate to the majority culture. For example, some parents insist that their children speak only English in order to minimize differences between themselves and other children, especially once the children attend school. Life histories recently gathered from Chicano college students in California and Texas indicate that the tendency to discourage children from speaking Spanish is not unusual. The most common reasons that parents gave their children were "So you wouldn't suffer like we did," and "We thought if you spoke English with an accent you would never get a good job," and so "you wouldn't be held back in school" (Ramirez et al., 1977a).

Although many Latino parents have been prompted to encourage assimilation in their children by the fear that they would otherwise not be accepted by their teachers, non-Latino peers, or prospective employers, another major determinant of this practice was that many parents were convinced that if their children did not speak English and assimilate at a very young age, then language and values confusion would result. (This argument is still put forth by opponents of bilingual, multicultural education even though research efforts of recent years have been demonstrating that such is not the case. For thorough discussion see Ramirez et al., 1977b.) This does not mean to imply that these parents wanted to deny their heritage or culture because they saw the dominant culture as better, but rather that many parents saw assimilation as the prerequisite to being allowed to function successfully (or at least have access to the means to do so) in this society.

Much less true today than earlier in our history is the preference of some parents for the familiarity of, and hence their relatively greater security in, the traditional modes of their culture, to the exclusion of changes within it as well as within other cultures. This response parallels Child's in-group reaction and may represent a retreat from intercultural contact. Yet it grows less possible daily for any parent to maintain such a position given the multicultural nature of our public education system and American society and the consequent need for development of intercultural competencies.

Latino parents are now increasingly voicing a desire for their children to maintain their first language, to learn about and be proud of their heritage, and to be active participants in their own culture as well as in the dominant American culture. For example, black and Mexican-American mothers in Texas overwhelmingly agreed with the following questionnaire items:

If parents have a culture of a background different from that of the majority of people in the United States, they should try to keep it and pass it on to their children. Parents who speak a language other than English should encourage their children to learn it [Ramirez and Castaneda, 1974].

Questionnaire and interview data collected from Mexican-American parents and community members for the purpose of identifying and ordering objectives for a preschool program, showed a strong desire that children receive instruction in Spanish as well as English and that Mexican-American culture be used as one of the foundations of the program (Ramirez et al., 1977b).

Surveys of parent attitudes and opinions by several bicultural/bilingual programs throughout the country have also found strong support for maintenance of minority languages and cultures. (For example, Yeager, 1975-1976; Herr, 1976; see also Ramirez et al., 1977b.) These goals are now finding a more receptive climate in American society because of changes in American attitutes toward diversity. For example, the results of a national poll reported in the *Los Angeles Times* in 1974 indicated that, in contrast to a similar poll conducted five years before, Americans no longer viewed differences among themselves as potentially dangerous and divisive; they further expressed the desire that everyone be allowed to explore and develop their differences.

In this more receptive climate there is evolving the understanding that rearing children for multiculturalism can have many positive consequences. Some of the recent thinking and research by scholars has highlighted some of these advantages in terms of development, identity, and functioning. Willie (1975) for example, speaks of a creative marginality in which there is identity in synthesis of groups, so each individual in the group (and each group) learns from the other(s) to obtain or become more than was possible without such synthesis. Adler (1974) discusses development of fluid, adaptable identities which transcend national and cultural boundaries. Fitzgerald (1971) describes bicultural persons' social and cultural identities: One can assume any number of social identities (that is, certain learned roles expected of an individual outside his first culture) without assuming a corresponding cultural identity (that is, the individual retains identity within his first culture).

One possible advantage of bicultural participation or development that has attracted some attention on the part of researchers is personality and intellectual flexibility. For example, Ramirez and Castaneda (1974) have found that Mexican-American elementary school children function effectively in their traditional Mexican-American homes, in a bicultural school and with both Anglo- and Mexican-American peers and authority figures in the community. The behavior and attitudes of these children indicate that they are in the process of developing a bicultural identity. These children also exhibit considerable flexibility in their behavior, using problem-solving strategies and perceptual modes of both the field sensitive and field independent cognitive styles depending on the characteristics of the situation and the task.

Another example of work in the area of flexibility is that of McFee (1968). Studying Blackfeet Indians in a bicultural reservation community, McFee emphasized the relationship of the situational context to the development and expression of flexibility of behavior. He hypothesized that, in the course of tribal acculturation, a bicultural social structure becomes established that provides both cultural models (white and Indian).

Fitzgerald (1971) stressed bicultural individuals' flexibility and capacity to shuttle between cultures, and flexibility of creative marginals, observing that they have a capacity to transcend the world of everyday premises in which most people are trapped, and are able to unite classes and races and help reconcile their differences.

Some of the research on biculturalism has focused on the role of socialization. Valentine's work (1971) on biculturation in blacks led him to the following conclusions:

> In any case, biculturation strongly appeals to us as a key concept for making sense out of ethnicity and related matters: the collective behavior and social life of the Black community is bicultural in the sense that each Afro-American ethnic segment draws upon a distinctive repertoire of standardized Afro-American behavior and, simultaneously patterns derived from mainstream cultural system of Euro-American derivation. Socialization into both systems begins at an early age, continues throughout life, and is generally of equal importance in most individual lives [p. 143].

Expanding on the influences of socialization he states:

> Ethnic cultural socialization is focused to some degree within family units and primary groups, with much mainstream acculturation coming more from wider sources. Yet this is by no means a sharp or consistent division of socializing influences. Ghetto homes expose their members from earliest childhood to many mainstream themes, values and role models [pp. 143–144].

Another research project assessed the degree and nature of participation in different cultural settings among Mexican-American college students and described processes by which the multicultural participation and positive attitudes toward multiculturalism developed (Ramirez et al., 1977a). Preliminary data give strong indication that several socialization factors contribute significantly to the development of multicultural functioning in Mexican-Americans. Also, several types of experiences can be identified as common to most of the subjects with extensive multicultural participation, and these could be encouraged by parents. These factors and experiences should be critically examined as possible starting points for programs intending to help parents promote multiculturalism or multicultural potential in their children. These preliminary findings are summarized below:

1. Parents of the multicultural subjects had strong ties with their extended families. Extended-family members frequently participated in child-rearing and were sources for oral family histories.
2. Parents of multicultural subjects had strong ethnic identification. They were also willing to share information about their culture and life style with others.
3. Spanish was the primary language of parents of the multicultural subjects. Parents encouraged their children to speak both Spanish and English.
4. Parents of multicultural subjects were accepting of their children's non-Mexican-American friends, even when they themselves had few friends who were not Mexican or Mexican-American. They did not reinforce ethnic stereotypes.
5. The multicultural subjects were bilingual.

6. The multicultural subjects had a strong ethnic identification.
7. They had acted as cultural facilitators or go-betweens, introducing members of other groups to their culture and preventing conflict and misunderstanding between people.
8. They were frequently active in sports and student government or had other group involvement.

Subjects who were identified as having a low degree of participation in two cultures could be divided in a general fashion into two groups: those who participated only minimally in the dominant culture and those who participated only minimally in the Mexican-American culture. Bearing in mind that the data are still preliminary, it seems that the subjects in these groups were not accepting of the experiences, values, and life styles of others, nor did they give evidence of being greatly desirous of developing interethnic understanding or competencies. Those subjects who functioned primarily within Mexican-American culture shared with the multicultural subjects a strong identification with the ethnic group, stress on family solidarity, and fluency in Spanish. These subjects, however, were not as active in sports, student government, or other extracurricular activities. These students and their parents viewed the value of school experience as being almost exclusively training in the basic skills areas of reading and math. Parents had not participated in parent-teacher groups or other group associations or functions, and seldom visited their children's school. In other domains as well, such as church, work, or recreation, these subjects interacted with few persons, either authority figures of peers, who were not Mexican-American. To a certian extent this would be accounted for by the nature of the subject's home community. However, this is probably not the case here since sites for the research were chosen that seemed to demographically facilitate cross-cultural contact.

The subjects in the group which participated minimally in Mexican-American culture, on the other hand, had interacted throughout their lives primarily with non-Mexican-Americans. Frequently these students were learning Spanish in school but had not learned to speak Spanish at home. Some expressed their uneasiness in Mexican-American group functions.

ENCOURAGING PARENTING FOR MULTICULTURALISM

From the available literature and the data being collected on multicultural subjects, we can begin to make some programmatic recommendations which could serve to encourage parenting for multiculturalism.

The first of these recommendations involves identifying the resources which are already available and planning strategies to optimize their use. For example, parents of multicultural children could be trained as leaders for parenting workshops. Films could be made of these parents so that their parenting strategies could be modeled. Multicultural parenting as a positive consequence of the minority experience in America could serve to benefit all Americans.

ATTITUDES TOWARD ETHNICITY AND MULTICULTURALISM

The finding that parents of multicultural subjects identified strongly with traditional Mexican or Mexican-American culture and values makes ethnicity a logical point from which to introduce parents to multicultural goals. This does not mean to imply that to raise children to be multicultural one must always have a strong ethnic identity, but that parents should be aware of their own feelings about ethnicity and of the goals they have for their children in this regard. Parents whose ethnic identity has not been important to them, for example, might be provided with information about their heritage and the history of their ethnic group, or they might be encouraged to recall their family history, or they might participate in cultural values clarification activities. On the other hand, parents whose ethnic ties are strong but who, because of negative experiences or misinformation about value or language confusion, have discouraged their children from identifying with their ethnic group, could be provided with information about today's changing attitudes toward diversity and research on the advantages of bilingualism and multiculturalism.

CHILDREN'S ETHNIC IDENTITY

The first step toward encouraging children to develop a positive and strong ethnic identity is accomplished if their parents are positive about their own ethnicity and realize the advantages and opportunities that multiculturalism can offer. Positive ethnic identity can also be actively developed or reinforced by strengthening extended family ties and by relating family histories including those about grandparents and great-grandparents, since these frequently depict cultural customs and values very clearly and are meaningful to the listeners.

A most critical goal may be encouraging bilingualism since language is a strong transmitter of culture in and of itself, and also because it allows greater communication to occur between generations. Parents who speak only English might be encouraged to acquire a second language along with their children.

A MULTICULTURAL ORIENTATION

To encourage the development of multiculturalism, parents should be able to help children learn about other cultural values and life styles as well as about cultural stereotypes and their causes. Parents should be prepared to deal with questions about prejudice and racism and conflicts between ethnic or racial groups. Children can be assisted in forming friendships with peers from other backgrounds as well as from their own ethnic group by enrolling them in schools that are ethnically diverse or by reinforcing their participation in team sports, group church activities, or youth groups that provide situations supportive of cross-cultural contact.

To assist parents in their efforts, parenting education courses which stress parenting for multiculturalism should be carefully planned.

Research programs are also needed in order to identify parenting strategies common to families of multicultural children. These programs should ensure that the information obtained through these research efforts will be made available to parents and prospective parents in attractive, interesting, and useful form.

POLICY IMPLICATIONS

Programs for multicultural parenting cannot have long-range success without supportive public policy. More specifically, we need a strong policy on recognition, maintenance, and continued development of the linguistic and cultural diversity in American society. This policy must discourage schools and other public institutions from attempts at forced assimilation, and encourage these institutions to examine the advantages offered by the sociocultural systems of different groups. This policy then should seek to implement the philosophy of cultural democracy, that is, to respect the right of the individual to remain identified with his/her own group while other sociocultural systems are explored.

A policy which encourages better community interethnic relations is also needed. Programs of school and community desegregation need to be planned carefully, expanded, and improved. Provisions must be made, for example, for dealing with interethnic relations employing multicultural people as facilitators and consultants.

CONCLUSIONS

Multicultural parenting can provide an avenue leading beyond the survival and coping levels toward greater quality of life and greater understanding among the different groups in our diverse society. Multicultural socialization could encourage the development of a philosophy of life and world view which enables the individual to learn from the experiences and world views of members of other sociocultural systems.

BIBLIOGRAPHY

Adler, P. S.   Beyond cultural identity: reflections on cultural and multicultural man. Richard Brison (Ed.). *Topics in culture learning.* Hawaii: East-West Culture Learning Institute, 1974, *2*.

Child, I. L.   *Italian or American? The second generation in conflict.* New Haven: Yale University Press, 1943.

Fitzgerald, T. K.   Education and identity—a reconsideration of some models of acculturation and identity. *New Zealand Council of Education Studies,* 1971, 45-57.

Herr, G.   Final Evaluation Report, San Jose Project Follow Through 1975–1976. Educational Systems Associates. July 15, 1976.

Madsen, W.   The alcoholic agringado. *American Anthropologist,* 1964, *66,* 355–361.

McFee, M.   The 150% man. A product of Blackfeet acculturation. *American Anthropologist,* 1968, *70,* 1096–1103.

Ramirez, M., and Castaneda, A.   *Cultural democracy, bicognitive development and education.* New York: Academic Press, 1974.

Ramirez, M.; Castaneda, A.; and Cox, B.   A biculturalism inventory for Mexican-American college students. Unpublished research report, 1977a.

Ramirez, M.; Macaulay, R. K. S.; Gonzalez, A.; Cox, B.; and Perez, M.   Spanish-English bilingual education in the United States: Current issues, resources, and research priorities. Center for Applied Linguistics, Monograph Series, 1977b, *41*.

Stonequist, E. V.   The marginal man: a study in personality and culture conflict. Ernest Burgess and Donald J. Bogue (Eds.). *Contributions to urban sociology.* Chicago: University of Chicago Press, 1964.

Valentine, C. A. Deficit, difference, and bicultural models of Afro-American behavior. *Harvard Educational Review,* 1971, 41, 2, 137–157.

Wheeler, T. C. *The immigrant experience.* New York: Pelican, 1971.

Willie, C. M. Marginality and social change. *Society,* July-August, 1975, 10–13.

Yeager, L. Survey of family attitudes, Cucamonga School District, Follow Through Project, Grantee Performance Report, 1975–1976.

6

Parenting in the Native-American Community

BILL J. BURGESS, ED.D.
Native American Research Associates, Inc.
Lawrence, Kansas

This chapter will concentrate on the nature of parent-child relationships within the native-American community. Generalizations about native Americans tend to distort the truth due to the difference in life styles between tribes, and the differences between rural-reservation residents and urban residents. The reader is cautioned to keep in mind that this overview of native-American life is based on the typical and traditional rural-reservation situation. No attempt is made to consider the urban native American or to deal with the middle class or professional groups.

First, this chapter will illustrate briefly the distinct position of the native-American community in contrast to the dominant North American society. Next, it will present an overview of the patterns of parent-child relations that are unique to the native-American community. Third, it will describe the differences in the behavior of native- and non-native-American children. Finally, it will review the problems that plague the native-American community and illustrate how these problems endanger good parenting relationships.

Whenever we use the term "native American," we must remind ourselves that this term cannot adequately describe a "people." For the most part, "tribalism," with pronounced differences in life-style and language, is paramount. Although these differences vary immeasurably among the tribes, from patterns conditioned during years of living as nomads to those of a sedentary domestic semiurban style, there are some common values or characteristics which consistently appear. A distinct pattern of parent-child and family relationships is one of those areas that appears with regularity within, as well as among, tribes.

The destructive forces to which native Americans were exposed for over two hundred years took a terrible toll. Among the effects were a variety of disruptions in family structure. Prior to the arrival of the "Anglo" ("Anglo" is the term used by many native Americans when speaking of the dominant society in the United States), tribal societies, customs, and traditional ways of life had developed. Family, and then tribal education, stressed and encompassed the principal social values of cooperation and collective organization, making possible both individual variation and tribal solidarity. In the collective, cooperative, and noncompetitive native-American society, the family, and through it the tribe, became the primary social and educational organization.

The conquest of native-American land and its people resulted in repeated and continued efforts to bring about the disintegration of native-American society and culture. The net results of these efforts, which left native Americans poor and powerless, speak for themselves:

> Per capita income averages around $1,500 per year, about one-half of the national poverty level, but individual cases are often worse. On some reservations, large families may have a total income under $1,000, and Native Americans tend to have large families. The birthrate is considerably higher than that of the country as a whole. And, the traditional extended family concept still prevails in many places. Therefore, when we are talking about such low income, we may be talking about a group of 10 or 12 people who must survive on these sub-poverty level earnings [Wax, 1963].

According to a 1975 report on young native Americans and their families:

> Native American peoples are survivors. They have survived through years of a government policy which has shifted from extermination to removal, to land allotment, to relocation, to termination which has ignored Native culture, tried to extirpate it through forced assimilation and only lately has given formal support to the strengthening of the language and cultural heritage of Native peoples. In spite of the multiplicity of problems, there is no justifiable reason why the American Indian and Alaskan Native population should not have a standard of living that provides what most people in this country consider the bare necessities of life and why they should not participate in the benefits of being in America. There is no justifiable reason why they should not have an education that honors and builds on their cultural heritage and provides the knowledge and skills that will enable them to determine their own future [Zimiles, 1976].

A major difference illustrating the uniqueness of the native-American community was reflected in a letter by the Honorable Edward M. Kennedy, Chairman, Special Sub-Committee on Indian Education (1969), which served as the foreword to the congressional sub-committee report. He stated that "the American vision of itself is of a nation of citizens determining their own destiny; of cultural differences flourishing in an atmosphere of mutual respect; of diverse people shaping their lives and the lives of their children." In the body of the same report which is entitled "Indian Education: A National Tragedy—A National Challenge," the following question was asked: "What happens to an Indian child who is forced to abandon his own pride and future and confront a society in which he has been offered neither a place nor a hope? Our failure to provide . . . for the American Indian has condemned him to a life of poverty and despair."

In spite of the conditions illustrated above and 200 years of paternalistic and degrading treatment by the federal programs responsible for the welfare of native Americans, there remains a distinct positive relationship between parents and their children.

Parenting in the traditional native-American community must be examined in the context of the extended family. And for many tribes, matriarchal influence is a tradition. Dennis (1940) writes about social organization among the Hopi:

The closest ties of a Hopi are with the members of his immediate family—his parents, his brothers and sisters ... he has a host of relatives, all of whom usually live in his own village and whom he sees almost daily. The sisters of his mother are called 'mothers,' although the young child knows which is his 'true' mother. The brothers of his father are likewise called 'fathers,' and all children of his mothers and fathers are called brothers and sisters, so that he is surrounded by a large number of relatives who, nominally at least, are very close to him. The mother's mother is, of course, his grandmother, as is his father's mother, but in addition all sisters of these grandmothers are also called grandmother.... Between the individual and any relative exist a number of mutual obligations which tend to bind them together. ...

Beyond the Hopi family is a wider group, the clan. The child's clan is the clan of his mother; that is, clan membership is inherited in the female line. All clan members consider themselves to be related, and they have a number of obligations to each other. There are numerous occasions when one would call upon a clan member for aid or services before asking the cooperation of others. The child owes obedience to his mother and father, to his mother's brothers, and to some extent to his father's brothers who are called "fathers." Grandparents are to be respected, but they are not disciplinarians and do not enforce obedience. The younger child usually obeys the older child, but in cases in which this does not occur, the older sibling must appeal to the parents: "Other people ... may not command the child, not threaten, nor punish the child, but they are free to reprove him for wrongdoing and to report his misbehavior to his parents" (Dennis, 1940).

Dr. Robert Bergman (Byler, 1977), a psychiatrist, noted for his work on the Navajo Reservation, describing the extended-family relationships of the Navajo, stated:

> One of the most significant differences between Navajo family structure and that of ordinary middle-class Americans is the relationship of the child to a number of caring people. In general, the relationship to aunts and uncles is much more important in the Navajo family than it is to the middle-class American family. A great deal more responsibility is given to other members of the extended family, and there is considerable attachment of the child to the entire group.... They (grandparents) would serve as models that the children would follow in their behavior—teacher, probably the final authority to which the children could appeal. In the ordinary good family they would be the leaders of the group, and the most respected people.

Generally, the extended-family concept is still practiced by native-American families, both on and off the reservation. During tenure as Dean of Bacone Indian College, Muskogee, Oklahoma, and Haskell Indian Junior College, Lawrence, Kansas, this writer can recall many incidents that illustrate the continuation of this practice.

- Very often in communication with grandparents, aunts, and uncles, an individual would refer to his "son" or "daughter" as if the relationship were an absolute, direct one.
- Students often arrived at college with expensive articles (baskets, rugs, jew-

elry, and so forth) that had been given to them by extended-family members, to be sold in the event they needed money while they were away.

- Young married students, upon the birth of a child, would bring the grand-mother to live with them so the child could learn tribal language and culture from the most respected teacher. This activity was endorsed and expected by all of the members of the extended family.

The role of grandparents in the parent-child relations of the native-American family is unique. Native-American children are taught to respect elders. Many Anglo and other non-native-American children are taught to love and respect their elders, but, this writer feels, not with the same intensity and depth as young native-American children. In addition, the advent of nursing homes and extended-care facil-ities has seriously diminished the effective role Anglo grandparents might have, or once had, in child-reading. It appears that, at best Anglo grandparents are utilized as babysitters, or as someone to visit on "special" holiday occasions.

The native-American child is taught that age is a gift, a "badge of honor," if you please. To have grown old is to have done the right things, to have pleased your crea-tor, to have been in "tune" with nature and your fellowman. In the native-American community, respect increases with age. Older people are expected to give advice and counsel. It is expected that grandfathers will take sons (grandsons or nephews) for long walks to talk about life, nature, and self, and that grandmothers will very care-fully arrange time and events during the winter to tell and retell stories of creation, culture, and relationships of nature and people. These teaching-learning activities are not happenstance or informal. They are structured and command adherence, partici-pation, and support by everyone concerned. Parents would not dare plan an activity or event that would break this traditional relationship.

In addition to those items mentioned above, one would need exposure to native American "values" to fully comprehend their effect on parent-child relationships. The traditional native-American community places particular emphasis on the values of brotherhood, personal integrity, generosity (sharing), and spirituality. Oftentimes, values of the native-American community are in direct contrast to those observed and reflected in the Anglo community. In addition, some values not in direct conflict with Anglo practices are taught and promoted with such an intensity that the net result is almost as if they were opposites. For instance, a native-American child is taught that wealth is measured by the amount that one shares with (gives to) others rather than the amount one obtains and keeps for his or her own personal welfare.

Native-American parents worry about these differences and are forced to give serious consideration to how to deal with them while rearing children through their early and formative years. Parents ask themselves: ·Are we holding to strict tradi-tional culture? Should we give up our traditional ways so that our children can "make it" in the Anglo world? Should we compromise, and hope that our children make it in both worlds? A dilemma is created by the conflicting values which exist between the traditional native-American society desiring to retain what it believes in, and a dominant society that has been unresponsive to these differences and reluctant to acknowledge the positive contributions of "cultural pluralism."

Observation and study through the years have led this writer to conclude that, in spite of the many problems which exist, positive parent-child relationships in the native-American community are equal to, and often better than, those of most other North American ethnic communities. The illustrations of some of the practices listed below are valued in most societies, but it is believed that they occur more frequently in the native-American community than in the non-native-American community. Some of the more significant characteristic elements that are visible in the native-American community follow.

- Children—from birth—are regarded as important units of the family and heirs to its concerns and belongings. Children are considered . . . by Native Americans . . . as more important than material possessions.
- Songs and lullabies sung to children by the parent and grandparents carry messages of hope and aspiration, the appreciation of beauty, sharing, and physical strength (so as to be of service to each other).
- Families engage only in those social activities which include their children; if the children cannot go, no one goes.
- Native American children are seldom, if ever, struck by an adult: not parents, uncles, aunts . . . no adults. This custom has enormous implications which may indicate the superiority of Native American parenting to Anglo-American customs.
- Considerable parental time and effort is devoted to making items for children to play with, or operate, or use when participating in popular activities and ceremonies. (Ex.: costumes for special dances, looms for weaving, tools for gardening, hunting, and fishing.)
- Respectfulness is taught by example as well as by precept. Respect is paid to a large number of worthy objects . . . parents, grandparents, members of the extended family, elderly people, various totem animals and objects, and various abstractions such as natural beauty and nature, dignity, and modesty.
- Talking loudly, especially while correcting children, is highly disapproved of.
- Spiritual qualities are taught and emphasized in special rituals and ceremonies.
- Artifacts (baskets, rugs, pottery, etc.) are made with *purposeful imperfections,* as a lesson to children that no one is perfect; we all make mistakes, and hence, censure and punishment are very minimal.
- Competition is considered acceptable as long as the object is not to get the best of (hurt) someone.
- Children are taught that the land . . . and all that grows . . . are only lent to us for our care and sharing, not for exploitation. [Menninger, to be published]

These features of the native-American family philosophy and parenting practice seem eminently healthy, wise, and useful for fostering parent-child guidance and development. They are conducive to self-confidence, serenity, and nonaggressive personality development. No doubt, the above list could be extended, but the major point is that children are extremely important extensions of the family and community; there is also a tendency to include the natural needs and activities of children in the whole of family and community life.

A classic example of conflicting values between the Anglo and native-American communities appeared as an advertisement in a major periodical that dedicated a particular issue to effective parenting (*Psychology Today,* 1976). The journal carrying the advertisement is generally accepted as respectable and knowledgeable. Some of the key phrases from the advertisement follow:

- Keep your kid ahead of the Jones kid.
- Get him the advantage of Montessori learning.

- Turn average kids into gifted ones.
- Your kid needs every advantage he can get to make it in this world.
- The difference between winning and losing is education.
- Make sure he doesn't bring home a discouraging report card and announce that "school is a drag."
- Don't wait another day. Time goes fast in a child's life.

It is difficult for this writer to relate in a positive manner the message of the advertisement to the goals and values of effective parent-child relations of any society or group. The goals mentioned, as well as those implied, are contradictory to the goals and methods supported by the native-American community in child-rearing. Native-American parents want their children to be successful, just as other parents do, but in a manner that is consistent with the cooperative and noncompetitive tribal, community, and family values and aspirations.

Non-native Americans, having an opportunity to observe parent-child relationships for the first time, are often amazed at the warmth that pervades this relationship. A noted early childhood educator from the eastern part of the United States visited our community recently during a period when a ceremonial was to take place. Knowing beforehand that most of the ceremony would be open to the public, he brought along his wife and three young daughters to observe the activities.

After the activities were completed, our friend related that he and his wife had enjoyed a new and pleasant experience. He reported that their three children were usually reluctant to leave their side while in public gatherings. During the ceremonial activities, all three children appeared to be relaxed and comfortable, although surrounded by complete strangers, most of them native Americans. The children felt secure enough to leave and return to their parents, and to permit themselves to be handed up and down rows of bleachers by persons they had never seen or met before. Without hesitation, they were willing to go to the concession stand, as well as to play by themselves or with unfamiliar children. Later, in discussing this phenomenon, the father remarked on the natural and wholesome relationship that apparently exists between parents and children within the native-American community.

He suggested that it might be helpful for the Anglo society to analyze this relationship and document both the cause and effect. He commented that the dominant society could probably benefit by observing the natural inclusion of the child in everyday life, as well as how native-American child-rearing remains in the center of family activities rather than exist an extension thereof.

If native-American parent-child relationships are equal to or superior to other societies and groups, one should see this manifested in the behavior of children. These children should display intellectual, social, and emotional characteristics that show the effects of this positive nurturing.

In terms of intellectual potential, there seems to be considerable research to indicate that the achievements of native-American youth, up to a given level, are equal to those of non-native-American children. Most studies show that the two groups are equal at school-entry level, and some studies reported native-American children to be at a higher level than non-native-American children. After that, a common pattern emerges. Native-American children fall behind non-native-American children in terms of traditional scores on achievement tests. This is especially true after the eighth grade.

In some instances, native-American children at an early age have shown higher achievement or intelligence potential than the non-native-American children in their community. One particularly important study is illustrated by Erikson. In reviewing a previous study that had been conducted by McGregor on the Dakota Sioux personality, Erickson (1963) stated: "To settle one question, which I am sure many a reader has wanted to ask: The intelligence of the Dakota children is slightly above that of White children. Their health, however, corresponds to that of underprivileged rural Whites."

There are a number of other studies to indicate that native-American children enter kindergarten or the first grade at an intellectual and social-readiness level that is equal to or superior to that of non-native-American children. If this is true, one might credit the family and community environment of the Indian children prior to school age with this achievement.

Native-American children, then, appear to have equal or superior intellectual potential, at least at an early age. Marked differences between native-American children and Anglo children can be found in affective measures—such as emotions and values. In fact, Erikson (1963) illustrates the Dakota Sioux child by stating: "My conclusion would be as before, that early childhood among the Dakota . . . is a relatively rich and spontaneous existence which permits the school child to emerge from the family with a relative integration, i.e. with much trust, a little autonomy, and some initiative."

An important comparative study of native-American children and others, *American Indian and White Children: A Sociopsychological Investigation,* was undertaken by Havighurst and Neugarten (1955). Their work studied the moral, emotional, and intellectual development of native-American children in six native-American tribes. The study included 1,000 children, age six to eighteen. A similar control group of white children was also studied.

The primary instrument utilized was the *Emotional Response Test* developed by Stewart (Havighurst and Neugarten, 1955). The test asks for open-ended responses to questions concerning children's feelings about happiness, sadness, fear, anger, shame, and the best and worst things that could happen to them. In this particular study, the Anglo children were asked to write responses in a group-test setting. The native-American children were interviewed, and translation from English to a native-American language was often necessary.

This study revealed differences in the emotional character of native-American and Anglo children, differences with roots in the culture of the two societies. Anglo children were more concerned about their personal achievement, were more self-centered in describing happiness and pleasure, and were more troubled about getting their own way. They were less concerned about property and possessions, possibly an indication of the relative wealth. The possession of food and clothing was an important factor in the daily lives of the native-American children, while Anglos probably took these essentials for granted.

An interesting difference was reported as a result of a measure of children's feelings about "shame." Answers for both groups tended to center around two basic interpretations of the word "shame": "embarrassment" and "guilt." More native American than Anglos reported shameful incidences in which they were simply embarrassed, such as falling down in public or doing something awkward in front of others. Anglo children, on the other hand, tended to associate shame with their own guilt—bad judgment, moral wrongs, transgressions for which they were caught. This behavior is consistent with the methods of control of children as practiced by native

Americans versus Anglos. For native Americans, warnings about the consequences of bad behavior are couched in community terms like, "What will people say—they will laugh at you." Rarely is a threat of physical punishment made. Shame, otherwise known as embarrassment, is a common disciplinary tool with native Americans.

Of significant importance were the differences in attitudes about family, as revealed by the Emotional Response Test. The study revealed that community members play a greater part in producing both pleasant and unpleasant emotions in native-American children. Both nuclear and extended families played a greater part in the statements about happiness, sadness, and the best and worst things in their lives. Anglo children did associate family members with their feelings, but were much more likely to associate them with punishment of negative emotions. Apparently the native-American community outside of the family has considerable influence on children, and native-American parents are less likely to be thought of in terms of punishment or unpleasantness.

In a study of the Hopi child, Dennis (1940) reflected,

> It seemed to us that the absence of a culturally determined goal of power and prestige has its effects upon the younger members of the community as well as the adults. We thought we saw less rivalry among Indian children, and less desire to be important, superior, and distinguished. This does not mean, however, that Hopi children make no invidious comparisons. . .but the ridicule which they deal out is as likely to be turned against the individual who tries to excel as against one who is aberrant in some other way. . . . Another guess which we hazard with respect to the Hopi child is that he has a world which he knows intimately and which accepts him completely . . . while the child may early learn the unfriendliness of the climate and the danger of starvation which faces the entire village, he lives in a social world in which he has an indubitable place.

Another important work is that of Beuf, *Red Children in White America* (1977). Beuf, in her work, studied native-American youngsters and their development of racial attitudes in the light of four concepts: institutional racism, nonconscience ideology, the principle of constancy, and associatedness. Beuf's research was conducted during the summer and fall of 1971 with preschool children from the southwestern and midwestern United States: A total of 229 children took part in the study, 134 native Americans, and 95 Anglo children from the Midwest and Southwest.

In summarizing her findings, Beuf reported that the midwestern and southwestern young non-native-American children tend to portray a rather placid and comfortable attitude in all four concept areas, while native-American children tend to tell stories and enact dramas which reflect the realities of their lives. The social hierarchies, which are both cause and consequence of the physical circumstances of their life, did not escape the attention and comprehension of the native-American youngsters.

Beuf also reported that native-American children, at the five- to six-year-old level, for the most part, were similar to non-native-American children of the same age in identifying racial preferences. She found that native-American children would select a "white"' doll as often as they might a "red" or "brown" doll to play with. A dramatic difference was observed in testing native-American and non-native-American youngsters in the early adolescent years. While being tested, the adolescent native-American children, with few exceptions, indicated a pronounced tendency to select native-American objects. The same adolescent children were permitted to observe during the testing of the younger children. The adolescent children reacted quite visibly and emotionally when the younger children failed to indicate a preference for native-American objects. Although non-native-American children showed a decided tendency to select objects reflective of their own race as they grow older, the tendency for native-American children to do likewise appeared to be considerably more consistent.

From these examples, it would appear that native-American children are different from their Anglo counterparts. In positive instances, it might be concluded that this could be due to the pleasant and wholesome environment directly associated with good parent-child relations which exists in the native-American community. Other differences, particularly negative, are due in part to the social and political burdens borne by the ethnic minorities of this country.

The final area to be considered in this chapter relates to the problems that endanger good parenting relationships within the native-American community. As in any society, the family is recognized as the central unit of all activities. If the family, as an institution, is disturbed or altered, then the entire group is affected. In a recent speech, Dr. Karl Menninger (1977), Dean of American Psychiatry, and renowned friend of native Americans, made the following statements:

> The family is the most wonderful educational and character shaping institution of human life. . . . It is similar everywhere in the world because it is biologically the same. It is the unit of *human* social life.
>
> In most cultures, the family structure . . . is not interfered with or impaired by design; accidentally sometimes, by death or disaster or war . . . but not by human intention.
>
> In the case of the American Indians, however, it *has been* interfered with, purposely—with good intention, no doubt, but we psychiatrists think wrongly and harmfully, however well intentioned.

The problems are many and varied; for example, the dynamics of native-American extended families are in danger. They are little understood by outsiders. A native American may have scores or perhaps more than a hundred relatives who are counted as close, responsible members of the family. Many outsiders, untutored in the ways of native-American life, assume only the parents to be responsible, and interpret the acceptance of responsibility for a child by persons outside of the nuclear family as neglect or abuse.

The extended family, by its example of sharing responsibilities for child-rearing, tends to strengthen the native-American community's commitment to its children. At the same time, it diminishes the capability of the nuclear family in mobilizing itself quickly if an outside agency acts to assume custody for a child.

Non-native Americans often show concern about the relative freedom a native-American child is given and what seems to be a lack of parental concern about his or her behavior. Although this may appear as excessive permissiveness or indulgence, in fact, it is often a different and perhaps more effective way of allowing youngsters to develop in a healthy way. Discipline may be administered in other ways and in other forms not noticeable to outsiders. Native-American children are not punished often, nor are they in continual fear of punishment. On the other hand, native-American children do not expect praise for doing what is required of them. Parents occasionally praise children for doing well, indicating approval through a smile or pleasant tone of voice, or a friendly pat. There is strong affection between parents and children; knowledge of approval and disapproval is undoubtedly, in itself, a powerful means of social control.

Current programs that take native-American children away from families and place them in boarding schools or in foster homes have created havoc in the parent-child relationships in native-American communities. There are two trends: (1) Native-American children are being placed outside their natural homes at an alarming rate, and (2) they are being given to non-native Americans for foster care. Children involved are subject to ethnic confusion and a sense of abandonment, which tends to adversely affect their own potential parenting capacities. There is a growing concern among native-American tribes and communities over the loss of children as well as the absence of appropriate child welfare services.

A number of research studies indicate overwhelming problems of institutional racism in the United States. These problems have a most disruptive impact on the native-American community and family. In a country that equates "brown" and "poor" as synonymous terms, it is a difficult task to ensure that young native-American children develop a positive self-image.

The continuing lack of recognition of native Americans as a people by the institutions and agencies empowered to direct native-American land, education, health, and social service activities, perpetuates disintegration of the tribal and family structure. Until those agencies and institutions, and the dominant society in general, are willing to recognize and respect the unique differences in social values of a collective, cooperative, noncompetitive society, the tribe and the family will continue to be threatened and disrupted. These conditions will continue to contribute to the overall conditions of powerlessness, hopelessness, and poverty which exist in the native-American community.

RECOMMENDATIONS CONCERNING NATIVE-AMERICAN PARENT-CHILD RELATIONS

1. Any and all native-American programs, including education, health, and social service programs, must reinforce native-American cultural fundamentals.
2. The national and international media must at every opportunity recognize the positive values of Indian culture and avoid stereotyping or emphasizing negative values.
3. Legal recognition must be given to the wider spread of a native-American child's blood relatives as caregivers. Official federal and state programs must recognize the natural role of the extended family.
4. Every program for native-American education, health, and social service must be based on the premise that children should be kept with their families if at all possible.
5. Native Americans must not be forced to copy Anglo child welfare services, which are based on the nuclear family, with no network and no coordination.
6. Native Americans must be involved in determining their own standards for child welfare services which reflect native-American values.
7. There must be an end put to the collusive de-tribalization and assimilation of Indian families and communities, and a restoration to tribes of their civil and

criminal jurisdiction (Public Law 53-280 permits certain states to extend jurisdiction over federal reservations, thus causing another source of conflict and uncertainty concerning the respective power of tribal and state governments).

8. Native-American communities must be provided with adequate means to overcome their economic, educational, and health handicaps. We must diligently seek to foster the economic incentives that will eliminate the existing conditions.

BIBLIOGRAPHY

Beuf, Ann H. *Red Children in White America.* Philadelphia: University of Pennsylvania Press, Inc., 1977.

Byler, William. *The Destruction of American Indian Families.* Steven Unger, Editor. New York: Association of American Indian Affairs, 1977.

Dennis, Wayne. *The Hopi Child.* The University of Virginia Institute for Research in the Social Sciences. New York: D. Appleton-Century Company, Inc., 1940.

Erikson, Erik H. *Childhood and Society.* New York: W. W. Norton and Company, Inc., 1963.

Fuchs, Estelle, and Havighurst, Robert. *To Live on the Earth.* Garden City, New York: Doubleday, 1972.

Havighurst, Robert J., and Neugarten, Bernice L. *American Indian and White Children: A Sociopsychological Investigation.* Chicago: University of Chicago Press, 1955.

McGregor, Gordon. *Warriors Without Weapons.* Chicago: University of Chicago Press, 1946.

Mead, Margaret. *Changing Culture of an Indian Tribe.* New York: Columbia University, 1932.

Menninger, Karl A., M.D. Speech, Navajo Nation Health Symposium, Navajo Community College, Tsaile, Arizona, August 22, 1977 (to be published).

Psychology Today, Vol. 10, No. 6, November, 1976.

Report of the Committee on Labor and Public Welfare, United States Senate Special Sub-Committee on Indian Education. "Indian Education: A National Tragedy—A National Challenge." Washington, DC: United States Government Printing Office, 1969.

Wax, Murray. *Indian Americans.* Department of Commerce, United States Census of Population, 1960 (Nonwhite Population by Race). Washington, DC: United States Government Printing Office, 1963.

Zimiles, Herbert et al. *Young Native Americans and Their Families: Educational Needs Assessment and Recommendations.* Bank Street College of Education, New York, 1976.

7

The Asian-American Family

BOB H. SUZUKI

Professor
School of Education
University of Massachusetts/Amherst
Amherst, Massachusetts

INTRODUCTION

Any anthology, such as the present volume, devoted to the American family and effective parenting, would doubtlessly be considered seriously remiss if it failed to include at least some mention of the Asian-American family. Indeed, due to their seemingly phenomenal success in American society, Asian-Americans have been hailed by many as the "model minority" that other minority groups might do well to emulate (Peterson, 1966; Anonymous, 1966; Alsop, 1971). Their widely extolled success appears remarkable considering their long history as an oppressed racial minority, and has been attributed largely to the unity, stability, and strength of the Asian family. While the validity of the model minority thesis is quite problematic (Sue and Sue, 1973; Suzuki, 1977a), few would question that a great deal might be learned about effective parenting by examining the nature and functioning of the Asian-American family.

What are some of the unique characteristics of the Asian-American family and how did they evolve? How do Asian-American parenting patterns differ from those of Anglo families and how do they affect the development of the Asian-American child? What has been the impact of racial discrimination and acculturation on Asian-American families? What are some of the major problems and issues facing Asian-American families today? The primary purpose of the present article is to attempt to answer these questions and to present, based on a retrospective analysis of the Asian-American family, a number of policy recommendations directed at the broader agenda of this anthology.

In order to achieve this purpose in a reasonably systematic manner, the article is organized into four major sections. These will cover, successively, the following topics: (1) the historical background of the Asian experience in the United States, (2) the cultural roots of the Asian-American family, (3) the characteristics of the contemporary Asian-American family, and (4) a summary of the article together with a list of the policy recommendations.

Since it will not be possible to present a comprehensive picture of all Asian-American families within the scope of this article, only the families of the two largest Asian-American ethnic groups, the Chinese and Japanese, will be treated. The term, Asian-American, will be used to refer to only those two groups, and not to other

groups, such as the Koreans, Philipinos, Pacific Islanders, East Indians, and In-
dochinese that are often included in the generic use of the term.

Moreover, given the wide range of variations that exists between and within
even Chinese and Japanese families, our approach will be that of modal description
and analysis. These families will be assumed to have enough characteristics in common that they may be generally described and analyzed as a single social entity. The
problem with this approach is that it tends to lead to broad generalizations at the
expense of important particularistic aspects. It also poses the very real danger that
such generalizations may be misused to stereotype all Asian-Americans. To partly
counter these inherent shortcomings in the approach, differences between and within
Chinese and Japanese families will be described whenever such distinctions are considered important enough to point out.

HISTORICAL BACKGROUND

Like all families, the Asian-American family is a changing, dynamic institution.
It can, therefore, only be fully understood through a knowledge of the historical experience of Asians in the United States. This section will briefly describe the following aspects and phases of that historical background: (a) immigration, (b) the early
Asian pioneers, (c) the "Yellow Peril" movement, (d) World War II, (e) the post-war
era, and (f) Asian-Americans today.

IMMIGRATION

The first of the Asian immigrants, the Chinese, began arriving in the 1850's,
lured initially by the discovery of gold in California and later by recruiters seeking
cheap labor for the sugar plantations in Hawaii and for railroad construction, mining, and agriculture in the western states. The vast majority were poor peasants,
nearly all men, from the Canton area of southeastern China. Most of them came to
earn money, hoping to return home reasonably prosperous after a few years. Those
who were married left their wives at home, while single men hoped to marry when
they returned. Only a few realized their hopes. The rest ultimately resigned themselves to remaining in the United States (Coolidge, 1909; Sung, 1967; Chinn, 1969).

By 1880, some 105,000 Chinese were living in the western states and another
12,000 in Hawaii. Men outnumbered women by more than twenty to one. In 1882, as
a result of a virulent anti-Chinese movement, Chinese immigration was brought to a
halt by an exclusion act passed by the United States Congress (Lyman, 1970).

The major proportion of the Japanese immigrants arrived in Hawaii and on the
United States mainland between 1890 and 1920. They were brought in to work as
cheap laborers in many of the same areas in which the earlier Chinese immigrants
had worked. Most of them were peasants or destitute small farmers in their twenties
who came from the more economically distressed prefectures of southwestern Japan
(Conroy, 1953; Daniels, 1962).

As in the case of the Chinese, males, predominantly unmarried, far outnumbered females. While most of them hoped to marry upon returning to Japan, they
later realized, like the Chinese before them, that such a goal would be nearly impossi-

ble to achieve. Their hopes further faded in 1908 when, under pressure from the United States, Japan began restricting emigration.

It was at this time that the practice of "picture-bride" marriages, arranged through photographs, became popular. These marriages redressed the male-female imbalance considerably among the Japanese immigrants. Nevertheless, thousands of Japanese men were still unmarried in 1924 when Japanese immigration was halted by the United States Congress, this time as a result of intense anti-Japanese agitation. At the time, there were about 110,000 Japanese living on the United States mainland, mainly in the three Pacific Coast states, and an equal number in Hawaii (Ichihashi, 1932; Hosokawa, 1969).

EARLY ASIAN PIONEERS

The early Asian pioneers from China and Japan made major contributions to the development of the American West and Hawaii. They provided much of the labor for the expanding agricultural industries of these areas and were largely responsible for building the vast network of railroads throughout the western states. Others worked in fields, and at jobs such as lumbering, fishing, mining, in canneries, at domestic work and gardening, in which the demand for cheap, unskilled labor was high (Chun-Hoon, 1973; Jacobs and Landau, 1971).

Since they were denied entry into most labor unions on the West Coast, Asian workers often engaged in their own collective tactics, such as work "slowdowns," to force wages up and improve working conditions. Some of them were accepted by a few unions and were involved in numerous strike actions (Yoneda, 1971). In Hawaii, thousands of plantation workers engaged in several work stoppages and strikes against the white oligarchy, known as the "Big Five," which controlled the sugar industry (Fuchs, 1961; Ariyoshi, 1976).

As their economic status improved, many of the immigrants leased or brought their own farms. Others moved into the towns and cities to enter other occupations or to start their own small businesses. Due to discrimination, they were forced to start their own largely self-sufficient communities—the Chinatowns and Little Tokyos —which could meet most of the needs of their Asian populaces (Chinn, 1969; Miyamoto, 1972; Light, 1972).

"YELLOW PERIL" MOVEMENT

The contributions of the early Asian pioneers are perhaps even more impressive when considered in the light of the intense discrimination encountered by them. The Chinese were particularly hard hit. They arrived at a time when both racism and violence were endemic in the American West. Moreover, they were viewed as a competitive threat by white workers. Consequently, they were victims of some of the most repressive and violent acts of racism ever directed against any minority group, including denial of citizenship, prohibition from testifying in court against whites, discriminatory taxes, segregated schools, race riots, and lynchings (Coolidge, 1909; Barth, 1964; Miller, 1969; Saxton, 1971).

Strong objections were also raised against the Japanese. As their numbers grew, labor unions, newspapers, and politicians all joined in a campaign to stop Japanese immigration. An abortive attempt was made to segregate Japanese children in the San Francisco schools and alien land laws were passed prohibiting Japanese immigrants from buying land. As mentioned earlier (Daniels, 1962; Kitano and Daniels, 1970) these and other efforts finally succeeded in bringing a halt to Japanese immigration in 1924.

The culmination of the anti-Japanese movement, however, was reached during World War II when most of the mainland Japanese, over 110,000 people, two-thirds of whom were American-born citizens, were removed from the West Coast and incarcerated in concentration camps. This tragic episode has been extensively chronicled in numerous studies (tenBroek et al., 1954; Girdner and Loftis, 1969; Daniels, 1971; Weglyn, 1976). While the Japanese in Hawaii were not incarcerated *en masse* (except for about 1,000 supposedly "high risk" community leaders), they were viewed with great distrust and subjected to many abuses and restrictions during the wartime period (Fuchs, 1961; Daws, 1968).

POST-WAR ERA

While discrimination against Asian-Americans persisted into the post-war era, the more overt forms prevalent during the pre-war period were now less frequently encountered, and American attitudes toward Asian-Americans gradually improved. Restrictions on Asian immigration were relaxed somewhat and Asian aliens were finally allowed to become naturalized citizens. Token compensation was provided to Japanese Americans for the enormous losses they suffered during the war. Many of the discriminatory laws against Asians were either repealed or declared unconstitutional (Sung, 1967; Chuman, 1977).

Moreover, during the decade of the 1950's, the job market improved measurably for Asian-Americans. This was due in large part to the unparalleled expansion in the technological/bureaucratic sectors of the American economy during this period. A high demand was created for appropriately trained technical-scientific workers. Since many Asian-Americans had gone on to college, despite the bleak outlook for jobs, and had been educated in these fields, they were in a good position to meet this demand when it arose (Lyman, 1974; Suzuki, 1977a). As a result, by 1960 the census showed that Asian-Americans had the highest median family income of any minority group and a higher educational level than whites (United States Bureau of the Census, 1963).

In order to achieve this rise in socioeconomic status, Asian Americans on the United States mainland generally adopted a low-profile strategy for advancement that would not attract too much attention nor elicit adverse reaction. They became known as quiet, hardworking, dependable, and accommodating—attributes that were viewed favorably by employers (Caudill, 1952). On the other hand, Asian-Americans in Hawaii, mainly the Japanese, chose quite a different strategy for gaining upward mobility. Since the Japanese constituted over one-third the state's population, Nisei leaders could clearly see the potential for gaining political power and decided to aggressively enter the political arena. By 1959 when Hawaii was granted statehood, the Japanese had succeeded in becoming a powerful political force in the Islands. Their success in politics was paralleled by their success in many other fields (Fuchs, 1961; Gray, 1972).

ASIAN-AMERICANS TODAY

According to the 1970 census, there were 591,000 Japanese and 435,000 Chinese living in the United States. Of these, nearly 70 percent lived in the three western states and Hawaii. Sizeable concentrations were also found in Salt Lake City, Denver, Chicago, Boston, and New York City (United States Bureau of the Census, 1973).

The 1970 census also revealed that Asian-Americans had made substantial socioeconomic gains since 1960. In particular, it showed ·'t the median years of schooling completed by the Chinese and Japanese was 12.. .ompared to 12.1 for the United States population as a whole, and that their median family income has risen above that of white families (Urban Associates, 1974). However, the latter comparison is somewhat misleading since it has been found that the median income of Asian-American males is still substantially below that of white males if adjustments are made for such demographic variables as education, age, and geographic location (Suzuki, 1977b; Cabezas, 1977).

While overt discrimination is rarely encountered by Asian Americans today, covert forms still are found in many areas. Hearings and investigations have shown that ethnocentric bias and subtle discrimination against Asian-Americans are pervasive in such areas as education, employment, social services, and the mass media (Governor's Asian-American Advisory Commission, 1973; California FEPC, 1970; California Advisory Committee to the United States Commission on Civil Rights, 1975). Furthermore, many Asian-American communities, particularly the inner-city ghettoes such as the Chinatowns and Little Tokyos, are currently beset with a multitude of serious social problems. These problems have been severely exacerbated in recent years by the large influx of immigrants and will be discussed at greater length in a later section.

Perhaps the single, most important influence on Asian-Americans in recent years has been the emergence of a movement which has brought together various Asian-American groups in united efforts to achieve common goals. Originating in the activism of Asian-American students on West Coast campuses during the 1960's, this movement quickly spread from the campuses to the communities and exposed many long-concealed and denied problems of the various Asian-American communities. As a result, there has been a reawakening of community concern and awareness, and many groups and organizations have been formed to address these problems at both local and national levels (Wong, 1972; Suzuki, 1977a).

CULTURAL ROOTS: THE FAMILY IN ASIA

The early Asian immigrants, like other immigrant groups, brought with them cultural values and behavior patterns deeply rooted in their countries of origin. As they struggled to survive in this country, often in the face of powerful forces against them, parts of their cultural baggage were modified and others discarded, leading to corresponding changes in the structure and functioning of their families. In order to provide a frame of reference for understanding this process of change, a cursory description will be given in this section of the following aspects of the traditional family in Asia: (a) cultural values, (b) family structure and relations, (c) child-rearing practices, and (d) kinship systems.

Before proceeding to these topics, two qualifications must be stated. First, generalizations about traditional Asian families are difficult to make because of both national and regional differences in their cultural patterns. Second, since there is a paucity of information on the families of the late nineteenth-century rural villages from which most of the immigrants came, we must sometimes rely on more recent studies of Asian families in rural areas where cultural change may be assumed to have been relatively slow. Notwithstanding these difficulties, a modal description of these families should prove to be of some utility, providing its limitations are kept in mind.

CULTURAL VALUES

To a large degree, the traditional cultural value systems of both China and Japan can be described, at least as desirable ideals, by the precepts of Confucianism, which has had a long and pervasive influence in both countries (Chan, 1963; Hane, 1972). It should be noted, however, that Confucianism underwent continual change under the influences of Taoism, Buddhism, and Shintoism. Moreover, even though the Confucian code of ethics was widely adopted, the lower classes did not always follow its rules and prescriptions (Wong, 1974; Pelzel, 1970).

Having stated these caveats, we will now describe the major traditional cultural values common to both China and Japan in terms of the following Confucian concepts: humanism, collectivity, self-discipline, order and hierarchy, wisdom of the elderly, moderation and harmony, and obligation. These concepts are discussed in much more depth by Chan (1963), Moore (1967), Nakamura (1964), Hsu (1953), and Benedict (1946).

HUMANISM

This concept, which is central to Confucianism, is based on the optimistic belief that human nature is basically good and that the inherent tendency of man is toward virtuous and benevolent behavior. Man is thought to have the potential within himself to achieve fulfillment and happiness during his earthly existence. However, satisfaction in life is to be gained not through the acquisition of power, wealth, or prestige, but through an individual's diligent and sincere efforts to conduct himself morally and to develop his full potentialities as a person.

COLLECTIVITY

This concept arises from the altruistic nature of Confucianism and its emphasis on kinship ties and mutual dependence. An individual is expected to subordinate or even sacrifice his personal interests for the greater collective good of his family, kinship group, village, or country. Since egocentricity is not compatible with such a value system, modesty and humility are considered important virtues.

SELF-DISCIPLINE

Confucianism teaches that a person should learn to control his emotions in order to think logically and make objective judgments. Control over both emotions and psychological and material gratification is thought to be necessary for cultivating the mind and self-improvement. A person is also expected to make every effort to utilize his own capabilities and resources to solve his personal problems and improve his life. Failure is attributed to either the lack of resolve or the result of fate beyond an individual's control.

ORDER AND HIERARCHY

Since Confucius's goal was to establish a stable and harmonious social order, Confucianism placed great emphasis on the proper relationships between man in all aspects of life. Since he believed that the cornerstone of these relationships was that between a child and his parents, he placed major emphasis on the virtue of filial piety. A child was expected to pay homage and give unquestioning obedience to his parents and be concerned and understanding of their needs and wishes. This expectation, in turn, was extended to all subordinates in their relationships with persons of authority above them. However, all of these relationships were supposed to be mutually dependent, entailing two-way obligations.

WISDOM OF THE ELDERLY

The pursuit of knowledge was highly stressed by Confucianism since knowledge was considered essential for wisdom and goodness. Learned scholars, especially the elderly sages, were highly respected because of their experience, knowledge, and wisdom. For the same reasons, the elderly in general were accorded much respect. These value orientations were reflected in the practice of ancestor worship, the high value placed on education, the respect given to tradition, and the emphasis on the past rather than the future. While these precepts insured social stability and cultural continuity, they also tended to make traditional Asian societies rigid and difficult to change.

MODERATION AND HARMONY

This concept is based on the idea that man should seek to maintain a balance and pursue a middle course between extremes of theory and practice, action and inaction. Thus, a flexible mode of thinking is promoted that values relativity and gradualism and prohibits rigid absolutes. Interactions between persons are generally characterized by politeness and restraint and by sensitive consideration for the position and feelings of others. Open confrontations and conflicts between persons are discouraged and tend to be avoided. Thus, Asians appear to be humble, modest, nonaggressive, and unemotional to many Westerners, who, therefore, often mischaracterize them as inscrutable.

OBLIGATION

We have already mentioned the mutuality of obligations involved in the concept of filial piety. The Japanese have extended these obligatory relations through a category of obligations known as *giri,* for which there is no equivalent in Chinese culture. They include gift-giving, mutual assistance, and other considerations (Benedict, 1946). Another type of obligation stems from the concept of collectivity. As part of his obligation to his group, an individual is obliged not to bring dishonor or shame to his family by socially unacceptable behavior. Consequently, Asians face considerable pressure to conform to social norms.

FAMILY STRUCTURE AND RELATIONSHIPS

Both the Chinese and Japanese kinship systems, though fundamentally different, generally led to extended families consisting usually of three generations living under one roof. In addition to the parents and their children, the residential family would often include the paternal grandparents. Contrary to popular image, however, the Confucian ideal of the large extended family of several generations and dozens of members was a rarity to be found only among the upper classes (Lang, 1946; Embree, 1939).

Perhaps the best known characteristic of the traditional Asian family has been its patriarchical structure. True to Confucian precepts, the father was the dominant authority figure in the family, while other members were in clearly prescribed, subordinate roles. However, the authoritarian role of the father has frequently been overdrawn (Wagatsuma, 1977; Wolf, 1970). In fact, in rural families in which the wife often worked alongside her husband, the mother also exerted considerable authority (Hsu, 1949; Fukutake, 1967).

The eldest son was accorded the next highest position in the family hierarchy, followed by his younger brothers. Females were considered inferior to males, and accordingly, daughters were relegated to lower-status roles. As Wong (1974) has noted, however, the position of females in Asian societies was probably not too different from that of women in traditional western societies.

The grandparents occupied a special position of honor in the family. As its most elderly members, their wisdom was respected and their advice often sought on important family matters.

While the children were expected to show filial piety to both the father and mother, their relationships with each were distinctly different. In order to command their respect and obedience, the father tended to establish a rather distant and formal relationship with his children, especially the older sons who often viewed him with trepidation. In contrast, the relationship of the children to the mother was generally one of greater intimacy, affection, and informality. Especially close, affective ties tended to develop between the mother and her sons, particularly the eldest son.

Due to the custom of arranged marriages and the hierarchical structure of the family, the husband-wife relationship was neither the strongest nor the most intense one within the family, and was usually overshadowed by father-son and mother-son relationships (Hsu, 1975).

Finally, the relationship between the mother and daughter-in-law has received much attention in Asian folklore. Stories about the suffering of new brides under the domination of a despotic mother-in-law are well known not only in Asia but also in the West. However, due to the strong tradition of extended families and the dictates of filial piety, the burden of the role in Asian societies was much less avoidable and probably more onerous (Lang, 1946; Benedict, 1946).

CHILD-REARING

In both China and Japan, the early years of childhood were characterized by the permissiveness of parents toward their children. By American standards, young children were indulged, receiving close attention, much soothing care, and little discipline. Close intimate contacts with the mother were continual during this stage of early childhood. The child was seldom left alone or to cry, and was almost always being fed, carried, soothed, or played with. Children usually slept with their mothers until weaning, which usually occurred at one or two years of age, but sometimes continued for years. Mothers seldom left their children alone. Thus, the infant was quiet and content most of the time, and came to relate the physical presence of the mother with emotional security (Hsu, 1949; Benedict, 1946).

At the age of five or six, children were assumed to have reached the age of reason and to be ready to begin their entry into the world of adulthood. Discipline was rather suddenly imposed at this age by both the father and mother as they began to more strictly control the conduct and behavior of the child. Minor infractions, such as boastful or selfish behavior, were controlled by ridicule or teasing. More serious misbehavior, such as emotional tantrums or fighting, was more sternly handled, usually by scolding or through the inculcation of shame and, in rare instances, by corporeal punishment.

In more direct ways, parents taught their children the ethics of good conduct, their obligations to the family, and the virtues of filial piety and self-control. They also soon learned that acts of serious social deviance such as stealing would greatly stigmatize the entire family; whereas, outstanding achievements such as success in school would be a source of much collective pride. Through this process, the child was gradually socialized from an egocentric to a family-centered orientation (Lang, 1946; Wolf, 1970; Embree, 1939).

Sex-role differentiation also commenced at about five or six years of age. Boys began to spend more time with their fathers, helping them in their work and following their example. Girls followed suit, only with their mothers. Although girls sometimes worked in the fields with boys in rural areas, they were trained primarily for household chores and subjected to many restrictions not imposed on boys. By the age of adolescence, sex roles were clearly differentiated.

Relationships between adolescents appear to have been quite different in China as compared to Japan. In China, adolescent boys and girls were usually kept apart in both work and play—even brothers and sisters were separated. Social relationships between boys and girls were strongly discouraged. Marriage was strictly a family matter to be arranged by the parents, and the parties to be wed had little, if any, say (Hsu, 1949). In contrast, in rural Japan, boys and girls often worked in the fields together and on some occasions had opportunities to congregate socially. Sexual mores were also more relaxed and premarital sexual relations, though frowned upon, were tolerated. While marriages were arranged by parents, the prospective mates met prior to wedding and, at least in theory, had to mutually consent to the union (Befu, 1971).

KINSHIP SYSTEMS

As previously mentioned, the Chinese and Japanese kinship systems were fundamentally different. In the Chinese system, the father's property was generally divided equally among all his sons, and the genealogical ties between brothers and along the patrilineal line were strongly emphasized and maintained. When sons married, their wives came to live in their households, whereas when daughters married, they went to live in their husbands' households and were no longer considered part of their biological families of origin. Kinship ties with more distant relatives were maintained through the patrilineal clan organization consisting of everyone with the same surname, all of whom were considered to be descended from a common male ancestor. A whole village would often be inhabited by a single clan consisting of thousands of individuals (Yang, 1959; Freedman, 1966).

The Japanese kinship system differed from the Chinese system in two basic ways. First, it was based on the concept of the corporate household, or *ie*. The *ie* consisted not only of the family's house and property, but also of its various organizational, social, and intangible assets. It was seen as having a life of its own which would endure through significant time. Its preservation was considered more important than the continuation of the patrilineal blood line stressed in the Chinese system. Secondly, the Japanese system was based on the rule of unigeniture under which one son, usually the eldest, inherited the father's *ie*, the main household. The other sons were expected to establish separate households, which often combined with the main household to form an extended kinship group called the *dozoku*. In rural areas, the *dozoku* was an economic and social unit which oversaw agricultural production and relationships between families. If a family lacked a son or a competent successor to the household head, a son would often be "adopted" through uxorilocal marriage to a daughter and assume the headship. Thus, in the Japanese system, genealogical lines were not as important and distinctions between kin and non-kin were not as sharp as in the Chinese system (Befu, 1971; Hsu, 1975).

While both the Chinese clan and the Japanese *dozoku* played important roles in the economic, social, and political life of their local communities, the degree and nature of their integration into the larger social systems of their respective societies were quite different. The Chinese clans were able to function almost autonomously from the central government (Freedman, 1966). On the other hand, the Japanese *dozoku* was a microcosm and a key building block of the total social system of Japan (Nakane, 1970).

THE CONTEMPORARY ASIAN-AMERICAN FAMILY

Having discussed the historical and cultural background of Asian-Americans, we are now prepared to examine the characteristics and relationships which are distinctive in their contemporary family life. To better understand its evolution, we shall begin by briefly surveying the sociohistorical changes undergone by the Asian-American family. We shall then describe the contemporary Asian-American family's sociocultural characteristics, structure and relationships, child-rearing practices, and kinship and community relationships. Finally, we shall discuss some of the major problems and issues currently facing Asian-American families.

The description and analysis to be presented were based on a variety of studies and sources. Among these were major works on Chinese-Americans by Lee (1960), Kung (1962), Sung (1967), Hsu (1971), Nee and Nee (1972), and Lyman (1974); and major works on Japanese-Americans by Ichihashi (1932), Broom and Kitsuse (1956), Kitano (1969a), Peterson (1971), and Kiefer (1974). Also utilized were works focusing on Asian-Americans in Hawaii by Fuchs (1961), Johnson (1972), and Ogawa (1973). All of these authors either specifically focused on or gave considerable attention to the family. Finally, numerous articles, papers, and reports were utilized and will be cited when appropriate. While much remains to be learned, the available information does allow us to draw a reasonably discernible, though very general, picture of the contemporary Asian-American family.

SOCIOHISTORICAL CHANGES

Since the Chinese and Japanese faced different circumstances at different times in history, the sociohistorical changes undergone by their families will be described separately for each group.

CHINESE-AMERICAN FAMILIES

Due to the exclusion act of 1882 and the resulting shortage of women, families were practically nonexistent among the early Chinese immigrants. The few Chinese wives present were married to the wealthier merchants. Although many of the immigrants had left families behind in China, most of them, together with their unmarried compatriots, were destined to live out their lives as homeless bachelors (Lyman, 1974).

It was not until the 1920's that the bachelor-society character of the Chinatowns began to change as families became increasingly visible (Nee and Nee, 1972). Many of these families were started by former laborers who achieved merchant status and were finally eligible to bring wives over from China. Others were started by marriages between immigrants and the few American-born Chinese women. Because wives were prized, they had more status than their counterparts in China, and indeed, sometimes assumed more authority than their husbands. Since grandparents were usually absent they also did not have to contend with the dictates of mothers-in-law. Moreover, the traditional extended patrifocal family was generally replaced by the nuclear family (Sung, 1967).

Many of the children in these early families grew up in the familiar surroundings of their parents' small shop, laundry, or restaurant, where they lived and helped in the family business. While most of them were subjected to strict, traditional upbringing, their early childhoods were generally secure and family-centered. However, when they began school and were exposed to Western ideas and values, cultural conflicts with parents frequently broke out and led to strained relations (Lowe, 1943; Wong, 1950). Parents were inevitably forced to make some concessions to this Americanization process, but still managed to inculcate their children with many traditional values and norms.

The number of Chinese families increased markedly in the aftermath of World War II as a result of special legislation which allowed thousands of Chinese women to immigrate into the United States (Kung, 1962). Husbands were reunited with their wives after decades of separation, and droves of immigrants went to Hong Kong to bring back wives, usually much younger than themselves. Such circumstances led to adjustment problems and familial patterns similar to those of the earlier immigrant families.

The post-war era was also the period when second-generation Chinese-

American families—that is, those in which both parents were American-born—began to emerge. The parents of these families were better educated and generally had higher-status jobs than the parents of first-generation families. Although they still faced widespread discrimination, many of them sought to escape the confines of the Chinatowns and managed to break into and find better housing in a few of the predominantly white suburbs (Lee, 1960). As a consequence, however, their families were subjected to more intense acculturation pressures. These pressures have produced familial patterns among second- and third-generation families that depart in a number of significant ways from traditional patterns.

More recently, during the past decade, there has been an increasing influx of Chinese immigrants into the United States. These recent immigrants now comprise over one-third of the total Chinese-American population. Their families must contend with societal forces quite different from those encountered by the earlier immigrant families. Consequently, they also face different problems and are undergoing different changes.

JAPANESE-AMERICAN FAMILIES

The early Japanese immigrants were more fortunate than their Chinese predecessors in that most of them were able to bring wives from Japan before the cutoff of immigration. Consequently, they were able to begin family life in the United States within a decade or two after their arrival. Since the majority were engaged in farming, they tended to continue many of the traditional ways of rural family life in Japan.

There were, however, a few significant departures from these traditional ways. As in the case of the early Chinese immigrant families, wives generally had more say in family matters than their counterparts in Japan, and the extended family was replaced by the nuclear type due to the absence of grandparents. Parental authority tended to diminish as the Nisei became Americanized through the schools and occasionally rebelled against traditional mores, such as filial piety (Masuoka, 1944; Iga, 1957).

The childhood of most Nisei was spent under the close, protective care and supervision of their parents either on the family's farm or in its place of business. In farming families, mothers often took their infant children out into the fields and cared for them as they worked. As the Nisei grew older, they were expected to help their parents on the farm or in the family business. Thus, except while they were in school, they were almost always in close contact with their parents. Even out in the Japanese community they could not escape scrutiny by relatives and family acquaintances.

Perhaps no event had a greater impact on Japanese-American families than the internment experience of World War II (Broom and Kitsuse, 1956; Thomas and Nishimoto, 1946). The sudden uprooting of families and the oppressive conditions in the concentration camps had traumatic, long-lasting effects on the family which even today have not been fully assessed (Morishima, 1973).

Many Japanese-Americans, especially the Nisei, felt deeply stigmatized by their internment experience. After their release from the camps many of them undoubtedly decided, consciously or unconsciously, to reject all vestiges of Japanese culture and to acculturate as quickly as possible into the American mainstream (Okimoto, 1971). This attitude appears to have had a strong influence on the subsequent development of familial patterns among the Nisei and Sansei on the mainland (Kiefer, 1974).

Since the Japanese in Hawaii were not mass-incarcerated and constituted a numerical majority, they were subjected to less intense acculturation pressures and appeared to have maintained more of the traditional familial patterns than their mainland counterparts.

Although Japanese immigration into the United States has also increased during the past decade, it has been of much smaller magnitude than Chinese immigration. Presently, recent Japanese immigrants comprise only a small percentage of the total Japanese-American population.

CURRENT CATEGORIES OF FAMILIES

The evolutionary process described above has led to a wide variety of Asian-American families. These could be grouped into an almost unlimited number of categories. However, since we are using a modal approach, we will assume that most of the families can be grouped into two broad categories: (1) families headed by American born Chinese and Japanese of second or third generation, and (2) families headed by recent Chinese immigrants. No attempt will be made to describe other smaller categories of families, such as those of recent Japanese immigrants, Asian scholars and intellectuals, or interracial marriages. It should also be noted that families headed by early Chinese or Japanese immigrants are practically nonexistent today.

In the four subsections to follow, discussion will focus primarily on the first category of families. For the most part, consistent with our modal approach, this category will be treated as a single social entity. Inasmuch as the high influx of Chinese immigrants is a relatively recent phenomenon, the second category of families will be covered in the final subsection on "Current Problems and Issues."

SOCIOCULTURAL CHARACTERISTICS

The contemporary Asian-American family's sociocultural characteristics will be described in terms of the cultural values prevalent among Asian-Americans today, and recent demographic data on family median income, family size, outmarriage rates, divorce, crime and delinquency, and mental illness among Asian-American families.

CULTURAL VALUES

The traditional Asian cultural values described earlier appear to have been modified, often significantly, through the process of acculturation. Generally speaking, third-generation Asian-Americans have acculturated to a greater degree than second-generation Asian-Americans, with Japanese showing greater acculturation than their Chinese counterparts (Sue and Kirk, 1973). Certain values, such as filial piety and respect for the wisdom of the elderly, appear to have depreciated more than others. Parents can no longer expect unquestioning obedience from their children, and relationships within the family have become more democratic. Furthermore, the knowledge and experience of grandparents no longer carry the weight they did in the past.

Despite such acculturative trends, both generations of Asian-Americans are still found to subscribe to many traditional values, though to a lesser degree than first-generation Asian-Americans. In particular, they believe more strongly than their Anglo counterparts in such values as respect for ethical behavior, duty and obligation to family, restraint of strong feelings, respect for authority, and modesty and politeness toward others (Kitano, 1969a; Schwartz, 1971; Fong, 1973; Sue, 1973).

However, Asian-Americans appear to be experiencing considerable psychological stress in attempting to maintain these values. They have been found to be more conforming, obedient, conservative, and inhibited than their Anglo peers. These personality traits appear to be the result not only of traditional cultural values but also of discrimination (Tong, 1971; Watanabe, 1973). Moreover, many of them are apparently suffering acute anxieties and conflicts as manifested by excessive conformity, lack of confidence, and feelings of self-contempt and alienation (Yamamoto, 1968; Sue and Sue, 1971; Sue and Frank, 1973).

FAMILY MEDIAN INCOME

According to the 1970 census, the median incomes of Chinese and Japanese families were $10,000 and $12,500, respectively, compared to $9,600 for United States families as a whole. The higher incomes of Asian-American families were primarily due to a larger proportion of such families having two or more earners than families in the general population (Urban Associates, 1974). As noted earlier, the median income of Asian-American males is still substantially below that of white males.

FAMILY SIZE

The 1970 census also showed that the average size of Asian-American families was somewhat larger than that of white families; namely, 4.0 for Chinese, 3.7 for Japanese and 3.5 for whites (United States Bureau of the Census, 1973). The larger size of Asian-American families is mainly due to extended family relationships, that is, the presence of grandparents, aunts, uncles, and so forth. In fact, 18 percent of all Chinese and 16 percent of all Japanese families were found to be of the extended type, compared to 12 percent of families in the total population (Urban Associates, 1974).

OUTMARRIAGE RATES

While the 1970 census showed that a high percentage (80 to 90 percent) of Asian-Americans were married within their groups, recent studies (Omatsu, 1972; Kikumura and Kitano, 1973; Sung, 1974) indicate that the rate of outmarriage has sharply increased in the past decade among the younger Chinese and Japanese, approaching 50 percent in many areas. A notable exception are the Japanese in Hawaii, whose outmarriage rates remain relatively low.

DIVORCE

In 1970, the proportion of divorced to married men was about 3 percent for both Chinese and Japanese, compared to about 4 percent for the total population. Correspondingly, the proportion of divorced to married women was about 3 percent for Chinese and 4 percent for Japanese, compared to about 6 percent for the total population. Again, these proportions were lower for the Japanese in Hawaii (United States Bureau of the Census, 1973). Of course, actual divorce rates, which cannot be obtained from the census data, are much higher and currently average around 40 percent for the general population (Bronfenbrenner, 1977).

CRIME AND DELINQUENCY

The low rates of crime and delinquency among Asian-Americans frequently have been cited as an anomaly among racial minority groups. Studies have shown that these rates are not only the lowest among minority groups, but are also lower than those of the white population (Kitano, 1969a; Sollenberger, 1968). However, there are signs that delinquency may be on the rise among Japanese youth (Peterson, 1971) and is reachinng alarmingly high rates among Chinese youth. This latter phenomenom will be discussed in the last subsection on "Current Problems and Issues."

MENTAL ILLNESS

The rate of mental illness appears to be extraordinarily low for this group. Data compiled by Kitano (1969b) for the period 1960-1965 show that in California the commitment rates of Chinese and Japanese to state mental hospitals were, respectively, one-half and one-third of the rate for Caucasians. He also found a similar pattern in Hawaii. However, as Berk and Hirata (1973) have pointed out, commitment rates do not necessarily reflect the relative amount of emotional disturbance among different groups due to cultural differences in the handling of psychological problems. Both the Chinese and Japanese generally have tried to cope with mental illness through their extended families and communities rather than relying on outside professionals or social service agencies.

FAMILY STRUCTURE AND RELATIONSHIPS

It has become almost axiomatic to describe the Asian-American family as patriarchal; that is, as vertically structured with the father as undisputed head and all others in subordinate roles (Kitano, 1969a; Sung, 1967). While this traditional structure may have prevailed in many first-generation families, it has almost certainly been modified in second- and third-generation families. In fact, as mentioned earlier, even in first-generation families the mother frequently assumed much more authority than her counterpart in Asia.

In second- and third-generation Asian-American families, husbands and wives appear to play complementary roles. One study (Johnson, 1972) of Nisei and Sansei families found that most husbands and wives made major decisions jointly and that their relationships were more often cooperative than disjunctive. Moreover, the investigator found that in such family matters as finances, social activities, and child-rearing, the wives were usually the decision-makers. Although more research is needed, these findings seem consistent with the impressions of many Asian-Americans themselves and are probably generalizeable to a large proportion of contemporary Asian-American families.

Paradoxically, despite such findings, the Asian-American male is generally seen as more chauvinistic than his Anglo counterpart (Fujitomi and Wong, 1973). Even in the study described above, most of the wives saw their husbands in the dominant position. The persistence of such views may be partly attributed to the strong mutual dependency that develops between Asian-American husbands and wives as a result of early socialization patterns (Caudill, 1952). One aspect of this relationship is the tendency for the husband to depend heavily on his wife to provide moral and ego support through responses that may appear indulgent and subservient by middle-class Anglo standards, even though their relationship may be more egalitarian in terms of actual power distribution.

Relationships between Asian-American parents and their children have also become more egalitarian. While they are still differentially socialized, boys enjoy little, if any, preferential treatment or status over girls with regard to the allocation of family resources. Furthermore, the duties and obligations expected of children are less demanding and restrictive than in the past. However, they are still generally subjected to stricter limits and constraints than their Anglo peers (Kriger and Kroes, 1972).

Verbal communication within Asian-American families is relatively restrained compared to that in Anglo families. This verbal reticence is not only rooted in traditional cultural norms but may also have been strongly reinforced by racial discrimination (Watanabe, 1973). On the other hand, there appears to be much greater utilization of nonverbal and indirect modes of communication. Family members generally become quite sensitive to using nonverbal cues and to reading between the lines of indirect statements.

Unlike traditional Asian families, contemporary Asian-American families are not dominated by parent-son relationships. The strongest relationships appear to be those between husband and wife and between the mother and her children. Husbands and wives appear to enjoy much closer companionship today than in previous years. Since mothers continue to assume most of the responsibility for child-rearing they develop the closest relationships with their children. Fathers still tend to maintain some distance from their children in order to engender respect and obedience. While fathers play with the children, they do not try to become close companions in the way that Anglo fathers do. Parents are more likely to show affection for their children in indirect ways (for instance, by sacrificing their own needs for their children's), rather than with words or overt displays of affection, such as hugging or kissing.

These relationships have served to make the Asian-American family a close-knit social unit. This cohesiveness is reflected in the social activities of Asian-American families, which tend to be more family-centered than those of Anglo families. Children are more likely to be included in Asian-American social gatherings since parents appear less comfortable about leaving them at home with babysitters (Hsu, 1971; Kitano, 1969).

CHILD-REARING

While acculturation toward Anglo middle-class patterns has taken place, many aspects of traditional Asian child-rearing practices appear to be continued among contemporary Asian-American families (Young, 1972; Sollenberger, 1968; Johnson, 1972; Kitano, 1969a). The early years of childhood are still characterized by close, nurturant care by the mother, who tends to be more permissive with the young infant than her Anglo counterpart. Infants are seldom allowed to cry for prolonged periods before they are picked up by their mothers. Mothers tend to feed their infants on demand rather than by scheduling. On the average, weaning takes place at a later age than for Anglo infants. Toilet training is also more gradual. Parents often allow the young child to sleep with them, occasionally tolerating such behavior even after the child begins school.

Such indulgences would very likely be viewed by middle-class Anglo parents as a sure way of spoiling the child and retarding his/her development into a mature, independent, and autonomous adult. However, such an approach to child-rearing develops close, affective ties within the family and the child's sense of belonging to the family. It also results in the child's becoming strongly dependent on the mother to satisfy his/her needs and, in turn, enables the mother to use various deprivation techniques to control the child's behavior. Moreover, even as the Asian-American mother caters to the needs of her child, she inculcates the child with a sense of obligation, which she continues to reinforce as the child grows older. Consequently, she is able to use shame and guilt to control behavior by appealing to this sense of obligation whenever the child deviates from her expectations.

Despite their seemingly permissive child-rearing methods, Asian-American mothers are able to use the nonphysical disciplinary techniques described above together with limited amounts of physical punishment very effectively to control their children's behavior. Although much childish behavior is tolerated, aggression, especially fighting, is strongly disapproved of and quickly admonished. Mothers maintain close supervision over all of their children's activities, carefully selecting their playmates and rarely leaving them alone or on their own. This protective care is reflected in the low childhood accident rates suffered by Asian-American children (Kurokawa, 1966).

Although their role appears to be increasing, most Asian-American fathers still play a relatively minor role in the rearing of children during their years of infancy. Since the time the father spends with his children usually is quite limited, he tends to take a rather tolerant attitude toward them, leaving most of the disciplining to the mother. However, when the children reach school age they are no longer indulged and begin to assume duties and responsibilities in the household. They also are subjected to stricter discipline and taught in various ways that their actions will reflect not only on themselves but on the entire family. In cases of serious misbehavior by older children, the disciplining often is done by the father since his authority evokes greater fear and respect. He also spends more time with the older children, particularly if they are boys, joining them in recreational activities and having them assist with household chores.

As Asian-American children reach adolescence, many of them join peer groups and begin showing interest in the opposite sex. Their friends are now even more carefully screened by the parents. Dating among Asian-American teenagers is often on a group basis, whereby girls and boys go out as a group without necessarily pairing off. Dating on an individual basis generally does not start until later; in fact, group dating patterns sometimes persist even into college.

Parental attitudes toward pre-marital sexual exploration are still relatively strict but are becoming more tolerant. In fact, it is not uncommon to find unmarried couples living together among Asian-American college students. However, while marriages among Asian-Americans today are based on romantic love and free choice, parents still exert considerable influence on their children in this matter.

KINSHIP AND COMMUNITY

The nuclear family consisting of the parents and their children is the norm today among Asian-American families. However, close ties are still maintained with many relatives outside the immediate residential family through frequent visits and telephone calls, mutual assistance, reciprocal gift-giving, and various social get-togethers. The bonds appear particularly strong between married sisters and between a mother and her married daughters. While grandparents generally do not live with their married children, they often live nearby and become quite involved with their children's families.

Due to the extent and closeness of these ties, the Asian-American family has been referred to as a modified extended family (Johnson, 1972). Although it is residentially nuclear, it is in many respects functionally extended. Such patterns appear to be particularly prevalent among Japanese families in Hawaii. To a lesser extent they are also found among second- and third-generation Asian-American families on the West coast (Kiefer, 1974; Nee and Nee, 1972) and in other areas, such as New York City, where there are relatively high concentrations of Asian-Americans.

Strongly complementing these family ties are the extensive networks of affiliations and communications that exist in the Asian-American communities. These include both informal networks, such as family friends and social groups, and formal networks, such as ethnic newspapers, churches, family and business associations, recreational clubs, and various other community organizations (Hsu, 1971; Kiefer, 1974). Many of these formal networks are outgrowths of those originally established by the early Asian immigrants through their adaptations of the Chinese clan and Japanese *dozoku* systems of kinship. In recent years, as numerous national Asian-American organizations have come into being, similar networks are developing even at the national level.

It is these networks that made the Asian-American communities very close-knit social entities. They strongly reinforce the sanctioning techniques of the family for controlling behavior by serving as very effective channels for gossip and news about both misdeeds and achievements of individuals in the community. Through such communications, the "good families" and "bad families" are readily identified. Thus, community members are quite aware that their actions will become widely known and ultimately reflect on their families' reputations.

CURRENT PROBLEMS AND ISSUES

Our discussion of the contemporary Asian-American family will be concluded with an examination of some of the major problems and issues currently facing it. These will be discussed under two broad categories: (a) those facing recent immigrant families, and (b) those arising from deculturalization.

Recent Immigrant Families

Since 1965 when discriminatory immigration quotas were finally eliminated, well over 200,000 Chinese immigrants have entered the United States, principally from Hong Kong and Taiwan. Most of them have crowded into the Chinatowns of San Francisco, New York City, Boston, and other major cities. These Chinatowns are stricken with some of the worst conditions to be found in any of the inner-city ghettoes, including increasing crime and delinquency, grossly inadequate health care, overcrowded and substandard housing, chronic underemployment, and a multitude of other pressing social problems (Chin, 1971; Wong, 1971; Lyman, 1974).

The families of these immigrants must contend with circumstances quite different from those faced by earlier Asian immigrant families. Parents no longer work and live with their children in small business establishments, but are now generally wage workers in restaurants, garment factories, and other large enterprises. Both parents usually must work, often ten hours a day, seven days a week, for subsistence-level wages. Consequently, they have little time to spend with their children and must live under poverty conditions (Chao, 1977).

Parents also no longer can rely on traditional techniques for controlling the behavior of their children. Unlike earlier Asian immigrants, most of the recent immigrants have come from urban areas, which have experienced major changes under the impact of modernization and Western influences. Values and lifestyles have undergone corresponding changes. Furthermore, the youth are far more sophisticated in their perceptions about the society in which they live.

All of these factors have subjected recent Chinese immigrant families to severe strains. Due to the absence of their parents and traditional constraints, the teenage youth of these families have been especially prone to acts of rebellion and social deviance. Since many of them cannot speak English and experience traumatic family/school discontinuities, they frequently become alienated from school, drop out and join their peers in street gangs (Sung, 1977). A large number of such gangs have formed over the past few years in all of the major Chinatowns and have been increasingly involved in crime and acts of violence, including an estimated forty-five killings attributed to intergang warfare (Wu, 1977).

These families also suffer from some of the highest rates of infant mortality and tuberculosis in the country. Furthermore, there are signs that mental illness and suicide are becoming serious problems. Many of these families may become trapped in these conditions of poverty inasmuch as the adult members are finding themselves in low-paying, dead-end jobs with little chance for upward mobility, and many of the young males are not able to find employment at all. These problems are exacerbated by the language and cultural barriers, which prevent immigrants from gaining access to social services and job programs. Unless these problems are ameliorated, the disintegration of immigrant families will undoubtedly continue for some time to come (Sung, 1976).

Deculturalization

A number of serious problems face second-, third-, and fourth-generation Asian-Americans as a result of their deculturalization, which is defined here as the combined process of both acculturation and discrimination. Although a wide range of these problems could be discussed, we shall touch just briefly on some of the major problems in the areas of education, employment, and mental health.

Despite their high achievement levels, Asian-American students face many subtle forms of discrimination in education due to the Anglo-centric orientation of most schools. The curriculum usually omits or badly distorts the experience and contributions of Asian-Americans. Teachers often stereotype Asian-American students as quiet, hard-working, and docile, and tend to reinforce conformity and stifle creativity. Therefore, Asian-American students frequently do not develop the ability to assert and express themselves verbally, and are channeled mainly into technical/scientific fields (Watanabe, 1973). As a consequence of these influences, many Asian-American students suffer from low self-esteem, are overly conforming, and have their academic and social development narrowly circumscribed.

Subtle forms of discrimination against Asian-Americans also appear widespread in employment. Although they have gained access to many professional occupations because of their high educational attainment levels, most Asian-Americans appear to be relegated to lower-echelon, white-collar jobs having little or no decision-making authority and low mobility. They are consistently passed over by Anglos for most supervisory and administrative positions, apparently because they are viewed as not having the requisite personality traits, such as aggressiveness, verbal fluency, and self-confidence, for such positions (Suzuki, 1977a).

Due to the anxieties, conflicts, frustrations, and suppressed anger generated by these and other problems of deculturalization, the mental strains suffered by Asian-Americans can be expected to increase. We have already mentioned some of the psychological problems that many Asian-Americans are currently experiencing. Ironically, traditional ways of dealing with these problems are being discarded as Asian-Americans acculturate. Yet, Western methods of psychotherapy do not appear particularly appropriate for effectively treating the psychological problems of Asian-Americans (Kitano, 1969b; Sue and Sue, 1971).

All of the problems discussed above could potentially have long-term, detrimental effects on the Asian-American family. In fact, if present acculturative trends continue, the rates of social deviance for Asian-Americans may well approach, or even exceed, those for Anglo-Americans.

Fortunately, there do appear to be countervailing forces at work. Perhaps the most important has been the emergence of the Asian-American movement, which has played a major role in raising the ethnic consciousness and social awareness of Asian-Americans. As a consequence, Asian-Americans are having second thoughts about the merits of acculturating further into the mainstream of American society, and are becoming concerned about preserving important traditional aspects of their own cultures. Many of them are also currently seeking to redefine their identity and role in American society on their own terms and can be expected to take a far less accommodating approach in this quest than in the past.

SUMMARY AND POLICY RECOMMENDATIONS

In this concluding section, we shall summarize our description of the Asian-American family, undertake a retrospective analysis of what we have learned from the Asian-American experience, and, finally, present a number of policy recommendations for guiding legislative action pertaining to the American family and effective parenting.

THE CONTEMPORARY ASIAN-AMERICAN FAMILY:
A SUMMARY

Several broad generalizations may be drawn from our description of the contemporary Asian-American family:

1. While they have acculturated toward middle-class Anglo norms, Asian-Americans still subscribe to many traditional Asian cultural values, such as group orientation and obligation to parents and family.
2. The educational level and median family income of Asian-Americans are among the highest of any ethnic group; and their rates of social deviance have been among the lowest.
3. Although the Asian-American family is often characterized as patriarchal, husbands and wives appear to enjoy a more egalitarian relationship than do their Anglo counterparts. However, except during early childhood, Asian-American parents tend to impose stricter discipline on their children. While verbal interaction between family members is relatively restrained, there is greater utilization of nonverbal and indirect modes of communication.
4. By middle-class Anglo norms, Asian-American mothers tend to indulge, if not spoil, their infant children. However, due to the close, affective ties that result from such an upbringing, mothers are able to very effectively employ nonphysical sanctions such as shame and deprivation to control their children's behavior.
5. By instilling their children with a strong sense of obligation to the family and with the idea that their actions will reflect not only on themselves but on the entire family, Asian-American parents are able to maintain a high degree of social control over their children. This control is strongly reinforced by the tightly knit Asian-American communities in which extensive networks of affiliations provide very effective channels for communicating both the misdeeds and achievements of individual community members.
6. The Asian-American family continues to be a close-knit, cohesive social entity. Although residentially nuclear, many Asian-American families are functionally extended due to the close ties that are maintained with many relatives outside the immediate residential family. Social activities tend to take place within the extended family and the ethnic community.
7. The families of recent immigrants constitute a significant proportion of all Chinese-American families. Most of them are crowded into Chinatown ghettoes and must contend with chronic underemployment, grossly inadequate health care, and overcrowded and substandard housing. Growing rates of social deviance, especially crime and delinquency, indicate that these families are experiencing serious dislocations. Language and cultural barriers prevent access to social services and job programs that could otherwise help ameliorate some of these problems.
8. The effects of deculturalization are creating serious problems for Asian-Americans in many areas, including education, employment, and mental

health. The resulting psychological strains could have long-term, detrimental effects on the Asian-American family. Perhaps the major countervailing force to deculturalization is the Asian-American movement, which has raised the ethnic consciousness and social awareness of Asian-Americans.

It must be reiterated that these generalizations should not be misused to stereotype all Asian-American families. Given the wide range of variations which exist among these families, one can be certain that many of them will not fit our modal description.

RETROSPECTIVE ANALYSIS

Prior to presenting our policy recommendations, it seems appropriate to attempt a critical, though brief, analysis of what we have learned about the family through the Asian-American experience. This analysis will be approached in two ways: first, by applying a general analytical framework and then by adopting a dialectical perspective.

A GENERAL ANALYTICAL FRAMEWORK

In general, we may delineate three broad influences which have shaped and directed the development of the families of all ethnic groups. These are (a) the cultural background of an ethnic group, (b) the socio-historical forces experienced by that group, and (c) its stage in the bio-social development of that group, or of any of its subgroups.

"Cultural background" refers to an ethnic group's values, beliefs, behavioral patterns, family structure, kinship system, and so forth. Most studies on ethnic families seem to focus primarily on this dimension, leading to various theories which have sometimes been used to make invidious comparisons between ethnic groups based on differences in cultural background (Ryan, 1971; Valentine, 1968). For example, the social deviance of Asian-Americans is low compared to other minority groups and has been attributed to their unique cultural characteristics. However, if culture were the only determinant it then becomes difficult to explain the alarming increase in delinquency among Chinese immigrant youth in recent years. These cultural theories are, of course, limited to the degree that they ignore the other two major influences on the family.

The term "sociohistorical forces" refers to the impact on the family of the larger social system, including the schools, political and economic institutions, mass media, and so forth. The action of these forces must be examined not only in the present but also in the past in order to determine their cumulative effects on the family. For example, it is possible that the virulent anti-Chinese movement of the late 1800's has residual effects on Chinese Americans even today. And the wartime internment experience has unquestionably had residual effects on Japanese-Americans today. However, like theories that focus only on culture, sociohistorical analyses will be limited to the degree that they do not consider the other two major influences.

"Stage of bio-social development" refers to the maturation level of an individual or group. While many theories of human development have been formulated (Reese and Overton, 1970; Sigel, 1972), most of them focus on the individual and assume that environmental conditions are primarily differentiated by culture; few, if any, consider interactions with sociohistorical forces. Yet, such interactions have significantly and differentially affected the bio-social development of Asian Americans. For example, the Nisei responded quite differently than the Issei to the crisis of the war-time internment and also suffered different residual effects. To take a more general example, the impact of the turbulent decade of the 1960's on college students may be compared with that on their parents.

These three broad influences on the family should be seen as interacting with each other both in space and over time. Projections about the future of the family would require predicting the course of these interactions into the foreseeable future. Given the complexities and independent proclivities of human behavior, such predictions have often proven to be quite wrong in the past, especially in the case of minority groups (Lyman, 1968). For example, few if any sociologists anticipated the black revolt of the 1960's (Blauner, 1972). It is also highly unlikely that anyone predicted even in 1940 that Japanese-Americans would be incarcerated in concentration camps in 1942. Yet these events had a profound influence on the families of each of the respective minority groups involved.

The above description should make it clear that projections about the future of the family for the purpose of policy formulation are difficult, if not impossible, to make. This may be particularly true for minority-group families, which have often been strongly affected by unexpected upheavals and crises. Therefore, we would probably be well advised to formulate policies on a tentative, provisional basis and question any highly specific prescriptions based on forecasts claiming scientific infallibility. And we should always be prepared to make appropriate corrections or adjustments in the light of unfolding socio-historical events and new evidence.

A DIALECTICAL PERSPECTIVE

As a small, powerless minority group, Asian-Americans have often had to adapt themselves to the indomitable forces of the larger society, even as they struggled for self-determination and the maintenance of their own way of life. This complex, dialectical interplay of necessity and autonomy in the lives of Asian-Americans has produced both strengths and weaknesses in their families. However, whether a given familial characteristic is viewed as good or bad may depend very much on the eyes of the perceiver.

To take only one example, the unity, stability, and cohesiveness of the Asian-American family are widely viewed as its major strengths. These familial characteristics are thought by many to explain the low social deviance, high educational achievement, and relatively favorable status of Asian-Americans in comparison to other minority groups. On the other hand, others believe that these same characteristics, within the context of a highly racially conscious society, have socialized Asian-Americans to become conforming, unassertive, inhibited, and conservative. As discussed earlier, this socialization of Asian-Americans is thought, in large part, to explain why so many of them appear to be suffering from serious mental strains. It may also partly account for the limited job mobility of Asian-Americans (Suzuki, 1977a) and the dearth of artists, writers, musicians, radical intellectuals, and other creative nonconformists among Asian-Americans (Watanabe, 1973; Ueda, 1974). Thus, from one perspective, particularly that of the dominant group, the above-mentioned characteristics of the Asian-American family may be seen as strengths which insure stability, order, and progress in society; whereas, from another perspective, they may be seen as weaknesses which insure the passivity, accommodation, and subordination of Asian-Americans.

Judgments of whether certain cultural characteristics are strengths or weaknesses may also depend on the societal context in which they are made. Many Asian-American cultural values and behavioral patterns, such as their group orientation, restraint of strong feelings, and modesty and politeness toward others, may be seen as highly compatible with a society oriented toward cooperation, harmony, and nonmaterialistic ethics. On the other hand, they may be seen as highly incompatible with a society oriented toward individualism, competition, and materialism.

In this regard, we may wish to closely examine the characteristics of upper-class Anglo families since most of the highest-ranking policy and decision makers in American society come from such families and exert a powerful and pervasive influence on the prevailing ethos of the society. Perhaps the most germane question might be: What are the socialization patterns in these families that lead to the values and norms subscribed to by their members? This question may not seem entirely facetious if one considers the wide-ranging impact on American families of the policies and programs initiated by high-ranking liberal reformers in the 1960's. It is probably fair to say that most of the reforms implemented in such areas as welfare, education, and child development did more to undermine minority-group families than they did to strengthen them, largely because of the culturally biased assumptions underlying them.

The point of the above discussion is simply that judgments about the strengths and weaknesses of families are very dependent on one's value orientation. We should, therefore, be quite suspicious of any claims to a purely rational, "scientific" approach for prescribing policies for the family. Such policies must ultimately rest on some underlying ideological, ethical, or moral bases (Schumacher, 1973; Connolly, 1974).

POLICY RECOMMENDATIONS

In line with the precautionary points made in the foregoing analysis, our policy recommendations for guiding legislative actions pertaining to the American family and effective parenting will be rather general and should be considered tentative and provisional. These recommendations, which are presented below, are based on what we have learned about the family through the Asian-American experience. No recommendations will be made outside this context.

1. Existing public policies and programs should be carefully assessed to determine the impact they have on the family. Special attention should be given to the impact on minority-group families, inasmuch as programs which help strengthen middle-class Anglo families may not necessarily have the same effect on minority-group families.
2. Programs intended to strengthen American families, especially those of minority groups, should be approached cautiously and deliberately to ensure that they do not adversely interfere with their functioning. There should be enough flexibility in these programs so that they can be modified or even

eliminated if evidence shows they are based on incorrect assumptions and/or projections.

3. Programs should adopt pluralistic approaches that are sensitive to the cultural backgrounds of families and that help develop self-sufficiency and supportive relationships among families.

4. In view of the apparent strengths of the Asian-American family, a more thorough examination of its characteristics should be undertaken to learn more about the sources of its strengths and to determine whether there may be important lessons to be learned for families in general.

5. Special attention should be given to the pressing problems and needs of the families of recent Asian immigrants. Language and cultural barriers which prevent access by these immigrants to education, social service, and job programs must be eliminated. Creative solutions must be found for alleviating their conditions of poverty and for arresting the further disintegration of their families.

6. More research should be conducted to explicate the subtle ways in which deculturalization adversely affects Asian-Americans. The American public, including Asian-Americans themselves, must be made more aware of its detrimental consequences. More effective ways of counteracting the effects of deculturalization should be explored and developed.

7. Family/school discontinuities experienced by Asian-American students must be reduced through the wider adoption of bilingual/multicultural approaches to education. Parents must be involved in more substantive and meaningful ways with the schools and in the education of their children.

8. More research should be conducted on how the family affects the cognitive development and achievement of Asian-American children and on how the schools and other institutions interact with the family in the socialization of these children.

9. Social service programs for Asian-Americans should give priority to family and community-based care over institutional care. More research and development should be undertaken to study and develop treatment and service approaches that are more culturally relevant and sensitive to the special problems and needs of Asian-Americans.

These few, broad recommendations will hopefully provide some general guidelines for the formulation of public policies that will help rather than hinder the future development of Asian-American families. From their past experience, Asian-Americans are quite mindful of the enormous impact the government can have on their families. If policy makers wish to avoid the mistakes of the past and develop policies equitable to all groups, they must give serious consideration to what can be learned from the experiences of Asian-Americans and other minorities. It is hoped that the description and analysis of the Asian-American family presented in the preceding pages will prove useful for this purpose and assist in the current quest for ways of strengthening and improving the quality of life for the families of all ethnic groups in American society.

BIBLIOGRAPHY

Abbott, Kenneth A. 1970. *Harmony and Individualism.* Taipei: The Orient Cultural Service.

Alsop, Joseph. 1971. "New American Success Story." *Los Angeles Times,* January 12.

Anonymous. 1966. "Success Story of One Minority Group in U.S." *United States News and World Report,* December 26:73–76.

Ariyoshi, Kòji. 1976. "Plantation Struggles in Hawaii." In *Counterpoint: Perspectives on Asian America,* Emma Gee (Ed.). Los Angeles: Asian American Studies Center, University of California.

Barth, Gunther. 1964. *Bitter Strength: A History of the Chinese in the United States, 1850–1870.* Cambridge: Harvard University Press.

Befu, Harumi. 1971. *Japan: An Anthropological Introduction.* New York: Chandler.

Benedict, Ruth. 1946. *The Chrysanthemum and the Sword.* Boston: Houghton Mifflin.

Berk, Bernard B., and Hirata, Lucie C. 1973. "Mental Illness among the Chinese: Myth or Reality?" *Journal of Social Issues,* 29(2):149–166.

Blauner, Robert. 1972. *Racial Oppression in America.* New York: Harper and Row.

Bronfenbrenner, Urie. 1977. "The Changing American Family." In *Early Childhood,* Barry Persky and Leonard Bolubchick (Eds.). Wayne, N.J.: Avery.

Broom, Leonard, and Kitsuse, John I. 1956. *The Managed Casuality: The Japanese–American Family in World War II.* Berkeley: University of California Press Reprint, 1973.

Cabezas, Amado Y. 1977. "A View of Poor Linkages Between Education, Occupation and Earnings for Asian Americans." Paper presented at The Third National Forum on Education and Work, San Francisco.

California Advisory Committee. 1975. "Asian Americans and Pacific Peoples: A Case of Mistaken Identity." Report to the United States Commission on Civil Rights, Los Angeles.

California FEPC. 1970. "Chinese in San Francisco, 1970: Employment Problems of the Community as Presented in Testimony Before the California Fair Employment Practice Commission." San Francisco.

Caudill, William, 1952. "Japanese-American Personality and Acculturation." *Genetic Psychology Monographs,* 45 (February):3–102.

Chan, Wing-tsit. 1963. *A Source Book in Chinese Philosophy.* Princeton: Princeton University Press.

Chao, Rose. 1977. *Chinese Immigrant Children.* Preliminary Report, Betty L. Sung (Ed.). New York: Department of Asian Studies, City University of New York.

Chin, Rocky. 1971. "New York Chinatown Today." *Amerasia Journal,* 1 (March):1–24.

Chinn, Thomas, (Ed.). 1969. *A History of the Chinese in California: A Syllabus.* San Francisco: Chinese Historical Society of America.

Chuman, Frank F. 1977. *The Bamboo People: The Law and Japanese Americans.* Del Mar, CA: Publishers, Inc.

Chun-Hoon, Lowell K. Y. 1973. "Teaching the Asian-American Experience." In *Teaching Ethnic Studies,* James A. Banks (Ed.). 43rd Yearbook. Washington, D.C.: National Council for the Social Studies.

Connolly, William E. 1974. "Theoretical Self-Consciousness." In *Social Structure and Political Theory,* William E. Connolly and Glen Gordon (Eds.). Lexington, MA.: D. C. Health and Company.

Conroy, Hilary. 1953. *The Japanese Frontier in Hawaii, 1868–1898.* Berkeley: University of California Press.

Coolidge, Mary R. 1909. *Chinese Immigration.* New York: Arno Press Reprint, 1969.

Daniels, Roger. 1962. *The Politics of Prejudice: The Anti-Japanese Movement in California and the Struggle for Japanese Exclusion.* Berkeley: University of California Press.

————. 1971. *Concentration Camps U.S.A.: Japanese Americans and World War II.* New York: Holt.

Daws, Gavin. 1968. *Shoal of Time; A History of the Hawaiian Islands.* New York: Macmillan.

Embree, John F. 1939. *Suye Mura: A Japanese Village.* Chicago: University of Chicago Press.

Fong, Stanley L. M. 1973. "Assimilation and Changing Roles of Chinese Americans." *Journal of Social Issues,* 29:2:115–127.

Freedman, Maurice. 1966. *Chinese Lineage and Society: Fukien and Kwangtung.* New York: Humanities Press.

Fuchs, Lawrence. 1961. *Hawaii Pono: A Social History.* New York: Harcourt, Brace and World.

Fujitomi, Irene, and Wong, Diane. 1973. "The New Asian-American Woman." In *Asian-Americans: Psychological Perspectives,* Stanley Sue and Nathaniel N. Wagner (Eds.). Palo Alto, CA: Science and Behavior Books.

Fukutake, Tadashi. 1967. *Japanese Rural Society.* Ithaca: Cornell University Press Reprint, 1972.

Girdner, Audrie and Anne Loftis. 1969. *The Great Betrayal: The Evacuation of the Japanese-Americans During World War II.* London: Macmillan.

Governor's Asian-American Advisory Commission. 1973. "Report to the Governor on Discrimination Against Asians." Based on hearings conducted in Seattle, Washington.

Gray, Francine du Plessix. 1972. *Hawaii: The Sugar-coated Fortress.* New York: Random House.

Hane, Mikiso. 1972. *Japan: A Historical Survey.* New York: Scribner's Sons.

Hosokawa, Bill. 1969. *Nisei: The Quiet Americans.* New York: William Morrow.

Hsu, Francis L. K. 1949. *Under the Ancestor's Shadow.* London: Routledge and Kegan Paul.

———. 1953. *Americans and Chinese: Two Ways of Life.* New York: Henry Schuman.

———. 1971. *The Challenge of the American Dream: The Chinese in the United States.* Belmont, CA: Wadsworth.

———. 1975. *Iemoto: The Heart of Japan.* Cambridge, MA: Schenkman.

Ichihashi, Yamato. 1932. *Japanese in the United States.* New York: Arno Press Reprint, 1969.

Iga, Mamoru, 1957. "The Japanese Social Structure and the Source of Mental Strains of Japanese Immigrants in the United States." *Social Forces,* 35:271–278.

Jacobs, Paul, and Landau, Saul. 1971. *To Serve the Devil.* Vol. 2: "Colonials and Sojourners." New York: Vintage.

Johnson, Colleen L. 1972. *The Japanese-American Family and Community in Honolulu: Generational Continuities in Ethnic Affiliation.* Ph.D. Dissertation in Anthropology. Syracuse: Syracuse University.

Kiefer, Christie W. 1974. *Changing Cultures, Changing Lives: An Ethnographic Study of Three Generations of Japanese Americans.* San Francisco: Jossey-Bass.

Kikumura, Akemi, and Kitano, Harry H. L. 1973. "Interracial Marriage: A Picture of the Japanese Americans." *Journal of Social Issues,* 29:2:67–81.

Kitano, Harry H. L. 1969a. *Japanese Americans: The Evolution of a Subculture.* Englewood Cliffs, N. J.: Prentice-Hall.

———. 1969b. "Japanese-American Mental Illness." In *Changing Perspective in Mental Illness,* Stanley C. Plog and Robert B. Edgerton (Eds.). New York: Holt, Rinehart and Winston.

Kitano, Harry H. L. and Daniels, Roger. 1970. *American Racism: Exploration of the Nature of Prejudice.* Englewood Cliffs, N. J.: Prentice-Hall.

Kriger, Sara F., and Kroes, William H. 1972. "Child-rearing Attitudes of Chinese, Jewish, and Protestant Mothers." *Journal of Social Psychology,* 86:205–210.

Kung, S. W. 1962. *Chinese in American Life.* Seattle: University of Washington Press.

Kurokawa, Minako. 1966. "Family Solidarity, Social Change and Childhood Accidents." *Journal of Marriage and the Family,* 28 (November):498–506.

Lang, Olga. 1946. *Chinese Family and Society.* New Haven, CT: Yale University Press.

Lee. Rose H. 1960. *The Chinese in the United States.* Hong Kong: Hong Kong University Press.

Light, Ivan H. 1972. *Ethnic Enterprise in America: Business and Welfare Among Chinese, Japanese, and Blacks.* Berkeley: University of California Press.

Lowe, Pardee. 1943. *Father and Glorious Descendant.* Boston: Little Brown and Company.

Lyman, Stanford. 1968. "The Race Relations Cycle of Robert E. Park." *Pacific Sociological Review,* 2 (Spring):16–22.

———. 1970. *The Asian in the West.* Social Science and Humanities Publication No. 4. Reno: Western Studies Center, Desert Research Institute, University of Nevada System.

———. 1974. *Chinese Americans.* New York: Random House.

Masuoka, Jitsuichi. 1944. "The Life Cycle of an Immigrant Institution in Hawaii: The Family." *Social Forces,* 23 (October):60–64.

Miller, Stuart C. 1969. *The Unwelcome Immigrant: The American Image of the Chinese, 1785–1882.* Berkeley: University of California Press.

Miyamoto, S. Frank. 1972. "An Immigrant Community in America." In *East Across the Pacific,* Hilary Conroy and T. Scott Miyakawa (Eds.). Santa Barbara, CA: Clio Press.

Moore, Charles A. 1967. *The Japanese Mind.* Honolulu: East-West Center Press.

Morishima, James K. 1973. "The Evacuation: Impact on the Family." In *Asian-Americans: Psy-*

chological Perspectives, Stanley Sue and Nathaniel N. Wagner (Eds.). Palo Alto, CA: Science and Behavior Books.

Nakamura, Hajime. 1964. *Ways of Thinking of Eastern Peoples*. Honolulu: East-West Center Press.

Nakane, Chie. 1970. *Japanese Society*. Berkeley: University of California Press.

Nee, Victor, and Nee, Brett D. 1972. *Longtime Californ': A Documentary History of an American Chinatown*. New York: Pantheon Books.

Ogawa, Dennis M. 1973. *Jan Ken Po: The World of Hawaii's Japanese Americans*. Honolulu: Japanese American Research Center.

Okimoto, Daniel I. 1971. *American in Disguise*. New York: Walker/Weatherhill.

Omatsu, Glenn. 1972. "Nihonmachi Beat." *Hokubei Mainichi*, January 12.

Pelzel, John C. 1970. "Japanese Kinship: A Comparison." In *Family and Kinship in Chinese Society*, Maurice Freedman (Ed.). Stanford, CA.: Stanford University Press.

Peterson, William. 1966. "Success Story, Japanese-American Style" *New York Times Magazine*, January 9.

————. 1971. *Japanese Americans: Oppression and Success*. New York: Random House.

Reese, H. W., and Overton, W. F. 1970. "Models of Development and Theories of Development." In *Life Span Developmental Psychology*, E. R. Goulet and P. B. Baltes (Eds.). New York: Academic Press.

Ryan, William. 1971. *Blaming the Victim*. New York: Vintage Books.

Saxton, Alexander. 1971. *The Indispensable Enemy: Labor and the Anti-Chinese Movement in California*. Berkeley: University of California Press.

Schumacher, E. F. 1973. *Small is Beautiful: Economics as if People Mattered*. New York: Harper and Row.

Schwartz, Audrey J. 1971. "The Culturally Advantaged: A Study of Japanese American Pupils." *Sociology and Social Research*, 55 (April): 341–353.

Sigel, Irving E. 1972. "Developmental Theory and Preschool Education: Issues, Problems and Implications." In *Early Childhood Education*, Ira J. Gordon (Ed.). 75th Yearbook. Chicago: National Society for the Study of Education.

Sollenberger, Richard T. 1968. "Chinese-American Child-rearing Practices and Juvenile Delinquency." *Journal of Social Psychology*, 74:13–23.

Sue, Derald W. 1973. "Ethnic Identity: The Impact of Two Cultures on the Psychological Development of Asians in America." In *Asian-Americans: Psychological Perspectives*, Stanley Sue and Nathaniel N. Wagner (Eds.). Palo Alto, CA.: Science and Behavior Books.

Sue, Derald W., and Frank, Austin C. 1973. "A Typological Approach to the Psychological Study of Chinese and Japanese American College Males." *Journal of Social Issues*, 29:2:129–148.

Sue, Derald W., and Kirk, B. A. 1973. "Differential Characteristics of Japanese and Chinese American College Students." *Journal of Counseling Psychology*, 20:142–148.

Sue, Derald W., and Sue, David. 1973. "The Neglected Minority: An Overview." *Personnel and Guidance Journal*, 51 (February):387–390.

Sue, Stanley, and Sue, Derald. 1971. "Chinese-American Personality and Mental Health." *Amerasia Journal*, 1:36–49.

Sung, Betty L. 1967. *The Story of the Chinese in America*. New York: Collier Books.

————. 1974. "It Figures: Chinese Interracial Marriage." *Bridge*, 3 (April):40–41.

————. 1976. *A Survey of Chinese-American Manpower and Employment*. New York: Praeger.

————. 1977. *Gangs in New York's Chinatown*. New York: Department of Asian Studies, City University of New York.

Suzuki, Bob H. 1977a. "The Education and Socialization of Asian Americans: A Revisionist Analysis of the 'Model-Minority' Thesis." *Amerasia Journal*, 4:2:23–51.

————. 1977b. "The Japanese-American Experience." In *In Praise of Diversity: A Resource Book for Multicultural Education*, Milton J. Gold, Carl A. Grant and Harry N. Rivlin (Eds.). Washington, D.C.: Association of Teacher Educators.

tenBroek, J.; Barnhart, E. M.; and Matson, F. W. 1954. *Prejudice, War and the Constitution*. Berkeley: University of California Press.

Thomas, D. S., and Nishimoto, R. 1946. *The Spoilage: Japanese-American Evacuation and Resettlement During World War II*. Berkeley: University of California Press.

Tong, Ben. 1971. "Ghetto of the Mind: Notes on the Historical Psychology of Chinese America." *Amerasia Journal*, 1:3:1–32.

Ueda, Reed. 1974. "The Americanization and Education of Japanese-Americans." In *Cultural Pluralism*, Edgar G. Epps (Ed.). Berkeley: McCutchan Pub.

United States Bureau of the Census. 1963. United States Census of Populations: 1960. Subject Reports. Nonwhite Population by Race. Final Report PC(2)–1C. Washington, D.C.: United States Government Printing Office.

———. 1973. Census of the Population: 1970. Subject Reports. Japanese, Chinese and Filipinos in the United States. Final Report PC(2)–1G. Washington, D.C.: United States Government Printing Office.

Urban Associates, Inc. 1974. *A Study of Selected Socio-Economic Characteristics of Ethnic Minorities Based on the 1970 Census*. Vol. 2: Asian Americans. Washington, D.C.: Office of Special Concerns, Department of Health, Education and Welfare (July).

Valentine, Charles A. 1968. *Culture and Poverty: Critique and Counter-Proposals*. Chicago: University of Chicago Press.

Wagatsuma, Hiroshi. 1977. "Some Aspects of the Contemporary Japanese Family: Once Confucian, Now Fatherless?" *Daedalus*, 106 (Spring): 181–210.

Watanabe, Colin. 1973. "Self-Expression and the Asian American Experience." *Personnel and Guidance Journal*, 51 (Feb.):390–396.

Weglyn, Michi. 1976. *Years of Infamy: The Untold Story of America's Concentration Camps*. New York: William Morrow.

Wolf, Margery. 1970. "Child Training and the Chinese Family." In *Family and Kinship in Chinese Society*, Maurice Freedman (Ed.). Stanford, CA.: Stanford University Press.

Wong, Aline K. 1974. "Women in China: Past and Present." In *Many Sisters: Women in Cross-Cultural Perspective*, Carolyn J. Matthiasson (Ed.). New York: Free Press.

Wong, Buck. 1971. "Need for Awareness: An Essay on Chinatown San Francisco." In *Roots: An Asian American Reader*, Amy Tachiki, Eddie Wong and Franklin Odo (Eds.). Los Angeles: Continental Graphics.

Wong, Jade S. 1950. *Fifth Chinese Daughter*. New York: Harper Brothers.

Wong, Paul. 1972. "The Emergence of the Asian American Movement." *Bridge*, 2:32–39.

Wu, Robin. 1977. "Front Page Chinatown: What the *** is Going on?" *Bridge*, 5 (Fall):4–7.

Yamamoto, Joe. 1968. "Japanese American Identity Crisis." In *Minority Adolescents in the United States*, Eugene Brody (Ed.). Baltimore: Williams and Wilkins.

Yang, C. K. 1959. *The Chinese Family in the Communist Revolution*. Cambridge: Harvard University Press.

Yoneda, Karl. 1971. "One Hundred Years of Japanese Labor in the U.S.A." In *Roots: An Asian American Reader*, Amy Tachiki, Eddie Wong and Franklin Odo (Eds.). Los Angeles: Continental Graphics.

Young, Nancy F. 1972 "Socialization Patterns among the Chinese in Hawaii," *Amerasia*, 1(Feb.):31–51.

8

The Puerto Rican Family: Its Role in Cultural Transition

JOSEPH P. FITZPATRICK, S.J.
Department of Sociology and Anthropology
Fordham University

LOURDES TRAVIESO
Director of the Center for Bilingual Education
New York City Board of Education and of the
Bilingual Teacher Corps Project
City College of New York

The Puerto Ricans now constitute one of the major minority groups in the eastern part of the United States. A special census of 1976 reported 1,753,000 Puerto Ricans, about one-third of all Puerto Ricans, residing on the mainland. Like all the Hispanic groups, they are a rapidly increasing population. They had increased by 22.6 percent over the 1,430,000 reported in 1970. They come from a small island in the Caribbean, about a thousand miles southeast of Miami, Florida. The island had been a Spanish colony from the time it was discovered by Columbus on his second voyage in 1493 until it was ceded to the United States after the Spanish American War in 1898. Citizenship was granted unilaterally to the Puerto Ricans in 1917; this was seriously resented by many Puerto Ricans who felt they had no choice in the matter. In 1948 they were granted the right to elect their own governor; in 1952, their present constitution, The Free Associated States (*Estado Libre Asociado*), generally referred to in English as The Commonwealth of Puerto Rico, was approved by the U.S. Congress and adopted by the people of Puerto Rico. They remain citizens and have a large degree of autonomy in their island government. They have no representatives or senators in Congress and do not vote for the President. They are subject to military draft, but pay no federal taxes. On the mainland they have all the voting rights of mainland American citizens. The political status of the island continues to be a point of controversy. The three major political groups are: the Parties seeking independence; the Popular Democratic Party (*Partido Popular Democratico*) which favors Commonwealth; and the New Progressive Party (*Partido Nuevo Progresista*) which favors statehood.

The inhabitants of the island when it was discovered were Tainos, a farming people who largely disappeared as a people during the conquest, either through

Selected parts of this chapter are reprinted with permission from Joseph P. Fitzpatrick, *Puerto Rican Americans* (Englewood Cliffs, New Jersey: Prentice Hall, 1971).

flight, disease, death in warfare, or absorption into the conquering Spanish population. Beginning in 1511, African slaves were brought to the island to provide the manual labor on the hot coastal plains. They replaced the decimated indigenous population. Over the years these three peoples—Tainos, Africans, and Europeans—intermingled and intermarried with the result that Puerto Rico's population consists of people of a wide range of color from pure caucasoid to pure negroid with all variations in between. Although the differences of color and physiognomy in Puerto Rico are striking, these characteristics become the source of serious problems when they come to the mainland where color often becomes an obstacle to opportunities in employment, housing, education, and social relations.

Puerto Ricans have been coming to the mainland since the last century, when New York served as the gathering place for militant leaders who were working for independence from Spain. Many of them were disappointed when this was not granted under American rule. Poor Puerto Ricans began to come to the mainland after the turn of the century, increased in numbers during the 1920's and after World War II, began a large-scale migration especially to the Eastern regions of the United States. The largest concentration, close to 60 percent, live in New York City. Since they are American citizens by birth there are no restrictions on their travel between the island and the mainland. Nevertheless, they are a Spanish-speaking people with a different culture; consequently, they face the problems of cultural uprooting, culture shock, and cultural adjustment in their transition to life on the mainland. Within recent years, there has been an increasing movement of Puerto Ricans returning to the island to live there permanently. The refrain of the song *"En mi Viejo San Juan"* by Noel Estrada epitomizes the sentiments and emotions of many Puerto Ricans:

Me voy, ya me voy, pero un dia volveré
a buscar mi querer,
a sonar otra vez
en mi viejo San Juan.

I am leaving, I am leaving now,
but one day I will return, to find my love,
to dream once again,
in my old San Juan.

Most other ethnic groups which settled here of their own volition came from distant shores as aliens and, for the most part, resolved to stay and make a go of it at any cost, in this strange and often hostile land. Puerto Ricans are unique in that they are citizens free to come and go as they wish, and with air travel that makes the journey very easy.

Migration back and forth enables Puerto Ricans to maintain a helpful and supporting contact with relatives and friends. But it is not without its difficulties for those who stay. In New York, Puerto Ricans are newcomers to the city; they are seen as strangers, culturally different. When they return to Puerto Rico, they are often considered *Newyoricans,* or *Neo-ricans.* In both cases there is a degree of alienation. The school-age child is often bewildered by differences in language—on the mainland the child may not speak English well enough; in Puerto Rico the child may not know Spanish well enough—they face differences of curriculum, methods of instruction, and general patterns of behavior.

The one institution that feels the shock of these changes most directly is the family; it is also the institution which provides the greatest strength and support to the individual in the face of cultural change. Puerto Ricans bring with them a style and structure of family life which has been formed by centuries of tradition on the island. In order to understand this family as it faces the difficulties of the mainland, the family as it exists on the island must be clearly understood. Once this is accomplished, the conditions and policies necessary to enable the Puerto Ricans to cope with their adjustment effectively will become clearer.

HISTORICAL BACKGROUND

Four major influences have contributed to the structure of family life, kinship patterns, and the patterns of family living of the Puerto Ricans: (1) The culture of the (Borinquen) Indians, now generally referred to as the Tainos, the natives on the island when it was discovered; (2) the influence of Spanish colonial culture; (3) slavery; (4) the American influence and economic development.

Very little is known about the culture of the Borinquen Indians, unlike those in other areas of the Spanish empire. Some speculations are available about their culture and family life, but little of it is reliable. New studies are now in progress.

SPANISH COLONIAL CULTURE

The great influence in the past and present on all levels of Puerto Rican family life was the Spanish colonial culture, the important features of which will now be discussed.

PREEMINENCE OF THE FAMILY

As in most cultures of the world, the individual in Puerto Rico has a deep consciousness of his membership in a family. He thinks of his importance in terms of his family membership. This is not a matter of prestige (as in belonging to the Ford or Rockefeller family) but a much more elemental thing, and it is as strong among the families of the very poor as it is among those of the very wealthy. The world to a Latin consists of a pattern of intimate personal relationships, and the basic relationships are those of his family. His confidence, his sense of security and identity, are perceived in his relationship to others who are his family.

The family is much more involved in the process of courtship than would be the case with an American family, although these patterns are changing rapidly in Puerto Rico. In America, boys and girls mingle freely, date each other, fall in love, and by various means ask each other to marry. If they agree to marry, they will advise their parents. If the parents agree, the marriage proceeds happily; if the parents disagree with the couple, they may go ahead and get married regardless. In Puerto Rico, intermingling and dating is much more restricted. A young man interested in a young woman is expected to speak to the parents of the girl, particularly the father, to declare his intentions. A serious courtship may never get started if the families disapprove. As one Puerto Rican sociologist explained personally to the authors: In America, courtship is a drama with only two actors; in Puerto Rico, it is a drama of two actors, but the families are continually prompting from the wings. Marriage is still considered much more a union of two families than it would be in America.

Finally, Puerto Ricans have a deep sense of family obligation. One's primary responsibilities are to family and friends. If a person advances in public office or succeeds in business enterprises, he has a strong sense of obligation to use his gains for the benefit of his family. Americans also have a sense of family loyalty, but to a much larger degree, they expect to make it on their own. Success does not make them feel obliged to appoint family members to positions, share their wealth with relatives, or use their position for the benefit of the family. They expect selection in business and government to be on the basis of ability and effort, not personal or family relationships. This is an oversimplification, since family influence operates in America and people in Puerto Rico are increasingly chosen on the basis of ability and effort. But in Puerto Rico the sense of family is much deeper. As economic development proceeds on the island, or as its citizens adjust to American life, the need increases to sacrifice family loyalty and obligation to efficiency. The Puerto Rican finds this a very difficult thing to do.

SUPERIOR AUTHORITY OF THE MAN

A second feature of the Puerto Rican family is the role of superior authority exercised by the man. This is not peculiar to Latin cultures; it is the common situation in most cultures of the world. The man expects to exercise the authority in the family; he feels free to make decisions without consulting his wife; he expects to be obeyed when he gives commands. As a larger middle class emerges in Puerto Rico, the role of the woman is in the process of being redefined. But in contrast to the characteristics of cooperation and companionship of American families, the woman in Puerto Rico has a subordinate role.

This must not be interpreted as meaning that women do not have subtle ways of influencing men. The influence of mother over son is particularly strong in the culture of the Puerto Ricans. Furthermore, women have played an unusually important role in public and academic life. In 1962, of the seventy-six municipios in Puerto Rico, ten had women as mayors, the most famous being Dona Felisa Rincon de Gautier, who was mayoress of the capital city of San Juan for twenty years. Women have played an important role on the faculty of the University of Puerto Rico. Oscar Lewis (1965) found the Puerto Rican women among the families he studied to be much more aggressive, outspoken, and even violent than the women in the Mexican families he had studied. Nevertheless, the role is culturally defined and ordinarily maintained as subordinate to the authority of the husband. Until recently, and still to a surprising extent, women will not make such decisions as consulting a doctor or sending children for medical treatment without seeking permission of the husband.

The superior position of the man is also reflected in what Americans call a double standard of morality in reference to sexual behavior. (See references to machismo in Stycos, 1955.) In Latin cultures, as in most cultures of the world, a very clear distinction is made between the "good" woman, who will be protected as a virgin until marriage and then be protected as a wife and mother, and the "bad" woman, who is available for a man's enjoyment. Puerto Ricans are concerned about their girls, and fathers and brothers feel a strong obligation to protect them. On the other hand, a great deal of freedom is granted to the boys. It is rather expected, sometimes encouraged, that a boy have sexual experiences with women before marriage. After marriage he may feel free to engage in what Puerto Ricans sometimes jokingly refer to as "extracurricular activities." These patterns of protection of the woman and freedom for the man are changing, but they are still quite different from patterns of sexual behavior on the mainland. It is also true that patterns of sexual behavior that are going through a revolution to greater sexual freedom in America involve boys and girls equally, and thus draw us even further away from the style of life in Puerto Rico.

COMPADRAZGO

Another consequence of the influence of Spain on the Puerto Rican family has been *compadrazgo,* or the institution of *compadres.* These are people who are companion parents, as it were, with the natural parents of the child; the man is the *compadre,* the woman is the *comadre.* Sponsors at baptism, for example, become the godparents *(padrinos)* of the child, and the compadres of the child's parents; this is also true of sponsors at confirmation. Witnesses at a marriage become *compadres* of the married couple. Sometimes common interests or the intensification of friendship may lead men or women to consider themselves *compadres* or *comadres.* The *compadres* are sometimes relatives, but often they are not. They constitute a network of ritual kinship, as serious and important as that of natural kinship, around a person or a group. *Compadres* frequently become more formal in their relationships, shifting from the familiar *"Tu"* to the formal *"Usted"* in speech. They have a deep sense of obligation to each other for economic assistance, support, encouragement, and even personal correction. A *compadre* may feel much freer to give advice or correction in regard to family problems than a brother or sister would. A *compadre* is expected to be responsive to all the needs of his *compadre,* and ideally, he supplies assistance without question. When Sidney Mintz was doing his anthropological study of a barrio of Santa Isabel, Puerto Rico, his principal informant was a remarkable man, Taso Zayas, a farm worker who cut sugar cane. Mintz reached a degree of close friendship with Taso and later decided to do his life history. Mintz describes the relationship that had developed between himself and Taso. Taso had reached a point at which he felt free to ask Mintz for money. "In his own words, he would not 'dare ask' if he were not sure I would respond; and failure to do so, if it were a matter of free choice would end our friendship" (Mintz, 1960). In other words, Mintz and Taso had become *compadres.*

SLAVERY

Another influence on family life in Puerto Rico was that of slavery. Slavery was a milder institution in Puerto Rico than in America. But slavery in the Western world has had a devastating effect on family life. Little effort was made to provide for the stability and permanence of the slave family; men and women, relatives, children, were bought, sold, exchanged, and shifted with little or no regard for permanent family union. Slave women were defenseless before the advances of free men.

The usual consequences of slavery in the broken family life of blacks have been as evident in Puerto Rico as elsewhere. A number of features of Spanish culture modified the effects to some extent. Consorting with a woman who was not one's wife was a practice of upper-class men in the Spanish colonial tradition and was not confined to black women. Therefore, the extramarital relationships of white men and black women followed a pattern similar to that of white men with white women. Cultural patterns formed around these relationships that provided some advantages to the women and children involved in them. However, the mother-based family—the family with children of a number of fathers and no permanent male consort—has been a common phenomenon in Puerto Rican history.

AMERICA AND ECONOMIC DEVELOPMENT

Within recent years, two other major influences have become important: (1) the influence of America has affected the island through the educational system, which for many years after annexation was in the hands of Americans and conducted on the American model; (2) religious influence from the mainland. Most of the Catholic priests, brothers, and nuns working among Puerto Ricans during the past eighty years have come from America. Protestant denominations have been established on the island since the turn of the century, and Pentecostal sects have preached a strong and effective gospel among the poor. Finally, and most important, Puerto Ricans returning from the mainland either to visit or to stay bring with them a strong and direct influence of mainland culture in relation to the family. The consequences, particularly of this last influence, will be indicated later.

FAMILY VALUES

Some aspects of the values of Puerto Rican family life have already been mentioned in relation to the influences that have helped to form it. In the following paragraphs, the range of values that distinguish the Puerto Rican family from the predominant middle-class family values of the mainland will be indicated. One of the best brief treatments of Latin values that are shared by Puerto Ricans can be found in Gillin (1960). Another good treatment is found in Wells (1969), Chapters 1 and 2.

PERSONALISM

The basic value of Puerto Rican culture, as of Latin cultures in general, is a form of individualism that focuses on the inner importance of the person. In contrast to the individualism of America, which values the individual in terms of his ability to compete for higher social and economic status, the culture of Puerto Rico centers attention on those inner qualities that constitute the uniqueness of the person and his goodness or worth in himself.

In a two-class society in which little mobility was possible, a man was born into his social and economic position. Therefore, he defined his value in terms of the qualities and behavior that made a man good or respected in the social position in which he found himself. A poor farm laborer was a good man when he did those things that made a man good on his social and economic level. He felt an inner dignity *(dignidad)* about which the Puerto Rican is very sensitive; he expected others to have respect *(respeto)* for that dignidad. All men have some sense of personal dignity and are sensitive about proper respect being shown them. But this marks the Puerto

Rican culture in a particular way. Puerto Ricans are much more sensitive than Americans to anything that appears to be personal insult or disdain; they do not take to practical jokes that are likely to embarrass, or to party games in which people "make fools of themselves." They do not "horse around," as Americans would say in an offhand, informal manner; they are usually responsive to manifestations of personal respect and to styles of personal leadership by men who appeal to the person rather than a program or a platform. Although the old two-class society in which these values developed has been disappearing, the values themselves are still very strong.

PERSONALISM AND EFFICIENCY

It is the personalism that makes it difficult for the Puerto Rican to adjust easily to what Americans call efficiency. For a Puerto Rican, life is a network of personal relationships. He trusts persons; he relies on persons; he knows that at every moment he can fall back on a brother, a cousin, a compadre. He does not have that same trust for a system or an organization. The American, on the other hand, expects the system to work; he has confidence in the organization. When something goes wrong, his reaction is: "Somebody ought to do something about this," or "Get this system going." Thus, an American becomes impatient and uneasy when systems do not work. He responds to efficiency. The Latin becomes uneasy and impatient if the system works too well, if he feels himself in a situation in which he must rely on impersonal functions rather than personal relationships.

THE PADRINO

Related to personalism is the role of the *padrino*. The *padrino* is a person, strategically placed in a higher position of the social structure, who has a personal relationship with the poorer person for whom he provides employment, assistance at time of need, and acts as an advocate if the poor person becomes involved in trouble. The *padrino* is really the intermediary between the poor person, who had neither sophistication nor influence, and the larger society of law, government, employment, and service. He is a strategic helper in times of need, but the possibilities of exploitation in this relationship are very great. The poor person can become completely bound to the *padrino* by debt or by obligations to personal service to such an extent that his life is little better than slavery. The role of the *padrino* has decreased in Puerto Rico, but the tendency to seek a personal relationship in one's business affairs is still strong.

MACHISMO

Another aspect of personalism is a combination of qualities associated with masculinity. This is generally referred to as *machismo*, literally, maleness. *Machismo* is a style of personal daring (the great quality of the bullfighter) by which one faces challenge, danger, and threat with calmness and self-possession; this sometimes takes the form of bravado. It is also a quality of personal magnetism that impresses and influences others and prompts them to follow one as a leader—the quality of the conquistador. It is associated with sexual prowess, influence, and power over women, reflected in a vigorous romanticism and a jealous guarding of sweetheart or wife, or in premarital and extramarital relationships.

SENSE OF FAMILY OBLIGATION

Personalism is deeply rooted in the individualism that has just been described; it is also rooted in the family. As explained above, the Puerto Rican has a deep sense of that network of primary personal relationships that is his family. To express it another way, he senses the family as an extension of the person, and the network of obligations follows as described above.

SENSE OF THE PRIMARY OF THE SPIRITUAL

The Latin generally refers to American culture as very materialistic, much to the amazement of Americans, who are conscious of human qualities, concerns, and generosity in American culture that are missing in the Latin. What the Latin means is that his fundamental concerns are not with this world or its tangible features. He has a sense of spirit and soul as being much more important than the body and as being intimately related to his value as a person; he tends to think in terms of transcendent qualities, such as justice, loyalty, or love, rather than in terms of practical arrangements that spell out justice or loyalty in the concrete. On an intellectual level, he strives to clarify relationships conceptually with confidence that if they can be made intellectually clear and precise the relationships will become actualities. He thinks of life very much in terms of ultimate values and ultimate spiritual goals, and expresses a willingness to sacrifice material satisfactions for these. In contrast, the American preoccupation with mastering the world and subjecting it, through technological programs, to man's domination gives him the sense of reversing the system of values, of emphasizing the importance of mastering the physical universe rather than seeking the values of the spirit. It is striking to note how many important political figures are also literary men with a humanistic flair. Former Governor Munoz Marin is a poet and is affectionately called El Vate, the Bard, in Puerto Rico; the former resident commissioner in Washington, Santiago Polanco Abreu, is a literary critic; some of the best known figures in public service in the Puerto Rican community in New York, such as Juan Aviles, Carmen Marrero, and Luis Quero Chiesa, are accomplished writers and artists.

FATALISM

Connected to these spiritual values is a deep sense of fatalism in Puerto Ricans. They have a sense of destiny, partly related to elemental fears of the sacred, partly related to a sense of divine providence governing the world. The popular song, *"Que sera, sera,"* "Whatever will be, will be," is a simple expression of it, as is the common expression that intersperses so much of Puerto Rican speech: *Si Dios quiere,* "If God wills it." The term "destiny" recurs frequently in Puerto Rican popular songs. This quality leads to the acceptance of many events as inevitable; it also softens the sense of personal guilt for failure. If, after a vigorous effort, an enterprise does not succeed, the Puerto Rican may shrug his shoulders and remark: "It was not meant to be."

SENSE OF HIERARCHY

The Puerto Ricans, like other Latins, have had a concept of a hierarchical world during the whole of their history. This was partly the result of the two-class system, in which members never conceived of a world in which they could move out of the position of their birth. Thus, they thought of a relationship of higher and lower classes that was fixed, somewhat as the various parts of the body were fixed. This concept of hierarchy contributed to their concept of personal worth as distinct from a person's position in the social structure.

THE PUERTO RICAN FAMILY ON THE MAINLAND

The institution that faces the most direct shock in the migration to the mainland is the family, and the progress of Puerto Ricans can be measured to a large extent by a study of the family. First, a statistical description of Puerto Rican families can be presented, followed by an analysis of the effect of migration on the family. Unless otherwise noted, data are based on U.S. Census Reports identified in the bibliography. The best analysis of the 1970 Census on Puerto Ricans and other Hispanics is found in A. Jaffee et al. (1976).

Puerto Rican families on the mainland are young families. The median age of Puerto Ricans on the mainland in 1976 was 19.6 years of age. The median age of second generation Puerto Ricans in 1976 was 9.7 years. This means that half the second generation Puerto Ricans (now close to half the population) are small children. There will be very large Puerto Rican teenage populations for another twenty years. When these large youthful populations reach marriageable age, even if they have only two or three children, the population of Puerto Ricans will continue to expand considerably. It is not clear yet how this increase will be affected by the availability of abortion. Although lower than that of the rest of the population, white or black, the rate of abortion among Puerto Ricans is very high. In 1977, among Puerto Rican women in New York City, there were 12,811 abortions, an increase of more than 800 over 1976. The percentage of all New York City abortions to Puerto Rican women was 14.8 percent about the same as the percentage of Puerto Rican in the population (New York City Department of Health, 1978).

Puerto Rican families are large families. In 1972, 20 percent of Puerto Rican families had 4.0 or more "own children," in contrast to 3.1 for total U.S. families. Puerto Rican families appear to be diminishing in size. The average family size of Puerto Rican families declined from 4.0 in 1970 to 3.76 in 1976.

Puerto Rican families are poor families—in fact, close to the poorest of all families in the United States. In 1976, 33.5 percent of all Puerto Rican families were reported by the Census Bureau as falling below the poverty level in contrast to 9.7 percent of all United States families. In New York, median family income of Puerto Rican is considerably lower than that of blacks.

Related to poverty is the high unemployment of Puerto Ricans: 14 percent in 1975 in contrast to 8.1 percent at that time for the United States as a whole. This unemployment must be seen in terms of its impact on the youth population. A report of the Bureau of Labor Statistics on August 1, 1977 named New York City at that time "the nonworking teenage capital of the country." Estimates indicated as many as 40 percent of black and Puerto Rican youths unemployed in Summer 1977. If this unemployment figure is related to the continued increase in numbers of Puerto Rican teenagers, the seriousness of the impact of unemployment on youth is more clearly perceived.

Large numbers of Puerto Rican families, 28 percent according to the 1970 census, were headed by women. This census indicates that in 1970, 25 percent of second-generation Puerto Rican families were headed by women, thus indicating that this condition is passing over into the new generation. The poverty level of so many Puerto Rican families is closely related to the high rate of female-headed families. These are families of the lowest median family incomes. Also related to the large percentage of Puerto Rican families headed by women is the increasing rate of out-of-wedlock children. This has increased among Puerto Ricans from a rate of 11 percent of all Puerto Rican births in 1956 to a rate of 46 percent in 1976.

THE SECOND GENERATION

Substantial educational improvement appears among second generation Puerto Ricans: Second-generation Puerto Rican men who were 18 to 24 years of age in 1970 had a median average number of school years completed of 11.5, almost as high as the median for the total United States male population at that age. In addition, a decided advance of second-generation Puerto Ricans, especially women, into white collar occupational categories such as clerical and sales jobs, is in evidence. Intermarriage with non-Puerto Rican whites increases considerably among the second generation, generally from about 6 percent in the first generation to over 30 percent in the second generation. Finally, the use of the Spanish language appears to be faltering. Of all persons of Hispanic origin in 1976, 25 percent spoke only English; 40 percent spoke English as a first language, Spanish as a second; 25 percent spoke Spanish as a first language, English as a second; only 10 percent spoke Spanish only.

CHANGES IN VALUES

Much more important than the statistical description of the Puerto Rican families in America or in New York City is the study of the changes in values that they face. Probably the most serious is a shift in the traditional roles of husband and wife. There is abundant evidence that this is a common experience of immigrants. It is provoked by a number of things. First, it is frequently easier for Puerto Rican women to get jobs in New York than Puerto Rican men. This gives the wife an economic independence that she may never have had before, and if the husband is unemployed while the wife is working, the reversal of roles is severe. Second, the impact of American culture begins to make itself felt more directly in New York than on the island. Puerto Rican women from the poorer classes are much more involved in social, community, and political activities than they are in Puerto Rico. This influences the Puerto Rican wife to gradually adopt the patterns of the mainland.

INTERGENERATIONAL TENSION

Even more direct and difficult to cope with is the shifting role of the Puerto Rican child. Puerto Rican families have frequently lamented the patterns of behavior of even good boys in America. Puerto Rican parents consider them to be disrespectful. American children are taught to be self-reliant, aggressive, and competitive, to ask "why," and to stand on their own two feet. Puerto Rican children are generally much more submissive. When the children begin to behave according to the American pattern, the parents cannot understand it. A priest who had worked for many years with migrating Puerto Ricans remarked to one of the writers: "When these Puerto Rican families come to New York, I give the boys about forty-eight hours on the streets of New York, and the difference between their behavior and what the family expects will have begun to shake the family."

The distance that gradually separates child from family is indicated in much of the literature about Puerto Ricans in New York. In the autobiography of Piri Thomas, *Down These Mean Streets* (1967), it is clear that his family—and it was a good, strong family—had no way of controlling him once he began to associate with his peers on the streets. The sharp contrast of two life histories, *Two Blocks Apart* (Mayerson, 1965), also demonstrates the difficulties of a Puerto Rican family in trying to continue to control the life of a boy growing up in New York. His peers become his significant reference group. A considerable number of scholars and social workers attribute much of the delinquency of Puerto Ricans to the excessive confinement that the Puerto Rican families impose in an effort to protect their children. Once the children can break loose in the early teens, they break completely. When Julio Gonzalez was killed in a gang fight on the lower East Side in reprisal for the murder of a black girl, Theresa Gee, in 1959, he was buried from Nativity Church. Julio's father, a poor man from a mountain town in Puerto Rico, was like a pillar of strength during the wake. He was a man of extraordinary dignity and self-possession. After the funeral mass, he went to the sacristy of the church, embraced each of the priests who had participated, and thanked them. Here was a man who sought to pass on to his son the qualities of loyalty, dignity, and strength. But when the son reached the streets, different definitions of loyalty and dignity took over. As Julio was dying, after the priest had given him the last rites of the Catholic Church, he fell into unconsciousness, mumbling: "Tell the guys they can count me; tell them I'll be there." For a lengthy discussion of this change of values and its relation to deliquency, see Fitzpatrick (1960).

Probably the most severe problem of control is the effort of families to give their unmarried girls the same kind of protection they would have given them in Puerto Rico. When the girls reach the early teens, they wish to do what American girls do: go to dances with boys without a chaperone and associate freely with girls and boys in the neighborhood or school. For a good Puerto Rican father to permit his daughter to go out unprotected is a serious moral failure. In a Puerto Rican town, when a father has brought his daughters as virgins to the marriage altar, he can hold up his head before his community; he enjoys the esteem and prestige of a good father. To ask the same father to allow his daughters to go free in New York is to ask him to do something that the men of his family have long considered immoral. It is psychologically almost impossible for him to do this. The tension between parents and daughter(s) is one of the most difficult for Puerto Rican parents to manage. It is frequently complicated because Americans, including schoolteachers and counselors, who are not aware of the significance of this in the Puerto Rican background, advise the parents to allow the girls to go out freely.

Finally, the classic tension between the generations takes place. The parents are living in the Puerto Rican culture in their homes. The children are being brought up in an American school where American values are being presented. The parents will never really understand their children; the children will never really understand the parents.

This conflict of generations appears to be more distressing for the Puerto Ricans than it has been for previous immigrant groups. The unique characteristic of the "Rican," "Nuyorican," or "Neo-Rican" must be noted. These are the second generation, either born on the mainland, or brought here at an early age and raised here. They have been described as "hybrid" persons who think and speak in both languages but yet are strangers in both lands. The Neo-Rican, having grown up in the ghettos and barrios, has adopted ghetto slang and life-style patterns and is often at odds with the older generation of Puerto Ricans who are seen as more passive—*hangotao* or with an *ay bendito* (submissive)—and often does not have the same feeling for returning to live permanently on the island. This has often perplexed and hurt the older generations of Puerto Ricans who see their children becoming very "Americano" and losing their traditional island values.

It is a difficult task to make a blanket statement about the Neo-Ricans because the term covers such a complex set of attitudes. On the one hand, having been forced to live in the ghetto creates a certain sharpness or "hipness" which enables one to survive the oppressiveness of this situation. Some young Neo-Ricans were drawn by the political movement of the 1960's into groups such as the Young Lords and the Real Great Society. Others have banded into gangs such as the Ghetto Brothers and the Savage Skulls. All of these young people share in trying to "cope" with the system in their own fashion, in attempting to ameliorate their substandard living conditions, education, and jobs, and in trying to carve out an identity which is uniquely theirs—to be a "Rican." Some "Ricans" are allied with political movements for independence, even though many of them may never have been to Puerto Rico. They are drawn to the philosophical concept of liberation of the Third World peoples and of having a "homeland." Still others are committed to staying here and making their permanent home in the continental United States, while at the same time maintaining their identity as Puerto Ricans or "Ricans" and maintaining the ties to the homeland or their "roots" to the island. Many of the contributions made by Puerto Ricans in the United States have been made by the "Nuyorican."

The "Nuyorican" may well hold the promise for the future as he forges ahead, creates a new ambiance, gains a measure of acceptance about himself as a person, and is able to unleash the creativity and expressiveness of his unique individuality. But the tension between the youth and the parents can become severe. Nevertheless, despite this, the loyalty of family to children is often striking. In a study of Puerto Rican addicts and nonaddicts in the Bronx, conducted by Fitzpatrick (1976), one major finding was the fact that Puerto Rican families do not reject their addicts as middle-class American families are likely to do.

WEAKENING OF EXTENDED KINSHIP

Apart from the conflict between generations, the experience of migration tends to weaken the family bonds that created a supporting network on which the family could always rely. To a growing extent, the family finds itself alone. This is partly the result of moving from place to place. It is also due to the fact that the way of life in mainland cities is not a convenient environment for the perpetuation of family virtues and values. The Department of Social Services provides assistance in time of need but not with the familiar, informal sense of personal and family respect. Regulations in housing, consumer loans, schools, and courts create a need for professional help, and the family is less and less effective.

REPLACEMENT OF PERSONALIST VALUES

Closely related to all the above difficulties, and creating difficulties of its own, is the slow and steady substitution of impersonal norms, norms of the system rather than norms of personal relationships. The need to adjust to the dominant patterns of American society requires a preparation to seek employment and advancement on the basis of merit or ability. To people for whom the world is an extensive pattern of personal relationships, this is a difficult adjustment.

The process of uprooting has been described before in the extensive literature about immigrants. It leads to three kinds of reactions or adjustments. The first involves escape from the immigrant or migrant group and an effort to become as much like the established community as possible in as short a time as possible. These people seek to disassociate themselves from their past. They sometimes change their name and their reference groups, and seek to be accepted by the larger society. They are in great danger of becoming marginal. Having abandoned the way of life of their own people, in which they had a sense of "who they were," there is no assurance that they will be accepted by the larger community. They may find themselves in a no man's land of culture. In this stage, the danger of personal frustration is acute.

The second reaction takes the form of withdrawal into the old culture, a resistance to the new way of life. These people seek to retain the older identities by locking themselves into their old way of life.

The third reaction results in an effort to build a cultural bridge between the culture of the migrants and that of the mainland. These are the people who have confidence and security in their own way of life, but who realize that it cannot continue. Therefore, they seek to establish themselves in the new society but continue to identify themselves with the people from whom they come. These are the ones through whom the process of assimilation moves forward.

QUESTIONS ON FAMILY POLICY

For many years sociologists and social workers have questioned why the United States has no family policy. Clearly one is needed, and in relation to Puerto Ricans, one is needed that relates to their particular cultural strengths and their particular needs as newcomers. But in view of the profound cultural changes taking place in the United States at the present time, there is little likelihood that a consistent family policy will be forthcoming in the very near future. Almost every aspect of public policy affects the family in some way, but it is precisely in the area of the implications for family life that policy questions quickly become controversial. One study in particular, *All Our Children,* published by Kenneth Keniston and the Carnegie Council on Children (1977), was a major effort to identify a family policy for the nation, but much more needs to be done in this regard. Four important areas of policy will be briefly indicated below.

ECONOMIC STABILITY

Keeping the family together was identified by the Carnegie study as the primary objective of family policy; it emphasized the close relationship of family stability to economic issues and economic policy. The information provided above about the severe economic distress of Puerto Rican families indicates the important impact of the economic factor in their case. Of all families in the nation, they are the ones who most need economic assistance. Thus, the proposals of the Carnegie Council, namely, the development of economic innovations which reward the nonsalaried work of the parent in the home, and which support family integration instead of weakening it as much of our welfare policy does are particularly relevant. The recent budget cuts which eliminated many resources for day-care service were regrettable. But more important than an institution which provides care for the child outside the home while the mother is gainfully employed would be an imaginative system of economic rewards for the work she could do in the home in the care of her family. Aid to Families with Dependent Children may appear to supply this, but it places a premium on the absence of the father. It is widely recognized that the problems of economic support for poor families is a very complicated issue and Congress has been wrestling with it for years. But it seems that something better could be achieved than a system in which New York State spends close to $20,000 to keep a Puerto Rican deliquent in a correctional institution while the delinquent's father is struggling to support a wife and six other children on a salary of $8,000. Indeed, the delinquency of the child may actually be related to the economic distress of the family.

FAMILY RESPONSIBILITY

However the issue goes far beyond economics. The Puerto Rican Family Institute in New York City has developed a very successful placement prevention program for Hispanic families. It has demonstrated in impressive fashion that support services in the Hispanic home in a style that makes sense to poor Hispanic families enable these families to take advantage of their own capacity for responsibility and keep their children in the home instead of making efforts to place them in child care facilities. Social workers often emphasize the importance of this kind of support service and, in particular, the unusual success of this program administered in Puerto Rican style and in Spanish. Such methods which foster a kind of gradual cultural adaptation process deserve much more attention than they are currently receiving.

From another point of view, the rapid increase of out-of-wedlock births and female-headed families among Puerto Ricans indicates the need for intensive family life education that touches not only on the biological aspects of sexual behavior, birth, and parental responsibility, but on a wide range of moral and spiritual as well as sociological and cultural aspects of life as well.

THE PROBLEMS OF INTERCULTURAL TRANSITION

There has never been an easy solution for this problem of intercultural transition for newcomers in the United States. Within the family, it requires a great deal of maturity on the part of parents, and a great deal of understanding on the part of children. It is not easy to achieve this. Grass-roots programs of the Puerto Rican community (such as Family Life Movements, Family Encounters, and religious and spiritual workshops) do currently assist many of the parents to cope with the problem of transition. However, far more extensive programs are needed, both in and out of school, for the children.

The non-Puerto Rican community has responsibilities here. The United States Commission on Civil Rights published its well known report, *Puerto Ricans in the Continental United States—An Uncertain Future,* in October 1976. It focused especially on the economic and educational problems of the Puerto Rican community. Attributing many of these problems to discrimination and prejudice in the larger American community, it presented a series of recommendations to correct this state of affairs. In short, the commission was convinced that many of the difficulties besetting Puerto Rican families will not be solved until the problem of prejudice and discrimination in the American community has been corrected.

BILINGUALISM

Finally, there is the important issue of language. Civil rights legislation has tried to call the attention of Americans to the fact that Puerto Ricans are native-born American citizens whose native language is Spanish. They have a civil right to participate in American life through the language which they know. A strange psychology, rooted in some fundamental insecurity, has troubled the Anglo-Saxon world in the areas of color and of language.

It is evident from the foregoing pages that the preservation of a sense of identity is a much more difficult problem for Puerto Ricans than it was for earlier ethnic groups. Preserving their Spanish language is an important element in this effort. For this reason, this cause has been taken up in a militant fashion by many mainland Puerto Ricans. It is, therefore, regrettable that so little has been done to evaluate the bilingual programs already in existence. While bilingualism as a cultural ideal has obvious advantages, bilingualism in education provokes sharp criticism and hostile reaction. A policy which promotes bilingualism helps enable children to keep their native language while they more effectively learn English; it is also directed toward giving the children a sense of pride in their cultural background and enabling them to retain a helpful sense of identity.

Another related current problem in Puerto Rico is the large number of school children returning from the mainland who do not know Spanish well enough to be instructed in it. Bilingual classes in English and Spanish have now become a necessity in Puerto Rico. Forty-five thousand children in schools in Puerto Rico in 1976 required special training in Spanish. Because so many children migrate back and forth between the island and the continent, there is a serious need for coordination between the school systems in the two locations on language instruction. As has been mentioned previously, many of these returnees are called "Neo-Ricans." The shock of moving to the island has a profound effect on their social patterns, particularly in the classroom. Many of them come from urban ghettos, where survival required one to be more "aggressive" and to hold onto a "piece" of one's "turf." Returning children often are shunned and ostracized by their Puerto Rican counterparts, not only because of their behavior but also for their inability to speak Spanish. The insistence on bilingualism in schools on the mainland will be helpful not only to Puerto Ricans on the mainland but for those returning to the island as well.

THE ROLE OF THE FAMILY

In the period during which the Puerto Ricans struggle for greater solidarity and identity as a community, the family remains the major psychosocial support for its members. In many cases, it is a broken family; in others, it is hampered by poverty, unemployment, illness. However it still remains the source of strength for most Puerto Ricans in the process of transition. In the turbulent action of the musical *West Side Story,* when Bernardo, leader of the Puerto Rican gang, sees Tony, a youth of another ethnic group, approaching his sister Maria, Bernardo pulls Maria away from Tony to take her home. He then turns to Tony in anger and shouts: "You keep away from my sister. Don't you know we are a family people!"

In 1966, the first presentation in New York of *The Ox Cart* took place. This is a play by a Puerto Rican playwright, Rene Marques, which presents a picture of a simple farm family in the mountains of Puerto Rico, struggling to survive but still reflecting the deep virtues of family loyalty and strength. Under the influence of the oldest son, the family moves to a slum section of San Juan in order to improve itself. But deterioration sets in as the slum environment begins to attack the solidarity and loyalty of the family members. The family then moves to New York. There the strain of the uprooting becomes worse, the gap between mother and children more painful, and the virtues of the old mountain family seem even more distant. After the violent death of the son, the play ends with the valiant mother setting out to go back to the mountains of Puerto Rico. There she hopes to regain the traditional values of Puerto Rican family life that were destroyed in San Juan and New York.

This is an ancient theme, and it may be as true for Puerto Ricans as it was for earlier newcomers. But if the Puerto Ricans "make it" on the mainland, it will be through the same source of strength that supported the immigrants of earlier times— the solidarity of the family.

BIBLIOGRAPHY

Fitzpatrick, Joseph. "Crime and Our Puerto Ricans." *Catholic Mind,* 1960, 58: 39–50.
———. *Puerto Rican Americans.* Englewood Clifffs, N.J.: Prentice Hall, 1971.
———. *Puerto Rican Addicts and Non-Addicts: A Comparison.* Unpublished. Bronx, New York: Institute for Social Research, Fordham University, 1976.
Gillin, John. "Some Signposts for Policy." In Richard N. Adams, et al. (ed.), *Social Change in Latin America Today.* New York: Vintage, 1960, pp. 28–47.
Jaffe, A. J.; Cullen, Ruth M.; and Boswell, Thomas. *Spanish Americans in the United States: Changing Demographic Characteristics.* New York: Research Institute for the Study of Man (162 E. 78 Street, New York, New York 10021), 1976.
Keniston, Kenneth, and the Carnegie Council on Children. *All Our Children: The American Family Under Pressure.* New York: Harcourt, Brace, Jovanovich, 1977.

Lewis, Oscar. *La Vida: A Puerto Rican Family in the Culture of Poverty—San Juan and New York.* New York: Random House, 1965.

Mintz, Sidney. *Worker in the Cane.* New Haven: Yale University Press, 1960.

Stycos, J. Mayone. *Family and Fertility in Puerto Rico.* New York: Columbia University Press, 1955.

Tyler, Gus. *Organized Crime in America.* Ann Arbor: University of Michigan Press, 1962.

U.S. Commission on Civil Rights. *Puerto Ricans in the Continental United States: An Uncertain Future.* Washington, D.C., 1976.

U.S. Department of Commerce. U.S. Census of Population: 1970. *Census Tracts, New York, New York, Standard Metropolitan Statistical Area,* PHC(1)–145. 3 vols. Washington, D.C.: Government Printing Office, 1972.

———. U.S. Census of Population: 1970. *Subject Reports. Final Report,* PC(2)–1C, "Persons of Spanish Origin." Washington, D.C.: Government Printing Office, 1973.

———. U.S. Census of Population, 1970. *Subject Reports. Final Report,* PC(2)–1D, "Persons of Spanish Surname." Washington, D.C.: Government Printing Office, 1973.

———. U.S. Census of Population: 1970 *Subject Reports. Final Report,* PC(2)–1E, "Puerto Ricans in the United States." Washington, D.C.: Government Printing Office, 1973.

———. U.S. Bureau of the Census. "Language Usage in the United States: July 1975." Series P-23, No. 60. Washington, D.C.: Government Printing Office, 1976.

———. U.S. Bureau of the Census. "Persons of Spanish Origin in the United States, March, 1976." Series P-20, No. 310. Washington, D.C.: Government Printing Office, 1977.

Wells, Henry. *The Modernization of Puerto Rico.* Cambridge, Mass.: Harvard University Press, 1969.

9

Implications for National Policy Decisions: The Black Family Perspective

MAGDALENE CARNEY AND ELIZABETH BOWEN
School of Education
University of Massachusetts
Amherst, Massachusetts

INTRODUCTION

The purpose of this chapter is to examine, in an abbreviated fashion, some of the realities affecting black family life in the United States and on the basis of that examination, to suggest, at some length, recommendations to guide and influence policy-making at the national level.

The chapter shows why the research emphasis of both black and white social scientists fails to deal meaningfully with real problems, assesses the way the federal government currently addresses human problems, cites racial prejudice as the root cause for the perpetration of inequities and injustices, and proposes the areas of health, education, economics, and the legal system as key points of leverage for affecting vitally needed changes in black family and community life.

Although many poor and oppressed groups may benefit by the implementation of such recommendations as those sketched in this paper, we have chosen to underscore the black family experience rather than to lump and label everyone else under the all-inclusive rubric of "nonwhite." We feel that such a practice does not do justice to the diverse needs and concerns of the various groups involved.

Black and white social scientists who study the black family experience in America differ significantly in their interpretations of the experience. That they hold contradictory views about the same phenomena stems in part from their differences in culture, motivation, and preference—factors that determine the purpose of their research, areas of focus, and interpretation of results.

According to most white social scientists, with the notable exception of Herbert Gutman (1976), black family life in America is a tangle of disorganization, instability, crime, and assorted pathologies presided over by tired, uncaring, disillusioned, inadequate matriarchs, and spawned by indolent, "absentee" fathers. In short, social problems, social disorganization, and social pathology form the lens through which black family life is viewed. Thus, wherever white researchers focus, they see only problems, disorganization, and pathology. This selective focus, of course, influences the kind of hypotheses they construct, the methodology they use to conduct their research, and the interpretation of their findings.

Zanden (1973), in his review *Sociological Studies of American Blacks* speculates that the apparent ideological commitment to *finding* blacks disadvantaged at all times and under all circumstances may be due in part to America's long tradition of racism. Indeed, there seems to be an obsession for constructing hypotheses that almost always place blacks in deficient, deviant roles, and for proclaiming that they perform consistently less well than whites.

Beyond the acknowledgement that racism permeates our society, a deeper issue underlies the treatment blacks receive in research studies. "Our efforts to create a productive and clear frame of reference," Howard (1972) says, "are impeded by the fact that there is little if any meaningful theoretical work being done in American psychology and, indeed, in American social science in general." This means that the theoretical and conceptual frame so essential for understanding the dynamics of black family life is missing. Lack of such frames of reference ensures that the research will be more descriptive than explanatory and suggests that it will highlight symptoms and fail to address root causes. Problems will be identified, but no solutions set forth (Billingsley, 1968; Turner, 1972).

Black researchers insist that "the validity of social analysis will be questionable as long as its interpretations of social reality are inconsistent with the actual (material) circumstances" (Turner, 1973). In other words, when someone describes "what is," he needs to also explain, "why it is," particularly in reference to comparative studies in which blacks are measured against so-called "white norms."

The traditional approach to black family studies ignores the vast domain of family diversity within the black community. Moreover, the role of religion, philosophy, folklore, legend, and myth in family development are likewise ignored (Turner, 1973). From the black researcher's point of view, the proper context for studying the black family is a developmental one that takes into account every aspect of experience. This includes the historical as well as the contemporary frame of reference with particular emphasis on the external forces that impinge upon the family. Research studies that could have value are those which (1) get organized around a theory of human development; (2) are longitudinal and interdisciplinary in nature; and (3) are problem-solution oriented and result in actions that improve the human condition.

This brief overview immediately brings to mind several policy recommendations which are as follows:

LAY THE GROUNDWORK FOR MUTUAL COLLABORATION BETWEEN BLACK AND WHITE SOCIAL-SCIENCE RESEARCHERS AND THEORISTS

This move is important because social-science researchers influence the shape and character of public policy by their reports and studies. In addition, these studies help policy makers determine what research gets funded, for how long, where, and by whom. Those studies that result in programs that aim at having a positive impact on the black community require collaboration between black and white researchers from an interdisciplinary perspective in order to avoid the theoretical and conceptual problems we cited earlier.

ABANDON ALL RESEARCH STUDIES THAT COMPARE BLACKS AND WHITES

Such comparison studies give us no new knowledge about human development. They are not only worthless, they are divisive and destructive. Apart from that, they distract scholars from attacking real problems and finding real solutions to them. Comparison studies assume that "the white norm" embodies an ideal that blacks need to measure up to. This assumption perpetuates an insidious form of racism that suppresses human development and impairs human relationships.

CHECK THE MOTIVATION OF SOCIAL-SCIENCE RESEARCHERS

Because research in the social sciences touches the lives of millions of people—perhaps everyone in some form or fashion—the motivation behind the research must meet the highest ethical standards. Thus, caution is required to protect the rights of subjects and to prevent the popularization of results beyond the original intentions of the researchers. Further, we think that this caution will help to put an end to the kind of research that denigrates, exploits, and maligns black families.

ORGANIZE REGIONAL RESEARCH CONSORTIUMS NATIONWIDE

Each of the geographical regions of this country has different needs and requirements. We envision the purpose of these centers as providing forums for ordinary citizens to air their views and share their concerns about local priorities and policy matters. In this way, national policy makers and planners will become better informed about the grassroots needs of various regions. Conscious efforts will have to be made to solicit the opinions of all the ethnic groups, particularly the ones whose voice is usually not heard.

In this section, we have attempted to alert you to a few of the limitations and blind spots in the social science research available on the black family. Our concern centers around the need for scrupulous integrity in scholarship, careful translation of research findings into policy recommendations, and courageous dedication to principle in carrying out such recommendations as they pertain to the black family. Similarly, we point out in the next section certain shortcomings in our national approach to human problems.

ADDRESSING HUMAN PROBLEMS

We will cite a number of problems in this study affecting black family life that have implications for national policy decisions. However, past experiences, current practice, and observations of the contemporary scene indicate that we cannot expect significant changes to be made given the way our government generally deals with human problems. Here are some of the primary reasons for our skepticism:

1. Too much national policy-making and planning develops in an *ad hoc* fashion in an attempt to respond to a perceived crisis.
2. National policies fail to be long-range in nature, and thus lack coherence and comprehensiveness.
3. Disorganization within and among governmental agencies almost guarantees that continuity and delivery of services will be at a minimum.

Let us examine each of these reasons in a little more detail.

RESPONSE TO CRISIS

Crisis-oriented policies and legislation seldom get to the root causes of a problem. A particular crisis (unemployment, drug abuse, juvenile crime) usually has been in the making over a long period of time and is inextricably bound up with numerous intervening variables. At present, however, social problems are defined and solutions are proposed on the basis of what is currently ideologically satisfying or politically palatable (Sowell, 1978). Thus, we continue squandering huge resources, proposing short-lived reforms, and treating symptoms only. Do we really believe that solutions are that simple? Can they be packaged, labeled "instant," and quickly produce the desired result as long as the directions on the package are faithfully carried out?

Crisis-oriented policies and legislation are often hastily conceived without the necessary background information that would make them effective and lasting. By the time the needed information becomes available, programs based on policies and guidelines previously in effect are already in motion. If modifications are called for, programs get changed to meet the new requirements. People barely get the new programmatic guidelines into operation when they hear that more information and new amendments are in the offing. Then too, the new set of guidelines may alter the program to such an extent that it is restricted, curtailed, or even abandoned.

This pattern of activity is an example of "ad hocism" at its worst because it leaves participants and personnel in the various programs frustrated and uncertain about what to expect. Approaching human problems in this fashion contributes to the perceived crisis rather than alleviating it. Moreover, we run the high risk of more fragmentation and duplication of efforts, wasting both human and material resources.

If we look beyond an immediate crisis, we see that effective policy planning needs to be made in the context of *preventing* societal disorders and pathologies rather than merely responding to them with brief, one-shot efforts at containment, rehabilitation, or treatment.

LONG-RANGE PLANNING

"Piecemeal" and "fragmentation" are two words which dominate the literature about planning for change. We complain to each other that our proposed solutions to problems are piecemeal, that our efforts are fragmented and often overlap with one another without our even being aware of it. In our view, there is little justification for the continuation of these conditions and complaints.

Long-range policy planning that focuses on human problems will be more effective when it draws upon coherent, comprehensive theories of human development. After sufficient conceptual work has been done, policy makers can view their task in a more holistic manner. They can realize that policies and programs aimed at satisfying immediate, short-sighted objectives rarely leave a lasting impact. They can understand that trying to solve long-range problems with short-range solutions perpetrates an unconscionable fraud on everyone, especially those a program is supposed to help. They can see to it that partisan politics do not interfere with sustained financial support for projects that need funding beyond the four-year political cycle.

If we are truly concerned about the achievement of more lasting results with human problems, sustained funding over at least a twenty-year period will become the norm rather than the exception. Given the long-range nature of human development, our policies have to be comprehensive and flexible enough to anticipate and to negotiate whatever contingencies arise in the course of that development. This brings us to the problem of evaluation.

Evaluation centers around an analysis of a system's energy use (means) to see how well or to what extent purposes (ends) are being achieved. Since energy use in a system is an ongoing process, evaluation likewise must be an ongoing process—one that examines every part of the program operation in order to provide immediate feedback so that timely modifications can be made. This type of evaluation contrasts sharply with the common method of waiting until the end of a program to do evaluation.

Evaluation as described here requires far more than the 1 percent funding usually allocated for human-service programs. Because everything is contingent upon the results of evaluation, more time and money must be invested in it.

DISORGANIZATION

What kind of administrative theory guides the functioning of our governmental agencies? To "administer" means "to serve." Yet a significant number of current organizational structures defeat the main purpose of administration. A system that does not provide for continuity of function and services over time becomes dysfunctional.

We see discontinuity and confusion most clearly whenever our national administration is in transition. What effect does this transition have on policy-making and implementation? First, information and communication channels are disconnected so that no one, including those working within the various agencies, knows what is happening, or where to direct others.

Secondly, those waiting in the field to carry forward the implementation of a program may experience incredible time lags for the receipt of resources. In short, equity, efficiency, and effectiveness diminish rapidly under disorganization.

Even if we could somehow eliminate the crisis-oriented, *ad hoc* approach in policy-making and planning; develop long-range, comprehensive policies; and replace dysfunctional administrative structures; at bottom we still have to deal with a most challenging issue in creating black family policy.

THE CENTRAL CHALLENGE

We can no longer avoid the real issue. The single greatest impediment to the establishment of a national family policy that deals with blacks equitably is injustice. The policies, practices, laws, structures, relationships, and conditions that are based primarily on racial prejudice reflect this injustice. Racial prejudice, supported by the fallacious doctrine of racial superiority, is so ingrained within our national fiber that nothing short of sincere, systematic, and sustained effort will suffice to eradicate it.

Personal transformation, by blacks and whites alike, on a scale heretofore unimagined, will be required to eradicate prejudice. It is the kind of transformation Manfred Halpern (1975) calls "the creation of fundamentally new and better relationships." That we need to create fundamentally new and better relationships is borne out by the fact that, historically, every advantage, opportunity, and privilege accorded to white citizens without question has to be fought for by black citizens. That blacks have repeatedly had to provoke a crisis in the nation before a modicum of justice has been secured, tells us that something is wrong with our system. Lerone Bennett, Jr. (1976), historian and senior editor of *Ebony* magazine charges that a policy of "malign neglect" is threatening the very foundations of the black community. Speaking out against a Great Black Depression, Bennett feels that the black community is facing its severest crisis since the end of slavery and that "generations of black people" are still being lost. As the following evidence shows, this tragic loss continues unabated and at an accelerating rate.

A recent survey from the Congressional Budget Office called *Income Disparities between Black and White Americans* (1978) cites an all too familiar fact: Whereas the median income for all white families in 1975 was $16,278, for black families it was $8,779. Fewer than 8 percent of white families were below the poverty income level in 1975, whereas 27 percent of black families were below the poverty level. The same report also notes that "blacks are disproportionately unemployed. Levels of educational attainment for blacks are much lower than whites," and "blacks are disproportionately centered" in low-pay jobs. Why is this the case? The report cites less advantageous black work experiences, educational attainment, occupational distribution, region of residence and discrimination. It finds "many forms of discrimination cutting across all other factors." Why the discrimination? This report and others like it stop short of admitting that rampant racial prejudice supports and nurtures discrimination.

The annual report of the National Urban League, *The State of Black America— 1978,* gives an even more devastatingly bleak picture. Teenage unemployment is 40 to 50 percent in many neighborhoods. Infant mortality among blacks is twice that of whites. Residential housing is a major source of frustration. Crowding in schools is another. For example, the state of New York has 740 school districts and 95 percent of the blacks are crowded into eleven of them.

Why do conditions like these prevail throughout the country? Roger Wilkin, a reporter for the *New York Times,* attempts to answer this question when he writes that "most whites believe either that the battle for racial justice in the United States has been won or that it is too costly in terms of the sacrifices white people have to make for the visions that the 1960's spawned to come true." Notice that hardly a decade has passed since the great reforms of the 1960's and some whites have already concluded, incorrectly, that all is well. Others have so quickly forgotten the inhumane sacrifices that blacks have endured for 400 years. No one should be surprised that attitudes such as these prevail. They reflect a typically widespread unawareness and unconcern that is covered up by an attitude of presumed rightness and superiority.

Another form of racism that undermines the black community operates in academic circles. It flourishes in educational policy research—set off by books such as Christopher Jencks' *Inequality: A Reassessment of the Effect of Family and Schooling in America* (1972). Arthur Jensen (1969) and his supporters are continually advancing biological deterministic theory which is under heavy attack by scientists. The latest version claims (1) that differences between individuals in schools and in socioeconomic success are chiefly the result of genetic differences and are therefore unchangeable, and (2) that differences in the average scholastic and socioeconomic levels among races (chiefly black and white) are mostly genetic and unchangeable. As long as hypotheses about the biological inferiority of blacks continue to flourish, coming generations of young scholars will be influenced, no doubt, to carry forward such "research."

Let us examine racial prejudice for what it is. The word prejudice is derived from "pre-judgment." It is an unfavorable opinion or feeling formed beforehand and without knowledge, thought, or reason. We tend to judge people or ideas on the basis of preconceived notions, without bothering to verify our beliefs or to examine the merits of our judgment.

Racial prejudice is an explicit expression of a preconceived opinion that certain people are inherently inferior. Racism in the United States has improvised a thousand variations on two basic themes. The first is that black people are born with inferior brains and a limited capacity for mental growth. The second is that their personalities tend to be abnormal, whether by nature or nurture. These concepts of inferiority and pathology are interrelated and reinforce each other.

Let us look specifically at what racial prejudice does.

1. Racial prejudice creates a social climate that practically guarantees the miscarriage of justice. Without justice, there can be no order, and without order, there can be no peace.
2. Racial prejudice distorts the inner life of the prejudiced person. He suffers because his kind of thinking is so rigidly compartmentalized that it is closed to new associations and new understanding. His psychological growth and development is thereby stunted. Such a person almost always exaggerates details about the objects of his prejudice, spreads rumors, passes on unfounded generalizations, and engages in many kinds of verbal character defamation.
3. Racial prejudice destroys bonds of trust and fellowship. It is exceptionally difficult for one who is the victim of racial prejudice and its numerous manifestations to forget and forgive.
4. Racial prejudice often leads to acts of aggression against others. Sometimes those acts of aggression spell extermination—through massacres, lynchings, and so forth.
5. Racial prejudice inevitably leads to numerous forms of discrimination. This lays the foundation for distinctions that exclude certain people from exercising their rights, having privileges, or enjoying opportunities to develop soul, mind, and body.

Now that we have some sense of what racial prejudice is, and what it does, where do we begin to effect changes in our attitudes and actions?

That question brings us full circle to Halpern's notion of transformation: "The creation of fundamentally new and better relationships." Among other things it operates on the personal level, at the grass roots of family and community. Therefore, the following recommendations are designed to assist us in transforming our characters in ways that may help us to rid ourselves of racial prejudice. They touch upon the moral ramifications of the issue. Let us:

1. *Make a firm and resolute commitment to eradicate racial prejudice in all its forms from our lives.* Why should we make a conscious commitment about this matter? First, it will help us to realize that the issue is far from being resolved. Secondly, it will force us to examine our presumptions without

"blinders" and to abandon our obliviousness and naivete for genuine awareness of the gravity of the situation facing each of us.

2. *Cultivate through everyday opportunities, genuine relationships with people of diverse races and classes.* By deliberately cultivating true friendships with diverse peoples, we may be able to exchange our stereotypic perceptions for a
   more realistic appreciation for diversity in the human family.

3. *Demonstrate in our public and private life our belief in the interrelatedness and
   worth of all peoples.* We often give lip service to this principle and yet it is not
   until we consistently exemplify it in our actions that it becomes a living
   reality.

4. *Develop a critical faculty for discerning evidences of racism.* Because so much
   racial prejudice flows from implicit assumptions, we are often immersed in
   racist experiences without even realizing it. For instance, our institutions,
   literature, and media bombard us so constantly with portrayals of inferiority-
   superiority relationships that we become psychologically numb and insensitive. Therefore, we must be alert to recognize these incidents and reject their
   false messages.

5. *Educate children and youth to appreciate and to welcome diversity.* In living by
   the above principles and encouraging our children to do likewise, we can help
   them to develop "fundamentally new and better relationships." Herein lies
   our greatest hope for the future.

POINTS OF LEVERAGE

A few of the major forces that impinge heavily on black family life are health,
education, economics, and legal services. The remainder of this study focuses on how
we might modify these forces through specific policy recommendations.

HEALTH ISSUES AND RECOMMENDATIONS

The World Health Organization's definition of health is, "A state of complete
physical, mental, and social wellbeing and not merely the absence of disease or infir-
mity" (WHO, 1960). Before black Americans attain equal opportunity to enjoy
health in its fullest sense, this country will have to undergo fundamental transformations in its character. What some writers refer to as a gap in health status between
black and white Americans has become a chasm, not likely to be bridged in the near
future without a dramatic reversal in our attitudes and policies. Let us cite a few examples.

The infant mortality rate is a very sensitive indicator of the health status of a
population. In the United States at the present time, the black infant has an 80 percent greater chance of dying during the first year of life than the white infant
(Lythcott et al., 1975). Most of the reliable statistical data list only white and nonwhite categories. Since 90 percent of the nonwhites are actually black, and because
precise data on blacks alone are rarely available, we have taken data on the nonwhite
population to be generally representative of the black experience. The terms "black"
and "nonwhite" are thus considered to be equivalent for the present documentation
(Haynes, 1975). This sharp contrast is evident in every age group and, in most cases,

it is widening rather than diminishing. Maternal mortality rates demonstrate this point. In the early 1900's the maternal death rates were high for both blacks and whites. Although the rates for both races have decreased dramatically, the black rate, which was formerly twice as high as the white rate, is now almost four times as high (Haynes, 1975).

For almost all of the leading causes of death, the rates for the black population are higher, often many times higher, than those for the white population. The death rate for hypertension and high blood pressure related diseases among blacks ages twenty-five to forty-four is fifteen times higher than that among whites (Yabura, 1977). The black death rates are four times higher than the white rates for tuberculosis; twice as high for diabetes mellitus, influenza and pneumonia, cirrhosis of the liver, and cerebral vascular diseases and one-and-a-half times as high for cancer and accidents. Because of such disparities, the life expectancy of blacks is 10 percent shorter than that of whites. On the average, the black American lives about seven years less than the white American; black men live to age sixty-one versus sixty-eight for white men; black women live to age sixty-nine versus seventy-six for white women (Haynes, 1975).

The preventable nature of the poor health and excess deaths that burden the black community is especially clear in the case of children's communicable diseases. It costs only $2.00 per child for a series of complete immunizations against polio, tetanus, rubella, measles, diphtheria, typhoid, and pertussis. Yet only about half of black children have protection against *any* of these diseases, including polio. Until immunization levels are raised, outbreaks of epidemics may be expected (United States Health, 1975).

To raise the health status of the black community, large resources are necessary over long periods of time. Realistic priorities should be set to provide an overarching framework for the accomplishment of specific manageable objectives within shorter time periods. In this way progress could be carefully monitored and evaluated. What follows are policy recommendations that, if implemented, would markedly improve the health status of black Americans.

INCREASE BLACK REPRESENTATION AT ALL LEVELS OF THE HEALTH PROFESSIONS

Many more health professionals are needed, especially in the black community. Although all health personnel should serve people of all races, there is still more of a need for health personnel in the black community than there is in the white community. Therefore, we should raise the quota of blacks to at least 12 percent of all health manpower in training programs within two years. Now, only 6.3 percent of medical students, 4.7 percent of dental students, and 7.7 percent of nursing students are black (HEW, 1975). Only 2.2 percent of practicing physicians are black. Whereas one in every 528 whites is a physician, only one in every 4,100 blacks is (Sullivan, 1977).

The absence of blacks is especially critical in the area of public health as this field deals with policy development, health planning, promotion of preventive health measures, and evaluation. There are fewer than 150 blacks in the country who have doctorates in public health, and of the 200 black students currently enrolled in graduate programs of public health, only 15 percent are in doctoral programs (Darity, 1977). A dramatic and rapid increase in the numbers of blacks entering health professions could give the black community significantly greater power in shaping the quality and distribution of health care.

REQUIRE ALL HEALTH PROFESSIONALS TO TAKE COURSES (PRESERVICE AND INSERVICE) ON THE CULTURAL AND ETHNIC DIFFERENCES OF VARIOUS MINORITY GROUPS' HEALTH PROGRAMS, RESPONSES TO ILLNESS, AND TRADITIONAL APPROACHES TO HEALING

Twenty percent of the American population belong to minorities that have distinctive disease patterns and unique views on these issues. This profoundly affects the delivery and outcome of health care. For instance, 75 percent of blacks have no choice but to be seen by white doctors. If prejudice and distrust prevail, coupled with ignorance of common black diseases, the result is disturbed communication, misdiagnosis, and destructive rather than curative treatment. This is appallingly common. Required courses for *all* health professionals, both preservice and inservice, could begin to address these problems. Such courses could begin immediately, be carefully evaluated and refined over the next five years, and be institutionalized in health and medical schools, hospitals, and clinics, within ten years. (For further discussion, see Wan, 1977; Ademuwagun, 1972; and Williams, 1975.)

ENSURE THAT ALL FAMILIES OBTAIN OPTIMUM NUTRITION

Current studies show that most of the major diseases affecting Americans—heart diseases, hypertension, cancer, diabetes, obesity, dental decay—stem, in part, from nutritional imbalances. Also, a growing body of research suggests that at least 75 percent of learning disabilities are directly related to nutritional and associated health disorders. (For specific policy statements and detailed documentation, see *Dietary Goals for the United States,* Senate Select Committee on Nutrition and Human Needs, 1977; Cott, 1974; Livingstone, 1975; and Birch and Gussow, 1970.)

DEVELOP COMPREHENSIVE HEALTH-CARE SERVICES AND MAKE THEM AVAILABLE TO ALL PEOPLE, REGARDLESS OF INCOME OR RACE

The United States is the only modern industrialized nation that does not ensure such services for all its peoples. Because minorities, expectant mothers, infants, and children are the most vulnerable groups in the population, their needs should be served first. Thus, as comprehensive, universal services are developed, their first targets should be those groups who are at greatest risk. Until this happens, health care in America will not be a basic right but a privilege. This is a complex and long-range task requiring that vigorous efforts be launched and sustained until the goal is met. (For specific policy suggestions, see Andreopoulous, 1974.)

PROVIDE BIRTH CONTROL AND FAMILY-PLANNING SERVICES TO ALL YOUTH AND ADULTS

There are significant unresolved issues relating to this point. Nearly 60 percent of married women report more pregnancies than wanted or pregnancies earlier than wanted *(Profiles of Children,* 1970). Some 80 percent of sexually active teenagers do not use contraception regularly, and indeed, do not have access to family-planning services. Among teenagers, one in four is already a parent. This poses major problems for them, their children, and their communities. Various options should be available to, and understood by, both men and women to help them time, space, and if so desired, avoid having children. (See Adams and Hatcher, 1977; and Wallace et al., 1973 for specific policy guidelines.) Also, a nationwide campaign to educate the public and especially the youth about the growing epidemic of venereal disease and its tragic effects is urgently needed.

PROVIDE APPROPRIATE PRENATAL, OBSTETRIC, AND PEDIATRIC (MATERNAL AND CHILD HEALTH) CARE TO ALL FAMILIES

In several countries, virtually all women obtain prenatal care, yet in the United States in 1973 only about 60 percent of white women and 35 percent of black women had continuous prenatal care (Haynes, 1975). Inadequate prenatal care is directly linked with high infant mortality rates.

Obstetrics is currently undergoing major transformations that call for restructuring maternity care so that labor and delivery are allowed to proceed as naturally as possible with medical and technological interventions kept to a minimum. This important development, which has profound implications for policy, is explained in detail in Klaus and Kennel, 1976; and Sugarman, 1977. (See also Jelliffe, 1971, for a detailed rationale for why breast feeding should be promoted over artificial feeding of any kind. One major reason, of course, is that it substantially reduces the risk of infection.)

PROVIDE ALL PEOPLE, ESPECIALLY MOTHERS, INFANTS, AND CHILDREN , WITH ADEQUATE IMMUNIZATIONS

This could be accomplished within months, yet only 60 percent of all children are now adequately immunized. This is a fairly simple, yet extremely effective and important measure.

ENSURE SAFE HOUSING AND NEIGHBORHOODS FOR ALL FAMILIES

This is crucial for infants and children, especially, and could lead to a marked reduction in accidents, lead poisoning, and other conditions associated with unsafe and unsanitary environments.

LAUNCH A NATIONAL PROGRAM TO EDUCATE THE PUBLIC ABOUT HYPERTENSION AND PROVIDE TREATMENT TO ALL HYPERTENSIVES AT LITTLE OR NO COST

Hypertension is the major health problem affecting adult black Americans, with at least 20 percent, or six million blacks, being affected (Saunders and Williams, 1975). Millions of people with hypertension do not even know they have it, and only 20 percent of those under treatment for chronic hypertension are receiving appropriate and effective treatment for it (Yabura, 1977). Remedying this situation would greatly improve the quality and duration of life for black Americans.

INTENSIFY RESEARCH ON THE BASIC CAUSES OF DISEASES AND THEIR PREVENTION

Today's medical profession is primarily crisis-oriented. It emphasizes "cures," rather than preventive measures. In contrast, we need to devote a far greater portion of our resources to examining the environmental factors that produce disease, such as inadequate nutrition, pollution, stress, lack of exercise, and other lifestyle variables. By modifying or correcting these negative influences, we can learn how to prevent disease and greatly enhance the health of millions of Americans, black and white.

EDUCATIONAL ISSUES AND RECOMMENDATIONS

Twelve years ago, Kenneth Clark (1966) made a statement that has as much relevance today as it did then:

American colleges and universities will demonstrate that they are relevant to the crucial issues of our times, that they are morally adaptive, and, therefore, that they can contribute to the survival of the human race, when they fully and functionally accept as their responsibility the need to train individuals of moral intelligence who demonstrate by the totality of their lives that they understand that an injustice perpetrated upon any human being robs them of some of their humanity and demands of them personal, constructive, and intelligent action for justice. Wisdom and moral sensitivity tempering human intelligence are not now ethical abstractions. They are survival imperatives.

What can we do now to translate this vision into reality? Because education in its broadest sense involves the release of our potentialities throughout our lives, the values and qualities that Dr. Clark calls "survival imperatives" must permeate the educational process from the earliest years. They must receive a special emphasis, particularly during the periods of early childhood and youth, when youngsters are developing the aims and ideals that will motivate and guide their lives. Because of the importance of character development in the education of the individual, education is inevitably a moral affair. The following recommendations suggest ways by which we can move toward equality of educational opportunity:

PROVIDE ALL CHILDREN AND YOUTH WITH THE BEST POSSIBLE TEACHERS THROUGHOUT THEIR DEVELOPMENT

We should put forward the best people we can possibly find as models to support, help and inspire our youngsters to pursue high ideals and develop their talents to the fullest. One way for the teaching profession to attract and hold the finest and best qualified people from diverse backgrounds is to provide commensurate prestige and pay. Another way, of equal importance, is to define the goals of education and to provide the conditions required to meet them. If, for example, we say we want to produce competent children, then we need to define competence, specifying what competent teaching means, and providing conditions in which this can take place.

In the absence of such recognition, clarity of purpose, and supportive conditions, it is extremely difficult for teachers to function, which then produces bitter frustration for them and for the children.

PROVIDE COMPREHENSIVE HOME-SCHOOL-COMMUNITY SUPPORT SYSTEMS FOR ALL CHILDREN AND YOUTH

One aspect of this is to see that all children get appropriate nutrition and health care so that their growth and development and their ability to learn will not suffer. Another is to attend to the special needs of handicapped youngsters at the earliest possible stage. A third is to provide excellent early childhood education programs in all communities as the preschool years are among the most decisive ones. To do this effectively, parents, grandparents, other relatives, and other community members need to join together to provide children with warm, consistent, and stable relationships with many diverse adults. This kind of adult-child interaction throughout the life cycle gives children many friends and role models beyond the limited confines of their immediate age-group peers. It greatly benefits everyone, and puts an end to the current unnatural segregation of adults from children.

PROVIDING CONTINUING EDUCATION PROGRAMS AT ALL HIGH SCHOOLS , COMMUNITY COLLEGES, COLLEGES, AND UNIVERSITIES SO THAT ALL PEOPLE CAN EASILY BETTER THEMSELVES

Women, minorities, youth, parents, and workers of all kinds are going back to school in increasing numbers. We need to make such schooling easily available, accessible, flexible, and manageable for more and more people. For schools, colleges, and universities to truly serve the needs of *everyone* in their communities, they will have to open their doors to lifelong learners.

PROVIDE HIGH-QUALITY EDUCATIONAL PROGRAMS ON RADIO AND TELEVISION , PUT MORE EDUCATIONAL MATERIAL IN NEWSPAPERS AND MAGAZINES, AND CONTINUE TO EXPAND AND DIVERSIFY THE SERVICES OF PUBLIC LIBRARIES

Many countries are moving rapidly in this direction, and there is no reason we cannot do likewise, given our vast technological resources. Technology and communications may be used to promote civilization or degradation.

Consider what the British have done. During prime time, they broadcast a series of very popular television programs by their foremost scholars in various fields ranging from archeology to Shakespeare. In addition to enjoying high-quality cultural entertainment, many of the viewers complete correspondence courses relating to the programs for university credit. Similarily, many developing nations are using radio programs to teach agricultural, health, and other kinds of valuable information to people who may have no other access to educational services. And yet, in this country, we have barely scratched the surface in exploring the positive ways we could use media to educate and uplift the public.

ECONOMIC ISSUES AND RECOMMENDATIONS

Economics broadly conceived refers to the production, distribution, and consumption of material resources. It appears that these three aspects of our economic system are unbalanced. What will it take to bring these elements into something approaching equilibrium? Perhaps a first step could be more collaboration and consultation among black and white economic theorists to reexamine the present system and its inadequacies and to devise new theories to guide our economic development. Then, we should:

PROVIDE VAST MONETARY RESOURCES FOR THE BLACK COMMUNITY AS THOUGH IT WERE A DEVELOPING NATION

This recommendation should be viewed as an investment rather than as a charitable handout. Over the long haul, it is far cheaper to prevent tragic and costly social upheavals by providing the means for people to contribute to the system. This kind of investment would enable the black community to develop its human resources as well as its material ones.

ELIMINATE UNEMPLOYMENT BY REVISING OUR CONCEPT OF WORK

We can no longer delude ourselves into thinking that our economic policies and practices are appropriate, efficient, or effective. At the heart of any effort to revise the system, we need an entirely new attitude toward work. The purpose of work is to be of service to society, and every individual needs to participate in this process, however modest his contribution may be. This means we need to reconsider our views on retirement practices, and the changing roles of women and youth in relationship to work.

ENCOURAGE BLACKS TO MIGRATE FROM OVERCROWDED URBAN AREAS BY PROVIDING ECONOMIC INCENTIVES FOR RESETTLING IN RURAL COMMUNITIES

Eighty percent of blacks are jammed into cities with the expectation of procuring steady employment and cultural advantages, which have not yet materialized. Therefore, we suggest a "Marshall Plan" type of aid program to help in the redevelopment and resettlement of rural, agricultural communities. This would not only alleviate the steadily worsening situation in cities, it would also allow people to have more control of their own food supply and provide more appropriate environments for rearing children and youth.

MAKE IT MANDATORY THAT EVERY CHILD'S EDUCATION INCLUDES COURSES IN FAMILY FINANCES AND BUDGETING

Each family goes through developmental stages in terms of its need and use of money. Over time, there are varying demands on the family income, such as a new baby, a new house, children's education, and medical expenses. How to manage and budget adequately for these transitions has to be learned early. (For further information on the economic condition of the black community, consult the 1978 National Urban League Report.)

LEGAL ISSUES AND RECOMMENDATIONS

Legal issues have no meaning apart from a clear conception of justice. Justice, as defined in the Oxford Dictionary means uprightness, equity, vindication of right, the principle of just dealing, and the exhibition of this quality in action. The experiences, past and present, of black Americans with the legal system fall far short of the attributes described in the above definition, as no fair-minded person can deny.

Isn't it ironic that the very system whose duty it is to deliver justice has institutionalized injustice? In spite of the maxim that we are innocent until proven guilty "beyond a reasonable doubt," blacks receive more than their share of harrassment, interrogation, and incarceration. For example, blacks are arrested four times as often as whites, found guilty twice as often as whites, and receive far stiffer sentences than whites (Ware, 1976). To deal effectively with these injustices, we must examine some very basic socio-political issues, one of which is representation.

One main reason for the miscarriage of justice is the exclusion of blacks from *meaningful participation* in such societal decision-making centers as banks, corporations, brokerage houses, government, and established law firms. Prosecutor, and judge are key governmental positions where blacks are underrepresented. In 1974, there were 58 blacks among 1,554 prosecutors in twelve major cities containing 24 percent of the nations's black population. Black judges are also scarce: In 1971–1972, they numbered 255 among 21,294 judges at the state and local levels and 31 among 475 judges at the federal level (Ware, 1976).

Blacks also need "meaningful access to the judicial decision making process" in quasi-judicial agencies such as the Interstate Commerce Commission, the Federal Aviation Administration, the Federal Trade Commission, the Federal Power Commission, the Securities and Exchange Commission, the Federal Communications Commission, the Federal Housing Administration, the Equal Employment Opportunities Commission, the National Labor Relations Board, and the Veterans Administration. Each of these agencies "is instrumental in the development of law . . . and thus instrumental in shaping and effecting this nation's economic, and political posture, including its response to the needs, aspirations, rights and privileges of Blacks" (Millender, Sr., 1976).

At the local level, blacks would benefit by equitable representation on police forces, juries, parole boards, and as officers in correctional institutions, probation officers, and counselors.

Injustices abound in courts of all kinds—in landlord-tenant relationships, in prisons, in juvenile cases, in politics, in labor, and management. When we witness in detail the gross inequities and injustices perpetrated on less powerful people, our consciences are jolted. We want to believe that these inhumane acts could not possibly happen. We long to believe that our legal system is indeed based on justice. However, in the absence of universal laws for organizing, regulating, and protecting human beings, we offer the following recommendations that may move us gradually in that direction:

INCREASE SUBSTANTIALLY THE BLACK REPRESENTATION AT ALL LEVELS OF THE LEGAL SYSTEM

Support systems are vitally needed to encourage, recruit, enroll, and sustain young black men and women to pursue careers in all branches and at all levels of the legal system.

MAKE IT MANDATORY THAT THE NATURE OF JUSTICE, THE LAW, AND THE
LEGAL SYSTEM BE AN ESSENTIAL PART OF EVERY CHILD'S EDUCATION

Parents need to realize that prejudice is solidly entrenched by the time a child is
three years old, perhaps sooner, depending upon his experiences. If prejudice can be
learned, so can justice and equity. We recommend that school curricula be organized
around concepts of justice, equity, law, how our legal system is structured, and how it
works.

PUT INTO LAYMAN'S LANGUAGE SUCH LEGAL DOCUMENTS AS LOAN
CONTRACTS, INSURANCE POLICIES, MORTGAGES, AND WILLS

Legal documents that come into our lives almost on a daily basis need to be simplified and written in standard English so that we can understand them without the
need for legal aid to interpret them for us. Moreover, we would all benefit greatly if
the "fine print" in contracts were highlighted.

A FINAL WORD

It was not the intention of this report to reflect the full story of the black family
in America. Rather, we have only emphasized some of the key problems that need
immediate and sustained attention. We have fashioned these recommendations for
policy in a spirit of optimism, for we know this nation has the potential to do what is
just and right.

BIBLIOGRAPHY

Adams, Jacob B., and Hatcher, Robert A. "The Perplexing Problem of Teenage Pregnancies."
    Urban health, 1977, 6(2), 26–27; 48–49.
Ademuwagun, Z. A. "Major Impediments to Effective Use of Public Health Services." *Health
    Education Journal,* 1972, 31(2), 22–20.
Andreopoulos, Spyros, (Ed.). *Primary Care: Where Medicine Fails.* New York: John Wiley and
    Sons, 1974.
Bennett, Lerone, Jr. Speech at ASALH Sixtieth Anniversary Meeting. *Negro History Bulletin,*
    1976, 39(2), 524–526.
Billingsley, Andrew. *Black Families in White America.* Englewood Cliffs, NJ: Prentice-Hall,
    1968.
Birch, Herbert G., and Gussow, Joan D. *Disadvantaged Children: Health, Nutrition, and School
    Failure.* New York: Harcourt, Brace and World, Inc., 1970.
Clark, Kenneth B. "Intelligence, the University, and Society." *The American Scholar,* 1966–67,
    36(1), 23–32.
Congressional Budget Office. *Income Disparities between Black and White Americans.* Washing-
    ton, DC: United States Government Printing Office, 1978.
Cott, Allan. "Treatment of Learning Disabilities." *The Journal of Orthomolecular Psychiatry,*
    1974, 3(4), 343–355.
Darity, William A. "Health Manpower and the Black Community." *Urban Health,* August
    1977, 6(7), 4.
Dietary Goals for the United States. Senate Select Committee on Nutrition and Human Needs.
    Washington, DC: United States Government Printing Office, 1977.
English, Richard A. *Social Research and the Black Community: Selected Issues and Priorities.*
    Lawrence E. Gary (Ed.). Washington, DC: Institute for Urban Affairs and Research, How-
    ard University, 1974.

Gutman, Herbert G. *The Black Family in Slavery and Freedom, 1750–1925.* New York: Pantheon Books, 1976.

Halpern Manfred, "The Politics of Transformation." *Main Currents in Modern Thought,* 1975, 31(5), 131–137.

Haynes, M. Alfred. "The Gap in Health Status between Black and White Americans." In *Textbook of Black-Related Diseases.* R. A. Williams (Ed.). New York: McGraw-Hill, Inc., 1975.

Health, Education, and Welfare. *Minorities and Women in the Health Fields.* Washington, DC: Health, Education, and Welfare Publication Number (HRA)76–22, 1975.

Howard, J. H. "Toward a Social Psychology of Colonialism." In *Black Psychology.* Reginald L. Jones (Ed.). New York: Harper and Row, Publishers, 1972.

Jellife, Derrick B., and Jelliffe, E. F. Patrice (Eds.). "The Uniqueness of Human Milk." *The American Journal of Clinical Nutrition,* 1971, 24(8), 967–1024.

Jencks, Christopher et al. *Inequality: A Reassessment of the Effect of Family and Schooling in America.* New York: Basic Books, 1972.

Jensen, Arthur R. "How Much Can We Boost IQ and Scholastic Achievement?" *Harvard Educational Review,* 1969. 31, 1–123.

Klaus, Marshal H., and Kennell, John H. *Maternal-Infant Bonding: The Impact of Early Separation or Loss on Family Development.* Saint Louis: The C. V. Mosby Company, 1976.

Lewontin, Richard C. "The Fallacy of Biological Determinism." *The Sciences,* 1976, 16(2), 6–10.

Livingstone, Robert B.; Calloway, Doris H.; MacGregor, John S.; Fisher, Gary J.; and Hastings, A. Baird. "U.S. Poverty Impact on Brain Development." In *Growth and Development of the Brain: Nutritional, Genetic, and Environmental Factors.* Mary A. B. Brazier (Ed.). New York: Raven Press, 1975, 377–394.

Lythcott, George A.; Sinnette, Calvin H.; and Hopkins, Donald R. "Pediatrics." In *Textbook of Black-Related Diseases.* R. A. Williams (Ed.). New York: McGraw-Hill, Inc., 1975.

Millender, Robert L., Sr. "Quasi-Judicial Agencies: Crucial but Ignored." In *From the Black Bar: Voices for Equal Justice.* Gilbert Ware (Ed.). New York: G. P. Putnam's Sons, 1976.

National Urban League. *The State of Black America—1978.* New York: National Urban League, Inc., 1978.

Profiles of Children. Summary Statistics of the White House Conference on Children 1970. Washington, DC: United States Government Printing Office, 1970.

Saunders, Elijah, and Williams, Richard Allen. "Hypertension." In *Textbook of Black-Related Diseases.* R. A. Williams (Ed.). New York: McGraw-Hill, Inc., 1975.

Sowell, Thomas. "Ethnicity in a Changing America." *Daedalus,* 1978, 107(1), 213–237.

Sugarman, Muriel. "Paranatal Influences on Maternal-Infant Attachment." *The American Journal of Orthopsychiatry,* 1977, 47(3), 407–421.

Sullivan, Louis, W. "The Education of Black Health Professionals." *Phylon,* 1977, 38(2), 181–193.

"The Complaints of White Men." *The New York Times,* November 27, 1977.

Turner, Clarence R. "Some Theoretical and Conceptual Considerations for Black Family Studies." *Black Lives,* 1972, 2, 13–27.

Turner, William. "A Position on the Question of Ethical Neutrality in Social Science." *The Journal of Afro-American Issues,* 1973, 3, 323–330.

United States Health 1975. (United States Health, 1975). Washington, DC: Department of Health, Education, and Welfare Publication Number 76–1232, 1975.

Wallace, Helen M.; Gold, Edwin M.; and Lis, E. F. (Eds.). *Maternal and Child Health Practices.* Springfield, IL: Charles C. Thomas, 1973.

Wan, Thomas T. H. "The Differential Use of Health Services." *Urban Health,* 1977, 6(1), 47–49.

Ware, Gilbert (Ed.). *From the Black Bar: Voices for Equal Justice.* New York: G. P. Putnam's Sons, 1976.

WHO-World Health Organization. *Constitution.* Geneva, December 1960.

Wilkin, Roger. "Racial Outlook: Lack of Change Disturbs Blacks." *New York Times,* March 4, 1978.

Williams, Richard Allen (Ed.) *Textbook of Black-Related Diseases.* New York: McGraw-Hill Inc., 1975.

Yabura, Lloyd. "Health Care Outcomes in the Black Community." *Phylon*, 1977, 38(2), 194–202.
Zanden, James W. Vander. "Sociological Studies of Black Americans." *The Sociological Quarterly*, Winter 1973, 14:32–52.

Part Three
Is There a Scientific Base for Child-Rearing?

There is currently a great deal of mistrust and apprehension concerning parenting research on the part of parents and social critics. Researchers themselves share this concern and openly suggest that their research is often taken out of context or used prematurely, and that some researchers are too eager to have their research transformed into policy. Furthermore, the methodology as well as the content of research is presently being questioned. Many critics contend that much of the research today is structurally biased and often discriminates against the poor and minority group members.

This section of the anthology gives special attention to questions that concern the structure and content of parenting research. The authors deal squarely with such issues as: What can research tell us about effective parenting? Do we know enough from research studies to guide public policy? Are there shortcomings in the methodology of parenting research? What are these? Can they be prevented? If the evidence from research is lacking, what are the consequences on improving parent effectiveness? What is the role of the expert, the professional, in the improvement of parenthood? What effect has professionalization had on the American family?

In the first selection, Robert D. Hess discusses the unintentional consequences of research and parent education. Hess warns that parent education, while attempting to improve the quality of family life, can eventually impair overall family functioning by undermining the parents' confidence and by creating external dependencies. In tracing the historical development of parent education, Hess discovers that parent-education programs and policies have been associated with the development and ultimate decline of both professionals and institutions in relation to the appearance of various ideologies and shifting intellectual emphases.

In the second selection, Michael E. Lamb exhibits the concern of many researchers that there is an increasing tendency for what is merely preliminary research to become the foundation for policy decisions. Lamb suggests that the principle of basing policy decisions on quantitative research may itself be unreliable because it literally ignores the variability and individuality of both parents and children involved in the family experience. Given the complexity of individual behavior and the inadequacies of current research, Lamb suggests that it is in the public interest for researchers to exercise caution and restraint with regard to parenting policy rather than to offer easy prescriptions.

In the final selection, Jean V. Carew elaborates on the methodological problems associated with parenting research. Carew discusses both direct observation and comparative research methodologies, and finds that they both contain inherent biases. With these limitations in mind, Carew reviews the current research on the relationship between child development and various environmental settings (home, day care, and so forth), and suggests that this research is of limited value until better research methods and concepts are created.

10

Experts and Amateurs: Some Unintended Consequences of Parent Education

ROBERT D. HESS
Lee L. Jacks Professor of Child Education
Stanford University
Stanford, California

The concern about the recent decline of the family in America and the problems of raising children in a time of rapid change has created a renewed interest in parent education. During the last century, concern about the way children are raised has emerged and then ebbed away in a "regular cycle of alarm, response and neglect . . . " (Downs, 1971). Family crisis has been periodically rediscovered. The current manifestation appears in several forms—papers presented at national conventions of relevant professions, research programs of federal and state agencies, and an outpouring of printed and filmed materials for parents. In this chapter, this movement is examined from the standpoint of the knowledge base from which it draws, its effectiveness in changing parent behavior, and its (perhaps unintended) impact upon the families it seeks to serve. I will suggest that the attempts to educate parents can impair family functioning by undermining the parents' sense of confidence, creating dependence upon external resources and diminishing the authority of the family as a socializing unit.

Parent education covers a range of topics and techniques, but a distinction can be made between two types of educational efforts. One is *knowledge-based*—an attempt to provide parents with useful information to which they can respond in specific ways. This includes information about immunization, warnings about the flammability of sleepware, and the importance of visual, dental, and health examinations.

Another type of parent education is *competence-based*. This is an effort to assist parents in their child-rearing practices. Examples are: instruction in methods of discipline, advice on how to deal with aggression or hostility, methods for handling extreme expressions of emotion, warnings about the consequences of rejection or neglect, and the like. This sort of instruction involves the parents' competence to nurture, teach, discipline, and interact with his or her child. The discussion in this chapter is aimed at the second of these two categories of parent education.

SOME HISTORICAL CHANGES IN PARENT EDUCATION

The attempt to instruct parents in their child-rearing duties is not a recent educational innovation. It has been around for at least a century and a half, perhaps longer. The development of social and educational policy toward children and their families is chronicled in Bremner's volumes, *Child and Youth in America: A Documentary History (1970–1974)*. A succession of actors have, at various times, marshalled their efforts in the attempt to rescue families. For example, in the seventeenth century, there were government-appointed agents in Massachusetts whose duty it was to oversee parents through direct intervention in the home. In the eighteenth century, church deacons, school teachers, and others acted informally as monitors of moral development and parental duty. The Sunday school of that time included attempts to teach appropriate social attitudes to lower-class parents and to upgrade the moral tone of the home (Schlossman, 1976). The involvement of governmental and religious institutions in family education continued into the twentieth century, justified by a philosophy of "benevolent intrusion" (Platt, 1969; Joffe, 1977).

There have been fundamental changes in the concerns of parent educators. Up through the early twentieth century, programs for helping parents deal with children were oriented toward moral and religious issues. The child-rearing literature of the early nineteenth century (1820–1860) was designed to help parents produce the ideal adult of that time—a person who was honest, moral, religious, and self-sufficient (Sunley, 1964).

The child was viewed as "doomed to depravity" unless given strict and careful guidance by parents and, ultimately, rescued through religious conversion. Sexuality was an ever present danger and specific means were employed to deal with masturbation, erotic impulses and acts. Personal cleanliness was a virtue; instruction in cleanliness was, of course, associated with toilet training. A central theme was the need to establish the will of the parent as law to insure that the child conform to parental authority through direct confrontation and mastery over the child's own will. Toward mid-century, there were signs of a moderating of the severity of child-training practices, with less emphasis on punishment, on strict obedience, and on the inherently evil nature of the child.

Although they were not dominant in the literature of the time, some contrasting views of the child can be found. These depicted the child as a tender creature, whose normal sexual and aggressive drives were benign unless distorted by improper upbringing. In these writings, the role of the parent was present as that of a guide and counselor, someone to help the child fulfill his needs and develop his potential (Sunley, 1964).

Among major themes of the literature of the early nineteenth century, according to Sunley, was the central importance of the mother in the internalization of moral standards. The father received little attention in the writings of the time. He was occupied with his work, relatively uninvolved in child-rearing. The phenomena of the absent father is not a recent event that emerged as a consequence of suburban living and a long daily commute to work. The father did, apparently, have a role in administering corporal punishment when needed, a disciplinary technique used widely both at home and at school, despite the vigorous opposition of many writers.

Professionals in child development have been active in parent education since the 1880's. G. Stanley Hall, president of Clark University, was largely responsible for initiating the scientific study of child development. He popularized the idea that research discoveries about child behavior could improve the child-rearing practices of parents (Schlossman, 1976). Parents themselves were not unwilling recipients of professional advice. Before Hall, there were organized groups of mothers as early as 1820 who met to discuss the best methods for improving the moral upbringing of their children.

The federal government got into the child-training business around the beginning of the twentieth century. In 1909 the first *White House Conference on the Care of Dependent Children* was convened. The conference recommended the establishment of *The Children's Bureau,* a federally regulated institution designed to collect and disseminate information about children. The mandate of this conference gave rise to the publication of the bulletin *Infant Care,* which appeared first in 1914 and was revised and reprinted for half a century. The most recent edition was published in 1964. Martha Wolfenstein (1964) describes the contrasts in advice offered to parents during the 1920's and the 1940's. In the earlier period, as in the literature of a century before, the danger of erotic impulses was a central concern, and specific devices and practices were recommended: the use of a stiff cuff that could be attached to the baby's arm so that he could not bend his elbow to get his thumb into his mouth, play with his genitals, and so on. In the 1930's, a major theme was the importance of regularity and firmness, intended to counter the danger that the child might dominate his parents. Training was scheduled (bowel training was to be completed by eight months) and carried out with unyielding determination.

The 1940's brought a dramatic contrast. The child suddenly became harmless; autoerotism was one manifestation of a natural desire to explore the environment and was probably pursued out of boredom. Toilet training was less rigid; it should begin at eight months or later and be conducted in a more flexible and easygoing fashion.

The theme of control and authority remained, but in a disguised form. The parents of the 1940's were told that if they picked up the child whenever he cried, he might become a tyrant. In toilet training, the mother was urged to avoid battles. If she tried to be tough, she could not win. This strategy of manipulation of the environment rather than direct confrontation with the child appears in other areas of child-rearing as well.

A theme common to many of these efforts is the presumed incompetence of parents, especially those from underprivileged backgrounds. Poor parents have most often been the specific target of intervention. The advice now presumably beneficial to parents, however, is not oriented exclusively toward parents from low-income backgrounds. Middle-class parents are probably the major market for professional counsel and support. The familiar parents' "bible," Spock's (1957) *Baby and Child Care,* saw more than 200 printings from the time it was published in 1946 to the mid-1970's. Seminars or classes for parents, such as Parent Effectiveness Training (Gordon, 1970), are available on the national level and locally through family associations, mental-health clinics, adult-education programs, and governmental agencies. Federal and corporate funds support the production of parent-training programs designed for public television. In addition, columns in the daily papers and magazines—Dr. Brothers and Dr. Salk are examples—offer tips to parents on how to understand and cope with problems of child-rearing. These publications cover the full range of socioeconomic backgrounds.

It is difficult to summarize the trends in current literature on child-rearing because of the diversity of sources and the large number of publications. Cursory examination of this literature, however, suggests that a conception of child-rearing as a form of interpersonal relations and behavior management is a familiar theme. During the past thirty years, a technology of human relations rooted in the behavioral sciences has been developed for use in industrial settings. This includes techniques of negotiation, bargaining, group interaction, and staff management intended to improve efficiency of the unit, reduce interpersonal stress, and raise morale. Some writers—Lasch (1977) is an example—see current parent-education efforts as an extension of this human-relations technology into the family.

There does appear to be less concern with the discipline and socialization of the child toward norms of adult behavior in the community; moral imperatives and issues do not dominate the tone of the advice to parents as they did a century ago. More often, concern about social effectiveness, mental health, individual fulfillment, and self-expression (Maslow is a familiar example) are the significant topics. Discipline, or child management, is not presented as a matter of imposing the authority of the parents on the child's will but of persuasion, sometimes behavioral manipulation, of the child toward rational choice. There is also an emphasis upon the here and now —a focus upon the present that is dramatically contrasted with the concern of the nineteenth century upon working and planning for future security and rewards.

In this new technology of child management, the focus is upon what a parent should do in particular situations, on the techniques that he or she should use in order to bring about a desired behavioral result, and on the principles and procedures that the parent can count on to regulate the behavior of the child. Sometimes the advice is explicit, as in the writings of behavioral psychologists for parents (Becker, 1971). Other literature, however, also instructs parents to respond in a way that will bring about a preferred response. This type of advice about child management is oriented not toward ongoing effective *relationships* between parents and children but toward *strategies* for altering specific observable behaviors.

Change in types of advice for parents parallels changes in the types of authorities who offer it. The experts are no longer the clergy. Psychiatrists, psychologists, social workers, physicians, and teachers are the authorities whose counsel now dominate advice-giving. Their competence is presumably based on accumulated knowledge of their respective disciplines; their status is bolstered by licenses, diplomas, and certificates.

Although the prevailing literature contains little of the "discipline and firmness" themes of the past, these have not disappeared from the minds of parents. A recent study by Yankelovich, Skelly, and White, Inc. (1977), of a national probability sample of 1,230 families in the United States showed that more than one-fourth (28 percent) of parents express strong agreement with the statement, "Strict, old-fashioned upbringing and discipline are still the best ways to raise children." Another 46 percent agree to some extent with the item. Almost three-fourths of the parents want to teach their children that sex outside of marriage is morally wrong. Ninety percent want their children to believe in "duty before pleasure". These are themes that are not often found in the contemporary literature. There is apparently a gap between the concerns of parents and professionals.

These brief glimpses into the history of child-rearing in the United States reveal some of the changes in the nature of advice given to parents. It is difficult, however, to document a relationship between historical circumstances and the popular ideas of any given period. One theme in the early child-rearing literature emphasizes the need to break the child's will. The prevailing religious ideology of the time, especially

Calvinism, probably influenced this conception of proper child-rearing in terms of taming the child's spirit. Other themes, such as the need to control and regulate children's schedules, evident in the 1930's, may have derived from the influence of corporate bureaucratization and popular theories of motivation. The gradual de-emphasis on restrictions of sexuality and aggression parallels the rise of pschoanalytic thought in the 1940's. It is possible to discern patterns in history and associate them with popular theories of child development; it is more difficult, however, to ascribe causation between a specific historical event and particular style of advice offered to parents.

Whatever the origins of the child-rearing themes of the past, it seems likely that the concerns of any given period were those of the family authorities of the time—clergy, representatives of governmental agencies, physicians, psychologists, and so forth. They did not emerge from a compelling body of scientific evidence or from the expressed needs of the parents themselves. Major shifts in the content of parent-education programs seem to represent changes in conceptions of human nature and behavior, especially those of the professional groups who dealt with the family. The history of advice to parents may well be the history of the rise and decline of various professions and the appearance of ideologies and fads in professional thought. These may, in turn, be linked to social movements that make certain types of advice especially attractive. Social and economic climates of the future will perhaps influence education for child-rearing. There is little reason to assume that the views popular today will be favored in 1990.

THE STATE OF KNOWLEDGE ABOUT THE EFFECTS OF CHILD-REARING PRACTICES

The authority of parent educators derives from two sources: 1) professional *prestige* that confers an image of special competence, or 2) a scientifically respectable body of *knowledge* about human behavior. Without attempting to deal in a comprehensive way with the state of theory and research in child development, some general observations are pertinent.

There has been a great deal of progress during the past quarter of a century in knowledge about child behavior and the conditions that affect it. Advances have been made in research on child language, modeling, behavior contingency management, social cognition, the effects of different types of family structure on sex-role development, the relationship of home and other environments to child behavior and other areas of growth and development. The series, *Reviews of Research in Child Development,* produced by the Society of Research on Child Development, is an impressive summary of current and recent achievements. However, it does not detract from the growing prestige of the field to admit that our understanding of the influence of family interaction and parent behavior on children is still primitive. Some of the reservations about the adequacy of our knowledge arise from the caution that accompanies rapid growth in any area of behavior science—today's discovery may be disconfirmed by tomorrow's research findings. Other reservations are specific to research on parent behavior.

A considerable amount of the research on parent-child interaction of the past ten years has been focused on the family's role in the growth of children's cognitive functioning. We know that a significant relationship exists but it is difficult to identify the specific parental behavior or cluster of behaviors that affect the development of a given cognitive ability. Although knowledge is progressing, it is still at an elementary stage. It is also very difficult to justify precise statements about the influence of child-rearing practices on affective and social outcomes in children. Where relationships between parental behavior and child outcomes are statistically significant, the level of correlation is low and cannot serve as a basis for making recommendations to parents about their own individual family situations.

Theories about language acquisition have been dramatically revised in the last fifteen years, even though the study of language has been part of systematic inquiry in developmental psychology for at least half a century. There is still controversy over the interpretations of data on language acquisition. Theories about the operation of the human mental system are being modified under the assault of information-processing theory and other aspects of a new cognitive psychology. The concept of intelligence as a general ability of the mind, the I.Q., notions of intellectual power, and the many techniques developed for assessing mental capabilities, once thought to be central to understanding mental behavior, are now regarded by many to be outmoded conceptualizations that may be misleading and even harmful when used in educational practice.

In other areas, the current level of research activity suggests that there will be rapid changes in both empirical evidence and theory. Social development, social cognition, and effects of family experience on interpersonal competence are fields that are expanding rapidly. The impact of day care, of divorce and father absence, and the effects of recent social changes in adult sex roles upon young children are also arenas of lively research.

The field of behavior management is, perhaps, one area of psychology that has been shown to be sufficiently effective to be included in parent-oriented programs. Its utility as a technique for shaping behavior is well established. What is not so clear is its long-term effect on social and emotional behavior in children. The use of behavior modification techniques is, of course, quite separate from decisions as to what behavior is to be modified or when the technique is to be used.

THE APPLICABILITY OF RESEARCH EVIDENCE TO PARENT EDUCATION

Much of the research literature cannot be generalized to family settings. The purpose of research is to identify relationships among variables. Because these relationships are never perfect, the reports of findings also usually indicate the level of confidence we have in the results. This is a useful procedure for describing relationships among variables for a scientific audience. Such statements of probable association between parental behavior and child outcomes for a large sample, however, are not useful as a basis for diagnosing or prescribing remedial strategies for the unique circumstances of an individual case. The use of a research finding as a basis for judgments about individual families is a hazardous, and conceivably unethical matter. It is appropriate to discuss the implications of data about psychological phenomena in a seminar room; it is less clear that they can be used to guide individual families. Or, they can be used only if the level of confidence in findings is extraordinarily high.

Despite these limitations of experimental research as a valid source of solutions for the problems of individual families, the courts have come to rely frequently on psychological evidence to support judicial opinion (Bradbrook, 1971). Agencies responsible for children draw upon research evidence to help justify their recommendations affecting child custody and other family matters. Valarie Vanaman, senior staff attorney for the Legal Aid Foundation in Los Angeles, recently described the attempts of attorneys on both sides of a custody dispute (parents and social-welfare agencies) to use research and other professional literature to support their arguments and detract from the validity of the opposing position. She added:

> It should be understood that the literature is being used only to enhance the authority of both sides. It is not being used, except in very broad terms, to help the trial judge understand the application of the "best interests" test to these two unique and individual children. Indeed, research literature in this field can rarely be used to absolutely dictate the "best interests" of any particular children since such literature is, of necessity, the aggregation of data designed to identify variables with statistical significance. [APA Division 7 Newsletter, December, 1977, p. 28].

There are other reasons why much of the research data in child development does not necessarily apply to families. Research data are usually generated in studies or experiments that are short-term, often completed in minutes or at most hours. The conditions introduced into the study or experiment are of short duration. Where special conditions are introduced for the purpose of examining their effects, there is rarely an opportunity to consider the long-term effects that might accumulate from such interventions. Even if experimental work demonstrates that a particular behavior can be modified, it does not deal with the possibility that a new bit of behavior may alter other patterns of behavior not the target of the experiment.

A study by Morton (1973) in which teachers were taught to modify a few specific actions illustrates this point. She identified teacher behavior that a previous study had shown to stimulate student interest. Reasoning that student motivation would be further increased if teachers used these techniques more often, she asked teachers to increase the frequency of the specific instructional techniques previously identified. They did so. The changes in these specific actions, however, had unintended consequences. The increase in frequency did not raise the level of attention of the students. In addition, there were unanticipated adjustments in other types of teacher behavior—some things increased, some decreased. Changes in one area triggered unexpected changes in other areas. Thus a relatively simple attempt to apply research findings to interaction in a classroom illustrates an important fact: Implementation of research results may have unpredictable outcomes.

The effort to apply research findings from psychological experiments to family settings is complicated in another way. Much of the data on adult influences on children's behavior is obtained from studies in which the adult who interacts with the children is the research psychologist or a staff member whose relationship to the children in the study is superficial and transitory. This feature of research designs is not accidental. It is intended to control effects of the unique patterns of interaction and affective bond that exists between the parent and child. These sources of variation might alter the effect of the treatment. The consequence, however, is to make the findings of the study nongeneralizable to family situations. In the family, the tie between the mother and child and the quality of their relationship are critical components of interaction. The transitory nature of the relationship between the adult and child in most studies also removes from the research situation the opportunity for the child to influence the adult. The action examined is often unilateral. Serious difficulties are involved in generalizing from the results of studies conducted under such artificial conditions. Family behavior is reciprocal interaction and draws from its own history (Gewirtz and Boyd, 1976). Bronfenbrenner (1974) described the limitations of research of this sort by his now classic comment "*much of American developmental psychology is the science of the behavior of children in strange situations with adults for the briefest possible periods of time.*"

Developmental psychology is, of course, only one of the sources of information for parent-education programs. Psychiatry, clinical psychology, and social work also contribute to the field. Data from the clinical professions, however, come from families who have sought treatment or have been referred to clinics or specialists by the courts or by physicians. The insights that arise from this type of analysis and experience have two serious drawbacks as sources for advice to parents. First, they are based on data from atypical families and their relevance for other families is not always clear. Second, these intensive examinations show that the origins of family behavior are exceedingly complex and are peculiar to the dynamics of a given family.

Another example of professional experience as a source of advice for parents comes from the rapidly growing field of child care and early education. There is, in the child-care field, a loosely bound body of principles for dealing with children. These may come in part from training programs and from the texts that are used in preservice preparation. They may also arise from the organizational demands and goals of institutions that deal with children, as Dreeben (1968), Kanter (1972), and others suggest. Whatever their sources, many professionals develop a special competence in child management, dealing with discipline, sexuality, aggression, anxiety, and other behavior that is common in preschool and day-care settings. The views they have of children and of the appropriate behavior that adults should use with them are not entirely congruent with the views and behavior of parents.

In a recent study, we have found differences between mothers and teachers in their interactive behavior with preschool children and in their expectations about child development (Hess et al., 1978; Conroy et al., 1978; and Dickson et al., 1979). The general pattern is that, compared with teachers, mothers are much more direct in their interaction with their own young children, expect mastery of developmental tasks at an earlier age, and appeal to their own authority more often in regulatory encounters. Teachers tend to be less candid in informing a child when he/she has made a mistake; they appeal to rules rather than their own authority in situations calling for control, and press less for mastery of certain individual skills.

Some examples from a study of mother-child and teacher-child interaction may illustrate this difference. Imagine two hypothetical incidents. In one, a child is writing with a pencil or crayon on the wall. In the other, a child is hitting another child with a block. We asked both mothers and teachers, with responsibility for four-year-olds, to tell us how they would respond to these two events.

In response to the child's writing on the wall, a mother said,

> I would tell him that the wall is not for painting, that there is paper for that purpose, and that he'd better help me clean it up; that the next time he tried anything like that he'd be in deep trouble.

To the same situation, a teacher responded,

I would probably get a sponge and some water—admire the picture and then say now we have to clean it off and next time you want to paint, we will use paper. If you use paper the next time, you can show it to someone, but if it's on the wall, we have to take it off.

In response to the block-throwing or hitting incident, a mother replied,

T_____, you know better than to throw your toys, and then I would make him apologize to the child for doing that, and if he didn't I would stand him in the corner or spank him.

To the same event, a teach said,

I would tell him that blocks are for building and when you throw them, that they hurt people and name the child that got hurt. I don't think he feels very good, but that's about all.

The relationship between child and parents is different in several ways from the relationship between child and caregiver. The mother-child relationship calls for and justifies more direct, intimate interaction, including anger and discipline as well as love and support. The roles are distinct; they evoke dissimilar behavior. My reading of the parent-education literature suggests that the most immediate tendency of professionals is to press parents to adopt the attitudes and behavior of the professional. Given their specialization, training, and experience with children, it is almost inevitable that they should do so.

IS PARENT EDUCATION EFFECTIVE?

As our knowledge about child development grows, attempts to utilize it in parent-oriented programs will continue. The current interest of federal agencies in "strengthening the family," and in parent-education programs for public television will probably not dissipate, especially if the divorce rate continues to rise.

Are these efforts likely to be successful? Brim's (1959) review of the effectiveness of parent-education programs does not give much basis for optimism. Programs developed in the past twenty years may, of course, be more effective than those he reviewed. However, his conclusions of two decades ago have been updated in a report prepared for the Advisory Committee on Child Development of the National Academy of Sciences. This report states, "the research literature provides little in the way of information for policies regarding parent education. If anything, the evidence seems to indicate that parent education is ineffective in altering child rearing practice...." (Amidon and Brim, 1972).

It is an extraordinarily difficult task to change parent behavior. Some information, particularly that having to do with such discrete matters as safety, nutrition, and innoculation, is relatively easy to transmit to parents. However, even such specific information is not readily translated into action. For example, roughly 20 million children in the United States do not have innoculations or immunizations for ordinary childhood diseases. The resulting threat of epidemic has forced some school systems to refuse enrollment to children who lack proof of this type of medical protection. In March 1977, Detroit enforced its revised School Entrant Immunization Law for the first time. After the enforcement program went into effect, almost 22 percent of children, mostly kindergarteners, had still not received the required immunizations (*Morbidity and Mortality Weekly Report,* January 6, 1978).

There are several reasons why parent education is not likely to be effective if pursued in its present form. The efforts of the past have not taken into account the processes through which parents learn to be effective parents. We know very little at the present time about how this kind of competence is acquired. Conventional wisdom is that teachers learn to teach in the classroom; I suspect that parents learn to be parents in their encounters with their children. It is the urgency of a particular situation that elicits a pattern of behavior. Parents' responses to aggression, to the refusal of a child to go to bed, or to eat are formed when the parents are faced with a problem. Parent-education programs are most likely to be successful if they can reach parents at these times of need. But there is little time in the midst of an encounter to consult the child-rearing cookbooks. Parents do not usually store up information to be applied in a future occasion; it is difficult to anticipate the problems and demands of developmental stages their children have not yet encountered. Parent-training programs designed for large audiences cannot provide information when it is needed and most likely to be utilized.

Programs of education are usually intended for mass markets, prepared to be used in a wide range of family situations. This strategy underestimates the degree of individual differences between families and between children of the same family. To be useful, information about child-rearing should be tailored to the specific situations of a particular family. This is virtually impossible to achieve except in direct involvement with individual families. There is not one best model of child-rearing that can be held up for emulation, except at a level of abstraction that is useless for most parents. Styles of parents differ; the cultures that families develop vary tremendously from one home to another. Even within families, the "best" way to deal with a given situation varies with the circumstances of the family at that time in its own history—number of children, spacing between births, sex of child, health, performance in school, friendship with children outside the family, and so forth.

The situations that parents encounter also are affected by the economic, social, and cultural backgrounds of the family. Parents who are affluent have different needs than parents who are poor; cultural and ethnic backgrounds influence the types of problems parents encounter and the solutions that will best serve their children. Single parents face problems not confronted by families where both parents are living together; parents without custody face still another array of needs and demands. The litany of family individuality can easily be extended, but the point is clear. To be effective, parent education must deal with the specific needs of parents, but these vary enormously from one family to the next. Perhaps efforts might be directed toward identifiable subgroups within the society. A start in this direction is the publication of books for black parents (Comer and Paussaint, 1975) and books for divorced parents (Galper, 1978). This solution, of course, does not deal with family-to-family variation within such subgroups.

Another problem is that parent behavior is determined by both parent and child. It is not a sequence of predetermined acts that parents learn in preparation for an event; it is behavior that emerges from the interaction between two (or more) individuals—a pattern of reciprocal responses between parent and child that develop over time. In the culture that each family develops, the child makes a major contribution.

The behavior of the parent is, in part, under the control of the child. There are recurring patterns of dependence, mistrust, aggression, resentment, and exploitation that must be faced again and again. The vignettes of parent-child problems and their solutions that appear in newspaper columns often do not correspond to real life. The history of the relationship is not thrown out with the newspaper; it remains to complicate attempts the parent may make to imitate the coping strategies described in the columns of child-rearing advice.

Even with good advice, parents can't always live up to their ideals. Those who realize that a particular pattern of interaction with the child often leads to a mini-disaster may not always be able to avoid it. Fatigue, stress, and frustration accumulated in work or other nonfamily areas of life erode the resolve and stamina required to be a perfect parent. Parents are part of a network in which they also respond to events; they are sometimes the victims of influences they cannot control.

If it is to deal with interactional processes, parent education is not education in the usual sense. It is an attempt to change established patterns of interpersonal behavior that have a history in the experience of the family members. The strategies that are developed in interpersonal exchange (Berne, 1964) are useful because they represent partial solutions to complex relationships with others. They are not easily relinquished.

These problems encountered by parent-education programs are enormous. It is difficult to provide information that is sufficiently specific to deal with the events of a particular family, to make it available at the time needed, to adapt it to the many variations of culture and economic conditions, to develop techniques that will give parents insight into the patterns of their family interaction, and to help them alter those patterns over time. These are barriers of the most formidable sort.

SOME UNINTENDED CONSEQUENCES OF PROFESSIONAL INTERVENTION IN FAMILY LIFE

The efforts devoted to parent education have been directed toward the *content* of the advice we should deliver rather than to the techniques that we use to get it to parents. Our concern with the interaction between parent and child obscures the possible effects of the relationship that exists between the professionals and parents. We suggest that the methods used by professionals deserve scrutiny. It is conceivable that the strategies through which advice is delivered have side effects that mitigate the potential benefits of such advice. The underlying messages conveyed by parent-education programs can alter the parents' view of themselves and erode their competence as parents.

Child-rearing in American society requires that parents develop their own values about a range of behaviors—T.V. viewing, common courtesies of social interaction, food habits, sex play, school performance, moral values, and a host of other specifics on which they must decide whether to take a stand. It is obvious to both parents and children that a number of different standards exist in the community. Parents do not usually have a supporting network of families that share their values and assist them in their child-rearing tasks. The (relative) absence of community consensus and support contrasts sharply with some other countries—China and Cuba are examples. In these countries, there is overwhelming agreement about the types of behavior that are approved. Child-rearing is the responsibility of all adults in the community. In the United States, parents often stand alone.

The lack of consensus about many of the behaviors that they deal with from day to day adds a particular burden for parents. They must create their own family culture; the authority of the community is weakened by the number of different options that are available. Children can usually find someone in the neighborhood who is permitted to do whatever their own parents would like to prohibit; T.V. shows not approved at home can be seen at a friend's house. The authority of the parents, not that of the community, is the central influence in child-rearing.

The authority on which the child-rearing is based is thin. The depth of a network of supporting institutions and community sentiment is often lacking. On some issues —violence in T.V. programming and commercials for sugar-coated snacks, for example—major institutions align against parents on the rationale that it is the parents' responsibility to protect their children from harmful effects of television fare.

Parents recognize their need for help. Some impressive evidence about the level of concern of parents comes from the Yankelovich, Skelly, and White, Inc. study. Many parents, especially those from one-parent homes, feel some lack of confidence in themselves as parents (Table 10.1). They express the need for help in dealing with a range of problems: drugs (49 percent); discipline (36 percent); solving problems of being parents (34 percent); and teaching children about religion (32 percent) or sex (31 percent) (Yankelovich, Skelly, and White, Inc., 1977, p. 120).

Other evidence of the need for help that parents feel are the sales figures of the advice-to-parents books on the market. They are impressive; some titles are claimed to have had sales of over half a million copies in the hardcover edition; paperback sales probably reach at least that figure and are still selling (Clarke-Stewart, 1978). Columns appear in newspapers and magazines written in response to parental interest. Teachers in preschools and elementary grades know from their own experience of parents' desire to discuss family and child-rearing problems.

In the past thirty years, there has been a rise in the number of professionals who deal with children and their families. The membership of the National Association

Table 10.1
SELF-CONFIDENCE IN SELVES AS PARENTS

	All Parents	Single Parents
Feel good about the job they are doing in raising their children	63%	45%
Worry about the job they are doing in raising their children	36%	50%

Note: 1 percent of all parents, 5 percent of single parents are not sure.
Source: Yankelovich, Skelly, and White, Inc., The General Mills American Family Report 1976–77, p. 64.

for the Education of Young Children, for example, grew from less than 1,000 in 1956 to over 28,000 in 1976. The American Academy of Pediatrics reports that its membership has grown from slightly over 5,000 in 1957 to more than 14,000 in 1977. The

American Academy of Child Psychiatrists had a membership of 102 in 1953, compared with 2,100 in 1978. Between 1954 and 1974, the membership of the American Psychological Association soared from 12,380 to 37,371. Roughly a third of APA members are clinical psychologists. Obviously, not all of the members of these professional groups deal directly with child-rearing, but the trends in membership over the past twenty years may indicate something of the increase in the number of professionals in specialities oriented toward families.

Professional groups draw their advice for parents from research and clinical experience, both of which have high prestige in the community. This prestige is bolstered by credentials, licenses, certificates, and diplomas, and by state laws that prohibit counseling without proper certification. The public reputation that professionals enjoy and their claims of special competence in dealing with children help persuade parents that their advice is to be respected.

The image of professionals as sources of expert advice is shared by the parents themselves. The survey of Yankelovich, Skelly, and White, Inc. (1977) included a question about where parents would turn for counsel about problems of raising children. Their responses show the dominant position of professionals in the parents' perception (Table 10.2).

Table 10.2
WHERE PARENTS WOULD BE MOST AND LEAST
LIKELY TO SEEK ADVICE

	Most Likely %	Least Likely %
Children's teachers	49	9
Family physicians	35	12
Priests/ministers/rabbis	37	18
Child psychologists	34	18
School principals	28	15
Own parents	27	24
Juvenile authorities	26	24
Family agencies	17	23
Friends	28	36
Social workers	15	27
Local clinics	10	28
Relatives	17	42

Source: Yankelovich, Skelly, and White, Inc., The General Mills American Family Report 1976–77, p. 119.

The most popular books written for parents present the twin themes of professional competence and the need of parents for training. A few excerpts from some of the best sellers illustrate these views. The quotes are not referenced; they are illustrative and are not intended to identify particular authors. Here is one example, from a book published in 1964:

The problems that our children present are increasing in frequency and intensity, and many parents do not know how to cope with them. . . . While working with parents and children for forty years, it became evident to me that the methods we suggest for the solution of family conflicts are indeed effective. They have been tested in the laboratory of our family counseling centers.

A second comes from a volume that appeared about a year later:

No parent wakes up in the morning planning to make his child's life miserable . . . yet, in spite of good intentions, the unwanted war breaks out again.

All parents want their children to be secure and happy. . . . Yet in the process of growing up, many children acquire undesirable characteristics and fail to achieve a sense of security and an attitude of respect for themselves and for others.

The purpose of this book is to help parents identify their goals in relation to children and to suggest methods of achieving those goals. . . . It is a practical guide: it offers concrete suggestions and preferred solutions for dealing with daily situations and psychological problems faced by all parents.

An author who presents another approach in 1968 writes:

Each year thousands of parents seek professional advice on how to handle problems with their children. . . . This poses a strange question. How is it that well-meaning, loving parents can have a child who behaves in a manner that makes him, his parents, and his teacher miserable?

We believe that it is quite easy for a parent to teach a child to develop problem behaviors. . . .

For several years (the authors and social scientists) have been working to develop a method of showing parents how to encourage desirable behavior in their children and gradually eliminate undesirable behavior. . . .

Any parent should be able to change the behavior of his or her children by using the method presented in this book. . . .

Two years later, in 1970, another author writes:

Parents are blamed but not trained. Millions of new mothers and fathers take on a job each year that ranks among the most difficult anyone can have. . . .

Yet how many parents are effectively trained for it? I took a very small step toward filling this void. . . . We have demonstrated. . . .that with a certain kind of special training many parents can greatly increase their effectiveness in parenthood. They can acquire very specific skills that will keep the channels of communication open. . . .

And they can learn a new method of resolving parent-child conflicts that brings about a strengthening rather than a deterioration of the relationship.

These are examples; many others could be offered. They serve to illustrate the image of authority and expertness that is projected to the reading audience. It is not argued that these claims are exaggerated, but evidence of effectiveness would be welcome.

The writers of parent-education materials share a mistrust of the family as an institution for raising children. Some of this view is evident in the above quotes. Occasionally, it is even more explicit. Evelyn Millis Duval (1943), the director of the Association for Family Living, claimed that "only one profession remains untutored and untrained – the bearing and rearing of our children." This unfavorable evaluation of parental competence also appears in more recent writings:

> The relatively few social scientists who have actually observed parents and children interacting at home have not been greatly impressed by all the mothers they have seen. For example, one of the writers recently spoke to a psychologist carrying out a large, long-term study of about forty young children and their families. When asked how many of these mothers she thought were really competent, who gave her no cause to worry about their effects on the children, physical or emotional, the psychologist thought for a moment and said, "Well, I don't believe in the concept of a 'good mother,' but I'd say about three." Indeed, a number of recent theories of schizophrenia have argued that the isolated nuclear family provides a fertile setting for driving children crazy [Skolnick and Skolnick, 1971, p. 306].

Contemporary views of early education specialists about the competence of many parents to prepare their children for academic achievement follow a similar pattern, with a few notable exceptions. Much of the literature on which Head Start and comparable programs were based presents a description of the family as a major contributor to the educational problems of children (Maccoby and Zellner, 1970; Chilman, 1973).

Parent-education programs thus seem to convey three messages to parents: First, they probably do not have the competence needed for child-rearing; second, knowledge and techniques for dealing with children are available; third, if they wish, they can acquire these skills. A fourth message is implicit but unavoidable – if parents are not successful, it is their own fault (Schlossman, 1978).

In a sense, programs and materials designed for parents create a para-social relationship between parents and professionals, even though there is no direct personal contact between them. In this relationship, parents are clearly amateurs. The prestige of the professional is very high, often bolstered by an institutional base – a clinic, a school, a day-care center, a welfare agency, a probation department, a community agency, or a university. The authoritative, confident tone of the child-rearing manuals contrasts vividly with the parent's awareness of her/his own struggles to deal with the complexities of raising children.

Parent-education programs can induce in parents feelings of powerlessness and dependence on the advice of professionals. Awareness of their own lack of skills makes them more vulnerable to voices of authority. Dependence erodes the parent's effectiveness with her/his children and feelings of inadequacy make it difficult for parents to acquire new skills. Research on learned helplessness shows that experiences and expectation of failure depress the ability to learn, the tendency to take initiative, and increase the desire to turn to others for assistance (Seligman, 1975). Confusion and uncertainty also mar the parent's potency as a model for the child, since models are more likely to be imitated and internalized if they have high status and power.

The effect of advice to parents on the self-image and self-confidence of the par-

ents themselves deserves closer examination. Attempts to advise parents have concentrated on the methods that parents should use with their children and have
neglected the methods that professionals use with parents. A thorough analysis of
parent education as a strategy of intervention is overdue.

SOME THOUGHTS FOR DESIGNING STRATEGIES FOR PARENT-EDUCATION PROGRAMS

I am suggesting in this essay that we examine the models from which parent-
education programs are designed and the consequences for parents of the approaches
that are traditional in the field. We have concentrated efforts on identifying the type
of advice that parents need. I suggest that the system through which the advice is
delivered is itself an important part of the program.

We do not now have a body of knowledge or theory about how competence in
child-rearing is acquired or maintained by parents. Perhaps the most useful step at
this time would be to undertake systematic studies of parental competence and the
processes through which parents learn. These studies could provide the basic information for decisions about future parent support and development efforts. The assumptions underlying programs of parent education may be unsound. Some skills are
not usually learned in formal instructional settings. Language and communication
competence, for example, are acquired outside the school. Competence in child-rearing may also be developed through processes not easily amenable to formal instruction. The most pressing need, perhaps, is to build a knowledge base about parental
skills and the influences that shape family interaction.

The instructional technique on which many of our attempts are based is, in the
classroom terminology, the lecture. We tell parents what they should do. We offer
information we believe to be accurate, assuming that parents will be able to make
good use of it. The "lectures" are delivered through books, journal articles, newspaper columns, and T.V. programs in which the actual contact between professional
and parent is distant and impersonal. While such channels may be useful in transmitting specific information about factual matters of health, safety, and the like, it does
not seem reasonable that these methods of "instruction" will significantly help parents in the interpersonal aspects of child-rearing and parent-child interaction.

It is not obvious that there are alternative models of parent education that are
economically feasible and realistic from the standpoint of organization. Alternative
strategies cannot be quickly or easily developed, but it may be worthwhile to consider some of the principles on which other approaches could be designed.

A reconceptualization of the respective roles of parents and professionals would
be a useful place to start. The relationship between the professional, as authority
(teacher), and the parent, as student, plays a crucial part in the educational process.
The usefulness of many programs of education is hindered by procedures that play
on the authority of the professional and the incompetence of parents. A different
view of the process is one that emphasizes the authority of the parent, as parent, and
casts the professional in the role of consultant. It is the parent, of course, who makes
decisions about child-rearing and takes personal responsibility for their consequences. Programs intended to assist parents can be designed to support parental authority by playing a supporting rather than an instructing role.

Effectiveness of parents is eroded by techniques that increase self-doubt and uncertainty. There is a directness and spontaneity of interaction that is diffused by hesitation or undue concern about what action to take. A program that supports the parent's objectives can also enhance the effectiveness of the parent, both as a model and as a source of guidance and authority.

A redesign of parent education could give parents a different perception of child-rearing by recognizing the complexity of the task. The tone of many parent-training publications suggests that their job is really very simple once the essentials are mastered. These descriptions only faintly resemble the realities that parents face. Child-rearing demands energy, patience, persistence, wisdom, self-control, executive ability, and stamina. It also has great rewards, but many of these are earned with considerable effort. This is especially true for households with one parent and for those where both parents work. It is not likely that parenthood will be given more acclaim and higher status in the society generally, but, as a starting point, professionals in parent education might recognize the difficulty of the task that parents face. It is demoralizing for parents to be told that child-rearing is a relatively simple undertaking when they find they are not able to deal successfully with some of the more "routine" events of parent-child interaction. As a considerable body of research on motivation shows (Weiner, 1974), a sense of effectiveness is a function of the perceived difficulty of the task. If the task is difficult, failure can be accepted; if it is perceived as easy, failure is a serious threat to confidence and self-esteem.

It might be helpful if we, as professionals, were more modest in our claims. The field of evaluation research is strewn with corpses of programs that looked good in experimental stages but could not survive transplanting into the real world. The helping professions have great resources to offer, but the task of helping families is difficult and our success rate will sustain only limited claims.

A reconsideration of our approach to parent education might take more seriously the established principle that initiative on the part of the learner is a crucial element in the development of a new skill. Teachers learn to teach when confronted by a classroom; perhaps parents also learn their role primarily on the job. Patterns of behavior are developed in the crucible of interaction. During these formative stages parents are in the best position to learn from others, especially from models. These can be provided not by professionals but by other parents.

A program of parent education might be based on a concept of self-help and mutual support among parents from different families and with varying levels of experience. The wisdom and experience of other parents may be the major resource available for developing competence. Groups of participating parents might themselves identify, through discussion of their own personal experience, the problems that they face and their techniques for dealing with them. There is an authenticity that comes from having shared an experience; to realize that another parent has been through the problem gives a sense of confidence in their judgment and advice.

Mutual support groups assist parents in another way. The realization that other parents have problems they find difficult to solve carries a unique reassurance. Parents who are unable to deal with a particular problem or find they have feelings of guilt or anger about their role or about their child often experience a great sense of relief when they discover that these feelings are shared by other parents. The fear that one is uniquely incompetent is dissipated by the knowledge that others have similar struggles.

A group of parents who support one another and share problems and child-rearing techniques also offer one another alternative ways to deal with a given situation.

This suggests to parents that there is more than one way to be effective—not a single, best, officially sanctioned method. Such group exchanges also help parents realize that each family is in some ways unique; a tactic that is successful for one family may not be the best for another.

Parents should become selective consumers of information and advice, choosing from each other and professionals the information that they need. Their confidence in the opinion of professionals would be based on their own shared experience, not on the authority of the institution or individual. They would be more prepared to select and to reject counsel. They would also be able to support one another in a way that no professional, packet of filmstrips, or printed material could—through personal interaction and friendship.

An approach of this kind would require the collaboration of the professional community. This is a very large order, indeed, since professionals use the techniques they believe to be most useful. Research on how parental competence is developed may help us redefine our own role. We can be available as resources to be called upon, supporting the authority and role of parents. Our efforts, despite their good intentions, have sometimes been an intrusion into the family network. Our function is quite different from that of public health officers who have an obligation to intervene for the health of the family. Such intervention, even when unwelcome, is appropriate in cases of clear danger to family members—child abuse or neglect, for example. It may be less appropriate for dealing with child-rearing functions of the society.

Some programs have been developed along lines consistent with the principles described here. Dave Weikart, in Ypsilanti, began an intensive parent-development program several years ago that used staff members to help parents achieve the goals they set for themselves. I have heard of other arrangements where mutual support programs are initiated and organized by parents. Perhaps the consciousness-raising format used by women involved in their liberation efforts offers an example of mutual support that could be adapted for parents. Although the organizational difficulties are serious, it would be worthwhile to examine the effectiveness of such groups and try to develop models that parents who wish to organize their own groups could use. Hopefully, we can return child-rearing to parents.

BIBLIOGRAPHY

American Psychological Association Newsletter, Division on Developmental Psychology, December, 1977.

Amidon, A., and Brim, O. G. What do children have to gain from parent education? Prepared for the Advisory Committee on Child Development, National Academy of Sciences, 1972 (mimeo).

Becker, W. C. *Parents are teachers.* Champaign: Research Press, 1971.

Berne, E. *Games people play.* New York: Grove Press, 1964.

Bradbrook, A. The relevance of psychological and psychiatric studies to the future development of the laws governing the settlement of interparental child custody disputes. *Journal of Family Law,* 1971, *2,* 556–587.

Bremner, R. *Children and youth in America: a documentary history.* Cambridge: Harvard University Press, 1970–74.

Brim, O. G. *Education for Child Rearing.* New York: Russell Sage Foundation, 1959.

Bronfenbrenner, U. Developmental Research, Public Policy, and the Ecology of Childhood. *Child Development,* 1974, *45,* 1–5.

Chilman, C. S. Programs for Disadvantaged Parents. In B. M. Caldwell and H. N. Ricciuti

(Eds.), *Review of Child Development Research* (Vol. 3). Chicago: The University of Chicago Press, 1973.

Clark-Stewart, K. A. Popular Primers for Parents. *American Psychologist,* April, 1978, *33,* (4), 359–369.

Comer, J., and Paussaint, A. *Black Child Care.* Pocket Books, Simon and Schuster, 1975.

Conroy, M., Hess, R. D., Kashiwagi, K., and Azuma, H. *Maternal Strategies for Regulating Children's Behavior in Japanese and American Families.* In press.

Dickson, W. P., Hess, R. D., Miyake, N., and Azuma, H. Referential Communication Between Mother and Children as a Predictor of the Child's Cognitive Development. *Child Development,* 1979, *50,* 53–59.

Downs, A. Up and Down with Ecology: The Issue Attention Cycle. *The Public Interest,* 1971, 39–50.

Duval, E. M. Growing Edges in Family Life Education. *Marriage and Living,* Vol. 5, 1943.

Dreeben, R. The Contribution of Schooling to the Learning of Norms. *Socialization and Schools.* Harvard University, 1968, 23–49.

Galper, M. *Co-parenting: Sharing Your Child.* Philadelphia: Running Press, 1978.

Gewirtz, J. L., and Boyd, E. F. Mother-Infant Interaction and Its Study. In H. W. Reese (Ed.), *Advances in child development and Behavior,* 1976, *11,* 141–163.

Gordon, T. *P.E.T.: Parent Effectiveness Training.* New York: Peter Wyden, Inc., 1970.

Hess, R. D., Dickson, W. P., Price, G. G., and Leong, D. Some Contrasts Between Mothers and Child Care Staff in Interaction with Four-Year-Old Children. *American Educational Research Journal,* 1979, *16,* 3, 307–316.

Joffe, C. *The Friendly Intruders.* Berkeley: University of California Press, 1977.

Kanter, R. The Organization Child: Experience Management in a Nursery School. *Sociology of Education,* Spring 1972, *45,* 186–212.

Lasch, C. *Haven in a Heartless World: the Family Besieged.* New York: Basic Books, 1977.

Maccoby, E. E., and Zellner, M. *Experiments in Primary Education: Aspects of Project Follow-Through.* San Francisco: Harcourt Brace Jovanovich, Inc., 1970.

Morbidity and Mortality Weekly Report, January 6, 1978.

Morton, A. R. The impact of changes in selected teacher strategies on expressive student engagement. Unpublished doctoral dissertation, Stanford University, 1973.

Platt, A. *The child savers.* Chicago: Chicago University Press, 1969.

Schlossman, S. L. Before Home Start: Notes Toward a History of Parent Education in America, 1897–1929. *Harvard Educational Review,* August 1976, *46,* (3), 436–467.

Schlossman, S. L. The parent education game: the politics of child psychology in the 1970's *Teachers College Record,* May, 1978, *79,* (4), 788–808.

Seligman, M. E. P. *Helplessness.* San Francisco: W. H. Freeman & Co., 1975.

Skolnick, A. S., and Skolnick, J. H. (Eds.). *Family in Transition.* Boston: Little, Brown & Co., 1971, p. 306.

Spock, B. *Baby and Child Care.* New York: Duell, Sloan and Pearce, 1957.

Sunley, R. Early Nineteenth-Century American Literature on Child Rearing. In M. Mead and M. Wolfenstein (Eds.). *Childhood in Contemporary Culture.* Chicago: University of Chicago Press, 1964, 150–167.

Weiner, B. *Achievement Motivation and Attribution Theory.* Morristown New Jersey: General Learning Press, 1974.

Wolfenstein, M. Fun Morality: an Analysis of Recent American Child Training Literature. In M. Mead and M. Wolfenstein (Eds.). *Childhood in Contemporary Culture.* Chicago: University of Chicago Press, 1964.

Yankelovich, Skelly, and White, Inc. *Raising Children in a Changing Society: The General Mills American Family Report.* Minneapolis, 1977.

11

What Can "Research Experts" Tell Parents about Effective Socialization?

MICHAEL E. LAMB
Assistant Professor of Psychology
Univeristy of Wisconsin
Madison, Wisconsin

This chapter will differ substantially from most in this volume. Instead of devoting a brief section to the presentation of policy recommendations, I will spend the entire chapter presenting my case for caution in the translation of research findings into policy recommendations. I choose to do this because, given the present state of our knowledge concerning socialization, I am uncomfortable about attempts to distill prescriptions for effective parenting from research findings. I am uneasy not because we know nothing of relevance, but because there is a distressing tendency for tentative findings to become hallowed principles, for essential qualifications to be forgotten, and more generally, for notions about *one* of the major inputs to the socialization process (the parents' contribution) to be portrayed as rules regarding the sole essential inputs to the process. Effective parenting and successful socialization depend on at least three considerations: (a) the goals and values of the parents; (b) the characteristics of the child; and (c) the practices and mores of the culture and subculture. Any description of effective parental behavior which fails to acknowledge the importance of the child's individuality, and the impact of other socializing agents (peers, schools, teachers, the media), and their implicit values, is at best misleading; at worst it is dangerously counterproductive. Unfortunately, however, policy applications can seldom make extensive allowance for individual variations of this sort, and we know too little about these complex issues to permit detailed and informed recommendations.

To illustrate the above, the first section of this chapter will comprise an outline of what one might view as the principal components of effective parenting. I will discuss only the conclusions for which there is substantial empirical support, and will stress the problems inherent in attempts to translate research findings into useful advice to parents. Thereafter, I will buttress my skeptical introduction with a brief discussion of the conceptual problems inherent in attempts to determine the characteristics of effective parents and to amend the process of socialization through the modification of parental styles. I will illustrate my argument by reference to one of the best studies—that directed by Diana Baumrind of the University of California at Berkeley. I will concern myself solely with socialization and the development of sociopersonality characteristics, whereas most of the other contributors focus on the facilitation of cognitive competence by parents. I believe, however, that my reservations apply whether one focuses on social or cognitive development.

THE CAUTIOUS PRESCRIPTIONS

Although one should not look to experts or researchers for easy formulae that purport to contain the essential principles of parenting, it is possible to make some cautious generalizations based on what we know about the effects of parents on children.

One key concept is clearly *sensitivity* or *empathic understanding*. Much of the work on mother-infant interaction suggests that the mother's sensitivity to infant signals (that is, her ability to interpret the baby's cues accurately and respond appropriately) is a major predictor of the quality of the relationship they develop (for example, see Ainsworth et al., 1974; Schaffer and Emerson, 1964; Blehar et al., 1977). The same may be true of father-infant relations, though the evidence is scanty (Schaffer and Emerson, 1964). Similarly, Baumrind's data suggest that the most effective parents—those who adopt an authoritative style—are notable for their willingness to "meet their children as persons, and maintain sufficient flexibility in the fact of their child's individuality that they can learn from it the kind of parenting to which it best responds" (Lamb and Baumrind, 1978). This sensitivity is probably related to the concept of nurturance which Mussen (1967) and Radin (1976) have emphasized in their discussions of identification. These researchers have shown that children are more likely to identify with warm and nurturant parents than with hostile, distant, or rejecting parents. Though the specific parental behavior that is appropriate obviously changes in relation to the child's age, therefore, the importance of sensitivity/empathy appears constant. This implies that effective parenting involves guiding children and encouraging the flowering of their individual propensities, rather than stamping in alien behavior patterns. Effective parents are able to determine the extent to which their children need guidance, and the extent to which they would benefit from the challenge of performing independently.

Unfortunately, sensitivity is a concept which is easy to describe verbally, yet remarkably difficult to concretize in a manner that may facilitate the training of parents and parents-to-be. Perhaps realistic information concerning the capacities and limitations of children of different ages would be most useful, inasmuch as it would provide parents with some basis for developing reasonable expectations. Too many books romanticize the wonder of children and the joys of parenthood; in so doing, they unrealistically portray the responsibilities and burdens of parenthood. It is easy, for example, for "experts" to speak rapturously of the recently bathed, powdered, rested, and healthy children they see in their offices or laboratories, but parents should know that babies can be frustrating, irritating, irritable, and burdensome, and that infants give precious little acknowledgement for "services rendered" for an unconscionable length of time. This does not mean that experts should aim to dampen the enthusiasm of young parents, or depict parenthood as an impersonal mechanical process. If we desire *better* parents rather than *more* parents, however, we need to communicate facts about attainments and capacities so that parents can formulate reasonable expectations regarding their children's development and can make appropriate demands of them.

Perhaps the most vexing dilemma for parents concerns the appropriateness and effectiveness of discipline and punishment. On the one hand, there are those who stress the importance of molding the child after the parents' image (the authoritarian viewpoint), while on the other, there are those who emphasize the self-actualizing propensity of children, and the dangers inherent in squelching this propensity (the permissive viewpoint). Baumrind's (1975a) studies suggest that both extremes are undesirable: that socially competent children are more likely to come from families that are "authoritative" rather than either "authoritarian" or "permissive" (Baumrind, 1975a). Authoritative parents are those who direct or guide their children in a rational issue-oriented manner. They tend, as noted above, to be sensitive to the child's needs and capabilities. Unlike authoritarian or permissive parents, they realize that children are immature and that they need guidance (mediated both by reward and attention, and by punishment and limit-setting) if they are ultimately to function optimally in the society.

A related modulator of familial influence is the *consistency* of parental demands. Nothing distorts the acquisition of socially approved behavior more thoroughly than parents whose discipline is capricious, whose attention and response are unpredictable, and whose wishes are ill defined. Effective parents should set reasonable and reasoned standards and should maintain these standards consistently thereafter. On the other hand—and this is why expert advice rapidly becomes confusing—they should not be inflexible and insensitive in formulating and enforcing their demands.

Successful socialization involves more than imposing demands and guiding children directly. It is increasingly apparent that what parents do *in front of* their children may be as significant as what they do *to* their children. Most children—particularly those whose parents are nurturant and accessible—are motivated to emulate their parents (Bandura, 1977; Mussen, 1967). By imitating parental models, children learn many complex behavior patterns, particularly those related to sex roles and (perhaps) morality. Although the early theoretical formulations stressed the noninvolvement of explicit reinforcement in these observational learning processes, it is evident that the effectiveness of modeling is greatly enhanced by parental encouragement of the identification, and by their explicit approval of the child's attempts to emulate its parents. The ideal course is to reward the motivation, while gently correcting the performance, bearing in mind the child's ability to render adult behavior patterns.

THE PRESCRIPTIVE CAUTIONS

Let's turn our attention now to the cautions: the reasons underlying my reservations about the inferences that can be drawn from research findings.

The major problem is inherent in the correlational research strategies upon which studies of socialization must rely—how can we determine the direction of effects? Eminent researchers like Diana Baumrind usually begin (implicitly or explicitly) with a description of what they believe to be the "perfect" child—the ideal outcome of the parenting process. They then seek to define parental characteristics that are correlated with the children's styles. For Baumrind, the ideal child is one who is assertive, autonomous, independent, socially competent, and not intrusive with adults; and her studies have provided reliable and replicable evidence about the characteristics and attitudes of the parents of such socially competent preschoolers (Baumrind, 1975a). In general, the most effective parents appeared to be those Baumrind called "authoritative." These parents attempted to direct their children in a rational issue-oriented manner; they encouraged independence while also valuing comformity to cultural mores. Permissive and authoritarian parents were not successful in producing socially competent children: They either provided insufficient guidance or thoroughly forbade independent effort, badly misjudging the developmentally appropriate needs of their children.

At first blush, then, it appears that we have here the "answer": careful research indicating quite clearly which patterns of child-rearing and parental behavior produce "appropriate" behavior patterns in young children. Unfortunately, however, Baumrind's subsequent follow-up failed to substantiate these seemingly robust findings (Baumrind, 1975b). Analyses across time failed to support the conclusion that parental practices *caused* reliable and predictable differences in the children's behavior. Although only preliminary findings from the longitudinal study have been reported, it appears that the differential effectiveness of the various patterns of child-rearing all but disappeared. By the time her subjects had reached nine years of age, Baumrind found no clear evidence that the children of authoritative parents were more socially competent than the children of parents with vastly different disciplinary styles.

Why the discrepancy? Well, if one looks at the original studies closely, one is struck by the troubling fact that they are entirely dependent on correlational data. In her interpretation, Baumrind had to assume that the social competence of the children at five years of age was a product of–was caused by–the behavior and attitudes of the parents. Unfortunately, parents and children were each assessed only once (all at roughly the same time) so the direction of effects is really obscure. It is quite conceivable that the apparent rationality and effectiveness of the authoritative parents was due, at least in part, to the fact that their children were significantly more socially competent, less intrusive–in short, more manageable disciplinary problems. In other words, perhaps the parents' behavior is as much a response to the children's personality styles as a cause of them. Thus the *cause* of the children's desirable behavior may remain partially (or completely) unexplained. This is not to say that cause and effect can never be elucidated in studies of socialization. Only longitudinal studies can yield the answers we seek, however, and the field's experience with longitudinal studies suggests that the answers are not easily attained!

One critical problem with research on socialization as well as with parent-education projects is the implicit assumption that all children are equally and similarly malleable. More crudely, certain parental practices are portrayed as the necessary and sufficient conditions for *forming* certain personality styles in children. This is, to my mind, an unreasonable assumption. Although it is certainly not true that the way children develop is uninfluenced by their parents (in particular) or their rearing environment (in general), we must appreciate that there are also innate differences in temperament and potential. These differences are not the sole determinants of a child's personality either. The "outcome" is dependent on an intimate and ill-understood *interaction* between the child's innate individual characteristics and the rearing environment. The findings of the New York Longitudinal Study illustrate this most clearly, the methodological inadequacies of the particular study notwithstanding. The children who eventually needed psychiatric attention, Thomas et al., (1968)

found, were not simply those who were characterized from early in life by their "difficult" temperaments, nor those whose parents were characterized by maladaptive
styles, but those for whom there was a *mismatch* between the infants' termperament
and the parents' styles.

Such an interactionist conclusion has practical as well as theoretical implications. Most important, as far as the goals of this volume are concerned, is the implication that there can be no hard-written prescriptions for effective parenting, because
the parental behaviors that are effective in achieving a given outcome (that is, a child
who behaves in the desired manner) will vary considerably depending on the nature
of the individual child concerned. To the notion that authoritative parenting may be
most effective, then, we must emphasize a qualification: Sensitivity to the needs, developmental level, and individual personality of the particular child with whom one
is dealing is of crucial importance, as is the ability to monitor one's own behavior
and demands so as to challenge but not overestimate the potential of the child.

Further qualifications are necessary when we bring into contention an additional complicating wrinkle–the societal mores. Unfortunately or fortunately, parents are not the sole arbiters of their offspring's future. Socialization is a complex
process, to which parents and siblings, as well as teachers, peers, and the media all
contribute. Further, socialization serves to prepare children to function independently and competently in the society. This has two implications for parents. First, to
the extent that parents may have legitimate but unconventional goals for their children, they have to compete with a variety of other socializing agents most of which
have a profoundly conservative function. With the possible exception of the adolescent peer group, all extrafamilial sources of influence exert strong pressures toward
maintenance of the *status quo* (compare Lamb, and Urberg, 1978). In addition, while
attempting to guide the development of their offspring, "counterculture" parents
have to bear in mind that the child must one day live in a wider society in which
others will expect the child to behave in accordance with different values or mores.
Parents may be forced, consequently, to compromise between what they believe to be
best for their child overall, and what will be best for the child in the context of a
given social framework. This, too, is likely to exert a conservative influence. Consider, for example, a "liberated" family that rejects traditional sex stereotyping because of the inequalities this imposes. The best-intentioned opposition to traditional
sex-role sterotyping becomes considerably more muted when a hypothetical problem
becomes an issue concerning how to raise one's own child. The problem is that while
they may oppose "unreasonable" inequalities (that is, aspects of gender role) most
parents wish their children to have secure gender *identities*–that is, to be content
with and proud of their status as male or female. Since neither parents nor experts
know which aspects of sex-differentiating treatment are necessary to ensure secure
gender identity and which are merely antecedents of aspects of gender role, parents
are forced to gamble on the basis of incomplete knowledge in making a decision that
may have important consequences for the course and quality of a child's life. The
least risky course is to conform: consequently, parental uncertainty may have a profoundly conservative effect.

There is another issue we need to address–one that is implicit in most studies of
socialization but is seldom considered directly. Is it the parents' *way* of posing demands in raising their children that is critical, or the *content* of the demands themselves? If we look closely at most of the research in this area we find a focus on style
rather than substance. Investigators have conducted research on the effects or effec-

tiveness of "punitiveness," of "permissiveness," of "nurturance," and so on, yet little research directly relevant to the concrete problems with which parents must deal. One reason for our current ignorance may be that the research endeavor often obliges us to address questions obliquely and abstractly. One consequence of this is that concepts like "punitiveness" are certain to be defined very differently by various researchers; we would expect—indeed predict—discrepancies among research findings depending on the methods and definitions adopted by the investigators concerned. Clear answers that are useful to parents may be possible only when we specify *what* demands are being made punitively or permissively, instead of papering over a multitude of parental styles and goals with labels like "punitive" or "permissive." it matters a great deal, I suspect, whether a parent punishes a one-year-old or a four-year-old for soiling itself; to call both punitive is to ignore the most important information. Classification of the content of demands is not easy, and I suspect this is why the issue has so often been avoided. Perhaps the value itself (for example, it is good/bad to fight back when someone hits you) is not as important as the age-appropriateness of the demand. This underscores the relation between the content of demands and parental sensitivity.

PITFALLS IN THE APPLICATION OF RESEARCH FINDINGS

In the above sections, I have emphasized the conceptual problems that make the generalization of research findings to recommendations concerning parent education hazardous at best. Next, I want to discuss specific examples of instances where available research evidence and the best intentions of those who formulate policy together fostered policies that, in retrospect, appear quite inappropriate.

SINGLE-PARENT FAMILIES

For several reasons, child-rearing is most easily and effectively performed by intact families. Single-parent families deprive children of a major role model, and make them the exclusive responsibility of a parent who lacks emotional and economic support from a spouse, and who is socially isolated. To this extent, therefore, government policies aimed at encouraging the maintenance of two-parent families appear to be well founded. On the other hand, *there is no reason to assume that nominally intact families reliably and assuredly provide children with two socially significant and accessible parents.* Children with psychologically absent fathers appear to be affected in much the same way as those whose fathers are physically absent (Blanchard and Biller, 1971; Hoffman, 1971). Marital hostility is also damaging to the personalities of young children (see Lamb, 1976). Thus, intact families are more effective and reliable as socializing agents than single-parent families only in cases where there are two happily married and committed parents (Lamb, 1977). Furthermore, it is important neither to understate nor to overstate the difficulties faced by single parents. Most aspects of personality development involve input from a variety of sources (mothers, fathers, siblings, teachers, peers, the media) and there is no reason to believe that any one source is irreplaceable. Contributions from all are generally not *necessary,* while none are *sufficient* in and of themselves (Lamb, 1978). This is so both because redundancy appears to be built into the socialization process and because others (such as siblings, teachers) may become adequate substitutes for the absent parents (Biller, 1971; Lynn, 1974).

In other words, then, a policy that aims to keep families together may harm some children even as it is beneficial to others. Unfortunately, we do not know the relative numbers involved. In the absence of these data, it is not possible to assess the net impact of such a policy. In such circumstances, it is probably unwise to institute policies that discriminate among families in order to encourage the maintenance of certain types. Any decision to do so must rest, not on empirical, but on philosophical and sociopolitical considerations.

SUBSTITUTE CHILD CARE

There is currently great concern about the children of working mothers and about a related issue—the effects of day care on developmental processes. The topics have been debated vociferously by both proponents and opponents; meanwhile, the evidence shows that both extreme positions underestimate the complexity of the issues. The children (particularly daughters) of working mothers, we find, tend to avow less stereotyped sex-roles than the children of full-time mothers (Hoffman, 1974; Vogel et al., 1970). In contemporary society, this is clearly a beneficial rather than a deleterious consequence. Second, children who are raised by dissatisfied women who would rather be working and pursuing careers risk greater psychological damage than those whose mothers are able to combine career and family roles in the way they choose (Birnbaum, 1971; Hoffman, 1974; Yarrow et al., 1962). A working woman may harm her children, in other words, only to the extent that she feels guilty or resentful at the abandonment of either her family or her career (see Hoffman, 1974).

As far as day care is concerned, it is now fairly well established that the daily separations from parents and the associated substitute care are not *in themselves* inimical to the normal course of sociopersonality development (see, for example, Doyle, 1975; Feldman, 1974; Roopnarine and Lamb, 1977; Schwartz, 1975; Schwartz et al., 1974). An important qualification is in order, however. Most research has been conducted in high-quality day-care programs, whereas most children are enrolled in inadequate (if not depriving) programs. No systematic effort has been made to compare the effects of high- and low-quality programs, though this may be a more important determinant of the child's fate than whether or not it is in day care.

In the heat of arguments about the effects of day care, furthermore, one crucial fact is often forgotten: Fewer that 10 percent of the children receiving some form of substitute care are enrolled in day-care centers! The majority are cared for by relatives, babysitters, or in "family day care"—a euphemism for the case where a mother agrees to look after other children in her own home. It is probably because children in day care are far more accessible to researchers that most researchers have focused exclusively on this comparatively small group, which is overwhelmingly comprised of the children of wealthier and better educated parents. While it is comforting to know that these children are not at risk, it is troubling to note how little concern is expressed about the fate of the majority. The findings of a pioneering and methodologically flawed study (Saunders and Keister, 1972) are certainly unsettling. Children in family day care, Saunders and Keister found, suffered more frequent changes of caretaker, had less competent caretakers, were kept in relatively unstimulating environments, and received markedly less attention from adults than did children in group-care facilities.

Again, then, it is clear that we know too little about the effects of various substitute-care arrangements to make reasonable assessments regarding the advisability of encouraging or discouraging a diverse range of child-care environments. All we can say is that quality-center day care is apparently not harmful to most children. Indeed the experience with peers may be valuable. Quality day care, however, is extremely expensive. Unless we find that other types of substitute care are harmful and thus merit eradication (achieved by providing free day care), the major policy issue here is not whether alternative modes of day care should be encouraged to function (I believe they should), but whether they should be publicly funded. This question has nothing to do with research expertise: It has everything to do with sociopolitical philosophy. Researchers, of course, have political opinions, and many who study children may feel especially strongly about issues concerning children. Nevertheless, their opinions are manifestations not of their expertise but of their philosophical persuasion. It is especially important, when dealing with socially volatile issues, to distinguish between recommendations based on empirical evidence and recommendations based on personal opinion. Unfortunately, strongly held opinions may easily be portrayed as products of special expertise.

DO RESEARCHERS LEAD OR FOLLOW?

The two preceding sections also highlight a particularly vexing impediment to the fruitful application of research data in the formulation of policy recommendations. In recent years, research focusing on working motherhood and the effects of substitute care mushroomed because so many mothers were working and so many children had substitute caretakers. However fascinating and extensive the research, I doubt whether the findings will have any major impact on the societal trends concerned. It is seldom the case that investigators of personality development are given free reign to engineer rearing environments in order to see what effects they have. They are left to study the environments created by others. This means that they do not guide the direction of the changes. Instead, they declare, in retrospect, what the effects of the changes have been. This fact is likely to moderate the impact that researchers have.

CONCLUDING NOTE

The tenor of this chapter may suggest that researchers have no role to play in shaping public policy. I do not believe this to be the case. Most researchers in this field, including myself, are in the field because they believe that the results of their investigations may have practical implications. Unfortunately, however, this is a relatively young science, and we need a great deal more basic research before reasonable policy recommendations can be wisely and confidently made. Zealous proselytization is simply not warranted. At this point, the interests of public policy and the credibility of researchers would best be served by humility and circumspection rather than by self-assured prescriptions.

BIBLIOGRAPHY

Ainsworth, M.D.; Bell, S.M.; and Stayton, D.J. Infant-mother attachment and social development: Socialization as a product of reciprocal responsiveness to signals. In M.P.M. Richards (Ed.), *The integration of a child into a social world.* Cambridge: Cambridge University Press, 1974.

Bandura, A. *Social learning theory.* Englewood Cliffs: Prentice-Hall, 1977.

Baumrind, D.M. *Early socialization and the discipline controversy.* Morristown, N.J.: General Learning Press, 1975a.

———. The contribution of the family to the development of competence in children. *Schizophrenia Bulletin,* 1975b, *14,* 12–37.

Biller, H.B. *Father, child, and sex role.* Lexington, Mass.: D.C. Heath, 1971.

Birnbaum, J.A. Life patterns, personality style, and self-esteem in gifted family-oriented and career-committed women. Unpublished doctoral dissertation, University of Michigan, 1971.

Blanchard, R.W., and Biller, H.B. Father availability and academic performance among third grade boys. *Developmental Psychology,* 1971, *4,* 301–305.

Blehar, M.D.; Lieberman, A.E.; and Ainsworth, M.D. Early face-to-face interaction and its relation to later infant-mother attachment. *Child Development,* 1977, *48,* 183–193.

Doyle, A.B. Infant development in day care. *Developmental Psychology,* 1975, *11,* 655–656.

Feldman, S.S. The impact of day care on one aspect of children's social-emotional behavior. Paper presented to the American Association for the Advancement of Science, San Francisco, February 1974.

Hoffman, L.W. Effects of maternal employment on the child: A review of the research. *Developmental Psychology,* 1974, *10,* 204–228.

Hoffman, M.L. Father absence and conscience development. *Developmental Psychology,* 1971, *4,* 400–406.

Lamb, M.E. The role of the father: An overview. In M.E. Lamb (Ed.), *The role of the father in child development.* New York: Wiley, 1976.

———. The effects of divorce on children's personality development. *Journal of Divorce,* 1977, *1,* 163–174.

———. Psychosocial development: A theoretical overview and a look into the future. In M.E. Lamb (Ed.), *Social and Personality Development.* New York: Holt, Rinehart and Winston, 1978, in press.

Lamb, M.E., and Baumrind, D.M. Socialization and personality development in the preschool years. In M.E. Lamb (Ed.), *Social and Personality Development.* New York: Holt, Rinehart and Winston, 1978, in press.

Lamb, M.E., and Urberg, K.A. The development of gender role and gender identity. In M.E. Lamb (Ed.), *Social and Personality Development.* New York: Holt, Rinehart and Winston, 1978, in press.

Lynn, D.B. *The father: His role in child development.* Monterey, California: Brooks/Cole, 1974.

Mussen, P.H. Early socialization: Learning and identification. In T.M. Newcomb (Ed.), *New directions in psychology III.* New York: Holt, Rinehart and Winston, 1967.

Radin, N. The role of the father in cognitive, academic and intellectual development. In M.E. Lamb (Ed.), *The role of the father in child development.* New York: Wiley, 1976.

Roopnarine, J.L. and Lamb, M.E. The effects of day care on attachment and exploratory behavior in a strange situation. *Merrill-Palmer Quarterly,* 1977, *24,* 85–95.

Saunders, M.M., and Keister, M.E. Family day care: Some observations. Unpublished manuscript, University of North Carolina, Greenboro, 1972.

Schaffer, H.R., and Emerson, P.E. The development of social attachments in infancy. *Monographs of the Society for Research in Child Development,* 1964, *29,* Whole number 94.

Schwartz, J.L. Social and emotional effects of day care: A review of recent research. Paper presented to the Society for Research in Child Development Study Group on the Family, Ann Arbor, Mich., October 1975.

Schwartz, J.C.; Strickland, R.G.; and Krolick, G. Infant day care: Behavioral effects at preschool age. *Developmental Psychology,* 1974, *10,* 502–506.

Thomas, A.; Chess, S.; and Birch, H.G. *Temperament and behavior disorders in children.* New York: New York University Press, 1968.

Vogel, S.R.; Broverman, I.K.; Broverman, D.M.; Clarkson, F.E.; and Rosenkrantz, P.S. Maternal employment and perception of sex roles among college students. *Developmental Psychology,* 1970, *3,* 384–391.

Yarrow, M.R.; Scott, P.; De Leeuw, L.; and Heinig, C. Child-rearing in families of working and non-working mothers. *Sociometry,* 1962, *25,* 122–140.

12

Effective Care-Giving—The Child from Birth to Three

JEAN V. CAREW

Senior Research Assistant and Lecturer
Harvard Graduate School of Education
Cambridge, Massachusetts

The popular literature as well as most research on child-rearing makes several critical assumptions as to the structure and functions of the American family that are obsolete and misleading as well as insulting and dangerous to the families who do not fit the model implicit in this writing. The crucial suppositions are that the white, middle-class, nuclear family—father at work, mother and children at home—represents the vast majority of American families, and research and advice-giving to parents still proceed as if certain major demographic changes in the American family that have taken place in the last twenty years had never come about. But fundamental changes have occurred—notably dramatic increases in the number of working mothers, in the number of female heads-of-households, and in the percentage of minority children in the population—so that it is probably true to say that currently only a *minority* of children live in the kind of family conjured up by this literature. The majority of American children are not middle class, and a substantial number are from minority groups. More than 30 percent of married mothers with children under age three work outside the home and 12 percent of families are headed by females most of whom also hold jobs (Bronfenbrenner, 1976; Hoffman and Nye, 1974; Snapper et al., 1975).

The purpose of this chapter is to examine critically some of the assumptions, methods, and findings of research on effective care-giving of the young child. My main thesis is that in order to understand the fundamentals of effective child-rearing, even within just the American culture, one must examine the influence of caregivers other than the mother, the effects of environments other than the home, and families other than those belonging to the white, middle-class mainstream.

In the following sections I shall first consider some newer methods being used in research—in particular the trend toward direct observation of the caregiver and child in natural day-to-day contexts. Although I welcome this new direction, I see certain dangers in the observation method that have not yet been confronted squarely. Second, I shall summarize briefly the research literature on effective parenting of the young child by the mother in the home. Although some of this research includes families of many social classes and ethnic groups, it is always designed, executed, and interpreted by middle-class researchers. This fact alone compels serious questions concerning the validity of results. This research is also always carried out by adults, and preposterous though it may seem, similar problems arise as to the validity of adult perceptions, interpretations, and assessment of child behavior. Next, I shall turn to research on two nontraditional caregivers: the teacher in the day-care center and the working mother who shares her care-giving responsibilities with someone else in or out of the home. The consensus that research has come to regarding effective parenting by *full-time* mothers may or may not apply to effective care-giving by these two *part-time* caregivers—the professional teacher and the working mother. Finally, I shall examine what we know about effective care-giving in minority families. I shall limit my remarks to black families, but the tenor of my argument applies to families of many other oppressed minorities.

DIRECT OBSERVATION IN NATURAL CONTEXTS: THE FUNCTIONAL, MICROANALYTIC APPROACH

The last ten years have witnessed a welcome trend in research toward the study of the child in "natural" day-to-day contexts. This new strategy relies heavily on direct observation of caregiver behavior and caregiver-child interaction to provide a *functional* analysis of the child care environment. By focusing on the relationship between child-development outcomes and observed caregiver *behavior*, this approach often achieves considerably more explanatory power than traditional strategies which typically merely relate dissimilarities in outcomes to differences in gross classifications such as socioeconomic status (SES) and ethnicity, ignoring both the behavior process mediating these outcomes and the enormous variation in process within SES and culture categories.

In my own work, I have developed and applied a microanalytic approach to the study of the home-care environments of the child between ages one and three. However, although I remain a strong advocate, I see several dangers in the growing use of this method. First, the microanalytic approach tends to encourage a "conceptual disconnection of functional systems from broader societal systems" (Fein, 1976). Studies of this type seldom go beyond child development considerations to address issues that sociologists, economists, and anthropologists might think vital to the interpretation of results (such as differences in economic, social, and political resources and differences in cultural norms, expectations, and values as factors influencing parental behaviors). Second, there are problems inherent in the observation and interpretation of behavior that few investigators employing the new method have faced squarely. Are the "same" behaviors equivalent in meaning or consequence for the child from one person, family, cultural group to another? Do observers see the "same" behaviors emitted by members of distinct social classes or cultural groups differently? Do observers from different social classes or cultural groups interpret the "same" behaviors the same way?

All such studies after all apply a common behavior coding system to all of their adult or child subjects. A different system is not used for middle-class and working-class parents or for black and white children in the same study. This recording framework necessarily reflects its designer's cultural background, life experience, education, and values, which are nearly always strikingly dissimilar from those of the subjects. Thus, males study females; whites study blacks; the rich study the poor; professors study the illiterate; childless women study mothers; working mothers study females who stayed at home to rear their children. Seldom are the subjects or people like them brought in to collaborate on the design of the research or to voice their views as to the interpretation of behavior. This practice is only defensible if we believe that behavior is constant in its meaning and consequence for child development through time, space, culture, and a myriad of life circumstances—a thesis in which few of us, I am sure, would be willing to place much faith.

Until these fundamental problems are overcome, we should treat skeptically research results such as those I shall soon be reviewing. Terms such as *restrictiveness, responsiveness, stimulation*, and *warmth*, even when concretely defined in terms of specific behaviors, still inevitably reflect the study designer's and observer's values and understandings of what constitutes their behavioral manifestations. Critically needed are studies designed to show in what ways behavior in natural contexts is spontaneously perceived and interpreted differentially by participants, by people like them, and by researchers. Quite different "psychologies"—different concepts, different ways of perceiving and interpreting behavior—might emerge from such a study with salutary results if it persuades the research elite to question its own sometimes self-serving biases.

Another humbling experience is to ponder how valid can be analyses of *child* behavior that are based solely on *adult* perceptions and interpretations. Researchers are virtually always adults. They are disposed to examine children's activities through the eyes of an adult. Child behavior that is like an adult's in its rhythm, concentration, systematic approach, and verbal quality is more easily understood, coded, and evaluated; hence the kind of behaviors that are accorded high scores in cognitive tests. Similarly, experiences which adults help to structure for the child are even more easily recognized as "intellectually stimulating" and assimilated to the researcher's recording and evaluating schemes. By comparison, "intellectually valuable" activities that the *child* fashions may not be detected so easily.

Research evidence on these points is scarce because the question itself has seldom been raised. However, in two independent studies (Carew et al., 1976a and 1977), my colleagues and I have examined longitudinally the functional environments of one- to three-year-old children reared at home and attending day-care centers. Both studies used the same observational procedures and focused on the relationship between the child's day-to-day experiences, in which the caregiver played a more or less active, structuring, participatory role, and the child's later cognitive development. The major results pointed to the critical and very similar role played by mothers at home and teachers in centers in creating, guiding, and sustaining *intellectually valuable* activities for the young child. In both studies, a large portion of the variance in test scores at age three could be predicted from knowing how often the child had had intellectually valuable experiences (especially those focused on language acquisition) in the preceding two years in which the child's caregiver had been actively involved as teacher, helper, playmate, or conversation partner.

These findings are very much in line with the many studies of mother-child interaction that highlight the key role of mothers in providing children with intellectual stimulation and influencing children's intellectual competence. However, an equally important finding in these two studies was the very *weak* relationship between intellectually valuable activities that children created *for themselves* in their independent play and their later test scores. These activities, by definition, required highly competent, well-organized, mastery-oriented behavior on the part of the children. For example, a child might build a tall tower of blocks, or undertake an experiment in flotation, or pretend to be a dinosaur eating up imaginary prey. These activities— clearly the kinds of experiences in which children manifest and build their intellec- tual competence—were nevertheless essentially unrelated to their later test scores and especially to their Binet I.Q.'s. High scores on the Binet were correlated almost exclu- sively with well-structured language experiences that adults provided for children and hardly at all to the large variety of intellectually stimulating experiences that the children created for themselves.

Perhaps the reason for these contrasting findings is the similarity between the test situation and the adult-structured natural experience. In both cases a principal component of the child's task is to listen to language input from adults and to carry out their directions. The point I wish to stress however is that it is *adults* who define children's "intelligence" in the test situation (for example, attentive listening and the carrying out of the adult's direction earn high scores) and similarly it is *adults* who perceive certain types of everyday experience (such as the teaching of language) as intellectually stimulating. Adults have difficulty conceiving of other forms of child behavior in the test situation (for example, originality, resisting the tester, tuning out) as intelligent, and similarly they have difficulty in perceiving child-generated exper- iences in the natural situation as intellectually self-stimulating. Thus, one would do well to be somewhat skeptical about the very research studies soon to be reviewed which claim that the caregiver's interactions are the key factor in the child's cognitive development. Until more valid "child-centric" measures of children's everyday ex- periences and intellectual competence are employed, the findings of such research are likely to be biased in favor of precisely this comfortable conclusion.

FULL-TIME MOTHERS

Direct observational studies of the home care-giving environment are difficult and expensive to undertake. Thus, relatively few studies provide detailed functional analyses of the home environment, and fewer still pertain to the very young child. Available research supports the following conclusions.

Birth to six months

Before the age of three months, babies seem to develop normally even under ex- tremely "deprived" home or institutional conditions in which they are seldom spoken to, played with, smiled at, or cuddled. After this point, depriving circumstances may begin to exert effects which are latent and cumulative, although reversible through appropriate intervention (Ainsworth, 1962; Dennis and Najarian, 1957; Dennis and Sayegh, 1965).

Some researchers see similarities between the radical forms of deprivation just referred to and that implied by low socioeconomic status. Social-class comparisons of maternal behavior, however, yield few differences in responsiveness, talkativeness, or affection to the infant. If anything, the environment of the average low-income home may be the more adequate in that some studies show that mothers in this group touch, hold, smile, and look at their infants more than do middle-class mothers, and that their babies tend to be more active, motorically advanced, and socially respon- sive. The main difference favoring the middle class has to do with the vocal interaction between mother and infant. Middle-class mothers are more likely to talk to their infants at close range, to respond to their babbles with speech, and to elicit "listening" behavior from them (Caldwell, 1967; Deutsch, 1973; Golden and Birns, 1968; Kagan, 1968; Lewis and Freedle, 1972; Wachs et al., 1971). These differences remind me of the effects of adult-structured language experiences demonstrated in my own research and may very well be the earliest antecedents of later differences in language acquisition between children from low and middle SES levels.

The main point, however, is that both within and across social classes there is substantial evidence indicating that the infant's perceptual and cognitive development is significantly affected by maternal behavior. The more the mother looks at, talks to, and plays with the baby, and the more age-appropriate, various, and responsive her stimulating behavior, the better the infant's performance on standard perceptual and cognitive tests (Gallas and Lewis, 1977). The mother's interactive behavior with the infant also strongly affects the baby's social and emotional development—a truism that much research has established as scientific fact. Infants of mothers who promptly respond to their babies' crying; who smile at, hold, and cuddle them frequently; who make eye-to-eye contact with them often; seem happier, less fretful, more socially responsive, and more securely attached to their mothers (Ainsworth, 1973; Bell and Ainsworth, 1972; Robson and Moss, 1970; Zelazo, 1971). These changes in the child's development, both cognitive and social, may very early influence the mother's perceptions of and behavior toward the child so that almost from the beginning the mother-child relationship is best described as a *reciprocal*, interactive dynamic in which the behavior of each member of the dyad is continually adapting to the other's.

Six months to three years

There is substantial research evidence demonstrating that children who spend much of the first three years of their lives in depriving institutional environments may consequently be severely retarded in cognitive, language, social, and motor development. Normal development of particular children in such institutions can usually be attributed to exceptional attention they received from a caregiver (Ainsworth, 1962; Dennis and Najarian, 1957; Skeels, 1966; Spitz, 1965).

Several studies report striking social-class differences in the behavior of mothers of children of this age. Again, the most pronounced differences are in the quality of verbal interaction, with middle-class mothers being seen as more verbal. Even with these very young children, middle-class mothers more often deliberately teach the use of language and symbols through labeling and explanation. They more often elaborate and expand their children's statements, explain events and functions, read, converse, and comment interpretatively on television programs. Their speech is also found to be more distinctive, complex, and varied. It contains more questions and suggestions and fewer commands, prohibitions, and corrections. Middle-class mothers also exercise greater control over the television programs their children are allowed to watch. They turn on programs like "Sesame Street" and switch off soap operas and Saturday morning cartoons. Middle-class mothers more often play with their children, use educational toys and creative materials, and exploit these occasions to teach the child skills similar to those assessed in cognitive tests. They also tend to put few restrictions on the child's exploratory activities and are more likely to sweeten commands and requests with explicit, verbal rationales (Carew et al., 1976a,

1976b, 1977; Clarke-Stewart, 1975; Kagan, 1968; Kessen et al., 1975; Schachter et al., 1977; Tulkin and Cohler, 1973; White et al., 1973).

Thus, a composite of highly correlated behaviors seems to distinguish mothers of high- and low-socioeconomic status. These differences apparently influence a number of competencies or dispositions which children acquire between six and thirty-six months, including language comprehension and expression, problem-solving skills, social sensitivity, the ability to express and control emotions, and the willingness to trust adults and to have confidence in oneself. Differences among children of different social classes on measures of intellectual development usually are not apparent until age eighteen or twenty-four months although the corresponding differences in maternal behaviors are discernible much earlier. In fact, about age one, children from lower socioeconomic groups may be relatively advanced on cognitive tests. By eighteen months however, this difference typically attenuates, and by thirty months it is reversed. Although many of these studies are correlational in design, the very high reported relationships between prior maternal behavior and later child outcomes make a causal hypothesis irresistible to many. This interpretation finds further support in the findings of the more successful intervention studies in which mothers were encouraged to adopt strategies of interaction with their children very similar to those referred to above, and positive changes in child functioning were observed.

Before ending this section, I should point out that the mother is typically not the only significant person in the child's life, even when she is the primary caregiver. Father, grandmother, siblings, the sitter, and even the ubiquitous television set may all play roles in the child's day-to-day experiences which may well rival in impact that of the mother. However, research has given very little attention to these "significant others" although they may often play a central care-giving role in some ethnic groups and among working mothers (Kotelchuk, 1973; Lamb, 1975; Lewis et al., 1972; Spelke et al., 1973; Wachs et al., 1971).

Finally I want to stress again the caveats previously introduced. As I mentioned, neither the framework used to record and interpret behavior nor the measures employed to assess child development can be assumed to be equally valid for all the subjects involved in these studies. In fact, both observations and tests are virtually always designed by researchers whose education and cultural background approximate those of some subjects (for example, middle-class parents) and are entirely alien to others (for example, welfare mothers). Moreover, the recording of children's everyday experiences and assessments of their cognitive development may also be fundamentally biased in the adult-centric sense that the research by Carew et al. (1976a, 1976b, 1977) described in the previous section seems to suggest. So again it is wise to be suspicious about research results. One can easily be beguiled by the apparent high agreement among researchers into thinking that the answers are already in. But in fact the consensus may be a spurious one traceable to the similarity of conceptualization and methods used by most investigators whose cultural background and training tend to be highly similar rather than to a convergence on the same conclusions by researchers with very different life histories and perspectives.

DAY-CARE TEACHERS

We turn now to research on another type of caregiver and environment, the teacher in the day-care center. Although most nonmaternal care of young children is provided in the child's home by relatives or nonrelatives or in the homes of other people rather than in centers, the former settings have seldom been studied. Most research on nonmaternal caregiving currently available focuses on teachers in day-care centers perhaps because it is easier to study a few caregivers and many children in one site than each caregiver-child dyad in a different home. We note that most day-care centers for young children are set up simply to provide good substitute care outside the home and are not concerned with accelerating development. Thus, studies on the effects of day care are typically designed to consider whether the day-care experience has *detrimental* effects on development—the explicit or implicit comparison being with children reared at home by their mothers.

ADVERSE EFFECTS

Strident claims that day care adversely affects the young child find little support from existing research. There is little or no evidence indicating unfavorable consequences, whether one considers intellectual development, peer relationships, responsiveness to adult socialization, or affective relationships between child and parent. However, this conclusion must be tempered with the realization that most research has been carried out in "high quality" centers (Caldwell, 1970; Kagan et al., 1976; Keister, 1970; Lally, 1974; Lewis, 1975; Ragozin, 1976; Ramey and Smith, 1976; Willis and Ricciuti, 1974). Only now are major research studies being implemented involving children enrolled in the broad range of centers characterizing the day-care market.

BENEFICIAL EFFECTS

High-quality, cognitively structured day-care programs probably do not enhance the development of children whose home environments are already supportive of normal development (that is, these children do not do better on assessments than control children from similar home backgrounds). On the other hand, such day-care programs may prevent the decline in intellectual functioning reported for children from considerably less favorable home environments or those judged to be at substantial developmental risk (Fowler and Kahn, 1975; Heber et al., 1972; Garber et al., 1976; Robinson and Robinson, 1971). High-quality day care may also have positive social consequences in the sense of fostering the child's ability to play harmoniously and productively with peers, to adapt to strange adults, and the like, but research on these issues is scant.

QUALITY OF CARE

Day-care centers vary widely in a number of aspects that have to do with "quality of care." These features include: caregiver/child ratios at different ages and group size; staff qualifications and turnover; the nature of the child's day-to-day experiences or "program" and available play materials; provisions for ensuring adequate health, nutrition, and safety; and communication with, support, and involvement of parents. High quality care refers to desirable components of variables which are thought to facilitate the children's intellectual, social, and emotional development and the relationship with their families. The problem is that not enough is now known as to the effects of variation on each of these characteristics and still less as to the many combinations that might define high- and poor-quality care.

In defining quality of care, Ricciuti (1976) suggests that the day-care center should approximate a "good" natural-home environment in the kinds of daily experiences it provides for children and that its goals for children should be the same as most parents'. Thus, the center should not only provide for children's basic physical, health, safety, and nutritional needs, but should also ensure that they are "cared for by familiar, responsive and affectionate caregivers who (a) foster through their interactions with the child an early sense of trust and confidence in salient, caring adults; (b) frequently create mutually enjoyable opportunities for learning through play and social interactions in the natural context of daily care-giving; and (c) are sensitive in dealing with the individual needs and characteristics of particular babies" (pp. 44–46).

There are some obvious problems with this definition of quality day care. What is a "good" natural home environment? What are the goals that most parents want for their children? Should the comparison be with a general norm or with the home environments and goals of most of the center's actual *clients*? This definition also glosses over some intrinsic differences between centers and homes which compel different strategies and goals for the two settings. The day-care center is intrinsically a *group* setting. The child in this setting usually has to learn to relate to more than one primary caregiver (at a time and over time) and to many children similar in age who also tend to come and go. Therefore, one of the most important aspects of effective care giving must be the caregiver's skill in helping children relate to many different people in cognitively, socially, and emotionally productive ways. Again, because it is a group setting, the individual child's experience in day care nearly always will include more accommodation to routine and rules, more waiting time, less privacy, more interruptions, more direction of activity from adults, more doing things in a group and with other children, and perhaps less one-to-one interaction with adults than in the average home. We are very far from being able to say how these obvious differences between center and home settings relate to development in children, but it would be a mistake to bias our answers in advance by assuming that the child's experience in a "good" home is the norm by which quality of care in centers should be measured.

THE WORKING MOTHER

In their recent book, Hoffman and Nye (1974) review many studies concerned with maternal employment as a factor relating to development in children. However, as the authors acknowledge, virtually none of these studies considers the very young child, and in most of the studies maternal employment is so confounded with other variables such a social class, type of job relative to qualifications, approval of mother's employment by family members and so on, that few generalizable conclusions can be drawn. The data as a whole suggest that the children of working mothers who obtain personal satisfaction from employment, whose decision to work is supported by family members, who do not feel guilty or anxious about working, and who have been able to make adequate household and child-care arrangements develop at least as well as children of nonworking mothers, and possibly better in certain areas such as sex-role attitudes. As we have already seen, this general conclusion was also supported by the research on children in day care, most of whom are children of working mothers.

Research on maternal employment, however, is sorely in need of redirection. Urgently needed are studies directly focused on the resources and skills required by the working mother for effective parenting. The problems a working mother faces, after all, are quite different from those of the mother rearing her children at home. First, the working mother is basically buying a service rather than performing one for her child. She must weigh the value of the service in terms of costs, convenience, quality, suitabililty to her child's need, and so forth, and typically she has few options, little knowledge about alternatives, and must reach a decision rapidly. Even when the working mother has the luxury of time and the choice of many alternatives, she is often unable to judge quality or suitability because few guides are available to help her distinguish poor from good centers or to discern differences between center and home care. Research on how mothers make this critical decision should be done because the choice of a center is likely to affect the daily fabric of the child's life and consequent development. Moreover, the mother's perceptions of the child's day-care world may (and should) consciously affect how she spends her time with the child at home and our definition of her parenting skill.

Most working mothers of children in day care see them only for a few hours each work day. In most homes these are hectic hours. Meals must be prepared, children fed, washed, dressed, and transported, and a multitude of housekeeping chores accomplished. The organizational, managerial, and interpersonal skills and attitudes required to get these tasks carried out efficiently are therefore as much a part of the working mother's parenting skill as the quality of her specific interactions with the young child. Where other adults or older children are available, her skill must include the ability to obtain adequate help from them in the routine performance of domestic responsibilities. It is estimated that full-time employment coupled with sole responsibility for domestic family needs demands a weekly investment of 105 hours of work—a burden few women can shoulder and still find the time, energy, and psychological resources to engage in positive interactions with young children (Howell, 1973). Again, research is sorely needed on this issue because, for the working mother, the carrying out of essential domestic tasks in a few crowded hours before or after a full day of work necessarily sets the main context in which interactions with young children can take place (Goldberg, 1977; Peters, 1976; Powell, 1977).

There is also a need for research to determine what aspects of mother-child interaction are important to the development of children when the mother works and the children spend most of their day with another caregiver. It cannot be casually assumed that the same variables defining effective care-giving for the mother at home or the teacher in day care apply to the working mother. In fact, it is plausible that a different composite of behaviors describes effective parenting for the working mother. For example, if she knows that the child is already bombarded with "intellectual stimulation" in day care, the working mother might profitably forego duplicating these experiences at home and concentrate instead on meeting needs that the other setting inadequately reaches. Obvious candidates might be the child's needs for overt affection and for experiences through which the child can learn to understand the personalities of family members, and achieve a sense of belonging and interdependence with others. Thus, for working mothers, the sociocultural aspect of interactions with young children is likely to be far more important than the cognitive if the child's intellectual needs are already well satisfied in day care. It is not sensible to assume that whatever defines good care-giving in one context also defines good care-giving in another.

BLACK MOTHERS

The themes I have touched on so far provide essential background for examining effective parenting in black families. Proportionately more than in white families, black mothers are employed, black children attend day care, black mothers are single heads-of-family, and black families are poor. These features do *not*, however, describe the majority of black families. The modal black family is still the hard-working, blue collar and white collar family in which two parents are present and the mother stays at home to rear her children when they are young. Thus each of the several bodies of research that I have summarized apply to some black families *if we disregard their race*.

To be black in America, however, is to be part of a culture that is different from and defensively resistant to the dominant Euro-American culture. These facts render invalid the application to black families of analytic and interpretative frameworks designed by nonblacks. As Pierce (1974), Nobles (1974), and others have pointed out, social science knowledge is rooted in social relations, and the predominantly race- and class-segregated society of the United States severely limits what a nonblack knows or can learn about the thoughts, feeling, and behavior of blacks. (It also severely distorts what a black, trained and educated in white institutions, can know about blacks not so acculturated.) The history of the black family vividly illustrates this point.

Traditionally, the black family has been studied as a pathological social organization, the perspective being that of a "sick" white family. Years ago, Dubois (1908) and then Frazier (1932) focused on "disorganization" in the black family which they related to oppressive economic conditions. More recently Moynihan (1965) claimed that the cause of black community deterioration was no longer its political and economic subjugation by a hostile wider society but the structure and nature of black families themselves. Other researchers have contended that the root causes of differences between black and white families lie in three centuries of slavery, servitude, economic oppression, and racism. Whether with benign or malevolent intentions however, researchers continue to view the black family as a social "problem." Their perspective is nearly always one that glosses over the uniqueness of the black family, ignores its strengths, and emphasizes its weaknesses. Only recently have scholars (Billingsley, 1966; Gutman, 1976; Hill, 1972; Ladner, 1971; Nobles, 1974, 1976; Peters, 1976; Staples, 1973, 1974) seriously turned to considering the coping strategies of black families that have enabled them to survive through centuries of economic, political, and cultural oppression.

In an insightful paper, Nobles (1974) emphasizes that the black family's "definition, character, form and function did not begin with the American experience of slavery and that as a system it has an historical continuation extending back in history to traditional Africa and its culture" (p. 37). The analysis of black family life must therefore take seriously its *Afro*-American heritage. Black family systems are "African in nature and American in nature." Nobles presents several examples of structure, roles, and behavior in black families that can be traced to their African heritage. These include parakinship ties where boys and girls have "play" brothers and sisters who have the same loyalties and responsibilities as blood relations; the extended family and the practice of informal adoption; flexible family roles in which black men and women more easily interchange the expressive/domestic and economic/instrumental roles that are normally sex-specific in white society; the more egalitarian pattern of relations between black men and women (which nonblacks often regard as evidence of female dominance). Knowing little of traditional African culture and history, I cannot say whether these features are truly African in origin. But certainly they are distinctive features of many Afro-American families that research usually ignores.

Pierce (1974, 1975a, 1975b) has presented a psychological analysis of the effects of racism and "the mundane extreme environment" on the behavior of black people which has enormous implications for how research is conducted and data are interpreted. First, he points out that black people have always lived in the United States under conditions of segregation and restricted mobility. Much of the life of a black individual is spent in all-black groups. Most black children spend the bulk of their time in an all-black family, neighborhood, and school setting, and for many, this pattern of minimal contact with whites continues all through adulthood.

Pierce defines racism as both a perceptual problem and a *folie à deux* in which both blacks and whites engage in complementary delusional beliefs. Racism is so pervasive in black-white relations that its effects are similar to terrorism. Blacks must constantly mobilize resources of body and mind to defend themselves against "micro-aggressions" by whites that are so routine and habitual as to be typically unconsciously committed by the white and unconsciously perceived by the black. This self-protective posture inevitably involves defensive thinking and defensive behaviors by blacks in the presence of whites.

Pierce couples his analysis of the effects of racism with an analysis of the effects of extreme environments on behavior. An extreme environment is one in which the magnitude of stress or wear and tear on the body is abnormally high. The urban ghetto is an excellent example of a *mundane* extreme environment; the South Pole or the moon or examples of *exotic* extreme environments. According to Pierce, both exotic and mundane extreme environments share the following stress-producing characteristics: forced socialization, density clustering, spatial isolation, inability to escape, fears of abandonment, noise/silence extremes, lack of information, and increased "empty" time. These stresses have discernible effects on thinking and behavior, requiring the victim to engage in greater than ordinary surveillance of the environment and constant mobilization against threat and hopelessness. The extreme environment also engenders problems of leadership and followership, time usage, planning, and decision-making. Dependency is increased and self-confidence is decreased as threats to one's survival multiply.

The behavior of most blacks then is fundamentally affected by their experience of racism and the stress of the mundane extreme environment in which they live. What does this imply for observational research on black families? The first implication is that blacks are likely to act differently in the presence of whites or of other blacks whom they may see as similar to whites or as carrying out their purposes. Indeed, the behaviors of parents toward young children are among those *most likely* to be affected by the presence of such an outsider in the home because this is the first context in which defense, wariness, and vigilance must be taught. Intensification of defensive behavior is automatic and is not likely to be much mitigated by the customary training of observers "to be friendly and respectful" because it is triggered as much by the black person's prior experience of racism and the mundane extreme environment as by the particular behavior of the observer/interviewer.

A second implication to be drawn from Pierce's analysis is that when the research instruments for recording/interpreting behavior have been conceived and designed by whites (or imitatively by blacks), these instruments are not likely to "fit" the behaviors of blacks. The basic concepts and definitions of behavior and the underlying values are likely to be inappropriate. For example, "control" is a category of behavior often used in observational research. Most middle-class white researchers regard "frequent" and "harsh" control of children as a bad thing, whether this takes the form of imposing ideas or controlling behavior. Pierce's analysis, however, suggests that in black families a high level of control over children may be critical to effective parenting insofar as it may protect the child from a hostile wider environment.

A third implication is that black and white observers, using the same recording and analytic framework, are likely to perceive and interpret the "same" behavior of a black person differently. No observation system can specify in advance how the large variety of behaviors observable in natural contexts should be recorded. Much must be left to the judgment of the observer who ultimately must rely on his/her own culturally and idiosyncratically determined ways of perceiving and interpreting behavior. Such basic categories as whether or not the mother "interacted with" the child are likely to be recorded dissimilarly by black and white observers who are differentially attuned to the meanings of nonverbal behavior. Similarly, "aggression," "affection," "responsiveness," "rejection" are categories of behavior that black and white observers are likely to define operationally in quite different ways.

One looks in vain for research on black families in which these all too real possibilities of bias are seriously assayed and finds instead only perfunctory attempts to train white observers to respect differences or to use black observers in black homes. The fact of the matter is that the research instrument, its designers, and users control the data, not the other way around. Until more valid concepts and methods for studying black families are created by those who know and have experienced black culture firsthand, it is fair to say that the accumulated research on black parenting is of limited authenticity and value.

SUMMARY

This chapter examines some problems with the assumptions, methods, and findings in research on the care of the young child. A major premise is that in order to understand the fundamentals of effective child-rearing, one must examine the influence of caregivers other than the mother, the effects of environments other than the home, and families other than those belonging to the white middle-class mainstream. At the same time a major thesis of the paper is that the assumptions, methods, and findings of currently available research leave much to be desired. Observation instruments and tests are virtually always adult-centric, ethnocentric, class-biased, and designed with the now outmoded model of the conventional nuclear family in mind. These biases are so strong and pervasive as to compel serious doubts about the validity of investigations involving lower-class children, children of working mothers, children in day care, perhaps *all* children studied by adult researchers. These doubts will not be allayed until researchers learn to take the perspective of the research subject more seriously into account and ensure that this perspective truly influences the research at every stage: conceptualization, design, execution, analysis, and dissemination.

BIBLIOGRAPHY

Ainsworth, M. D. The effects of maternal deprivation: a review of findings and controversy in the context of research strategy. *Public Health Papers*, 1962, *14*, 97–165.

Ainsworth, M. D. The development of infant-mother attachment. In B. M. Caldwell and H. N. Ricciuti (Eds.), *Review of Child Development Research*, Volume 3. Chicago: University of Chicago Press, 1973, pp. 1–94.

Bell, S. M. and Ainsworth, M. D. Infant crying and maternal responsiveness. *Child Development*, 1972, *43*, 1171–1190.

Billingsley, A. *Black Families in White America.* Englewood Cliffs, N.J.: Prentice-Hall, 1966.

Bronfenbrenner, U. Research on the effects of day care on child development. In *Toward a National Policy for Children and Families.* Washington, D.C.: National Academy of Sciences/National Research Council, 1976.

Caldwell, B. M. Social class level and stimulation: Potential of the home. *Exceptional Infant*, 1967, *1*, 455–466.

Caldwell, B. M., Wright, C. M., Honig, A. S. and Tannenbaum, J. Infant day care and attachment. *American Journal of Orthopsychiatry*, 1970, *40*, 397–412.

Carew, J. V., Chan, I., and Halfar, C. Observed intellectual competence and tested intelligence: their roots in the young child's transactions with his environment. Paper presented to EPA and SRCD, April 1975. To be published in *Child Development: A Study of Growth Processes*, Second Edition (S. Cohen and T. J. Comiskey, Eds.). Itasca, Ill.: F. E. Peacock Publishers, Inc., 1977.

Carew, J. V., Chan, I., and Halfar, C. *Intelligence and Experience in Day Care.* Final report to National Institute of Mental Health, August 1976a.

Carew, J. V., Chan, I., and Halfar, C. *Observing Intelligence in Young Children: Eight Case Studies.* Englewood Cliffs, N.J.: Prentice-Hall, 1976b.

Clarke-Stewart, A. *Child Care in the Family. A Review of Research and Some Propostions for Policy.* Report to the Carnegie Council on Children, 1975.

Clarke-Stewart, A. Early child care arrangements: variations and effects. A research proposal presented to the Bush Foundation, 1976.

Cochran, M. A comparison of group day care and family childrearing patterns. Unpublished manuscript, Cornell University, 1976.

Dennis, W. and Najarian, P. Infant development under environmental handicap. *Psychological Monographs*, 1957, *71*.

Dennis, W. and Sayegh, Y. The effect of supplementary experiences upon the behavioral development of infants in institutions. *Child Development*, 1965, *36*, 81–90.

Deutsch, C. P. Social class and child development. In B. M. Caldwell and H. N. Ricciuti (Eds.), *Review of Child Development Research*, Volume 3. Chicago: University of Chicago Press, 1973, 233–282.

Doyle, A. Infant development in day care. *Developmental Psychology*, 1975, *11*, 655–656.

Dubois, W. E. B. *The Negro American Family.* Atlanta: Atlanta University Press, 1908.

Fein, G. The changing ecology: economic uncertainty, families and children. Proposal submitted to the National Science Foundation, 1976.

Fowler, W. and Khan, N. The development of a prototype infant and child day care center in Metropolitan Toronto. Year IV Progress Report, 1975.

Frazier, B. F. *The Negro Family in Chicago.* Chicago: University of Chicago Press, 1932.

Gallas, H. and Lewis, M. Mother-infant interaction and cognitive development in the 12-week-old infant. Paper presented to the Society for Research in Child Development, New Orleans, 1977.

Garber, H., Heber, R., Hoffman, C. and Harrington, S. Preventing mental retardation through family rehabilitation. *TADS Infant Education Monograph.* Chapel Hill, N.C.: TADS, 1976.

Goldberg, R. Material time use and preschool performance. Paper presented at SRCD meeting, New Orleans, 1977.

Golden, M. The New York City Infant Day Care Study. Symposium presented at SRCD biennial conference, New Orleans, March 1977.

Golden, M. and Birns, B. Social class and cognitive development in infancy. *Merrill-Palmer Quarterly*, 1968, *14* 139–149.

Gutman, H. *The Black Family in Slavery and Freedom: 1750–1925.* New York: Pantheon Books, 1976.

Heber, R., Garber, H., Harrington, S., Hoffman, C. and Falender C. *Rehabilitation of Families at Risk for Mental Retardation.* Rehabilitation Research and Training Center, University of Wisconsin, 1972.

Hill, R. *The Strength of Black Families.* New York: Emerson Hall, 1972.

Hoffman, L. W. and Nye, F. I. *Working Mothers.* San Francisco: Jossey-Bass, 1974.

Howell, M. Employed mothers and their families (I). *Pediatrics*, 1973, *2*.

Kagan, J. On cultural deprivation. In D.C. Glass (Ed.), *Environmental Influences.* New York: Rockefeller University Press, 1968, 211–250.

Kagan, J., Kearsley, R. and Zelazo, P. The effects of infant day care on psychological development. Paper presented at AAAS, Boston, February 1976.

Keister, M. *A Demonstration Project: Group Care for Infants and Toddlers.* University of North Carolina at Greensboro, 1970. Final Report.

Kessen, W., Fein, G., Clarke-Steward, A. and Starr, S. Variations in home-based infant education: language, play, and social development. Final report to OCD, 1975.

Kotelchuk, M. The nature of the infant's tie to his father. Paper presented to SRCD, Philadelphia, April 1973.

Ladner, J. *Tomorrow's Tomorrow: The Black Woman.* Garden City, N.Y.: Doubleday, 1971.

Lajewski, H. C. *Child Care Arrangements of Full-Time Working Mothers.* Washington, D.C.: Children's Bureau, 1959.

Lally, R. *The family Development Research Program.* Syracuse University Progress Report, 1974.

Lamb, M. E. Fathers: forgotten contributors to child development. *Human Development*, 1975, 245–266.

Lewis, J. *Family Developmental Center: A Demonstration Project.* San Francisco: Family Services Agency Final Report, 1975.

Lewis, M. and Freedle, R. Mother-infant dyad: the cradle of meaning. Paper presented at University of Toronto symposium on "Language and Thought," March 1972.

Lewis, M., Weintraub, M. and Ban, P. Mothers and fathers, boys and girls: attachment behavior in the first two years of life. Educational Testing Service, 1972.

Low, S. and Spindler, P. B. *Child Care Arrangements of Working Mothers in the United States.* Publication 461. Washington, D.C.: Children's Bureau, 1968.

Nobles, W. Africantry in Black families. *The Black Scholar*, June 1974.

Nobles, W. A formulative and empirical study of Black families. Final report to OCD, 1976.

Peters, M. Nine Black families: a study of household management and childrearing in Black families with working mothers. Doctoral dissertation, Harvard Graduate School of Education, 1976.

Pierce, C. M. Psychiatric problems of the Black minority. In S. Arieti (Ed. in Chief), *American Handbook of Psychiatry*, Volume 2. New York: Basic Books, 1974, 512–523.

Pierce, C. M. The mundane extreme environment and its effects on learning. In S. Brainard (Ed.), *Learning Disabilities; Issues and Recommendations for Research.* Washington, D.C.: National Institute of Education, DHEW, 1975a.

Pierce, C. M. Poverty and racism as they affect children. In I. Berlin (Ed.), *Advocacy for Child Mental Health.* New York: Brunner and Mazel, 1975b, 92–109.

Power, D. The coordination of preschool socialization: parent-caregiver relationships in day care settings. Paper presented at SRCD, New Orleans, 1977.

Prescott, E. A comparison of three types of day care and nursery school-home care. Paper presented at SRCD, Philadelphia, March 1973.

Ragozin, A. Attachment behavior of day care and home reared children in a laboratory setting. Seattle: ADAI report, University of Washington, 1976.

Ramey, C. and Smith, B. Learning and intelligence in disadvantaged infants: effects of early intervention. Paper presented at the Council on Exceptional Children, Chicago, April 1976.

Ricciuti, H. N. Effects of infant day care experience on behavior and development: research and implications for social policy. Cornell University: 1976.

Robinson, H. and Robinson, N. Logitudinal development of very young children in a comprehensive day care program: the first two years. *Child Development*, 1971, *32*, 1673–1683.

Robson, K. S. and Moss, H. A. Patterns and determinants of maternal attachment. *Journal of Pediatrics*, 1970, *77*, 976.

Ruopp, Richard, Travers, Jeffrey, Glanz, Frederick, Coelen, Craig. *Children at the Center: Summary Findings and their Implications.* Vol. 1, Final Report of the National Daycare Study, Abt Associates, March 1979.

Schachter, F., Marquis, R., Bundy, C. and McNair, J. Everyday speech acts of disadvantaged and advantaged mothers to their toddlers. Paper presented at SRCD meeting, New Orleans, 1977.

Snapper, K., Bariga, H., Baumgarner, F. and Wagner, C. *The Status of Children 1975.* Washington, D.C.: George Washington University Social Research Group, 1975.

Spelke, E., Zelazo, P., Kagan, J. and Kotelchuck, M. Father interaction and separation protest. *Developmental Psychology*, 1973, *9*, 83–90.

Spitz, R. A. *The First Year of Life.* New York: International Universities Press, 1965.

Staples, R. *The Black Woman in America.* Chicago: Nelson-Hall, 1973.

Staples, R. The Black family revisited: a review and preview. *Journal of Social and Behavioral Sciences*, 1974, *20*, 65–78.

Tulkin, S. R. and Cohler, B. J. Child-rearing attitudes and mother-child interaction in the first year of life. *Merrill-Palmer Quarterly*, 1973, *19*, 95–106.

Wachs, T. D., Uzgiris, I. C. and Hurt, J. McV. Cognitive development in infants of different age levels and from different environmental backgrounds: an exploratory investigation. *Merrill-Palmer Quarterly*, 1971, *17*, 283–317.

White, B., Watts, J. C., Barnett, I., Kaban, B., Marmor, J. and Shapiro, B. *Environment and Experience: Major Influence on the Development of the Young Child.* Englewood Cliffs, N.J.: Prentice-Hall, 1973.

Willis, A. and Ricciuti, H. N. Longitudinal observations of infants' daily arrivals at a day care center. Research Program in Early Development and Education, Cornell University. Technical Report, 1974.

Zelazo, P. Smiling to social stimuli: eliciting and conditioning effects. *Developmental Psychology*, 1971, *4, 34–42.*

Part Four
Improving Parenting at Home and in the School

The home and the school are the two most important institutions in a child's early development; for the most part, the individual child's physical, emotional, and intellectual development take place in relation to these institutions. Yet, despite their importance, these institutions are often in conflict. Each institution is willing to take responsibility for successful social adjustment on the part of the child while blaming the other for any dysfunctional behavior which develops.

This section of the anthology explores the relationship between the home and school. The contributors deal with such issues as: What role has the school played in the education of minority children? Has the school been responsive to the multicultural characteristics of the students and their families? What has been the relationship between home and school in minority communities? Is there a home/school partnership? Should there be? Can there be? Should the school become a support structure for improved parenting? How can collaboration be developed? What are the policy ramifications of a home/school approach to parent education?

The first selection of José A. Cárdenas and Gloria Zamora describes the failures of the compensatory programs which were instituted in the late 1960's to support or modify the relationship between the two institutions. From their perspective, these programs were unsuccessful because they often failed to take into account the vast cultural and societal differences which exist between poor and minority group children and those providing the assistance. In the future, Cárdenas and Zamora advise, fundamental changes are necessary in educational philosophy, in the use of individualized and multicultural instruction, and in school governance and staffing.

The second selection by Mario D. Fantini joins Zamora and Cárdenas in calling for greater collaboration between the home and the school. It suggests that parenting is a learning process that in many cases has been systematically lost as schools have been asked to expand their responsibilities. This trend must be reversed and parents must be socialized to their parenting role. According to Fantini, this is best achieved in a pluralistic society by providing options in terms of parent-education programs, and by better preparing both this generation and the next for their parenting roles within the educational context.

The final selection by Terrell H. Bell advocates greater participation by parents in the child's educational development and a more active role on the part of schools in parent education. Bell urges families to reassess the quality of their relationship in terms of emotional and educational support, community and neighborhood interaction, and communications. Further, he insists that due to its unique position in society, major responsibility for the improvement of parenting must fall upon the school.

13

The Early Education of Minority Children

DR. JÓSE A. CÁRDENAS AND DR. GLORIA ZAMORA
Intercultural Development Research Association
San Antonio, Texas

THE AMERICAN FAMILY

Much has been written about the important role that the family plays in the education, socialization, and nurturing of its children. Next to the family, the school is recognized as the second most important influence on the development of the child. Thus, it can be said that two powerful influences—home and school—are shaping and molding our children. Are these institutions at odds or do they work together? Should they work together? How can they work together? This paper will address itself to these important issues.

The American family is recognized as the basic unit of our society, but there is much concern regarding its survival. In a report to the then Governor Jimmy Carter, Joseph Califano (1972) stated:

> Families are America's most precious resource and most important institutions. Families have the most fundamental, powerful, and lasting influence on our lives. The strength of our families is the key determinant of the health and well-being of our nation, of our communities and of our lives as individuals [p. 2].

In the same report, Msgr. Lawrence J. Corcoran, Executive Secretary of the National Conference of Catholic Charities, was quoted as saying:

> The American family is our primary national resource. Its strength is our nation's strength. The values it nurtures in its children are the mainspring of our nation's values. History demonstrates that the family is the most effective institution for nurturing the newborn, for developing within the newborn all the biological, psychological, intellectual and spiritual capabilities which produce a mature, loving human being [pp. 2–3].

In short, there is no doubt that a good, strong, emotionally healthy family can have positive effects on the development of its children.

In Hispanic culture, the family, *la familia*, is an especially significant institution.

It is the focal point during special celebrations, and is a unifying element. The Mexican family is usually larger than the American family and extends to include grandparents, aunts, uncles, cousins, and so forth. Much respect is shown to older members of the family and women have a special place—daughters and wives are protected and mothers are revered.

FAMILY SURVIVAL

But the American family, across all ethnic and racial lines is in trouble. In fact, there is question as to its survival. The rapid move from rural to urban centers, undereducation, high unemployment, high mobility, changing social and cultural values, are all assaulting families, and today's children are growing up in environments drastically different from those of a few decades ago.

If schools and families are to work together to help our children grow up to be emotionally healthy, fully functioning adults, then we must understand the kinds of changes that are taking place in America's families:

1. In the last 25 years, the number of working mothers has doubled. One-third of the mothers have preschool age children; one-half of the mothers have school age children.
2. There are drastically high mobility rates. The average American moves fourteen times in his lifetime and 20 percent of our population moves each year.
3. Two out of five marriages in the United States now end in divorce. The rate is higher for teenage marriages.
4. Approximately one out of eight births are to unwed mothers.
5. Six-hundred thousand children are born each year to teenage mothers who have a higher than average risk of birth defects.
6. Television now occupies more of the average child's time than does school. [Califano, 1972, p. 4]

PROBLEMS IN MINORITY EDUCATION

The education of minority children has received much attention in recent years. The social-reform efforts of the Great Society programs in the 1960's placed a great deal of emphasis and resources on the educational needs of minority and disadvantaged children. The early years of the Great Society revealed that certain segments of the population were being denied many of the fruits of this bountiful land. Blacks, Hispanics, and the disadvantaged of other groups were found to be caught in cycles of poverty that precluded access to job opportunities, housing, upward mobility, the administration of justice, and a voice in the political system. Basic to the plight of the minorities was education. The lack of education and job skills in the minority adult population paralleled the performance of minority children in schools. Drop-out rates, retention in grade, underachievement, incidents of suspected mental retardation, and disciplinary measures all attested to the deplorable performance of minority children in school.

Cognizant of the fact that success/failure in the adult society is very much determined by the benefits acquired from educational experiences, it is not surprising that much of the reform effort was directed toward education. Thus, we see in the 1960's the National Defense Education Act being replaced by the Elementary and Secondary Education Act with Title I investing huge amounts of money in support of new programs for minority and disadvantaged children. Subsequent to this, other programs such as bilingual education, desegregation, Follow-Through, Right To Read, Education Professions Development Act, and others were implemented to assist this target population. Legislation of the 1960's also led to the implementation of Head Start, an education program for three-, four-, and five-year-old children which would prepare them for succes in subsequent educational activities. In the 1970's, interest in such programs has somewhat diminished, and though substantial amounts of money are still being expended for the original purposes, the intensity of the 1960's is over. As stated by Dr. Roger Heyns (1976), President of the American Council on Education, "We are witnessing a flagging of activities and interest in many aspects of the problem . . . most of the forms of institutional commitment installed in the late 1960's are still here, but some of the vigor, sense of urgency and vision has gone out" (p. 16).

Although a certain amount of the lack of intensity can be attributed to the institutionalizing of programs, a large amount of the lack of interest can be attributed to dissatisfaction with the limited success of the Great Society programs. This is not to say that benefits have not been derived from each and every one of the educational interventions implemented by federal and state governments, but rather that, as is most common in social programs and research, there is an absence of clear-cut, demonstrable gains attributable to the effects of the program. It would be extremely advantageous and supportive to be able to demonstrate conclusively that each of the children who has participated in a Head Start or Title I program shows large and consistent gains in comparison to the nonparticipants. Unfortunately, this is not and cannot be the case.

The reasons for the limited success of educational programs for the minorities and disadvantaged are varied, but the following suggestions must be considered:

1. The quantity of intervention is limited. Time constraints, limited resources, time span of children, and practical limitations preclude extensive amounts of participation in any programmatic activity. Regardless of the program, administrative details, basic necessities; pupil-adult ratios and many distracting activities result in the program participant receiving limited amounts of treatment, especially so when compared with the amount of time spent in nontreatment activities. In many cases, and this is especially true in the elementary and secondary schools, programs for the disadvantaged did not replace traditional programs, but rather were added on to traditional activities. In such cases, the intervention was usually presented only after traditional educational activities had already been conducted. Similarly, the funding of treatment activities was supplemental to existing resources, and when the existing resources were meager and insufficient, the special programs were built on an inadequate and shaky foundation.

2. The quality of the intervention left much to be desired. In elementary and secondary schools, the same teachers who had been unable to teach the children during the day were employed to tutor them in the evenings. The same teachers who had not been able to teach the children for nine months were employed to continue the treatment during the summer. The same materials which had been most inadequate for the minorities and disadvantaged were enlarged by the ever-present overhead projector. Concern with pupil-teacher ratios inevitably led to a reduction in the

number of pupils for all teachers, though the treatment afforded children did not vary in any way. In many instances, the entire intervention for minority and disadvantaged children consisted of providing the necessary resources for the schools to do the wrong things better.

Regardless of the direction of the intervention, all the newly instituted educational programs suffered from a lack of appropriate materials available to them, not enough adequately prepared teachers, and from the presence of inexperience and confusion. Head Start programs were bombarded with conflicting and competing rationales, and no sooner were materials made available than they were made obsolete by new models based on the newest theory or philosophy.

It is interesting to note that even today, Head Start programs complain of inadequacies in instructional materials and methodologies. Although Head Start had been around for many years and has been serving 15–20 percent of the language-minority children, it is only within the last two years that an effort has been initiated toward the development of bilingual materials, and such programs cannot be marketed for several more years.

3. Interventions have been unable to control dependent variables. Unlike the immaculate laboratories in the hard sciences, social scientists are unable to manipulate variables outside of their programmatic activities and sometimes even within the program itself. Teacher attitudes, teacher competency, efficiency of interaction, and level of interaction have to be assumed as constants, though in practice we know they are not so. Outside the program, the child is continuously bombarded with experiences which may have an impact on his or her subsequent educational performance. The effect of interactions with an older sibling is completely uncontrollable in a research and evaluation activity, though quantity and quality of the interaction may be of more consequence than anything being attempted in the education program.

4. There has been a lack of significant changes in the larger society in which we live. To a certain extent, the implementation of innovative programs assumed that changes in the education of children would parallel changes in the larger society. There has been a most naive assumption that the larger society is prepared and receptive to the social changes which can be brought about by a successful effort in bringing about equality of educational opportunity. It is naive to assume that the exclusion of minorities in the fruits of the land could be attributed solely to the minorities' lack of preparation for participation.

Such changes in the larger society did not come about, which is not surprising when significant changes did not come about in the education community itself. Thus, children successfully participating in Head Start programs did not enter the first grade in a climate receptive to their changed characteristics and prepared to expand upon the experiences of the early years. In the relationship between Head Start and the elementary school, the big problem was not preparing Head Start children for the first grade, but rather preparing the first grade for Head Start children.

5. To a great extent, Head Start programs were developed on a deficit model. Minority and disadvantaged children were perceived not only as different but as inferior. The culture, language, and economic class characteristics reflected by the children were perceived by the educator as negative attributes which should be eliminated or compensated for before the child could hope to succeed in the traditional educational programs designed by and for middle-class populations. Thus, the minorities and the disadvantaged were bombarded by middle-class values, traditions, orientations, language, behaviors, and attitudes in the hope that the blackness or His-

panicness of the child would be removed, allowing the child to fit in the middle-class mold afforded by traditional middle-class education programs.

HOME AND SCHOOL COOPERATION

A well-prepared learning environment is vital to the child's intellectual and physical development, and the time and effort spent in developing it is time well spent. Thus, good teachers always work hard to prepare a learning environment that will arouse the interest of their students. Great care is taken to provide the right kind and quantity of materials that will help children develop their large muscles, their small muscles, their coordination and their cognitive and language skills as well.

One area, however, is often overlooked because it is an area that cannot be physically touched or seen, but it can be felt! This area concerns the psychological safety and well-being of students. It concerns the feelings children develop about themselves. This area is temendously important, because it *sets the stage for learning.*

Learning is a complex mental process. There are many theories about the best conditions for facilitating learning, but one thing appears to be fairly certain—learning is a highly complex process which can best take place if certain basic and prerequisite needs have been provided for.

Setting the stage for learning begins to occur long before the child enters the classroom. The process begins at home in earliest infancy with parents serving as the first teachers. The quality of the interaction between child and parents will determine, in large measure, whether the child develops a positive or negative sense of self which will carry over to his school years and his adult life. Therefore, it is important that both parents and teachers understand the psychological needs of children as well as the cultural context within which these needs are met so that their efforts to create a learning environment may be complementary and continuous rather than contradictory and discontinuous.

EARLY PSYCHOSOCIAL NEEDS

One of the earliest needs of the infant is to develop a sense of attachment to an important figure—usually the mother. Erikson (1964) describes this period as the first of the eight psychosocial stages or "Ages of Man" which begin in infancy and go through adulthood. This is the period called "trust versus mistrust." Erikson describes trust as the general state of being in which the child has learned to depend on the continuity of care provided by the caregiver. Trust versus mistrust is a conflict; finding an enduring solution to this conflict becomes the first task of the ego. The quality of the maternal relationship determines the amount of trust that is developed. By combining "sensitive care of the baby's individual needs and a firm sense of personal trustworthiness within the trusted framework of their culture's lifestyle" (p. 249). Mothers can create a sense of trust within their babies, essential to the development of a positive self-concept.

Following this stage are two others that are especially important for those who care for young children. These are: autonomy versus doubt, and initiative versus guilt. Biehler (1974) provides a clear and concise description of these first three stages.

trust vs. mistrust

Adequate care and genuine affection lead to a view of the world as safe and dependable. Inadequate care and rejection lead to fear and suspicion.

autonomy vs. doubt

Opportunities for the child to try out skills at this own pace and in his own way lead to autonomy. Overprotection or lack of support may lead to doubt about the ability to control self or environment.

initiative vs. guilt

Freedom to engage in activities and patient answering of questions lead to initiative. Restriction of activity and treating questions as a nuisance lead to guilt (p. 109).

The implication of these stages for schools and teachers is obvious. They must continue to build the good foundation we assume the parents have begun. The child's sense of trust can be developed by accepting and including his culture and language in the curriculum; his autonomy and initiative can be developed by matching the curriculum to his developmental level and dominant language, thus giving him a sense of pride in his ability to learn.

It is inconceivable to the writers of this essay that a child could develop a sense of trust in his school and his teacher in an environment that is inconsistent and incompatible with his home culture and home language. Thus, setting the stage for learning means providing continuity of care and experiences from home and school.

THE PROCESS OF BECOMING

"Self-actualization" is the term used by Abraham Maslow (1954) to explain the force that motivates man to fulfill his potential. However, Maslow maintains that this can best happen if prior, more basic needs are gratified. He has arranged these needs in a hierarchy that can be visualized as in Figure 13.1.

Figure 13.1 *Maslow's hierarchy of human needs.* (Source: *Maslow,* Motivation and Personality, *1954.*)

Physiological needs refer to the basic biological needs such as food, water and temperature regulation.

Safety needs refer to such things as the need that one has to maintain a sociable, predictable, orderly, and nonthreatening environment.

Love and belongingness needs refer to the need to love and receive love in return; the need to be a member of a group such as a family group, ethnic group, and so forth.

Self-esteem needs refer to the need to have a high opinion of yourself; the need to know that others hold you in high esteem.

Self-actualization refers to the need to develop fully; to become what you are capable of becoming; to be self-fulfilled.

Maslow states that the first four of these are "deficiency needs." The young child depends on others, most significantly his parents and teachers, to satisfy these needs. Self-actualization is called a "growth need." The implications of Maslow's theory are powerful! Teachers should do everything possible to help their students satisfy these deficiency needs *so that the stage is set for learning.* This must include designing the school environment so that it is compatible with the child's home culture and language. Should schools and families work together? It is abundantly clear that they must.

The development of a fully functioning human being depends largely on an individual's development of a healthy, accurate, accepting concept of self. The success of this development has its roots in earliest infancy.

Growing crime statistics and child-abuse statistics point to the need for action. Clearly, families need a variety of support services so that their relationships may be strengthened. Prospective parents need to be prepared for successful parenting. In child-care centers, Head Start centers, and schools, staff who are actually surrogate parents must be well prepared in order to fulfill this role and skillfully prepare parents for providing the nurturance, reinforcement and culturally consistent care and learning that Erikson (1968) describes as a vital need if children are to develop a sense of trust in their work (and the people in it). This large order will require commitment, money, and a variety of creative responses.

One way of looking at problems in the education of minority and disadvantaged children is by perceiving the child with a whole array of characteristics being placed in an educational program requiring a completely different set of characteristics. The educational problem does not lie in the characteristics of the child or the characteristics of the educational program, but in the incompatibility between the two. The teaching of minority children is analagous to the placement of a round peg in a square hole. Neither of the two shapes precludes the successful completion of the activity; it is the incompatibility between the two which constitutes the problem.

One way of bringing about a match between the characteristics of minority populations and education programs is by analyzing the characteristics of nontypical populations and developing programs consistent with these characteristics. The following is such an analysis, based on the work of the author and Dr. Blandina Cárdenas. This analysis served as the conceptual design for the exemplary and highly successful Edgewood Early Childhood Education Program.

AREAS OF INCOMPATIBILITY

POVERTY

Many of this country's minority children are raised in a poverty situation. Much has been written about the effects of poverty on the development of the individual. In general, it can be concluded that the growth of a child in a poverty situation leads to a nontypical developmental pattern which differs from the developmental patterns of middle-class children.

Large child-to-adult ratios lead to the development of atypical speech patterns when the amount of interaction between children and adults is constrained. The frequent absence of one of the typical adults in the home, and the dissipation of adult energies in meeting the basic essentials of life further compound this problem.

The relative absence of communication media in terms of T.V. sets, radios, newspapers, magazines, and books contributes to the development of an atypical developmental pattern. An absence of success models and an academically oriented tradition develop differing concepts toward schools and schooling. Poverty also leads to the relative unavailability of intellectually stimulating toys, games, and activities. The deprivational effects of inadequate housing, malnutrition, and poor health similarly influence the development of poor children.

Evidence of this type has led educators to an erroneous conclusion, namely, the development of a deficit philosophy which attributes the poor school performance of poverty children to an inadequacy brought about by growing up in a deficient environment. Although educational developmental retardation frequently exists in such cases, it is our opinion that this retardation is not a serious educational handicap. The retardation can be overcome by the placement of the child in a school environment which can stimulate learning and rapidly produce an accelerated development in those areas critical to educational success in typical school situations.

Poor children are educationally handicapped when they are placed in an educational program which fails to take into account the unique early developmental patterns and assumes and requires the same developmental level which is normally found in middle-class children. For example, it has been extensively documented that children growing up in the noisy environment of an overcrowded ghetto home located in an undesirable residential area develop listening skills in a different manner from children raised in the relative quiet and order of a middle-class home. Children raised in poverty situations tend to learn to block out sounds rather than to learn finer and finer sound discriminations as is the case with middle-class children. Upon entering school, it is possible to place a poor child in an auditory-discrimination program. In a matter of weeks, the auditory developmental retardation may be successfully overcome. Instead of being placed in such a program, however, he is usually placed in a typical reading-readiness program which assumes that the child has the auditory-discrimination development of the middle-class child for whom the program was designed. The results of such a placement are disastrous.

Therefore, the failure of the child in this case is not due to the type of home in which he was raised, but rather to the type of school program in which he was placed. Auditory-discrimination retardation is not an educational problem. The incompatibility between the existing level of development and the level of development assumed in the instructional program are needed for success in the educational program.

CULTURE

A second incompatibility between the characteristics of minority children and instructional programs is in the area of culture. The incompatibilities between minority children and most school systems can be summarized in three generalizations:

1. Most school personnel know nothing about the cultural characteristics of the minority-school population.
2. The few school personnel who are aware of these cultural characteristics seldom do anything about it; and
3. On those rare occasions when the school does attempt to do something concerning the culture of the minority groups, it always does the wrong things.

Much as been written about the cultural irrelevance of instructional materials. In general, typical instructional materials developed by and for white, Anglo, middle-class personnel present surroundings, situations, dialogue, and conclusions which are foreign and incongruous to the culturally atypical child. The absence of minority traditions, values, and orientations in instructional materials makes them irrelevant, meaningless, and inferior in educational value for utilization by minority children.

School responses to this incompatibility have been dysfunctional. The use of black or brown ink to color the physical features of some of the people portrayed in some textbooks has done little to reduce the incompatibility. The inclusion of negative stereotypes has frequently aggravated this problem rather than diminished it.

Although incompatibilities in instructional materials have received much attention in recent years, no such attention has been drawn to the incompatibilities in instructional methodologies. Professor Lessor at Harvard conducted some interesting experiments which gave us some insights into the nature of this problem. In studying learning characteristics of children from different ethnic backgrounds, he discovered that children from different ethnic groups display some marked preference for ethnically compatible learning styles. For example, Jewish children did better than Chinese children in instructional activities based on verbalization. On the contrary, Chinese children outperformed Jewish children in instructional activities presented in the abstract. Regardless of socioeconomic background, the amount of learning correlated with the ethnicity and the preferred learning style.

In a similar experiment at UCLA, Kagan and Madsen conducted learning activities with Mexican national, Mexican-American, and Anglo children. In a learning activity based on typical middle-class Anglo competition, the Anglo children outperformed the Mexican-American children, who in turn outperformed the Mexican children. Upon presenting the same learning activity, but basing it on cooperation rather than competition, the Mexican children outperformed the Mexican-American children, and both groups outperformed the Anglo children.

The findings of these and other similar studies indicate that the amount children learn in a classroom is dependent on their race or ethnicity, the related cultural characteristics, their culturally related, preferred learning styles, and the style used by the school. Obviously, if learning styles compatible with Anglo children are utilized exclusively, the instructional program is biased and incompatible for minority children.

In distinguishing between these first two areas of incompatibility, the school is warned that it is responsible for differentiating between the "culture of poverty" and "cultural poverty." Responsiveness to the characteristics of poverty is a prerequisite to providing equal access to the full benefits of the educational program for minority-group children. It is incumbent upon the school district to remove the constraints which poverty places on the educational success of children and to compensate for deprivations that are correlated with poverty.

There is a fine distinction, however, between the effects of poverty and the effects of culture. While it is the school district's responsibility to eradicate the effect of poverty, it is not the school's prerogative to reverse the effects of culture. Mexican-American and black children are culturally different children who are deprived because they are poor; cultural difference becomes cultural deprivation only after culturally biased institutions succeed in damaging the fabric of culture through consistent attack.

LANGUAGE

Language is an element of culture so significant in its role as an impediment to learning that it must be listed as a separate incompatibility. It is apparent that an incompatibility exists when a Spanish-speaking child is placed in an English-language instructional program. The incompatibility is not so apparent when the language differences are attributed to dialect (as in some black children) or to socio-economic background. The language utilized in most textbooks in the early grades is so incompatible with the language of minority and disadvantaged children that it frequently appears to the child to be a foreign language.

We make no value judgment as to the relative worth or adequacy of the various languages and dialects which can be utilized in our country. The important point, as in the two preceding areas of incompatibility, is that a child cannot be taught successfully in a language system which he does not understand.

Past attempts to eliminate this incompatibility have been detrimental to the minority child. Psychologically, the trauma produced by the sudden immersion into an incomprehensible situation coupled with the identification of the native language as undesirable, detrimental, and inadequate still remains with many of us. Pedagogically, the cold turkey approach into the acquisition of a new language commonly requires that the beginning child master a new language, plus basic skills in that new language such as reading and arithmetic, and a variety of content materials—all at the same time. The common failure of the child to achieve all three marks the beginning of the cumulative deficit phenomenon.

The introduction of English as a Second Language (ESL) program may have improved the situation but this single phenomenon, in itself, failed to solve the problem. The postponement of basic skill development and content acquisition until a new language system has been mastered led to the delay of a child's progress for periods of as long as one year with a resultant academic retardation. ESL, with the inevitable nonacceptance and subsequent elimination of the Spanish language associated with it, gave the child a sense of language valuing which indicated to him the inferiority of his native tongue.

The only sensible solution to come about for the elimination of this incompatibility has been the development of bilingual education programs in recent years. Typically, bilingual programs consists of three basic elements presented simultaneously:

1. The continued cognitive development of the child, with accompanying development of basic skills and content acquisition in his dominant language;
2. The development of English as a second language; and
3. The further extension of his native language system.

MOBILITY

To a large extent, the instructional program for typical children is one designed for a geographically stable population. Such a program is incompatible with a highly mobile child. Although this characteristic was originally identified in the children of migrant agricultural laborers, it was soon apparent that urban minority children are no less mobile. The advent of urban development with the accompanying urban renewal and government-subsidized housing coupled with financial and social problems, led to the mobility of minority and disadvantaged children.

The typical instructional program with built-in continuity and sequence which assumes that the child in the classroom today was here yesterday and will be here tomorrow is incompatible with the mobility characteristic. The program-discontinuity problem must be faced with either a mobile curriculum or with a highly individualized instructional program.

SOCIETAL PERCEPTIONS

The last area of incompatibility presented here is that which exists between the instructional program and the way the minority child is perceived. Minority children tend to perceive themselves in negative terms. If the child does not have negative perceptions upon entering school, the alien environment with its continuous negative valuing of the child, his home, his language and culture will rapidly aid in the development of this negative self-concept.

Typical instructional programs are developed for dominant-culture children who have positive, often very positive, concepts of self. The instructional materials and methodologies do not have the frequent, strong, and immediate positive feedback mechanism needed in order for the child to change his concept and perceive himself as a successful learner in a learning situation. On the contrary, the erroneous assumption of the existence of prerequisite skills, the large increments of difficulty, and the inadequacies of the program tend to develop or strengthen a negative concept. Yet, just as nothing succeeds like success, nothing is as educationally motivating to a child as experiencing success in a learning situation.

A similar situation exists with regard to the perceptions which the school has of the minority child. In general, the negative feelings which schools hold and express to minority children lead to the development of very low levels of expectancy for the performance of these children, and all children tend to perform in keeping with what is expected of them. Just as Jacobson and Rosenthal were able to improve children's school performance and subsequently even intellectual abilities by giving teachers false information about the innate potential of children in their classic experiment, *Pygmalion in the Classroom,* so too can teachers downgrade the performance of minority children by low levels of expectancy based on equally false information.

SUMMARY

In general, the Cárdenas-Cárdenas Theory of Incompatibilities attributes the poor school performance of minority and disadvantaged children to the differences between the characteristics of the children and the characteristics of typical instructional programs developed for typical children. No deliberate attempt is made to criticize instructional programs when utilized with the children for whom the programs were developed. On the other hand, no criticism is made of the characteristics of minority children. The situation is analogous to trying to put a square peg in a round hole. The incompatibility between the two shapes does not allow them to get together.

PRINCIPLES OF INCOMPATIBILITY

INTERRELATEDNESS AND INTERDEPENDENCE

Two additional principles are necessary for understanding the educational implications of the Theory of Incompatibilities. The first is the principle of interrelatedness and interdependence. Up to this point, the various areas of incompatibility have been presented individually. It is dangerous to assume that each of these areas is an independent variable which can be studied, analyzed, and responded to, independent of the other four areas. The five areas are so interrelated that it is impossible as well as fruitless to consider one in the absence of the others. For instance, it has been stated that mobility is an area of incompatibility which accounts for the poor academic performance of minority and disadvantaged children. Yet, we can cite many examples of other types of "mobile" children such as the children of military personnel, chain store executives, and certain civil-service workers who experience a similar degree of mobility and still do not suffer from the effects of program discontinuity. In fact, many of these children, in spite of or because of their mobility, tend to outperform children from geographically stable homes.

Therefore, mobility can be an asset or a liability. It is only when mobility is coupled with poverty, culture, language, or societal perceptions that it becomes a liability for the minority child. Perhaps it is the combination of some, or perhaps all the other areas of incompatibility with mobility that produces the disastrous educational effects characteristic of mobile minority children.

Another example is the incompatibility of language which is frequently described as the cause of all of the educational problems of Mexican-Americans. Yet, educators who have taught along the Mexican border where there is a large influx of new immigrants are well acquainted with a phenomenon characteristic of these children. Although immigrant children who have previously attended school in the mother country may enter our schools without any knowledge of the English language, after a brief period of instability as they acquire English language skills, they will consistently outperform native-born minority children.

Therefore, the incompatibility of language, even coupled with culture, is not the sole source of the problem. It is language, and culture, and poverty, and mobility, and perceptions in tandem which account for the poor performance of minority children.

This principle has two major implications for our purpose. First, the development of education programs which respond to one of the incompatibilities and ignore the others is doomed to failure. This principle accounts for the past failure of our school systems to develop successful programs for minority children. In most cases, billions of federal dollars have been poured into programs aimed at responding to some characteristics of the minority child in the absence of the others and have failed to make a significant change in the performance of the children. The second implication is that the development of an education plan which responds to the needs of minority children must be a comprehensive plan which takes into account all the areas of incompatibility rather than a piecemeal effort. A bilingual program, a black-studies program, a poverty program developed in the absence of a comprehensive attack will not bring about the improved performance of minority children.

ADAPTABILITY

A second principle which must be considered prior to the development of an educational plan is the principle of adaptability. It was previously stated that an incompatibility exists between the characteristics of the minority child and the characteristics of the instructional program. One of two options exists: Either the child must be changed to fit the instructional program or the instructional program must be changed to fit the child.

Past attempts on the part of school systems to develop functionally responsive instructional programs indicate an eclectic philosophy. When the atypicality was a characteristic falling within the area of the dominant cultural group, the school had modified its program to fit the child. Thus, we commonly see elevators for handicapped children, Braille materials for the blind, and elaborate schemes, materials, and equipment to fill the needs of a limitless assortment of atypical children. But when the atypical characteristic has been attributed to race or ethnicity, the school has placed the burden of adaptability on the child. Thus, schools have acted in a racist manner in the application of this double standard for adaptability.

In addition to the inherent racism in the concept of having minority children adapt to a typical program, such an approach can no longer be tolerated for the following reasons:

1. It has been a failure. There is no way to change a nonwhite into a white or to change a Mexican-American boy or girl into a child of northern European descent. Mass efforts in welfare legislation have barely made a dent in the incidence and extent of poverty. Past legislation in various states prohibiting the use of any language other than English for instructional activities in schools did little to reduce, let alone eliminate, the speaking of Spanish among Mexican-Americans.

2. The melting pot myth is rapidly being replaced by concepts of cultural pluralism. Before attempts to change the characteristics of the learner are implemented, it is necessary to raise the question: Is it desirable to do so?

3. Changing the individual in order to produce compatibility between the instructional program and the learner is futile unless the changed individual is also accepted into the larger society. Social, political, military, and economic discrimination against blacks and Mexican-Americans in this country will continue to constrain any ethnic disposition to change for the sole purpose of participating in the educational program.

4. The process of change is destructive when it calls on blacks and Mexican-Americans to reject themselves in order to assume a new identity.

ELEMENTS OF AN EDUCATIONAL PLAN

A comprehensive education plan aimed at eliminating the incompatibilities between the school and the minority children cannot be effective if it addresses itself only to the physical assignment of students or the implementing of a smattering of isolated programs. The entire institution must develop a sensitivity to the problem and all aspects of the school must be affected. A course for the educational improvement of minority children is valueless if the teacher is not trained to teach the course. The assignment of children to mixed classes on the basis of racial equality is useless if the child encounters racist manifestations in school policies, the curriculum, materials, or on the football team. Therefore, the education plan must consider a wide array of changes, a comprehensive program "coupled with an intense and massive compensatory program for the students if it is to be successful." It must involve the entire community, the board, the school staff, and the pupils, and incorporate the following elements of school activity:

EDUCATIONAL PHILOSOPHIES

Problems in the education of minority children would be eliminated almost overnight if educational institutions would develop and implement positive educational philosophies concerning minority education. One would hope that educational institutions would develop such philosophies of their own accord, but in the absence of such initiative, it is necessary that these philosophies be imposed by external agencies. Thus, a court order may lay down the philosophies under which schools are to operate.

Basic philosophies which must be adopted regardless of origin include the following:

1. Minority children can learn, regardless of any characteristic which they may exhibit due to economic, cultural, language, social, ethnic, or racial background. There is nothing inherent in minority children which is an impediment to learning. Past failures of minority children are the result of inadequate school programs and not the fault of the child and his background.

2. Cultural pluralism is a desirable condition in our society. It is the pluralistic element in our society which made this country great. It is impossible to predict those cultural characteristics which will be conducive to the continued development, or perhaps survival, of our society. The coexistence of differing lifestyles will allow alternatives which provide the natural variations needed for subsequent selection.

3. The capability of utilizing more than one language is a desirable educational goal. The United States is probably the only country in the world where a person is considered educated in spite of an inability to speak a foreign language. Though schools pay lip service to this philosophy, neither the teaching of foreign languages, nor the retention and expansion of non-English native languages has been accomplished by our schools. The cost of this shortcoming in terms of international relations, economic, social, diplomatic, political, and military effects has been disastrous.

4. The individualization of instruction is an essential element of all instructional programs for all children. The different characteristics of children lead to different needs, interests, effort, motivation, style, and programs. The lock-step concept of education with similar programs for all children has led to the waste of a good portion of our personal resources—the minorities, the disadvantaged, the gifted, and the handicapped.

5. Children, all children, are a natural resource of our country. As humans they have an intrinsic worth; as resources they have a potential value. Each child must be developed to the point that he becomes an integral and positive part of our society, a contributing member, and a participant in the fruits of this bountiful land.

6. The end result of an educational program for minority children, and for all children, is freedom. Freedom is manifested through freedom of choice, and freedom of choice in turn requires feasible alternatives from which to choose. It is incumbent upon the schools to develop in children the necessary skills which make feasible alternatives available to them. Vocational choices, lifestyles, economic levels, and so forth, should be determined by an individual's free choice, and not by accident of birth, parents' economic conditions, geographic location, race, ethnicity, or any of the monolithic cultural constraints now found in social institutions which lock out people through the absence of alternatives.

GOVERNANCE—POLICIES, RULES, AND REGULATIONS

The racism inherent in our social institutions commonly manifests itself through racially biased policies, rules, and regulations. These forms of governance are usually biased in favor of the dominant cultural group in that they reflect its values, traditions, and orientations. Thus, it is necessary for the school system to analyze its forms of governance as they affect economic conditions, culture, language, mobility, and perceptual characteristics of children.

SCOPE AND SEQUENCE

The scope and sequence of the instructional program must be flexible in order to meet the needs of individual children and the varying elements in the community. For example, a barrio-raised child may benefit greatly from early intervention by the school. The nutritional aspects of a free lunch at the age of three may require that such a program be made available to him. The educational level of an adult group may be such that considerable benefits could be derived from an adult-education program.

CURRICULUM

The changes which the school must make in order to eliminate incompatibilities between child and school are most evident in the curriculum element. Much of the discussion on the areas of incompatibility has been in terms of curriculum. In general, it is necessary that the school identify, acquire, adopt, and develop instructional materials and methodologies which are compatible with the characteristics of minority children.

STAFFING

The implementation of an adequate curriculum requires that schools devote considerable attention to the area of staffing. In this area, four concepts must be included in the education plan:

1. It is the responsibility of the school district to identify, recruit, and employ educational personnel sufficiently cognizant of the characteristics of minority children to insure the adequate development and implementation of a responsive instructional program.

Not only must training and experience be taken into consideration, but at least a portion of this staff must be reflective of the characteristics of the minority child. Teachers who are members of minority groups have the highest propensity for understanding and responding to the characteristics of minority children. It is the responsibility of the system to acquire minority staff at least in equal proportions to the numbers of minority children.

2. Staff Differentiation Patterns—An educational institution may react negatively to the seemingly awesome implications of this education plan. The chances of successful implementation are considerably diminished in the light of the staff expertise which will be required. For example, a recommendation that all Mexican-American children be placed in a bilingual education program may seem like an unreasonable if not impossible demand especially so if Mexican-American children are to be mixed with Anglo children at all elementary schools. The implications of such an order is that all children may need a bilingual teacher. To expect the school system to furnish a bilingual teacher in each elementary school position is inconceivable.

Yet, much of the seriousness of this problem may be attributed to a tendency to think of staffing in terms of traditional staffing patterns. As long as staffing is perceived as the placement of a certified teacher in each classroom who spends her time interacting with *all* students at the *same time*, a problem persists. However, if a teacher is perceived as a director of learning activities who utilizes a wide array of personal and material resources for instructional purposes, the problem is greatly diminished.

Staff differentiation is the utilization of a variety of professional and paraprofessional personnel for instructional purposes. The type of personnel is very much determined by the skills required for a specific instructional activity. It may appear that the entire array of skills needed for the implementation of an instructional program, including the diagnosis and prescription of instructions, is awesome and requires many years of training through an M.A. or Ph.D. program. However, when instructional activities are broken down into these component elements, it is apparent that not only do they not require an advanced college degree, but in fact some elements can be successfully implemented by a moderately trained layman. Specific types of school personnel which can be utilized by the school system in order to guarantee that each child has some adult with whom he can relate include assistant teachers, teacher aides, student interns, student teachers, paid lay persons, secondary school students, and volunteer parents.

For school systems faced with large staff needs and limited financial resources, the last two types of personnel should be of special interest. Youth-tutoring-youth programs which utilize high school students for instructional purposes have demonstrated many benefits over and beyond the low cost of the service. Minority high school students have shown more sensitivity to minority elementary-school-aged children than have regular teachers. The concept of sibling assistance is inherent and strong in most minority cultures. The provision of laboratory experience in homemaking, child care, psychology, and social studies courses has done much to make these courses meaningful and beneficial to high school students. Analysis of the tutor-tutee relationship has repeatedly demonstrated that though the younger children (tutees) make gains, the tutor tends to make even larger and more significant gains in the subject matter areas in which he tutors. Unbelievable as it may sound, the best way to teach a high school nonreader is to have him teach a group of third graders a reading lesson.

Indirect benefits also accrue as a result of this involvement. In one experiment, a group of 240 minority high school potential dropouts, plagued by disciplinary problems, truancy, and underachievement were enrolled in an elementary school classroom-assistant program. In one year, 240 students made signficant gains in the subject-matter areas to which they were assigned, did not have a single serious disciplinary problem, truancy disappeared, and amazingly enough, not a single one dropped out of school while enrolled in the program.

Volunteer parents have likewise proved to be an unexpected gold mine in teaching minority children. When given limited training they can conduct simple instructional tasks with individual and small groups of children. In the previous program, the goal of one volunteer parent per classroom each day was easily reached. Perhaps the teacher slogan of "a parent a day will keep the doctor away" accounted for the initial interest of the teachers in the program. Within a short time, teachers found this assistance indispensable in the offering of an individualized and relevant program to disadvantaged minority children.

A feasible objective in differentiated staffing is that during the day each child have an adult with whom he can communicate and relate in his preferred mode of communication.

3. The successful implementation of this plan will require a massive effort in the training and retraining of all levels of educational personnel. Beginning with the basic assumption that traditional practices have not been successful and alternative programs must be developed and implemented, it is apparent that an in-service teacher training program must be implemented for the understanding and synthesis of the rationale of this education plan. Further training would be needed for the identification of the characteristics of minority children, the development of alternative activities, and the acquisition of the necessary skills for program implementation. In sum, the development and implementation of a staff training program will require the identification and acquisition of personnel resources very different from the conventional higher-education trainers of teachers, locked in their ivory towers, and cranking out dysfunctional teachers completely unprepared to teach the atypical minority child.

4. Staffing also implies the development of a program that affords upward and lateral mobility for minority personnel. The use of minority persons in para-professional positions may become detrimental when the child perceives that assistants and aides reflect minority characteristics, but professional personnel and authority figures

always refelect an alien cultural group. An adequate staffing program will also provide the necessary training and experience for minority teachers to move into counseling, supervisory, and administrative positions. This upward mobility must extend to the highest level administrative position of the school system.

CO-CURRICULUM ACTIVITIES

The effective integration of minority children must extend beyond the confines of school integration and an integrated instructional program. The various co-curricular activities must provide an opportunity for the minority children to perceive themselves as equal participants in those activities. Various impediments such as cost, policies, and procedures must be reviewed in order to afford minority children a full opportunity for effective participation in all aspects of school activities.

STUDENT PERSONNEL SERVICES

The various services provided to students such as advisory, counseling, guidance, and health usually contain the same incompatibilities found in the classroom. The use of invalid and biased tests have been extremely detrimental to minority children. This aspect of the school program must be drastically revised in order to afford equality of educational opportunity.

NONINSTRUCTIONAL NEEDS

Not all the needs of minority children can be met in the classroom. The effects of hunger, malnutrition, inadequate housing, and poor dental and medical attention have a direct and strong influence on educational outcomes. A failure to provide adequately for the noninstructional needs of children can be a contributing factor to lack of school success.

COMMUNITY INVOLVEMENT

Schools have generally failed to effectively involve some segment of the community in planning, implementing, and evaluating school programs. Sometimes this failure can be attributed to preconceived notions that the school and the larger society has of the minorities. An erroneous myth still persists that minority cultures do not have an interest in their children. Anthropoligical studies support the rejection of this myth. The fact that minority communities have different customs not understood by the schools, the failure of the schools to communicate effectively with parents, and the negative relationship which exists between the two, fail to provide the necessary bridge for the chasm that exists between the school and the home.

Parents continually complain that they are degraded and insulted in school interactions. The communicating with parents only when a negative situation develops such as a disciplinary problem makes parents shy away from any relationship.

The failure of schools to provide personnel congnizant of minority lifestyles and fluent in the language of the home creates a barrier to an effective relationship.

EVALUATION

The evaluation designs, materials, and techniques commonly used by the school are frequently most inappropriate for utilization with minority populations. Not only are the tools inadequate, but conclusions based on cultural and language biases can be extremely erroneous and detrimental to the pupil. Incompatibilities existing between the element and the characteristics of minority children must be elminated.

THE DEVELOPMENTAL MATRIX

Consideration of the five areas of incompatibility (poverty, culture, language, mobility, and societal perceptions) juxtaposed with the ten elements of an education plan produces a developmental matrix which gives fifty cells. Each of these cells is the intersection of an area of incompatibility with a school element. For example, the incompatibility of language relates to educational philosophies, school policies, scope and sequence, curriculum, staffing, co-curricular activities, student services, noninstructional needs, community involvement, and evaluation.

In a similar manner each of the elements of school activity intersects with each area of incompatibility. For example, the curriculum must be compatible with the minority characteristics of poverty, culture, language, mobility, and societal perceptions. The same is true for each element in the list.

Table 13.1 is the developmental matrix produced by the interrelationship of incompatibilities and element. This matrix serves as the basis of an instruction program which will improve the performance of minority children, protect the rights of minority children, and provide equality of educational opportunity (See Table 13.1).

CONCLUSION

The American family and the educational system—the two major institutions that influence the development of children—are apparently in trouble. Educational programs designed for a homogeneous society have become irrelevant; Johnny (and much less Juanito) is not learning to read and write; all over the country citizens are demanding from educators accountability for learning. American families are under tremendous stress. Family structures and life styles are changing; young people are running away from home and committing suicide in ever-increasing numbers; family life is threatened by unemployment and lack of adequate income (Califano, 1976).

The goal of American education has always been to help children develop into competent, emotionally healthy, fully functioning citizens. While for some children this is happening, we must recognize that for millions of children education has become a meaningless, frustrating experience. Families and schools must heed the warnings and accept the challenge to work together to create compatible environments where children may feel secure and loved and where they can develop positive and accurate concepts of self so that they may grow into mentally healthy, self-actualizing adults.

If strong families are the barometer of a strong nation, let us do all that we can to strengthen them, recognizing that we are shaping today's children to become the adults who will build the families of the future.

Table 13.1
THE DEVELOPMENTAL MATRIX

Elements of an Educational Plan

Area of Incompatibilities		Philosophies	Policies	Scope and Sequence	Curriculum	Staffing	Cocurriculum	Student Services	Noninstructional needs	Community involvement	Evaluation
	Poverty	1	6	11	16	21	26	31	36	41	46
	Culture	2	7	12	17	22	27	32	37	42	47
	Language	3	8	13	18	23	28	33	38	43	48
	Mobility	4	9	14	19	24	29	34	39	44	49
	Societal Perceptions	5	10	15	20	25	30	35	40	45	50

BIBLIOGRAPHY

Biehler, Robert F. *Psychology Applied to Teaching*, 2nd ed. Boston: Houghton Mifflin Company, 1974.

Califano, Joseph A. *American Families: Trends, Pressure and Recommendations* (A preliminary report to Governor Jimmy Carter). Unpublished paper. September 17, 1972.

Cárdenas, José A., and Cárdenas, Blandina. *The Theory of Incompatibilities*. San Antonio: Intercultural Development Research Association, 1977.

Erikson, Erik, H. "Eight Ages of Man." In *Childhood and Society*, 2nd ed. New York: W. W. Norton, 1964.

Heyns, Roger W. "Equality of Access to Postsecondary Education for Full Participation in American Society." *Chicanos in Higher Education* (proceedings of a National Institute on Access to Higher Education for the Mexican American); Henry J. Casso and Gilbert D. Roman, Editors. Albuquerque: University of New Mexico Press, 1976, p. 16.

Maslow, Abraham H. *Motivation and Personality*. New York: Harper and Row, Publishers, 1954.

Zamora, Gloria R. "Roots in Infancy for Later Development." *Understanding and Nurturing Infant Development*. Washington, D.C.: Association for Childhood Education International, 1976, pp. 47–53.

14

The Parent as Educator: A Home-School Model of Socialization

MARIO D. FANTINI
Dean, School of Education
University of Massachusetts
Amherst, Massachusetts

INTRODUCTION

We have known for a long time that parents are teachers, that the home is a "school" with its own "curriculum" in which children learn many things before moving into the formal classroom. We have also known for some time that parents as teachers significantly affect the physical, emotional, and intellectual world of their children from birth onward. However, what has up until now escaped our scrutiny, and not received nearly the attention it deserves, is the process by which parents learn their roles—more specifically, the process of *parental socialization*. Recently, the themes of "parent effectiveness" and "improved parenting" have become popularized. In one sense, these developments reflect a "back-to-basics" trend. The family and parents are viewed as *basic* agents in the education of the young, a strong family structure being crucial in fostering the kind of values that will enable children to develop into mature, responsible adults who will ultimately contribute directly to making the world a better place.

In early times, when society was less industrialized, the family appeared to have more of a "built-in" parenting socialization process. More often than not, the young were exposed daily to an extended-family support structure which formed the major social context in which they learned their responsibilities. They acquired skill in child-rearing by being immersed in a context in which adults carried out their tasks routinely, as had been the custom and tradition for decades. Thus, in earlier centuries, manpower needs were determined by intergenerational transmission. Sons and daughters followed in their parents' footsteps because the job situation was rooted in an agrarian economic system.

Technology and urbanization changed much of that. The national manpower needs of modern business and industry required that workers be mobile (more than 20 percent of the work force moving each year) and retrainable—modifications in the means of production occasioned the need for retooling. The place of employment changed from rural to urban and metropolitan areas where services related to production needs were more cost effective. Cities became the centers of the marketplace. Since the process by which families attempt to keep pace with the demands of a changing economic system has a decided impact on life style, earning a living is naturally central to family survival. Attempting to adjust to twentieth century economic realities has resulted in the uprooting of traditional familial arrangements. Add to this the changes initiated by "rights" groups (for example, blacks, women, the elderly, and so forth) and the net result is a change in the home environment of many families. This change has, in turn, also influenced child-rearing practices.

Thus, the contemporary American family is experiencing an erosion of the older, established parenting pattern in favor of more formal learning patterns. The old supports, such as the extended family (grandparents, relatives, and the community neighbors), are gradually being replaced by books, courses, television programs, self-help groups, and so forth. In the process, some viewers believe that parents have to shift their reliance from "instinct" to greater cognitive knowledge.

This trend had influenced modern parents to turn increasingly to what has become a major contemporary source for seeking answers to their parenting needs: the advice of professional experts. Such consultation has taken the form of reading books and magazines on the subject by such authors as Dr. Spock, or of seeking out counselors. More recently, parent groups have been formed which give parents the opportunity to learn and profit from sharing their experiences.

The main point I wish to emphasize is that, even today, adults must still *learn* how to be effective in their role as parents. Whereas in earlier times, this process was more informal and, as it were, built in to the social fabric of the agrarian society, today's parents must seek a process for learning their roles that is appropriate for an industrial society. Some feel that this relinquishing of intergenerational socialization to specialized professionals and their institutions has led, in part, to severe strain on child development—a few even going so far as to believe that the increase in delinquency rates can be traced to this process. In addition, this change has resulted in a professionalization of the methods of child-rearing in which experts have the greatest authority and influence. Some observers believe that professionals have a monopoly on child-rearing which must be broken. Effective parenting is viewed as a way of reclaiming the authority parents have lost over the decades.

The so-called back-to-basics sentiment currently in vogue, appears also to be developing within the family with increased numbers of parents seeking recall of authority lost to professionals in their child's development. Many parents want more authority for making decisions about their children's education, for example, in which the trend toward family choice in education is a case in point (for example, tax benefits, vouchers). Educational vouchers, for instance, would permit families to redeem their vouchers at a private or public school of their choice. On the other hand, the impact of modern society has often resulted in the need on the part of many parents to *delegate* to other agencies responsibilities for child-rearing and education. The phenomenal rise in child care is one prime example. Many parents want the opportunity to pursue their own careers and see economic advantages to having their children participate in a day-care program, for example. Thus, whatever its manifestation, the impact of contemporary society on families and their functions has greatly affected the overall process by which parents learn their child-rearing roles.

HOW DO PARENTS LEARN TO BECOME EDUCATORS?
A SOCIOLOGICAL PERSPECTIVE

Trying to really grasp this dimension of parenting today is a difficult task. However, one way to gain some insight into this process is through sociological analysis. Employing the sociological concepts of *socialization* and *role* gives us some tools with which to probe further. According to role theory, roles are learned through a patterned set of formal and informal interactions of the individual with a culture including its language. Thus, the context or setting in which the role is actually performed becomes crucial. That is to say, a person is socialized in role-appropriate settings. The more powerful these role-related settings are, the more powerful the process of socialization. Conceivably, by creating ideal role settings in which parents have opportunities to learn the skills and competencies associated with their role, the more competent they will become as educators.

Hence, in the socialization of doctors, we see the creation of internships and residency, of teaching hospitals and clinical professors. These become the role-appropriate settings in which future doctors are socialized. Clearly, the certified doctors who also perform in these settings become models of role behavior, whose language and style become role-appropriate behavior for those being socialized. Continuous immersion in these contexts eventually results in the assimilation of the normative behavioral pattern by most medical professionals. Doctors learn a new language and manner in addition to an array of diagnostic and prescriptive procedures. In short, the doctor has learned the appropriate behavior by being systematically socialized. Left to happenstance, it is unlikely that this transition from layman to doctor could attain the same results. We use this type of conceptual framework to guide the process by which we prepare our doctors, lawyers, teachers, and so on; that is to say, what goes into the conversion of a layman into a lawyer, doctor, teacher, and so on. Fulfilling the role of an effective parent might be encouraged if more attention were given to the process by which parents learn their skills as well.

This sequence of experiences by which parents learn their roles can be so informal as to be considered a "natural" occurrence. There are those who believe that the more natural this process, the more the innate maternal and paternal instincts become the main determinants of behavior with the young. By "trusting their feelings," parents are able to draw on their "inner senses" that may be "genetically programmed" and therefore not only powerful, but perhaps reliable as well. For others, instinct needs to be supplemented or even superceded by the development of alternative capabilities; still others need a combination of internal and external resources to perform their roles adequately.

As human behavior has increasingly become the subject of more disciplined inquiry, the knowledge base has increased; this has given rise to specialists—child and abnormal psychologists and psychiatrists, geriatricians, family counselors, therapists, and so forth. The trend appears to have evolved as follows: The more the knowledge base has been extended, the more professionals as experts have assumed responsibility for that particular aspect of human behavior which is their area of expertise. As this trend has developed, parents have become increasingly influenced by what the experts say. An entire professional language system has been created to diagnose and explain different aspects of human behavior: *aggression, the Oedipus complex, identification fixation, sibling rivalry, delayed gratification,* and so forth. This technical language has served to communicate to parents their own inadequacies, the suspect nature of following their own instincts. How to gain the knowledge necessary to perform their role as parents more effectively and how to use it have become major challenges for contemporary parents.

Consequently, a central question remains: How does a parent learn his or her role today? Does the parent view himself or herself as an actor who has to learn a part? Does the parent learn a script prepared by professional experts which he or she then practices at home? Is this script evaluated by the response of the child? What happens if the child does not respond as expected? Is there another script, and still another? Which one is the "best" script?

It appears clear that roles do develop out of some interaction of the person seeking or performing the role and those who either have performed the role or who are viewed as knowing how the role should be performed. In the more stable agrarian period to which reference has been made, the new parent had his or her mother, father, and grandparents as models who, if close at hand, were actually their "on-the-job trainers" in a type of apprenticeship or internship system. Certainly, in this older, informal socialization process, a "language" depicting various aspects of the child-rearing function was used as were particular methodologies (for example, *spare the rod, spoil the child; duty before pleasure; spoiled; ornery*). The home environment and the participants constituted, in essence, a clinical setting in which the prospective parent began to learn his or her role under the supervision of more experienced friends and relatives.

Today, the clinical setting of the home still exists. The context may have been altered somewhat, with such powerful new participants as radio and television, but the need to perform a parenting role is still present. Parents now can turn on the television set and see experts advising millions of parents on particular techniques. The parent may be advised to get a particular book or may hear about a particular course being offered at a local school or college.

Thus, given the realities of being a parent today, this chapter is based on the assumption that the majority of parents from all socioeconomic levels and cultural orientations will seek outside assistance in their quest to improve their skills as educators. I will suggest that an important dimension in the contemporary development of the parents' role as an educator is the interaction between home and school, for the agency closest to parents and the one to which most parents will first turn for help is the school. (Clearly, there are other agencies and institutions that also relate to the family such as religious and medical centers, but for my purposes, the school will be emphasized as a key socializing agent in parenting.) In fact, a poll conducted in 1977 revealed that nearly half of all parents surveyed reported that they would prefer to approach their children's teachers, as opposed to any other individuals or institutions, on parent-effectiveness issues (Yankelovich, Skelly, and White, Inc.). Teachers and the schools are geared to youth. The professionals are trained in and dedicated to child development. Therefore, the school and its personnel are in a logical position for performing important support roles in the contemporary socialization of the parent as educator. This function of the parent thus becomes another form of parent participation, an extension of the contemporary community involvement trend in education which has resulted in parent councils for Title I, Head Start, councils in local schools, and so forth.

The emergence of the school (including day-care centers, Head Start groups, and the like) as a central agency in the community and in the life of the child and the family has thus made this institution an important force in the socialization of parents. To begin with, *all future parents go through school.* Later, as mothers and fathers, they continue to be functionally linked to schools through their children. The proximity of the school to the home, the natural relationships and system of communication that emerges around the needs of the child, the fact that parents and school personnel are united in the mutual goal of furthering child development, makes the school and its resources important *support* structure for parent socialization. This is not to say that there are not shortcomings associated with any plan to "professionalize" parenting and that is not the intention here. Rather, such an approach merely provides *one* of the many possible ways of supporting the development of maternal and paternal educational roles in parenthood.

A close school/home partnership built around the best interest of the learner has always been sought. Historically, we have viewed parents and teachers as key allies in the education of the young. In recent years, there has been a "strain" on school/community relations, but this may be a phase occasioned by the changing political picture in the schools; for example, the case of teacher unions' involvement in collective bargaining, school finance issues, and so forth. Although the emergence of teacher unions, for instance, has necessitated that the schools adopt a different type of "political" connection with the family and community, as far as the child's education is concerned, the parent and teacher, the home and school, are still inevitably tied as first principles in community organization.

Returning to such first principles today, in fact, will require a new and more effective bond between modern parents and teachers. Their functions as primary agents of socialization will ultimately bring them together around the developmental needs of the learner. If personalized, a mutually supportive home/school structure can bring the concerns of the family and school, of the parent and teacher together in cooperative planning to guide a child's development.

What needs to be different today in our conceptualizing the home/school, parent/teacher relationship is a mutual realization that *both are primary educators, both directors of learning environments* that shape the mind and heart of the child, and both often in competition with other "teachers" such as the peer group, the media, and the like. This would necessitate that parents play a larger role than ever before in directing their child's education. Therefore, we need to give much more careful and deliberate thought to the socialization process appropriate to the parent as educator.

THE PRESERVICE AND INSERVICE TRAINING OF PARENTS AS EDUCATORS

There are two aspects of parental socialization which the school should consider implementing: (1) the preparation of the *next* generation of parents, and (2) the retooling or delivery of appropriate education for those who are *currently* parents. At one level, this may appear to be a "curriculum and instruction" problem, and to a considerable extent it is. The school is often viewed as an institution which has, as one of its objectives, the preparation of children for the major societal roles (citizen and consumer) which they will one day assume. Certainly, the role of the parent would fit in this category. Urie Bronfenbrenner (1974), a leading child-development expert at Cornell, makes the point directly:

It is commonplace among educators to affirm that the task of the school is to prepare the child "for life." There is one role in life the overwhelming majority of all children will ultimately play but for which they are given virtually no concrete preparation. It is parenthood. In cross-cultural observations I have been struck by the American child's relative lack of ease in relating to infants and young children, engaging their interest and enjoying their company. With the important exception of certain minority groups, including blacks, many young people never had experience in extended care of a baby or a young child until they have their own.

A solution to this problem, which speaks as well to the need to give young people in our society genuine and consequential responsibility, is to introduce truly functional courses in human development into the regular school curriculum. [p. 60]

However, we have learned from past experience that the preparation of parents is not simply a matter of reading a book on the subject or forming a committee of teachers and developing a curriculum guide or a course of studies. Bronfenbrenner (1974) sketches his view of a curriculum that gives the usual "family life" programs sometimes found in our secondary schools:

Now the material is typically presented in vicarious form, that is, through reading or discussion or possibly through role-playing rather than actual role-taking. In contrast, the approach being proposed here would have as its core a responsible and active concern for the lives of young children and their families. Such an experience could be facilitated by locating day-care centers and pre-school programs in or near schools so that they could be made an integral part of the curriculum. The older children would work with the younger ones on a regular basis, both at school and in the young children's homes, where they would have an opportunity to become acquainted with the youngster's families and their circumstances. [p. 6]

To begin with, the so-called knowledge (or competencies) necessary to mount such a program does not reside mainly in the schoolhouse or with school personnel. A serious approach to the socialization of parents would require that the expertise of the various human services of the community—for example, psychiatrists, pediatricians, child psychologists, nutritionists, human development specialists, linguists, clergy, and so forth—be tapped. The classroom teacher, along with the school counselor, psychologist, and administrators can and should become key "orchestrators" or "facilitators" who see to it that the fullest utilization of these resources takes place for the parents requesting such services. The pedagogical goal of such orchestration is to harness these diverse talents in a carefully planned curriculum within and outside of the existing school program. Further, the clinical dimensions of socialization (that is to say, the contexts in which future parents practice their roles) need to be planned. These contexts could be something as commonplace as "peer tutoring" or something more elaborate like "internships in day-care centers." In any case, establishing the necessary theory and practice of parenting would legitimize the concept of parenting in our schools and communities.

At the inservice level, a range of avenues for reaching today's parents should be considered. Again, the schools, as a central community agency, can play a key role. Programs for parents during the day, in the evening, and on weekends can be instituted. The school can help coordinate the talents of other community agencies. Business, industry, and labor can help create on-the-job opportunities such as flexible working hours, which would allow parents to engage in parent-effectiveness training. The medical and mental health communities can help plan programs on this subject which would include the delivery of such services. Universities can also assist in opening their doors to these new learners with programs that focus on the parent as teacher. Obviously, there are many ways of approaching both preservice and inservice education for parents, but there are certain basic key factors which must be taken into account in advancing a home-school approach to effective parent socialization. What follows is a discussion of these considerations.

ONE MODEL FOR HOME-SCHOOL COLLABORATION

One model for this home/school partnership views the *parents as the ultimate decision-makers* and the *professionals as counselors or advisors* who are engaged in providing relevant input for the educational development of the child. The parents of particular cultural persuasions might solicit the advice of those professional educators most familiar with the values and style of that culture. They may ask the professionals for a recommendation on a particular decision, or even *delegate* to certain professionals the opportunity to make the decision for them. In each case, however, the parents make the ultimate decision. Even if they delegate this responsibility to professionals, they have made the decision to do so. The point to be stressed is that such a collaborative effort deliberately attempts to acknowledge the rights of parents as the *primary educators* of their children, defining the professional role as that of a *support resource whose unswerving commitment to the needs of the child provides a natural link to the parent's own intrinsic motivation in this regard.* The trust developed in working toward this common goal—the child's best interests—coupled with a mutual respect for the parent's right as educational decision-maker, becomes an essential ingredient in the home-school relationship.

COLLABORATION IN THE RESOCIALIZATION OF PRESENT PARENTS

Once this core relationship is established, the next step is to personalize the assessment of parental concern. That is to say, to develop an individualized approach which will lead to a determination of the major problem which the parents perceive they have in raising their children. Once this major problem is identified, the next phase is to survey the resources within the school and community that may potentially be tapped by parents to assist them in solving the problem. These resources may be nutritionists, child psychologists, pediatricians, reading specialists, bilingual teachers, and so forth. Again, it must be underscored that the parents and their professional school advisors view the needs of the child as paramount at all times. Moreover, given the *individualized* nature of this collaboration, the *parent is free to choose from a variety of resources* those that are felt to be most appropriate to the parenting task at hand. At no time is any one pattern or service imposed or forced on the parent. The goal is to increase the parent's capacity (on the parent's own terms) to acquire the skills necessary for effective parenting. In this model, the collaborative *process* is, in itself, educational for parents and professionals alike.

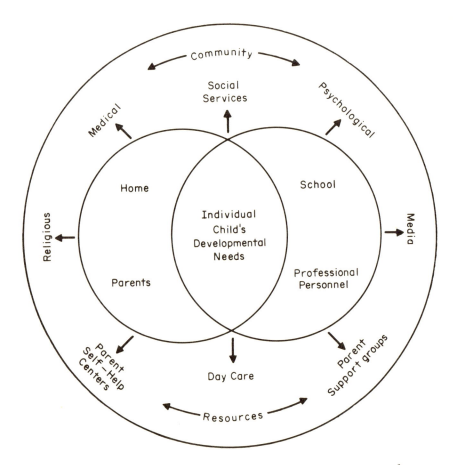

Figure 14.1 *A model for home/school, parent/professional collaboration on effective parenting.*

Figure 14.1 portrays the interaction of parents with professional school personnel. The latter play a supportive role as advisors in tapping and tailoring available resources to fit the unique parenting situation identified as suited to meeting the developmental needs of the child and the expressed concern of the parent.

Such a model satisfied the concerns which we suggested earlier. Therefore, in setting up this model, the following guidelines have been kept in mind:

1. The ultimate objective, and the heart of the process, should always be the child's needs.
2. The parent should be the central decision-maker.
3. The professional educator is a chief advisor to parents on their needs in relation to the child's. The professional offers suggestions and provides information on the basis of which parents can make their own decisions.
4. The cultural orientation of the family should be respected and remain of primary importance.

5. The talents of various school personnel as support agents close to the family and child should be maximized.
6. The parent/professional relationship should be personalized.
7. The resources available in the community (health, recreational, religious, cultural, and so forth) should be utilized and orchestrated.

By giving the school a support role in the socialization of parents as teachers, the goals of community education (that is, the long-held vision of the home and school coordinating the rich talents and resources of the community on behalf of enhanced learning for youth and adults alike) is furthered. Within this conception of "community education," parents and learners who want to do a better job of child-rearing can seek and obtain the assistance of various resources in the community with help and guidance from the school. Perhaps a community-school plan with flexible scheduling might enable school personnel to be available at all hours, including evenings and weekends, to work with parents. Further, with the decline in the school-age population, more professionals are available for working with parents.

Once the community resources are identified and tapped, the next phase involves utilizing the newly gained information, insight, or skill with the child at home. This parental testing of child-rearing practices accompanied by continuous evaluation of their potential impact and the reporting of these results to advisors, occasions the necessity for planning and for further modification of these procedures. Thus, we see created the beginning of a systematic process of parent socialization. The parents are pursuing a process of learning to be more effective in their roles as parent educators. As such, they are deliberately engaging in a planned sequence of resocialization, accomplished in a manner which fits the parents' unique learning style.

COLLABORATION IN THE SOCIALIZATION OF FUTURE PARENTS

The other process of socialization which the schools should give serious thought to implementing involves the preparation of the next generation of parents as educators. Maintaining the home-school, parent/professional collaborative relationship, the schools may consider adapting their curriculum to emphasize the *preservice* education of parents as teachers. Again, the parents have a right to choose or reject a program in which their children are learning to be parent educators. If parents decide in favor of it, then a school program from early childhood through secondary levels might include the ongoing study of human development, opportunities to work continuously with other children and adults in various contexts, carefully developed techniques in self-analysis and clinical observation under appropriate supervision. More specifically, such a developmental program might begin with children teaching and helping other children at all levels, performing assistantship and apprenticeship roles in day care, Head Start, or nursery schools, neighborhood youth centers, school health offices, school food service facilities, pediatric wards of hospitals and clinics, special state schools, and so forth. The focus of the curriculum is to learn how people grow, to seek answers to such questions as: What are the conditions that seem to promote or retard positive development? How can we learn to help others reach their potential? Where can we go for help?

Curricula, such as the one just sketched, are being prepared. For example, the

Educational Development Center in Newton, Massachusetts, with a long history of pioneer efforts in curriculum development (for example, "Man: A Course of Studies, Elementary Science Study"), has produced a series entitled, *Exploring Childhood.* This program provides a comprehensive structure and process for school-age students, their parents, and teachers to systematically approach the content of human development. The curriculum sequence is divided into modules such as *Working with Children, Seeing Development,* and *Family and Society.* Each module is carefully structured to promote conceptual understanding, skill, and competence building as well as applied research techniques.

Each module also includes a projection of the learning goals anticipated. For instance, in Module I, *Working with Children,* some of the learning objectives for teachers and parents are as follows:

- demonstration and recognition of the universal needs and patterns that underlie individual development in oneself and others
- illustration and understanding of development as a lifelong and multifaceted process
- use of the development theories of Erikson and Piaget as hypotheses in understanding the behavior observed in children
- demonstration of knowledge of cultural values held in different societies, values that influence the behavior and emotional patterns of caregivers and children
- careful observation of and listening to children in order to be sensitive to their needs, interests, and perspectives and to identify when children need help and when they are best left alone
- recognition and expansion of opportunities for children to express themselves and stretch their emerging capacities (for example, through art, fantasy, vigorous play, or manipulation of materials)

This module is expected to result in students being able to:

- consider the point of view of others involved when solving problems
- work cooperatively with adults at the fieldsite
- show respect for the traditional lifestyles and values of families different from their own

The curriculum is buttressed with multi-media materials, including booklets, filmstrips, films, records, and posters. The themes of safety, nutrition, health (including mental health), play, and cultural and individual diversity are all addressed. Clearly, it is not our intent to review the entire *Working with Children* module, but rather to suggest that future parent curricula are emerging that can be considered by parents and school personnel who are interested in providing such options.

In terms of role development and socialization, such programs provide sequenced patterns of focused learning, combining theory and practice in an ongoing blend of clinical contexts in which students have opportunities to perform caregiving rolls in such real life situations as Head Start and day-care centers, peer tutoring programs, pediatric wards, family-therapy clinics, child-development institutions, and the like. In each learning environment, the future parent is exposed to the theory underlying the practice by experienced and qualified persons who supervise each setting. The home and school can work closely in a joint effort to provide planned opportunities to learn these care-giving competencies. Social settings that provide such

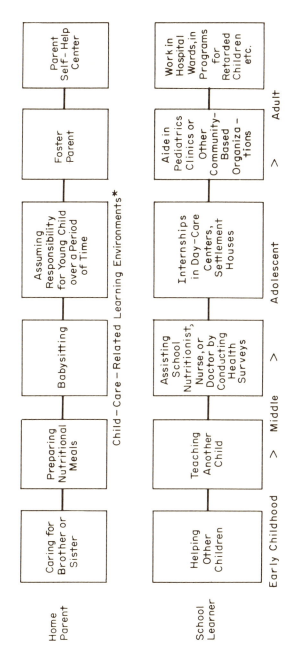

Figure 14.2 *A developmental approach to the preparation of future parents as educators.*

This diagram represents examples of the type of child-care-related learning environments which may be tapped in this home-school interrelationship.

field experiences can be arranged in a developmental pattern over the years as Figure 14.2 illustrates.

MATERNAL AND PATERNAL TEACHING STYLES

In attempting to approach the parent as an educator in a more substantive way, the personal and cultural dimensions of the role always assume critical importance. The shorthand way of dealing with these more elusive ingredients is to place them all under the rubric of "style." Clearly, different maternal and paternal teaching styles exist, depending on the personality and cultural orientation of the parents.

On the personal level, each parent brings certain values, concerns, feelings, attitudes, needs, and aspirations to his or her role. These psychological components converge on all parent/child relationships, making both parent and child behavior to each situation difficult. Nonetheless, to predict the effective socialization of major parental rolls necessitates fuller consideration of such emotion-laden variables and their influence on child growth and development. Such situationally oriented dynamics reinforce the importance of the setting itself and the "clinical judgments" of those associated with the process of socialization. Moreover, the cultural or ethnic dimension of the family involved also becomes crucial in shaping the appropriate style of teaching. In certain cultures, the dominance of one parent will create a certain environment in child-rearing. In those cultures in which extended families are functional, "team teaching" will be the result.

More specifically, maternal and paternal teaching styles will include modes of *social control* and *pedagogy*. Social control refers to the parents' orientation to disciplining the child. Does the parent appeal to the child on a personal basis? For example, does he or she say "do it for mommy or daddy"? Or, does the parent appeal to the child on the basis of external standards by saying "they don't allow that here"? Pedagogy refers to the technique and method employed to promote intentional learning. How does the parent ask questions, use materials and toys, read to the child, watch television with the child, teach the child to read, walk, quantify, sing, dance, and so forth. Subcultural family orientations appear to emphasize certain modes over others, making any quest for cross-cultural norms increasingly difficult. Some cultures are more emotionally expressive than others; some cultures use touch in their personal interactions while others shy away from body contact; some cultures expect eye contact in personal interactions while others may view such patterns as connoting disrespect. Moreover, a parent who is overly preoccupied by life's daily problems or major decisions is likely to relate in a different way to his or her child than a parent who is less burdened by these kinds of considerations. Some parents may develop a personal preference for teaching the child through examples, others for answering question after question, and still others for "mini-lectures." Suffice it to say that both cultural and personal styles become important factors that affect parental teaching styles. These styles in turn influence the child directly and provide an important means by which the learner develops his or her own style of learning.

CONTINUITY AND DISCONTINUITY AMONG PRIMARY SOCIALIZING AGENTS

The evidence compiled thus far in the behavioral sciences underlines the critical role played by parents in all phases of a child's growth and development; this role may have its most crucial influence before the child reaches school age. In any case, the parent is the pivotal agent, the most influential factor in the child's development.

Under ideal conditions, it is hypothesized that there are two master teachers in the educational environment of the home, a father and a mother. Each assumes responsibility for different complementary aspects of the child's learning. Generally, the mother satisfies the child's immediate physiological needs and ministers to baby's comforts. Long before the child can comprehend the meaning of her words, mother soothes and reassures the child with her voice, thus setting the patterns for speech as well as cognitive and emotional grasp of the immediate environment. The father provides opportunities for the child to socialize through games, conversations and other, often more physical, activities in which male interests and feelings are projected.

As yet, we know very little about mothering and fathering, and the changes which have surely taken place in the traditional roles of the past have yet to be assessed. Furthermore, different children respond differently to the same parental patterns, making pinpointed comparisons virtually impossible. However, the overall impact of mothering and fathering on the child is another matter. The role of the parent as teacher in the socializing process continues even after the child enters the kindergarten classroom doors. To be sure, the importance of parental interaction increases since the child is in a continuous state of becoming, developing a more acute awareness of his environment, one in which the school accounts for about 22 percent of his waking hours. If we accept the role of the parent as educators, then we must, in turn, accept the proposition that the child's development would be enhanced in a style in which continuity among the primary socializing agents were achieved—for example, the home, the school, the peer group, and the community. Discontinuity among the socializing units may be preferable in those cases in which parental impact has resulted in dysfunctions such as autism or where child-abuse practices are identified.

Facilitating the interaction of complementary environments where the two most important socializing agencies—the home and the school—contribute to the growth and development of the child, should be a primary goal of the coordinated planning involved in such an undertaking. This may require that the school make available more learning options for the family. Continuity in the process of socialization between home and school may mean matching teaching/learning styles. To be sure, parents have different styles of teaching than do school personnel. For many, the present school structure does not foster the creation of opportunities for teachers to *choose* a preferred style or for parents to *select* from among these styles. With certain families, for example, bilingual learning environments may be necessary in many schools to maximize such continuity. In other situations, some children may need noncompetitive environments, while others may require competitive structures. In short, the parent and teacher should be in continuous collaboration with one another, for together, they are responsible for orchestrating the resources that are deemed appropriate to facilitating the maximum development of the child. The parent as educator must be seen as an equal, or perhaps more than an equal, partner in this educational development process. From the outset, the educational criteria developed in this partnership should be *unified* to avoid the existence of conflicting methods and goals for the child, but never *imposed* upon parent and/or child.

If models for effective parenting are to foster stronger bonds between the home and the school, then early childhood education policy makers must not continue seeing either of the parents as the primary *cause* of their children's learning difficulties at school. The goal is for these informed parties to form a mutual pact in which they assume mutual accountability for the maximum development of the child. Together, parents and teachers can support one another and really pool their talents for the child-rearing task at hand. Together they can personalize and individualize the education of the child, thereby increasing the chance for continuity in the process of socialization. Through this process, parents can gain important insights into child development which contributes significantly to increasing their effectiveness in rearing their children.

This renewed link or bond between home and school which we are proposing, therefore, would entail the development of a unified strategy by parent and teacher in the creation of educational programs which meet the multifold needs of the child. Every word, every action, and every educational policy should be derived from and consistent with these needs. The parent, by concerning himself/herself with the teacher's style of teaching as well as with the classroom environment, should serve as negotiator for the child; the teacher, by providing information and insight to support the parent in reaching a decision, should assume an advisory role—that of a professional colleague—in this relationship.

What we are suggesting here is an updated conception of parent/teacher linkages, a new support system in which parents and teachers and other educational personnel are the key agents. This interaction is essential for effective parenting in the home and effective teaching in the school. Ironically, although in certain quarters strains of contemporary society have served to weaken the ties between parents and teachers *at the political level,* the demands of our society necessitate the development of such a support system. It is our belief that the learner-centered support group suggested in this chapter can help reunite these key agents *at the educational level.*

We are well aware of the political ramifications of the effective parenting movement. Efforts to influence the growth and development of new generations of children are not new. The institution of the public school itself was initiated as an attempt to socialize children through the inculcation of values and ideals not necessarily provided by the family from which they came. In fact, some critics of the schools point to the maintenance of this "hidden" curriculum which socializes students in a "subversive" fashion. In their view, such socialization is viewed as serving the interests of the established economic system and the professionals who control the schools. Public interest in the family has gradually, over the years, expanded to include high school youth and, perhaps increasingly and more importantly, kindergarten age, prekindergarten and preschool children as future parents. At this juncture, the most effective way for reaching this youngest group of children is through their parents, many of whom are not fully aware of the psychological intricacies of child growth and development. The study of these intricacies are fields in their own right. Familiarity with the lessons of effective parenting could, therefore, be of crucial benefit to each family member.

POLICY CONSIDERATIONS

A concensus could probably be reached on the basic goals of effective parenting: Parents want to be more effective; family oriented professionals want parents to be more effective; children want their parents to be more effective; the courts seek the same ends. Moreover, all parties might agree that the desirable ingredients of effective parenting include such things as:

- facilitating linguistic development
- assuring adequate guidance in issues involving nutrition, health and safety
- facilitating the child's intellectual development
- developing problem-solving and decision-making skills
- setting examples for the development of moral and ethical values in the child
- facilitating a feeling of self-esteem and fate control in the sense of control over one's own destiny
- promoting basic skills (reading, studying, writing, mathematics), learning how to learn, critical thinking, and the formulation of the world view
- enabling cultural transmission and ethnic orientation to take place
- fostering the development of individual styles and standards of performance within the context of our society
- utilizing learning resources effectively (for example, television, toys, enrichment activities, books, paper, crayons, pencils, and so forth)

Nonetheless, although the creation of a home environment that is appropriate for the child at different developmental stages in his/her life and the development of these (and other) competencies associated with effective parenting during the early years of the child's life is by and large widely recognized, a wide gap remains between principles and practice. Extensive research has been conducted to assist parents in reaching such desired ends, but the results are as yet inconclusive. (For example, in a search of the literature in this area, the ERIC System identifies over 800 entries.) There is, in addition, considerable disagreements among professionals, parents, and cultures on the *means* of attaining the common goal of effective parenting.

Therefore, we believe that a public policy which advocates *options* for parents seems to make the most sense educationally, economically, and politically. A flexible policy which encourages parents to choose from among a variety of possibilities which appear justified in the context of any given time is preferable to one dominant pattern to which all must adjust. That is to say, parents should be able to *choose* from among support groups, family counseling, course work, and so forth, as well as choose the means for increasing their competence in parenting. Such a policy which advocates alternatives and choices avoids the problem of imposing one orthodoxy on parents, a consideration which seems especially important in our pluralistic and individualistically oriented society.

However, to add to the conventional educational process which exists today, a didactically oriented course on parenthood for high school pupils (for example) may not be effective, and may only make an already overloaded and unwieldy educational system more inefficient and unwieldy. As things stand, the schools are simply not equiped to deal with this aspect of education. Instead, the basic educational system must be reformed to integrate the emotional and intellectual education of future parents into the educational process from the outset. The revised educational system would perhaps build parent education into the curriculum while also assuming a major support role as an advising center for present parents on improved child-rearing. The scope of this curriculum and support service would be to *assist* and not to *supplant* the role of the parent. It should be emphasized again that the idea is not to "professionalize" parenting by structuring the experience of parenting into professionally oriented parental roles. Rather, perhaps starting in preschool classes (where play-oriented activities are an ideal context for beginning education in parenthood) and extending through the middle and upper grades to junior and senior high school classes in the biological, emotional and social realities of marriage, childbirth, and child development (where the older children can help the younger pupils), the school can do much toward facilitating the development of parents who are fully aware of their roles. Throughout this sequence, instruction and guidance must be consistent and geared to the individual realities of the family and the child.

BIBLIOGRAPHY

Bronfenbrenner, U.   "The Origins of Alienation," *Scientific American,* August 1974, Vol. 231, No. 2, p. 60–61.

Yankelovich, Skelly, and White, Inc. "Raising Children in a Changing Society." *The General Mills American Family Report,* 1977.

15

The Relationship Between Home and School: A Commentary on the Current Scene

TERREL H. BELL
Commissioner of Higher Education
Salt Lake City, Utah

It is both a curious and lamentable phenomenon that the home and school have never had a wider span of psychological distance separating these two basic institutions than the one that exists today. Both have (or should have) a commitment to promoting the child's health, emotional maturity, and intellectual growth. Between preoccupations with career and social life, parents are leaving the responsibility for education almost entirely to the school; this problem is further compounded by the fact that teachers are too busy teaching to find much time for parents. Also, educators often caution their colleagues that they should not invite too much parent participation for this leads to meddling in matters that are strictly for the professionals. All too often school personnel operate on the assumption that the children will be sent to school–that they will not be bothered too often, and that periodically, they will send home a report or hold a twenty-minute parent-teacher conference

The school often cautions parents not to teach but to leave such matters to the teachers because the parents may make matters more difficult for the child. But the fact is that parents do teach–for good or ill; they teach incidentally as they share in the lives of their children. Indeed, many parents are the most powerful teachers that children ever have. And many of these powerful parent-teachers are powerfully destructive. They destroy confidence. They nurture negative attitudes. They teach poor health habits. They damage self-image. And they often do so unwittingly, thinking that they are doing what is right–that they are discharging their duties as parents. Such parents cannot follow the school's admonition to leave the teaching to the school teachers, because life and living teach all human beings. We learn from life and from our daily living experiences. Moreover, parents are the central part of the life of the child.

No agency has a greater stake in the outcome of effective parenting than does the school. The best school on earth cannot totally remediate and restore the damage caused by inadequate and misguided parent behavior toward the child. The school must receive the child as a teachable human being, ready and anxious to learn. This calls for a healthy child who has never been starved for either good food or parental love and active concern. The child's social maturity, physical health, and organic vigor are products of the home. And these are vital requisites to any measure of success that the school might have.

Many eminently successful parents in the business and professional world have suffered heartache and deep remorse because they have reared an unhappy, maladjusted child. There can be no doubt that parents have a reciprocal need for the school despite the fact that many may not recognize it.

The schools need strong, stable, educationally oriented families. From time to time, a distinguished family is recognized for the outstanding accomplishments of all members. Some families seem to have unusual success and every child seems to be highly motivated, well adjusted, and distinguished insofar as accomplishments are concerned. What are the characteristics of these unusual families? What do parents do and what practices should they follow to encourage in the home the behavior that will lead to these unusual accomplishments?

There are no simple answers and we must beware of overly simplified generalizations. But the writer has concluded from his studies and from observations, and particularly from discussing these questions with many outstanding family groups, that there are some fundamental guidelines that will enhance the probability of success. Following are ten such guidelines that might be helpful to parents interested in evaluating and improving the quality of family life. In discussing these guidelines, it should be emphasized that not many families will meet all of the standards outlined below, but the concepts should be helpful to parents.

1. *The family is deeply involved in learning.* This involvement includes continuous conversation about learning and about topics that stimulate the mind and generate an overall desire to acquire knowledge and to be intellectually competent. Before, during, and after school, the children from such families are oriented toward intellectual activity. There is strong encouragement and stimulation towards thinking and toward utilizing the mind in seeking lofty goals and in perpetuating high ideals.

2. *The family is psychologically close.* There is an atmosphere in the home of warmth and caring for each other. The members of the family identify as a family unit. This psychological closeness is usually created by a large number of activities in which the entire family participates. This lifestyle is contrasted with many aspects of modern day family life where each member goes his own way and sees the home only as a place for sleeping and eating. The family members have a genuine regard for each other and a feeling of responsibility toward the family and toward helping all other family members to reach goals and to attain a feeling of fulfillment.

3. *The family members are oriented toward the neighborhood and community.* They may make contributions to others less fortunate than they themselves. The family members give of themselves when no particular reward is expected. In addition to meeting their own needs as individual family members, they are actively involved in helping others and in participating in community activities that tend to lift up the less fortunate among them.

4. *The children in the family largely govern themselves and settle problems among themselves with very little parental intervention.* Personality conflicts are few in such families. Talking and the exchange of ideas among brothers and sisters seem to help this self-governance characteristic. Rare is the case where a dispute has to be arbitrated by the father or the mother.

5. *The conversation among family members is quite clear and spontaneous.* The

family members speak freely and have a sense of openness and a lack of tension in conversation. The children grow up in a family atmosphere where clear expression and spontaneous relating of one's thoughts and feelings are encouraged. Communication among family members is, of course, very important. The achieving family encourages this free expression and establishes a pattern of living and a sense of emotional interrelatedness that makes this free expression easily attained.

6. *The conversation is generally constructive.* Most of the comments made by family members to each other are positive. This all reflects a certain maturity and understanding among the family members. There is a sense of duty and willingness to contribute toward a constructive emotional climate in the home. Mutual encouragement is offered to others within the family. Even criticism is framed in positive ways. The conversation is oriented toward placing the needs and the well-being of the other person very high in the hierarchy of values. This attitude offers a considerable amount of reinforcement for good behavior and for positive thinking in the home.

7. *There is very little distortion in the conversation.* Family members tend to tell things as they are. They don't create problems for each other more than they need to or exaggerate them for the sake of emphasis. The family members tend to be modest and ego-seeking is low key. This approach provides healthy reality therapy on a continuous basis for children growing up.

8. *The parents hear differences of opinion and behave toward children in a way that will encourage expressions of difference.* Through this listening to differences of opinion, and through this approach that does not compel agreement, the parents are able to detect problems as they develop from conversation. This openness to hear differences is encouraged by keeping distortion of differing views to a minimum, and by letting children know that parental egos need no feeding because the level of maturity is beyond this.

9. *The life history of family members during the growing time is one of increasing independence with age.* There is a gradual taking on of more work, added responsibility, and independent decision-making opportunities. Each member of the family feels that it is natural for those older and more mature to have more privileges and also more responsibilities. This gradual transition toward independence is very important and is a characteristic of family life that should be encouraged.

10. *Both the father and the mother are very active participants in family affairs.* One of the parents will act as the hearing examiner on serious difficulties. Both parents have a rapport with all members of the family that communicates interest, strong support, and an active orientation toward the family as being of central importance in their lives. The parents are a source of stability and strength to the family members. As heads of the family, they provide a sense of support, understanding, and encouragement. Most of the decisions in the home are cooperative ones which the parents share extensively before decisions are made. This helps to build family identity and family concern for working together in a way that will help ensure the wisdom of major decisions made on behalf of the entire family.

There is little doubt that most parents and all of our schools would like to see family ties, commitments, and life styles that resemble the outline of the ten guidelines above. The emotional relationships and the psychological climate can be attained in most homes, for they are simply common sense ideas in applying concepts that are well known.

As one contemplates the foregoing and considers the common ground and common cause that should tie the home to the school and vice versa, one cannot help but wonder why we have the psychological distance that does exist between these two institutions. Why do schools wait until age five to become concerned about the child? Why have educators not attempted to educate parents, those most influential of all teachers that will ever come into the lives of the children? And why have so many parents been unwilling to work closely with the school and with their child's teacher?

Each of these institutions has an unreasonable expectation of the other. Parents "send" their children to school to be educated. They pay their taxes. They send and they pay and they expect that to be their share. The schools expect the child to come to school always teachable, always positive and well behaved. If the child does not learn in the school environment, many educators quickly blame the home. They are often–but not always–right. Too many educators fail to seek out and improve the source of the bad behavior they witness at school by reaching out with a helping and understanding hand to the home.

Both the home and the school have been negligent in grasping mutually supportive opportunities. Modern technology, new economic forces that demand two salaries, bigness and impersonality in our institutions, 17,000 hours before the T.V. tube and 12,000 hours in the classroom at age seventeen, and a life style that is less stable and serene–these are all the factors–and many more–that erode the quality of parenting and the resultant opportunity for a normal, serene life during the crucial early years as well as the turbulent teens.

The neighborhood school stands in the midst of all the residences of America's children. The schools are numerous and they are almost omnipresent in their strategic placement on the streets and in the neighborhoods where parents rear their children. There simply should and there positively must be a closer working relationship between home and school. It must by systematically developed, for it does not exist to the extent that the needs of our times demand.

THE RELATIONSHIP BETWEEN HOME AND SCHOOL: A SUMMARY OF MAJOR ISSUES AND POLICY RECOMMENDATIONS RELATED TO THE PROMOTION OF MORE EFFECTIVE PARENTING

This chapter moves from the foregoing discussion to the basic premise that the school systems, having the major responsibility for providing primary and secondary education for the citizens of the nation, should do all things that are necessary to enhance the educational opportunities of America's youth. Growing from this premise is another: Parents are the child's first teachers and the home is the first classroom. Emerging from these two facts, there then follows the precept that the schools must do much more in the future than has ever been done in the past to help parents and all others with child-care and child-rearing responsibilities to perform their duties in a manner that will enhance the health, as well as the physical, emotional and intellectual growth of children of preschool and school-attending ages. It is assumed that, while we have much more to learn about child-rearing and nurture, there is a limited but significantly important body of knowledge that can and should be taught to parents and to others involved in child-care and child-rearing activities.

Since this has not traditionally been a prime role of the schools in our society, schools are not prepared to carry out this responsibility. While responsibility for effective parenting is not an exclusive responsibility of the schools (other institutions in our society must shoulder much of this burden), the school systems of America must make a deeper and more lasting commitment to the advancement of effective parenting.

MAJOR ISSUES

1. How can school administrators and school boards be persuaded to recognize and support activities to enhance effective parenting in the homes of current and future pupils of their schools?

Most school leaders believe that the American family is the cornerstone of our society. They also acknowledge that the family is in deep trouble today. They also know that effective parenting has declined, as evidenced by unacceptable levels of infant mortality, child abuse, youth delinquency, abusive uses of drugs and alcohol, and so forth. All of these problems compound the headaches of those with the responsibility of educating our youth. Schools must help to enhance the effectiveness of parents and to promote active parent concern for child nurture, child development, and childhood learning in the home. Before we can have more active parent concern for children, we must attain more active school concern for the advancement of effective parenting. This must come through a change in the thinking and in the priorities of school administrators and school board members. Most school systems do not deliberately ignore parents and the family unit. They have simply concentrated on the child as he or she comes to school and have treated the parent and home with benign neglect. They think of teaching the curriculum to the child in the traditional academic setting, and the school program has devoted little attention to the parent and the home as an educational institution of significance and power that either educates or miseducates. The school budget, the program of instruction, the expertise and time commitments of personnel in the school system must all focus upon the advancement of effective parenting and *the enhancement of active parent concern* as major objectives of the school system.

Before this can be accomplished, we must gain the recognition and commitment of the school system policy makers and executives. How to do this is a very vital issue that must be resolved.

2. Given the premise that schools have a significant responsibility in promoting effective parenting, and given the premise that many other institutions and entities also must assume a large role in the enormous task of enhancing parent effectiveness and in promoting more active parent concern for the total nurture (physical, emotional, and intellectual) of their children, how can more effective cooperation be established between (and among) the school, the social worker, the health institutions, the church, the juvenile judiciary entities, and other governmental and nongovernmental entities?

Fragmentation and lack of communication are major obstacles to the delivery of services to children and to parents. Timely health care would eliminate many barriers to learning. Diagnosis of early symptoms of emotional disturbances would do the same. Schools must attain more awareness of other agencies and these agencies must be more cognizant of school problems and potential. Unhealthy rivalry and bureaucratic jealousy must be replaced with close, effective working relationships. This issue is related to the proper orchestration of all the services to children and to parents that can strengthen the home and promote effective parenting. How can this be done? It's a big problem and an enormous headache.

3. Educators have been taught—mostly in colleges of education—how to organize and effectively teach the traditional subject matter to the child. Given the expanded responsibility to teach parents and promote active parent concern and awareness, *how can we teach the teachers to become effective parent educators?* Is this an expanded role for the school of education on the university campus? Must we begin here if we are to gain the commitments mentioned in issue number one above?

4. Can the experts who have done the most significant research and who have written the best books on the subjects of effective parenting and child development prepare a body of knowledge as an academic discipline and as a total curriculum that schools could utilize in promoting effective parenting?

We will never reach the point where we know all that is needed to be learned from the research. We must continue to push back the frontiers of knowledge in this field. But we must also concern ourselves with today's children. They should be beneficiaries of *what we do know;* but they should not, of course, be the victims of false knowledge. How can we organize the validated subject matter that we do have into a teachable form? Subject matter on parenting must be organized in a sequential series of ideas that will begin with simple points and lead steadily to larger and more complex concepts. Most curriculum specialists organize subject matter in a format that moves from the simple to the more complex. Most knowledge can be taught to willing and able learners. We have a limited but significant body of knowledge. It must be organized in teachable format so that educators and others can master it so that it can be taught, in turn, to parents. How can this best be done?

5. How can the schools promote readiness, awareness, and active concern on the part of parents? Before we can solve a problem, we must recognize that we have one. Ineffective parents and parents who are actually creating barriers and obstacles to proper child development and learning must be reached. They must learn that they are the key—the turnkey—to success or failure for the child. Most parents love their children and aspire to the best for them. Many parents willingly sacrifice for their children. How can we harness these drives and concerns to enhance the parents' capabilities by persuading them to want to learn more about parenting? How can the schools do this? Parents must want to learn to become more effective parents. They must be *actively* concerned about their roles as parents. They should learn, for example, that the first five years of life prior to their child's entry into kindergarten are the most crucial months of all and that they as parents can give their child the greatest possible advantage, or cause the child to develop the deepest resentments and the most hangups that will plague him all of his years. This crucial role must be understood by the father and the mother at the time that the first pregnancy occurs. How can the schools reach parents with the messages that parents must receive? How can those who need it the most be reached?

There are other issues related to the home and school, but these five are of enormous importance. Their resolution would see us well on the road to establishing the school systems of the nation as involved in a very vital and hightly crucial new mission in American society.

POLICY RECOMMENDATIONS

The traditional role of the school systems of America must be expanded through legislative action (and also by appropriation of funds) to charge the educational system of the nation with two additional major responsibilities:

1. Effective parenting principles and practices should be taught to the secondary-school students of the nation as a basic skill that is as vital to American society as is a mundane (but important) subject like driver training.
2. Today's parents should be contacted and vigorously recruited to participate in a school-sponsored program of parent effectiveness training. This expanded mission should be encouraged by the federal government, state legislatures, state boards of education, and chief state school officers.

Schools of education on university campuses and departments of family living and child development should be charged with the responsibility of developing and teaching school leaders about the problems, promises, and prospects of effective parenting programs under public and private school-system sponsorship. The best practices and the validated research should be drawn together and organized so that specialists in this field can be trained and placed in the school systems of the nation. School administrators, curriculum directors, and school principals should be offered course work in effective parenting. They must learn much more and become more sophisticated in this field if they are to advocate and provide generally effective leadership. State departments of education should modify certification standards to recognize, encourage, and support schools of education and their colleague departments of family living in this new realm of responsibility and service to the school systems of the nation.

Public and private schools nearest to the parents' residences should be established as centers for the delivery of services to parents and children. These centers should become the focal point of coordination and cooperation of all agencies and entities providing health, social welfare, recreational, and economic assistance to parents and children. As such, these centers should not be educator dominated. The fact that the neighborhood school building hosts the headquarters for the delivery of services should not lead to a feeling of "eminent domain over the territory." To be successful in placing these services under one roof there must be a new era of outreach and mutually supportive activity on the part of all agencies. The neighborhood school should take the lead because of its strategic location, for given the current decline in elementary school enrollments, space is increasingly made available to house these new services and expanded programs.

PROPOSED FEDERAL INITIATIVES TO IMPROVE PARENT EFFECTIVENESS

Given the interest of the federal government in schools and learning, it follows that effective parenting would also be part of the priority concerns of programs enacted by the Congress. What ought the federal government to do to improve the quality of childhood through enhancing the effectiveness of parents?

There are several federal programs currently being given hundreds of millions of dollars of federal support that could be modified in focus and thrust to greatly accelerate the improvement of parent effectiveness. Such federal initiatives would now demand vast new federal dollar outlays. Much could be done by modification and shift of emphasis of some programs and by broadening the purposes and scope of others. The following are a few examples.

COMPENSATORY EDUCATION

The largest single federal aid program is Title I of the Elementary and Secondary Education Act. This effort to give special assistance to schools with concentrations of low income and disadvantaged children reaches over 95 percent of the school districts in the United States. With outlays now in excess of $3 billion per year, the program attempts to bring special, individualized assistance to disadvantaged children.

Congress should modify and enlarge the emphasis of Title I to mandate more parent involvement, parent education, and parent awareness of the home's role and potential to enhance learning opportunities in the child's total environment. Although such program thrusts are not prohibited in the current laws and regulations, they are not highlighted. Very little is being done, and some Title I administrators lack understanding and commitment.

Title I needs a new thrust. It needs some additional emphasis on parenting and the home environment if it is to ever fully realize the goals for which this very large and nationally pervasive program was established.

As a first step under existing national legislation, Title I should, by congressional mandate, extend its emphasis to meet an urgent need and a prime opportunity to reach the wellspring of childhood learning problems and life adjustment difficulties.

BILINGUAL EDUCATION

A relatively small program that has been expanding rapidly is the nation's major emphasis on bilingual and bicultural education. More attention to parenting and bilingual parent education should become a major component of this very significant program.

The school-based efforts need not be abandoned. A parenting component would add the enriching depth that this program needs to serve a very important segment of America's total population.

EDUCATION FOR HANDICAPPED CHILDREN

The Education for All Handicapped Children Act was passed in 1976. This new federal emphasis requires that all states meet the needs of handicapped students. More emphasis on early childhood education and parent education for the handicapped should be provided in new amendments to this act. Federal dollar outlays are being expanded dramatically in this new program thrust.

It would be a serious omission to fail to add a strongly mandated program thrust in this act aimed at parent effectiveness and extensive parent participation.

In no educational effort is early diagnosis more essential than in educating handicapped children. And in no program is parent participation and parent enlightenment more vital. Before these new thrusts become firmly established in routine and the dollars firmly rooted in the bureaucratic structure, Congress should add, greatly strengthen, and strongly mandate a parenting component to this relatively new law that is still in the implementation process.

OTHER FEDERAL EDUCATION STATUTES

In all federal legislation designed to strengthen American education there should be a parenting component that adds this vital dimension to the total thrust. The Vocational Education Act, for example, ought to have more parenting elements in the legislation. The Career Education Act is almost totally devoid of any emphasis upon parenting and parental participation, notwithstanding the fact that parents are essential to all career decision-making by students in the school setting.

The Indian Education Act needs a stronger parenting component. The Higher Education Act, with its heavy emphasis on assisting men and women to have broader access to higher education, ought to give cognizance to the fact that many couples and single parents are attending college while trying to cope with the problems and burdens of parenting. The specific purposes of this act ought to be expanded to encompass the expenses and burdens of parents who are attending college.

The United States Department of Labor administers the Comprehensive Employment Training Act. Billions are spent annually to prepare the unemployed and the underemployed for useful and productive work. This act (CETA) should have a more explicitly mandated parenting section in it. Family strength and parenting effectiveness are vital elements in the total framework that comprised CETA's purposes. New legislation enacted by Congress should be extended to encourage the use of CETA funds in developing parenting skills.

If we are to bring the American family and the home's needs into proper perspective in all our efforts to enrich the lives of our citizens and bring equality of opportunity to its full fruition, we must weave into the fabric of all our social legislation concern for the role of parents, families, and the home. By doing so, we will reach the very source of our problems and, at the same time, we will also gain more benefit for the dollars we are spending. We do not need massive new federal programs so much as we need enlightened articulation and coordination of our current legislation to focus upon the family and strengthen parenting performance. We have been narrow in our past perspective by either totally ignoring the vital role of parenting or by giving it woefully little emphasis in our school, welfare, health, and economic development legislation. By weaving into the fabric of all our social legislation the strong and distinct thread of parenting improvement and family strengthening, we will make all our federal programs more effective.

BIBLIOGRAPHY

Bell, Terrel H. *Your Child's Intellect.* Salt Lake City: Olympus Publishing Company, 1972.
———. *Active Parent Concern.* Englewood Cliffs, N.J.: Prentice-Hall, Inc., 1976.
Briggs, Dorothy C. *Your Child's Self-Esteem.* New York: Doubleday, 1970.

Burton, Alan DeWitt. *The Authentic Child.* New York: Random House, 1969.

Cohen, Dorothy M. *The Learning Child:* Guidelines for Parents and Teachers. New York: Random House, 1972.

Evans, Thomas W. *The School in the Home.* New York: Harper and Row, 1973.

Fantini, Mario D. *What's Best for the Children?* New York: Anchor Press Doubleday, 1974.

Gesell, Arnold. *The First Five Years of Life: A Guide to the Study of the Preschool Child.* New York: Harper Bros., 1940.

Ginott, Haim C. *Between Parent and Child.* New York: Macmillan Company, 1965.

————. *Between Parent and Teenager.* New York: Macmillan Company, 1969.

Gordon, Thomas, *Parent Effectiveness Training.* (paperback) New York: New American Library, 1975.

Hunt, J. McVicker. *Intelligence and Experience.* New York: The Ronald Press Company, 1961.

Larrick, Nancy. *A Parent's Guide to Children's Reading.* New York: Doubleday, 1969.

Spock, Benjamin. *The Common Sense Book of Baby and Child Care.* New York: Duell, Sloan and Pearce, 1945.

White, Burton L. *The First Three Years of Life.* Englewood Cliffs, N.J.: Prentice-Hall, 1975.

Part Five
Support Systems For Parenting

As the material in previous sections of the anthology has suggested, there has been a proliferation of new parent-education programs in recent years. Some involve simply reading a book or watching television, others require more active participation such as group therapy. Although many of the programs have been initiated in the sincere belief that they are providing a valuable service, may critics maintain that these programs have done a disservice to parents by encroaching upon parental authority and ignoring variations in parenting style and customs.

This section of the anthology will focus on the support sytems that exist outside the home and school and will recommend ways in which these services can be improved. These chapters focus sharply on such issues as: What are the vehicles for delivering parenting services? What are the characteristics of these support services? What is the role of existing family-service agencies in community-based parent-education services. How are these services paid for? What are the political implications of such modes of delivery? Are there policy guidelines for such delivery systems?

In the first selection, James A. Levine discusses the current skepticism over the many new approaches to parent education. He maintains that many of these programs tend to serve the needs of professionals and their institutions, while ignoring many of the most common informational needs of parents. To meet this parental need, Levine suggests that community-based information and referral centers should be developed. These centers would provide specific information about local child care and social services and would be active in evaluating and developing parenting services.

In the second selection, David P. Weikart discusses the improvements that could be made in organizing parent-education programs. For both philosophical and economic reasons, he recommends a community-oriented parent-education model which provides direct services to parents. This model requires that professionals, paraprofessionals, and parents work closely as equals in developing local support systems. Unlike the first two chapters in this section, the final selection by Tobias H. Brocher is more concerned with the content of parent-education programs. It is Brocher's perspective that while most parent-education programs are concerned largely with child development, parental development itself has been too long neglected. Since parents are not prepared for parenthood in any formal or educational sense, parenting often becomes both a reflection of and reaction to the parent's own childhood experiences. Brocher advocates a parent-involvement model that involves groups of parents working together in developing parenting skill while examining their own experiences.

16

An Alternative Perspective on Parental Support: Child-Care Information and Referral Services

JAMES A. LEVINE
Research Associate
Center for Research on Women
Wellesley College
Wellesley, Massachusetts

There is no lack of assertions these days that parents need help, and no lack of attempts to meet the need. Guidebooks on child-rearing seem to appear almost as frequently as babies themselves to assure parents that they, too, can raise children even if they are not experts in child development; as Dr. Burton White (1975) put it in *The First Three Years of Life,* "I am convinced that most families, given a little help, are potentially capable of doing a good job of raising their children" (p. xii). Increasingly, federal programs are being designed or redesigned, with parents as their target population. HEW's Administration for Children, Youth, and Families, for example, has added a parent-education component called Home Start to the politically popular Head Start Program, and is currently redemonstrating the effectiveness of its Parent-Child Development Centers, which emphasize working with parents and children together. As one project report summarizes, with a backward glance at the "early intervention" programs of the 1960's, "Tutoring the child without helping the parent to develop her teaching abilities, formally or informally, was a waste of time" (Schlossman, 1978). To make sure that enough parents are able to develop their teaching abilities, colleges and universities are gearing up to train new cadres of professionals with degrees in parenthood education. Meanwhile, at the high school level, commercial publishers are getting into the act, offering curriculum materials—fancy packages of readers, filmstrips, and worksheets—to prepare future generations of American parents for the realities that lie ahead. Educating parents is big business!

If I sound skeptical, it's not because I'm against parent education *per se.* If truth be told, I have not only read books on parenthood, but have attended workshops on parent education, both of which have been useful. However, I am wary of what might be called the "bandwagon effect" in social programming, the almost inevitable tendency among professionals to develop programs in response to what can be funded, thereby reinforcing the impression that what can be funded is somehow "right." In the case of parent education, I am concerned that the bandwagon effect may be leading us to serve the needs of professionals for new markets while bypassing many of the everyday practical needs of parents. Moreover, I share the concern expressed so well by historian Stephen Schlossman, psychologist Alison Clarke-Stewart, and others, that parent education is, to a great extent, being seen as a new social panacea, as an "intervention" that can resolve many of the complex social-structural problems that were left untouched by the Great Society programs of the 1960's (Schlossman, 1976; Clarke-Stewart, 1978 and unpublished).

In the 1960's, at the height of the Great Society, the dominant model of parental support was service oriented, not education oriented. Professional energies were devoted much less to the development of programs to teach parents how to be better parents, and much more to programs responsive to daily parental coping, such as day care, the area I am most familiar with. As prospects of a national day-care program were dimmed by the Nixon veto of 1971 Comprehensive Child Development legislation, and by the nation's growing mood of fiscal conservativeness, the needs of parents for educational programs began to increase, or at least to be asserted more by professionals. Political and fiscal constraints of the 1970's have led to a shift in notions of parental support for service to education. Parent education has become, in effect, a less costly stand-in for some of the broader social programs of the 1960's.

I realize, of course, that the pattern I am sketching may seem too schematic, too simplistic. In practice, distinctions between service and education can not always be made so neatly. Day-care programs, even in the 1960's, often had parent-education components, and some of today's parent-education programs include service components. Nevertheless, I would argue that there has been a shift in emphasis in our notion of parental support that is reflected in policies and programs at both the federal and state levels. To cite but one example of the latter, the state of South Carolina when faced with a cutback in funds for its day-care program, recently began developing a parent-education program as a substitute. The new program may, in fact, be excellent in its own right, and I am not arguing against it. The point here, a point rarely acknowledged as educational programs replace service programs, is that teaching parents about child development simply does not fulfill the same function as providing child care so that they can go to work.

In asserting my concerns, I am not suggesting that we should or could return to the Great Society programs of the 1960's. There is simply no denying the fact that we are operating with a new set of political and fiscal realities. But, as someone who has been working in one capacity or another for the last ten years to expand parental options for child care, I also cannot deny the persistence of stress on families in this country who are in need of reliable child-care arrangements. The mainstream of parenthood-education programs, as I see them, does little to alleviate such stress.

In their volume, *All Our Children: The American Family Under Pressure,* Kenneth Keniston (1977) and the Carnegie Council on Children have given us a useful analysis of some of the sources of stress on parents today. Summarizing and interpreting from that work:

- The role of parents in today's society includes coordinating and negotiating services for family members.
- Parents have a need for a variety of types of information to help them in their role.

- Parents have a need for such information on a regular basis, and not just in times of dire emergency or crisis.
- Parents at all income and social status levels have such needs; it is normal, not pathological, to have such needs.
- Parenting advice given by experts has often tended to undermine rather than to reinforce the parents' role.
- Parenting advice needs to be given in a way which reinforces the parents' role.

Building on Keniston's perspective, this chapter focuses specifically on the widespread parental need for information about child care and describes the operation of a type of community-based service designed to meet that need. For the purposes of this discussion, this service prototype will be referred to as child-care information and referral, and abbreviated as I&R. Although such services are not educational in any formal sense—that is, they do not attempt to train parents to be "better parents" —they provide an ongoing resource for parents to learn about various aspects of child care and other services to children, to become better informed consumers. In that sense, I&R services provide an alternative perspective on many current efforts of parent education. This paper calls for the investment of public and private resources to stabilize the development of existing I&R services and to spur the development of new ones.

Consider the following situations.

Carol Tuccio, who has just separated from her husband, can't even begin to think about going back to work as a secretary until she finds child care for her two-year-old daughter. Carol's parents live some 1,500 miles away, she has few friends in the area, and she has heard that "day care" is harmful to children. She is scared stiff, and she doesn't know what to do or where to turn.

It is Friday afternoon and Donald and Shirley Jackson have until Monday to make arrangements for the care of their three young children. For the last seven months, while he was unemployed, Donald had been taking care of the children during the day while Shirley was at work as a department store cashier. Now Donald has landed a day-shift job in a nearby tool and dye factory. It starts Monday morning, Shirley can't skip work, and they need the income. But how can they make suitable child-care arrangements in two days?

Angela and Robert Brown and their two children, eight-year-old Susan and five-year-old Brian, have just moved into a brand new suburban house—their fourth such house in the fourth suburb in the last four years. Once again, Robert has been transferred. Once again, in a community where they know virtually no one, the Browns are trying to figure out how they can ease the transition for the children, let alone for themselves. But where do they turn this time to find a kindergarten for Brian, who is mildly handicapped with cerebral palsy, and an after-school gymnastics program for Susan?

If these situations sound familiar, it's because they are repeated in one version or another countless numbers of times each day in inner cities, in suburbs, in outlying towns, and rural communities. Throughout the country, working parents, mobile parents of "special needs" children—regardless of differences in means, social standing, and racial or ethnic group—find themselves looking for support, for a helping hand in taking care of their children.

Given the amount of attention being paid these days to helping and educating parents, it is somewhat ironic that the sort of information needed by Carol Tuccio, the Jacksons, and the Browns is so hard to come by. The fact is, however, that most of our parenthood-education and other social programs tend to ignore people's basic need for reliable information. We assume that people rely on social networks, that there is a friend to call, someone to turn to in a moment's need; but that just isn't the case.

In a few communities throughout the country, however, the needs of parents for information about child care is being recognized and responded to in a prototype of a program that could serve as a model for other communities. If, for example, Carol Tuccio, Donald and Shirley Jackson, or Angela and Robert Brown lived in San Francisco, each of them—in their moment of need—might have turned to the Childcare Switchboard. Every day the switchboard receives almost 100 calls from parents who are trying to find day-care centers, nursery schools, and babysitters, as well as pediatricians, eye clinics, summer camps, recreation programs, and an assortment of other services. Even if it can't provide instant solutions, the switchboard can often help parents clarify their needs and steer them toward a range of possible solutions.

In response to Carol Tuccio's worry about the effects of day care, for example, switchboard staff might have suggested that she think about a home-based, family day-care arrangement, described several factors to consider in choosing a family day-care home, and then offered the names of several family day-care providers in the neighborhood. For Donald and Shirley Jackson, the switchboard might have offered a list of people who did short-term emergency care and suggested a visit to the switchboard office to go through the files on more permanent center-based arrangements. For the Browns, the switchboard might have provided not only the names of several different types of kindergartens, but also the names of other parents with even more information.

The Childcare Switchboard began operating as a pilot project in December 1972, after a study funded by the Rosenberg Foundation determined that the number one social service need among young families in San Francisco was for information about child care. Staffed by a dedicated group of young parents who had all experienced that need firsthand, the switchboard operated for several years on a shoestring budget; by 1978 it was receiving some 2000 calls per month, had an operating budget of some $130,000 (provided in part by the Ford Foundation and in part by the state of California), and had established a local and national reputation as a multipurpose resource center for parents and other caregivers. At the Toy Farm, for example, a storefront adjunct to the switchboard, parents can drop in to borrow or make toys for their preschoolers. Jigsaws, bandsaws, masonite, plywood, old photographs—most of the material is there for puzzles, lottos, and simple board games, along with equipment and plans for much more. Among its other services the switchboard offers training and supportive services to a network of some eighty family day-care homes, runs workshops on a host of child-related topics (health care, legal issues, day-care licensing, nutrition, and so forth), maintains a single-parent resource center with an ongoing weekly rap group, and acts as a coordinating body for childcare advocacy throughout the city of San Francisco.

A number of similar services have developed along parallel lines—and for similar reasons—in communities scattered throughout the country. In 1971, in Cambridge, Massachusetts, for example, a group of working women who wanted to help other women overcome the problems they had faced in finding child care started the Child Resource Center. By 1975, the resource center had become such an essential and well-known service in Cambridge that the telephone company listed it on the cover of the phone book (along with the fire department and police); the city began allotting it $30,000 per year out of revenue-sharing funds, and state day-care and social-service officials began relying on it regularly to advise *them* about matters ranging from community needs to federal legislation and the state budget.

In Minneapolis, a Child Care Resource Center and Library has been operating since May 1973, when a group of community people who could not find space that could be licensed for a day-care center decided on an alternate approach to meeting parental needs. After a shoestring start the Minneapolis center now operates with an annual budget of some $35,000, most of it from the city. In addition to its daily work of helping parents locate suitable child-care and other services, the center conducts accredited workshops for family day-care providers (who need six credits per year to maintain certification in Hennepin County), provides technical assistance to local groups which are developing child-care programs, and mails a monthly newsletter with a listing of all local children's activities to over 1,500 people.

Parental needs for information about child care is not, of course, just an urban phenomenon, and neither are child-care information and referral services. In upstate New York, to cite one example, the Day Care and Child Development Council of Tompkins County has developed a highly successful strategy for creating child-care links in the midst of a highly dispersed population. Council staff identify "day-care neighbors," women knowledgable about child care who act as informal satellite resource centers for parents to contact. On a regular basis, day-care neighbors meet to exchange ideas at The Gathering Place, the council's home-like headquarters, where parents, providers, and children are always welcome to drop by and talk, read, make toys, and so forth.

Looking across the country, and including both urban and rural areas, there are now some two or three dozen agencies comparable to the council, the switchboard, and the Child Care Resource Center, agencies devoted primarily to meeting the needs of parents for child-care information. No matter where they are located, and no matter what particular differences in organizational structure or operational style they have, all tend to have the following characteristics and components which distinguish them from the mainstream of parent-education programs:

CONSUMER ORIENTATIONS

Most of the child-care I&R services have been developed for parents by parents, not by professional educators. Their emphasis is on transmitting practical information in response to parent requests, rather than on transmitting a packaged body of knowledge, program, or curriculum on "parenting." This approach reduces the risk, inherent in many parent-education programs, of undermining parental confidence.

CULTURAL DIVERSITY

Because they are community based and community generated, most I&Rs are responsive to what are often significant differences in the information and support needs among different populations of parents. Rather than assume a uniform model of parenting, I&R tries to offer choices to parents that demonstrate sensitivity to cultural diversity.

SITUATION SPECIFIC

I&R services respond to the real ongoing and everyday needs of parents for support, advice, and information; and they respond at the moment of need. Typical telephone conversations with parents range from five minutes to thirty minutes. Very often parents aren't sure what they want, have an incomplete picture of what services are available to them (or what they are eligible for), and aren't always sure about how to choose once they have the appropriate information. The phone work of information and referral, then, usually requires more than the dispensing of a piece of information; it involves active listening and the sensitive asking of questions to respond to individual situations.

MULTI-PURPOSE PARENT SUPPORT

Because child-care needs are so often inseparable from needs that affect other areas of parenting—such as needs for housing, medical care, and other services—most of these services have become multi-purpose. In a sense, they respond to the "whole parent," rather than to a more narrowly defined set of educational needs.

COMMUNITY CHANGE AGENTS

I&R services usually become active as agents for developing better services for parents and children. Because they gather information about parental needs on a daily basis, I&Rs often become the most reliable mechanism for community-needs assessment. They can play an important role in local planning for service development or for the improvement of the quality of services. More broadly speaking, they can actively educate their communities, acting as advocates on behalf of both parents and children.

Given such attractive features, one might expect a greater national proliferation of community-based child-care information and referral than we have at the moment. Why aren't there more such services? Why has there been so little financial support available for parents or for professionals who do want to develop such services? And why aren't such services a main thrust of the parent-education movement?

I think it can be argued that some of the very features that make I&R such a potentially important model of parental support have militated against its development. For one thing, unlike many of the parenthood-education programs, I&R does not rely on any special body of knowledge that requires help from experts. Rather, it relies on parents making accessible to other parents information that they otherwise would not have or would find very hard to get. Because it places decisions so squarely in the hands of consumers, I&R has offered relatively little incentive for an expanded professional role.

Moreover, child-care information and referral services operate from a nonpathological premise. They assume that all parents need help, at some time or another, with child-care arrangements, and that services should be accessible to all parents on a regular basis. By contrast, most federal and state social-service programs assume that only certain "target populations" need such help. Because I&R is at fundamental odds with current governmental policy, it has found few advocates from within the system.

Last, but not least, information is not tangible the way other direct services are; even though planners and policy makers all rely on information from friends or colleagues every time they make decisions about what physician to use, or what detergent to buy, or what neighborhood to live in, information is a very elusive service. It is hard to measure and hard to sell.

In effect, then, I&R as an alternate model of parent support is stymied by several paradoxes of public policy; we are reluctant, it seems, to pay for something so seemingly inconsequential, so seemingly accessible, as information. It seems, in many ways, too simple to be effective. And yet, the experience of a select group of services scattered throughout the country suggests that it may be highly effective as a means of offering a much-needed type of parental support.

What, if anything, can be done to bring this alternate model of parental support to greater public attention? What can be done to further develop and test the effectiveness of community-based child-care information and referral services? A number of strategies can be implemented by the Lilly Endowment and other foundations, either acting alone, or preferably, in cooperation with the public sector. These include:

Identification of successful I&R models

At the present time, I&R is a relatively unrecognized concept. Foundation dollars could be used to identify successful models of I&R, to profile their operation, and then to disseminate profiles to community planning agencies, parenthood-education organizations, and so forth.

Identify patterns in the use of public Title XX dollars for I&R

Ironically, the 1975 enactment of the Title XX amendments to the Social Security Act stipulated that states had to use some Title XX money for information and referral services that would be available without income-eligibility criteria. That is, there is an existing base in public policy for the further development of I&R. However, most of the Title XX I&R money appears to end up being used for "internal" I&R—that is, for the administration of state welfare departments. Foundation dollars could be used to monitor Title XX activities in several states and to document a case for violation of the intent of federal law. In a complementary approach, foundation dollars could be used to identify any instances in which states are effectively and appropriately using Title XX funds for the development of I&R.

Research and demonstrate different approaches to I&R

One of the biggest problems facing the few model I&R services identified in this chapter, as well as others not mentioned in this chapter, is stabilization of funding. Enormous amounts of time and energy are currently consumed by I&Rs in attempting to secure funding from year to year. Multi-year demonstration funding by the federal government would simulate the conditions of stability, during which time the effectiveness of different types of I&Rs could be more adequately assessed. A demonstration program of this type could be launched with a standard RFP (Request for Proposal) process under the Administration for Children, Youth, and Families and/ or the Children's Bureau in OHD.

RESEARCH AND DEMONSTRATE THE EFFECTS OF I&R ON SELECTED POPULATIONS OF PARENTS

Rigorous examination of the effects of different I&R strategies with different populations of parents would provide an initial data base for the development of any major policy initiatives relying on this alternative approach to parent support.

GRANTS TO STATES AND LOCALITIES FOR CAPACITY BUILDING

Federal support for research and demonstration of I&R could be made contingent upon state and/or local financial participation, facilitating the use of state Title XX money for I&R.

RESEARCH AND DEMONSTRATE I&R AS MEANS OF PARENT EDUCATION

One of the most effective means of facilitating what I have called an "alternate model" of parental support may be to link it to the dominant educational model. Under the parent-education rubric, research and demonstration grants could be given by NIE or other federal agencies to assess the ways in which the giving of information serves, in effect, as another type of education. I suspect that the results of such an experiment would be most dramatic, that the two models I have differentiated would be found, in fact, to be quite compatible.

BIBLIOGRAPHY

Clark-Stewart, A. "Popular Primers for Parents," *American Psychologist,* April 1978.
————. Unpublished manuscripts critiquing parent education.
Keniston, K. *All Our Children.* The Report of the Carnegie Council on Children, Harcourt Brace Jovanovich, New York, 1977.
Schlossman, S. L. "Before Home Start: Notes Toward a History of Parent Education in America, 1897–1929," *Harvard Educational Review,* August 1967, Vol. 46, No. 3, pp. 436–467.
————. "The Parent Education Game: Politics of Child Psychology in the 1970's," *Teachers College Record,* Vol. 79, May 1978, galleys p. 106.
White, B. L. *The First Three Years of Life,* Prentice-Hall, Englewood Cliffs, N.J., 1975, p. 12.

17

Organizing Delivery of Parent Education

DAVID P. WEIKART, Ph.D.

High/Scope Educational Research Foundation
Ypsilanti, Michigan

INTRODUCTION

Effective parenting has become a matter of public concern, setting the stage for a clash between individual family values and public goals. The basic concerns revolve around the management of child growth by the family in response to the pressures of a society in flux. Is the family knowledgeable enough to rear children properly? Does the family know how to provide the necessary experiential enrichment to maximize the child's social and intellectual growth? Is the family sufficiently attuned to the issues of nutrition, health, and physical development to provide effective care? Is the family able to generate rapport and nurturing to help the child develop such crucial traits as self-confidence, creativity, responsibility, and the capacity to initiate and sustain long-term relationships?

This concern for the family and its competence has not developed in a vacuum, nor have the problems appeared suddenly. The great social movements of the 1960's altered the social context of the family. The "generation gap" and the sexual revolution, the civil rights movement, the divisive debate on the Vietnamese War, the concern about population growth, food supplies, and the environment are among the many antecedents now reflected in immediate problems. More women working outside the home, persistent unemployment, underemployment, and inflation, and smaller families with both fewer children and fewer adults are only current manifestations of fundamental changes. This broad mix of issues has produced considerable dissonance among those proposing solutions. For example, at a recent conference on the family, one speaker emphasized the need for parents, especially fathers, to spend time at home with their young children. The next speaker reported the damage to children caused by unemployed fathers who are at home with their families. Another pointed out the importance of the development of an attachment between a mother and her infant, only to be followed by a speaker advocating day care for infants so that mothers would not be "forced" to provide child care if they desired to accomplish other things.

Child-rearing is no longer a private concern of the family, and the situation ap-

243

pears to be rapidly approaching the juncture where society will be assuming increased responsibility for the upbringing of children. Thus, the stage is being set for massive conflict between the right of self-determination for families that desire children, and the goals established for *all* children through national family-policy decisions. Ultimately the conflict will be between society's need for a healthy and productive citizen and the family's right of self-determination.

At issue, of course, is the definition of what society means by "healthy and productive citizens." Society represents converging political alliances organized to either obtain or retain particular benefits. Certain philosophical and attitudinal positions must be accepted by the members of society or there will be a shift in the social format to some alternative from the present compromise. Today it is this general social format that is increasingly in conflict with the individual family goals, especially as it relates to child-rearing. For example, the society needs disciplined workers to operate its means of production. These workers need education which both teaches the skills needed to produce goods and creates the willingness to consume the goods produced. Individual families may have goals which simply do not conform with such overarching societal goals. For example, religious groups such as the Amish prefer to limit the education obtained by their children and to provide what is allowed within the context of their own community. The state's insistence on standards in textbooks, length of daily and yearly attendance, and teacher preparation are in direct conflict with the well-defined goals of the Amish religious community. The state standards are established to provide workers for the general production goals of the society at large; the religious community standards are established to continue the ethical goals of that community. At the present time, this conflict is simply unresolved, though the state appears to be able to enforce its "will."

While the problem of conflict is clearest in the small tightly knit and recognized religious-group situation, it also exists in the broad community on an individual family basis. Mindless television programmed for the lowest common denominator audiences, fast foods, and endless advertising to increase consumption represent concerns for some parents regarding the impact upon their children. Yet these aspects of our lives represent supposedly necessary avenues of support for the society at large.

Child-rearing in the home by the parent has not been directly controlled by society in the past. Certainly the indirect influence has been profound not only through the mass media but also as a result of the general change brought about within the context of the urban to suburban migration, the increased affluence that has raised the expectations of all families, and so forth. In the past several years, however, increased discussion has focused on the family and its child-rearing functions with children under six years old. Kindergartens have become all but national in availability in the last ten years. The recent highly positive findings on the long-term impact of preschool education at three and four years of age by researchers at the High/Scope Foundation (see Weikart et al., 1978a; Weikart et al., 1978b; and Weber et al., 1978) will increase the amount of funds available for such programs at both the federal and state levels. Various federal and state initiatives in programming for parents, such as Child and Family Resource Center and parent-child centers, have made planned programs readily available to families. While these programs are seldom directive ones transmitting specific information to individual families as determined by some state policy, they do raise the basic question of state control of family self-determination. In this rapidly evolving social context, the need for information about effective parenting has increased in importance. It is equally important, however, to give some attention to the *manner* in which programs for parents are "delivered," because the total program amounts to more than the information conveyed—it shapes the personalities of those involved.

This chapter will first examine some basic assumptions made about the parents' role in programs related to child-rearing (a more complete discussion is presented in Lambie et al., 1974), and then look at some of the implications of different model delivery systems. One particular model will be discussed as an illustration of one method of supporting parents and building community competence in child development.

ASSUMPTIONS ABOUT THE PARENTS' ROLE

Most parent-education programs make implicit assumptions about parental involvement that both influence and reflect their attitude toward parents as child-rearers. These assumptions may or may not be consciously recognized by the people responsible for program operations, but most programs admit one of these positions. The following statements summarize three distinct sets of assumptions.

- *Parents need the benefit of expert knowledge* and special training to raise their children effectively. In order to learn these essential skills, they must be involved and trained in infant education programs derived from laboratory and field research.
- *Parents know what they need as parents.* They can run effective programs and find the needed resources to accomplish their goals.
- *Parents and educators can be resources for each other,* working as co-equals in determining the goals and practices of effective child-rearing.

PARENTS NEED EXPERT KNOWLEDGE AND TRAINING

Programs with this view that parents need the benefit of expert knowledge and special training to raise their children effectively assume that parents must be trained and involved in infant-education programs in order to learn the essential skills.

Knowingly or unknowingly, these programs assign parents a passive role in the educational program. The implicit assumption in this orientation is that parents are the receivers of predetermined information transmitted by educators or professional staff. Programmed instruction or preplanned curricula in which there are finite numbers of correct conclusions or behaviors to be learned by parents are obvious manifestations of this assumption. This approach to parent education is not always rigid in its sequence of application. Its widespread use in programs reflects the basic philosophy underlying traditional views of education and learning. Such programs are usually designed to achieve goals formulated by experts and based on desired outcomes of the development of the child. Although this approach is conceivable given current research information and technologies, it represents a philosophical position that is currently unacceptable to many members of ethnic minority groups and others who prefer to emphasize the values of diversity.

PARENTS KNOW WHAT THEY NEED

Some programs assume that parents know what they need as parents—that they can run effective programs and find the needed resources to accomplish this goal. Co-op day-care centers in the United States and neighborhood playschool groups in England are the most typical examples of programs in which parents (most frequently mothers) are almost totally responsible for the program operations. Educators or professional staff may serve as resources for the parents, but their involvement is generally only at the request of the parents. Some parent-child centers in the late 1960's began with very active parent groups and, with assistance from organizational staff, found facilities for the program, built or remodeled equipment and play materials, and sought community resources for additional support of the program. This position will not be discussed further in this chapter as it typically is not in broad use at this time.

PARENTS AND EDUCATORS CAN BE RESOURCES FOR EACH OTHER

In some programs, parents and educators are considered resources for each other, working as equals in determining the goals and practices of effective child-rearing. Expert knowledge may be utilized to help educators be responsive to and supportive of the individual needs of parents and children. The objective is not to retrain parents but to facilitate self-determined behavior.

This position assumes that parents have the capacity to adequately rear their own children, but need support to overcome specific problems that are common to families in all sectors of society but often more pressing among those with extremely limited resources. The child-rearing role of parents is considered primary, and the task of persons (educators) working with the family is to provide assistance and opportunities for parents to achieve self-determined goals. Infant-education programs of this nature provide parents with opportunities to clarify the goals and aspirations that they hold for their children and to develop an open, problem-solving approach to child-rearing. At the same time, the rights, abilities, and individuality of parents are acknowledged and respected. The educational process that typifies this assumption about parents is interaction between the parent(s) and the educator. The educator does not assume the dominant role in the educational process, nor are the parents the only active agents in the program. Each participant acts as a resource for the other and a balance is struck between the collective and individual sources of information and activity. The role is difficult for the educator because any tendency to subtly dominate the relationship must be strictly avoided if the program is to be successful.

DESIGNING THE DELIVERY OF PARENT-EDUCATION SERVICES

When the staff of a parent-education program selects methods for delivery of services, critical decisions are made about the basic character of that program. While the words utilized by different parent-education programs are often the same, the actions generated by the different approaches are, in fact, very different. (See Weikart, 1977, for a contrast of two home-teaching approaches.) At the same time, a particular parent-education philosophy does not dictate a particular delivery system. Television, books and pamphlets, group instruction, and so forth, lend themselves to the delivery of expert knowledge more easily than to other philosophies but they can be adapted to "parents-as-equals" models. The home-teaching format utilized by many of the programs which are currently under development or which have evolved during the past decade is compatible with either basic parent-program philosophy. The parent-education model selected by the program sponsors limits the manner in which the delivery methods selected will be employed, but the delivery method itself does not commit the program to a specific philosophy. The critical issue is how five basic questions are answered.

1. *How is information provided?* Expert-knowledge programs supply systematic information that generally implies a right and a wrong way of proceeding or of thinking about problems. The information flow is unidirectional from the expert to the learner. In parents-as-equals programs, information is shared between the program staff and the recipient. The program staff member has general knowledge about child development, but the parent has specific knowledge about his or her own child—and the clear implication is that through sharing, richer and more complex information is produced.

2. *How is adult interaction viewed?* Expert-knowledge programs assume that the adult receiving the program is a passive listener, or one who carries out instructions to arrive at known solutions. Education is the process of learning answers that experts know to questions experts ask. Parents-as-equals programs assume that the program and the participant have equal and active responsibility to achieve shared goals. The process and content, as well as the outcome, of the experience are the responsibility of both parties.

3. *How are individual differences reflected in the program?* Expert-knowledge programs are usually centrally developed and applied to a broad spectrum of individuals. Large audiences are identified but, aside from different "pacing," individualization is seldom feasible. Parents-as-equals programs ask questions leading to differentiation of the program based on a child's age, rate of development and ability level, and on a parent's special life experiences and level of personal development and learning. Issues of efficiency and appropriateness of specific program activities for the learner are carefully considered because of the value the program places on the learner's initiative and active participation.

4. *How are differences in cultural and linguistic patterns reflected in the program?* Expert-knowledge programs can be adjusted to categories of potential learners but under the assumption that most participants match one program variation or another. Parents-as-equals programs specifically reflect the different goals and values of individual families which are integrated into the program. This flexibility permits the program to match a wide variety of individual life situations.

5. *How are the goals for children identified?* Expert-knowledge programs tend to have specific skill or ability outcomes defined in performance terms as goals for the child. These are frequently drawn from standardized growth or other measurement indices. Parents-as-equals programs accept a wide range of parent-established outcome goals for children. The specific goals desired by these programs tend to reflect process orientations rather than arbitrary standards.

If one assumes the position that parents need expert knowledge, perhaps television is the most obvious vehicle. It has the power to transmit information over great distances, and the cost per receiver is relatively small. Programs may be generated by groups of knowledgeable experts working with skilled media staff under relatively controlled conditions of time and funding. Products can be made of high quality and in easily handled units. The problems come at the receiver end, not in the creation and transmission phases. In order for the program to be effective, the parent need only turn on the television and watch it. Skilled production presents a format that "grabs" attention and keeps the parent watching, but the central problem is the match between the program and its content on the one hand and the parent and family needs on the other. What do the actual words of the program and its situation mean to the parent? The problems of individual differences in development, culture, and language are critical.

Building from a philosophy of parents as equals, it is also possible to utilize television as a means of developing parenting skills. Effective programming which supports the parents-as-equals goals can be built around situations that admit multiple alternative solutions. Television can examine the range of problems faced by different families in child-rearing and explore the solutions that each attempts; it can focus on the complexity of family interaction so that viewers gain empathy for the reality experienced by the families; it can support the development of observation skills by providing opportunities to view various family situations that can be interpreted in different ways. If the goal is to transfer specific information regarding child-rearing, in certain respects, television is the poorest choice of assistance to families because of the impossibility of matching the specific information with specific families, their needs, and their realities. However, television does hold out great promise: It can portray alternative solutions to problems and show concretely the variability of issues and perspectives among families.

Broadcast television specials, books, video disks and tapes, and discussion programs all have a role to play in creating effective parenting. The point is that every message, regardless of method, carries with it a philosophy of learning and of the rights of the learner in the learning process. Learner-controlled education, for example—a new catchword employed by some behaviorists—can be more than the selection by the learner of a didactic course of study.

If one approaches parent education with the philosophy of parents as equals, the most obvious format is home teaching. Home teaching carried out by a professional or paraprofessional and based on a developmental curriculum and a supportive attitude toward parents offers a simple vehicle to address the five major questions listed above. Home teaching is especially effective in the delivery of service programs adjusted to individual families. Such a model need not make value judgments about differences among parents or children, but may attempt to respond to specific needs of each family, avoiding a highly uniform programmed approach. At the same time, it assumes that the actual level and extent of general development of each child is not only a product of the family's cultural tradition but of child-rearing patterns that derive from adaptations to economically difficult life conditions.

In the High/Scope Foundation's parents-as-equals home-teaching model, the home visitor's role is to provide service to the parents rather than "expert" translation of middle-class social wisdom into universal child-rearing practice. Of course, this position is not the traditional one for a teacher; nor is it a comfortable one. It calls into question the assumption that professionals can effectively develop a universal "curriculum."

What is generated in a parents-as-equals home-teaching program is an open and supportive relationship with the mother, with the focus on helping the mother become the creative teacher of her child. The mother is helped to recognize and state the goals she has for her child, and to develop the skills necessary to support the growth of her child toward those goals. If the teacher will be patient, the mother will teach her how to proceed. For example, watching how the mother handles the infant and her other children gives a very real sense of how she acts and thinks, and this enables the home visitor to begin interacting with the things the mother finds most important, rather than with some predetermined system in mind. It is essential for the home visitor to sit back, watch, and *then* act in such a way that her basic respect for the mother and for the integrity of the home is evident. Helping a mother effect *her* goals and aspirations for her child is the major task of the home visitor; it is understood to be the reason why the mother has accepted the visitor into her home in the first place.

Of course a teacher or paraprofessional working in a home has ideas, goals, and things to do, which the mother is aware of from the start if the relationship has been honest. But a respectful teacher doesn't impose an oral or written blueprint for the entire period of contact. The *action* taken with the child will provide the mother with sufficient clues as to how the teacher feels about her and her child. Abstract terminology is a poor substitute for this kind of deeply personal interaction.

Regardless of the delivery system or the philosophy of a parent-education program, two issues must be faced by the program staff. First, educational programs have implications beyond the particular families served; that is, they affect family life within the community and ultimately in the society as a whole. Second, programs must devise ways to operate at low cost so that it is feasible to enact large-scale projects that can meet the needs of society. Unfortunately, the history of social-service programs with respect to both of these issues is not encouraging.

Generally in the organization of services to clients, the social-service professions have focused on "adjusting" the individual to the expectations of specific institutions; thus their services are endlessly needed because the pressures that actually generate the problems are not in the least diminished. While examples of this situation abound, the educational system provides the most obvious. Schools provide special-service programs for the children who do not fit expectations: the delinquent, the emotionally disturbed youngster, the truant, the classroom disrupter. While the behavior of these children is often the result of extreme conditions within the community and family, frequently, and more than we would like to admit, it is at least partially a product of or a response to the schools themselves. It represents the failure of schools to provide sufficiently differentiated programs to match the vast range of individual differences in the population. "Adjusting" these individuals to the needs of schools is a major task of agencies that serve the *schools,* and not the child. Rigid curricula produce discipline problems, grading systems make some children chronic failures, and teaching methods focus so narrowly on the mechanics of learning that they sacrifice whatever may be broadening and deepening in the learning process. The result is that large segments of society miss the chance to develop fully such essential capacities as critical thinking and innovative problem-solving; more precisely, they miss the chance to develop the skills that will make a difference in the quality of their own lives.

As service programs come to depend more and more upon experts, the costs of the programs tend to rise. In parenting education, costs will continue to accelerate unless new programs are evolved which reduce costs either through efficiency measures or by evolving systems that are built essentially around volunteers. One example of the latter approach is the High/Scope Community-Oriented Parent Education Model.

A COMMUNITY-ORIENTED PARENT-EDUCATION MODEL

The organization of a community-oriented model is presented in Figure 17.1. This is a system that provides for direct benefits to families at minimal costs.

There are four levels of participants involved in the program. A supervisor/director, in the only paid and permanent staff position recommended, assumes the basic responsibility for organizing the program and maintaining its operation. The educational supervisors are mothers who have both participated in the service program and served as educational assistants, for a two-and-a-half year total commitment to the program. The educational assistants are mothers who have participated in the service program, for a one-and-a-half year total commitment. The participant mothers are in the basic service program for one year. All levels of involvement represent a one-year experience, with promotion to the next level based upon interest and screening for effectiveness by the mothers who have previously held the position. It is recommended that no positions be paid, although the educational supervisors might be. All participants should be women from the geographic and cultural community served.

The program is phased in the following manner. There is a four-month orientation period for the group of sixty-four mothers selected for the program. During this time, the sixty-four mothers are visited in their homes once a week by an educational assistant (one of sixteen selected from the previous wave of sixty-four). At the end of the four months, sixteen mothers are selected to be trained as educational assistants for the next wave, and they both continue in their program and receive additional training for a two-month period to become educational assistants. While they continue to receive their own visits and supervision from their own educational assistants, they begin service to the new wave as educational assistants. They and the remaining mothers of their wave complete six more months of visits. At the end of their service program, four are selected as educational supervisors to work with the educational assistants of the following wave and so on.

This cycle of waves in the service program can filter throughout the community as long as the service is needed. Indeed, parallel waves can be created to increase the rate of service, or the months between orientation and training of the next wave of educational assistants can be spread out to delay the rate of new wave formations.

What is critical in this service-delivery model is that, since the program is based on a local volunteer network rather than on a paid professional force, it becomes rooted in a local community. Moreover, the participants rotate throughout the program—so that in the entire community there could be a project mother in every apartment building or on every block who has experienced the program at some level (or all levels), and who is available for informal "extended family" contact through the regular neighborhood channels.

While this community-oriented parent-education model has yet to be utilized in a full-scale trial, it has evolved from a decade of work with families. After a tightly controlled research project to examine issues in parent-infant education, the recent

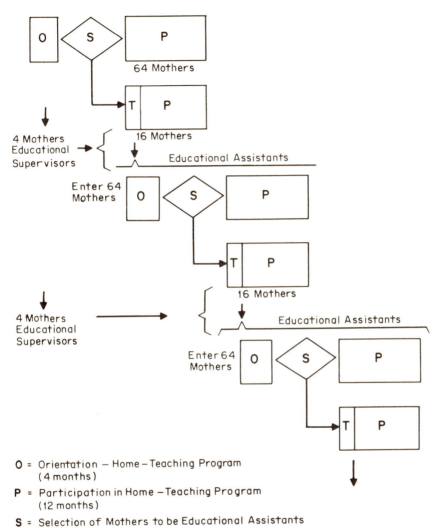

O = Orientation – Home – Teaching Program
    (4 months)

P = Participation in Home – Teaching Program
    (12 months)

S = Selection of Mothers to be Educational Assistants

T = Training to Prepare Educational Assistants for Home Teaching
    (12 months)

Figure 17.1 *Community-oriented parent-training model.*

High/Scope work has focused on evolving programs to train parents to assist parents. A small Michigan community has found that volunteers are willing to aid their neighbors and that mothers welcome assistance from other mothers. The use of low-cost program methods provides the opportunity for community-based services which, with careful program operation, will produce the expected high quality results.

Providing programs to families to enable them to become more competent in child-rearing is an admirable undertaking given today's social context of rapid change. Inherent in each program, however, is a series of critical decisions about the fundamental rights of families. These decisions, either implicitly or explicitly, guide the actual delivery of services. The use of service models based on television, books, group meetings, and so forth, generally reflect an expert-knowledge orientation. Parents-as-equals programs are typically delivered through home-teaching systems. Such teaching systems provide direct services to participating parents through individualized contact in the parents' own homes. These services blend the general knowledge of the trained professional, paraprofessional, or parent with the specific knowledge of the parent receiving the service, so that the resulting interactions are directly related to the parents' needs and experience. It is this relevance of service that gives parents-as-equals models their strength. Parents-as-equals models can be delivered in such a manner that they build the strength of communities through supporting groups of people to help each other in various ways. Through the use of volunteers, the system both reduces costs as well as builds a knowledge base among the participants. Our task is to insure that action taken on behalf of the community strengthens that community.

BIBLIOGRAPHY

Lambie, D. Z. *Adult support of early learning.* Ypsilanti, MI: High/Scope Educational Research Foundation, 1977.

Lambie, D. Z.; Bond, J. T.; and Weikart, D. P. *Home teaching with mothers and infants: The Ypsilanti-Carnegie Infant Education Project: An experiment.* Ypsilanti, MI: High/Scope Educational Research Foundation, 1974.

Weber, C. U.; Foster, P. W.; and Weikart, D. P. *An Economic Analysis of the Ypsilanti Perry Preschool Project.* Ypsilanti, MI: High/Scope Educational Research Foundation, 1978.

Weikart, D. P. Educational processes in mother-infant interaction. A paper presented at the International Symposium on the Ecology of Care and Education of Children under Three; Berlin, February 1977.

Weikart, D. P.; Bond, J. T.; and McNeil, J. T. *The Ypsilanti Perry Preschool Project: Preschool Years and Longitudinal Results Through Fourth Grade.* Ypsilanti, MI: High/Scope Educational Research Foundation, 1978a.

Weikart, D. P.; Epstein, A.; Schweinhart, L.; and Bond, J. T. *The Ypsilanti Preschool Curriculum Demonstration Project: Preschool Years and Longitudinal Results.* Ypsilanti, MI: High/Scope Educational Research Foundation, 1978b.

18
Toward New Methods in Parent Education

TOBIAS H. BROCHER, M.D.
Director of the Center for Applied Behavioral Sciences
The Menninger Foundation
Topeka, Kansas

INTRODUCTION

The history of parent education in the United States demonstrates remarkable changes between 1914 and 1955 as illustrated in the official government publication on child-rearing, *Infant Care*. Although one cannot assume that all parents followed the recommendations given in this publication (which was thought of as a support for parents given to them by their regional congressman), the contemporary knowledge about and attitude toward children is mirrored in the basic data about child development which were passed on to parents in great candor. The theme of parent development as the primary causative factor for difficulties in child-rearing was not raised until the early 1950's. That parenthood is a developmental phase in the life of the parents and needs closer observation, now seems to be common knowledge, but the focus and intention of child-rearing practices has been mainly on the child and his developmental stages, thereby neglecting the fact that parents unconsciously repeat part of their own childhood history in their affective-emotional relationships with their children. It remains an open question which has not yet become the subject of serious research how far generations raised under the recommendations of *Infant Care* from 1926 to 1938 (that is, the current adults of the age group thirty-nine to fifty-one) have a basically greater obsessional attitude (for example, strong sense for time urgency, punctuality, regulating everything by the clock, need for domination and competition, and so forth) than the following generations which were raised under nearly the opposite principles recommended in *Infant Care.*

As a basic experience we have to assume that parents were not prepared for parenthood in any formal or educational sense, although all industrialized cultures provide formal educational procedures for all professional tasks except for how to be a parent. As a result, parents generally repeated the child-rearing patterns they had experienced themselves during their own childhood with the variation of either doing the same as their parents did to them, or from their subjective perspective, doing the opposite, or mixing both attitudes in an unpredictable manner.

However, following the contemporary preference for cognitive-intellectual learning, the potential for experiential-emotional learning was merely neglected and left to the subjective experience of the individual parent and his or her interaction with the child. The historical background, the meaning of childhood, the scientific knowledge of child development, as well as parent development and the social and societal conditions and values, have changed remarkably during the last seventy years. The historical period of *200 Years of Children* (as documented by the United States Department of Health, Education, and Welfare in 1976) provided neither any systematic educational help nor sufficient medical help for children *and* parents until 1907 (first Division of Child Hygiene in New York City).

The first White House Conference on Children in 1909 led to the establishment of a Children's Bureau on April 9, 1972. Julia Lanthrop as the first chief of the Children's Bureau asked Mrs. Max West, a mother with some writing skills, to prepare information that would be useful in the care of infants as well as in the care of pregnant women. *Prenatal Care* was first published in 1913; *Infant Care,* the first official government publication, a guideline for mothers and parents, first appeared in 1914. The basic changes and partial reversals of values and beliefs in the practice of child-rearing are documented in Martha Wolfenstein's report on infant care from 1914 to 1952 (1953). In 1930, President Herbert Hoover convened the White House Conference on Child Health and Protection which produced the Children's Charter.

However progressive these various steps could be considered in light of the historical development, the fact remains that even then the focus was mainly on the physical health and growth aspects of child-rearing rather than on the infants' psychological development and the importance of the interaction between parent and child. The simple explanation lies in the fact that the specific research data were not available because they developed slowly after 1945 without direct application, although most of the findings were systematically published. As Ortega y Gasset has pointed out, the time span before a new awareness and insight developed by a progressive elite become common knowledge, encompasses about seventy to eighty years. We can conclude that the understanding and need for a systematic way of educating parents might still meet much resistance throughout the next decennium, although the historical beginning of the first thoughts in this direction lead back to Rousseau, Pestalozzi, and other educators of the seventeenth century. Contemporary thought tends to focus on parent "effectiveness," thereby following a basically technological and economic assumption as the preferred belief system and "Zeitgeist" which neglects emotional development. It seems highly questionable, especially in comparison with other cultures and American subcultures of different cultural origin, whether such rational-cognitive orientation can meet the need of parent education. From all research data we have to conclude that the period of early childhood not only determines the basic reaction-formation and defense mechanisms in the lives of all human beings, but also the fact that the highest preparation of learning processes (especially experiential-emotional learning) takes place during the first six years of life, as Bloom (1964) has documented.

Therefore, we would have to distinguish clearly between parent "training" and parent education. While the former implies a pragmatically "how to" intention, the latter tries to take into account the fact that the development of a parent is experientially and emotionally closely intertwined with the development of the child. As the fate of many firstborn children has demonstrated in the past, his or her development is mainly determined by the uncertainty of inexperienced parents who behave differently with the following children. As Toman (1970) has proven, the sibling sequence also often determines emotional reactions of parents toward their children, depending on their own sibling position and experiences.

The stages of *Parenthood as a Developmental Phase* (Benedeck, 1959), that is, age, duration of marriage, previous experience with children, planned or unwanted pregnancy, social background, life experience, and so forth, need clarification in any systematic approach to parent education. The newest developments in various experimental approaches (for example, Minnesota Early Learning Design, Minneapolis) have demonstrated that parents who expect their first child need a different type of experience than parents with children of different ages, especially during early school age and when their children enter puberty and adolescence. In the latter case, many parents are already approaching the midlife transition as a different stage of their own development, which leads to the mobilization of their own repressed adolescent dreams and visions in comparison with the behavior of their children. Unfortunately, many efforts at offering support systems to parents often fail because the critical developmental problems of the parents which influence the child's development are underestimated or completely neglected; it is assumed that parents are parents and, therefore, a scheme of successful gimmicks or recipes can be sold to them and make them successful. The fact that this prevailing "teaching" approach has failed in the past becomes more understandable when we recognize that even in most scientific studies, the focus is mainly on child development as the various institutions in the United States and elsewhere clearly demonstrate in the label "child guidance."

On the average, these institutions are characterized by the principle of using experts who measure educational goals in comparison with scientific theories. In the extreme, this approach has led to community-based institutions such as child-guidance clinics which have been considered by many parents as a kind of "repair shop." The contrast between the specific knowledge of professional experts in child development and the average lay parent has created a specific dynamic where child behavior is measured against an immanent ideal of normality which does not exist in reality. Urie Bronfenbrenner (1977) has recently pointed out that the overestimated expert role has not only created an increasing alienation between parents and the so-called experts, but has also contributed to the often recognized irrational assumption that the expert could solve conflicts between parent and child.

Tyler (1976) has pointed out that the more open, multicultural society has diminished the influence of values cherished by the parent generation which no longer insists on a particular code of conduct. The basic change which has taken place in most industrialized countries can be characterized by an increasing awareness of the impact of parents' behavior on the development of the child. Therefore, since World War II many countries—especially in Europe—have shifted the original focus from the child to the parent-child interaction. More than twenty-nine years of research, such as is documented in the *Psychoanalytic Study of the Child* (Freud et al., 1945-1976) as well as in Piaget's and Inhelder's publications (1973), have confirmed the interdependence of early parent-child relationships and internal object representation as motivation for behavior.

At this point, we are confronted with six main approaches of theoretical models expected to offer solutions to parent-child interaction as a basis for early socialization and adaptation processes:

1. The educational-teaching didactic model
2. The behavior modification model

3. The psychoanalytic-object relations model
4. The family therapy (group) model
5. The parent involvement (school-for-parents) model
6. The unsystematic, eclectic mixture of various parts of the above models

In the interest of concentrating on the purpose of methodologies in parent education, the following discussion is limited to a description and discussion of Number 5, with the assumption that models Numbers 1 to 4 will be presented by other participants.

METHODOLOGY OF PARENT INVOLVEMENT

Four main assumptions are based on observation of parent groups since 1953:

1. Parents are adults who don't want to be told anything by a stranger, even if he is an "expert." They feel easily infantilized and either regress to opposition and defiance, or to helpless dependency, thereby seducing the "expert" into an omniscient-omnipotent role in which he may faii in the long run.
2. Contemporary educational methods most often underestimate the motivations underlying emotional and affective forces which determine the parent-child relationship and interaction. Denying the unconscious factors in human interactions is an oversimplification and does not eliminate their existence. As a consequence, many of the short-cut methods either fail because they are not applicable for many parents or, worse, these methods contribute to long-term repressions of important developmental steps which will have to be acted out at a later developmental stage–a typical symptomatology many modern societies are facing in the current behavior of teen-agers.
3. The growing child stirs up all the unsolved and repressed conflicts each parent has had with his own parents (Benedek, 1959). As a consequence, many interactions between parents and children are overdetermined by unconscious expectations, fears, repetition-compulsion, and false identifications based on early object representations of each parent.
4. Parents who have learned to support, teach, and understand other parents have a higher credibility than the "expert" who may have more difficult problems with his own children and family, or no experience at all as a parent. This is usually one of the first questions asked by parents who seek help and advice.

Parent-involvement methods have been used in different ways in various places throughout the last two to four years. The first "school for parents" was initiated in 1919 in Berlin, Germany, within the framework of adult education. During the 1930's the concept which had not been continued in Berlin because of a lack of leadership, was taken up in Switzerland in a different way, one based mainly on the Swiss Pestalozzi tradition. The program was backed up by various legislators, and contributed to a nationwide campaign, *pro juventute*, which is now part of a national program.

During the process of redemocratization after World War II, new laws for the protection of youth were introduced in West Germany. Within the framework of this nationwide campaign it became evident from evaluation reports of more than two hundred child-guidance clinics that the traditional "teaching" methods in parent education were not very successful although the government had spent respectable amounts of money to involve selected teams in workshops and seminars for parents in connection with the national network of adult-education sources in all cities and districts with a population of over 50,000. As a result of this campaign, the new methodology of the school for parents was developed by a small team in Ulm and Stuttgart, West Germany. The support of this program led to a nationwide regular broadcast TV series, and the school for parents became a national movement which was also picked up by neighboring countries such as Switzerland, Austria, France, Holland, Norway, Denmark, and Sweden.

The new principle of involving parents (and teachers) in situations in which they could relive and experience emotionally the critical events of their own childhood development, has spread rapidly. This increasing interest was apparently due to the fact that the focus of this method is on the parent and his or her emotional problems or midlife-transition difficulties rather than on the child. Helping the parent automatically helps the child.

In addition, the parents are never "taught" because most experiences are deemed self-evident, with the parents themselves observers of their own interactions in sharing continuously their real experiences, and relating them to the behavior of their own children as well as to the past behavior of themselves toward their own parents. This model also takes into account the various developmental phases of parenthood as well as the fact that usually three to four different generations interact with each other at the same time, on the same life stage, in the same social environment. The social mix of parent groups, coming from different social strata and economic backgrounds, thus contributed to a better understanding and solution of social (and racial) prejudices.

In comparison with other methods, this parent-involvement model, also later designed as "empathy workshops" (at the Menninger Foundation) has enabled most parents to include *emotional learning* which is usually neglected in most other approaches based on *overintellectualizing* assumptions. The actual distrust of professional promises which cannot be delivered may have intensified the search for new methodologies which are neither based on a certain I.Q. level nor on social disadvantages but take into account basic common emotional experiences in childhood which are generally independent from social, racial, or economic factors—this despite the fact that the development of parenting skills depends highly on the economic and political support of opportunities for emotional learning of parenting skills.

Further advantages of this model have developed because of the *changing role of the parent educator* who is neither putting himself in the role of an omniscient expert nor is he perceived as a "teacher." In a simpler formula, the essence of the model could be expressed as follows: *Parents are helping parents to learn parenting.* The basic principle of this model presupposes that this goal cannot be achieved without an opportunity for the individual parent to reexperience his own childhood relationships which he or she considers as hang-ups on an emotional level. Instead of imitating their own parents' behavior toward their children, most parents begin to change their parenting approach according to the emotional experience and *secondary* intellectual insight they have gained from being confronted with their unconscious *repetition-compulsion* in their behavior toward their children.

THE NEED FOR COMPARATIVE STUDIES

Currently, all of the six models mentioned before are used throughout the United States. Depending on the individual institution and its basic theories, the definition of success and the awareness of the need of each child to be a person in his or her own right, each model can reach different levels of consciousness for the difficult task of parenting. Without more clarification of goals, comparison of parent-education models and the impact of political and societal support or neglect, it is difficult to predict which of these approaches will be an accepted bridging and coping device for the most important future task: To build a national network of community-supported, ongoing learning groups for parents during their varying developmental phases of parenthood.

As long as the selected model does not meet the emotional needs of *all* sorts of parents it remains either a middle- and upper-class franchise operation with questionable "adjustment effectiveness," or it becomes obsolete because, focusing solely on the child, it does not serve the interests of the parents' development. The traditional focus on the child, with its subtle implications of consulting the "repair workshop" of child experts, might be useful in pathological cases although the pathology of the parents has to be included. The real problem is not the child but the parent, because as long as the parents are hung up on their own infantile, internalized parent relationships and their emotional consequences, the child cannot grow emotionally unless he or she is genetically blessed with strong inherited capacities which permit enough independent and autonomous development, either without or against the parents' ill-advised methods of parenting. However, this independence can rarely be reached or expected during early childhood developmental phases. Therefore, the most important consideration which must guide any future parent education model is *the need for educating parents emotionally about the specific developmental steps during the first six years of the child's life.* This would enable the parents to react appropriately in ways which would serve to promote the growing intellectual and emotional autonomy of the child.

PARENT EDUCATORS

TRAINING

From our experience (in the United States as well as in European countries) we would conclude that, despite many teaching methods in parent education which are used in various institutions and agencies throughout the country, parent educators, like any other professionals, need primarily a safe emotional basis for their exposure. In principle, each parent educator should be familiar with the fact that this exposure in working with parents inevitably triggers transference and countertransference reactions which can become counterproductive to his or her work as long as it is primarily theoretically based without enough opportunities for experiential-emotional learning.

Theoretical knowledge—as sophisticated as it may be—loses credibility when it is not accompanied by emotional understanding, sensitivity, and realistic perception. In other words, the *discrepancy between knowing and being* becomes counterproductive to the task of the parent educator if he or she is unable to feel and experience what he or she knows and/or tries to teach others. Therefore, the experiential side of any training process should be used as the basic experience, secondarily followed by theories which confirm congnitively the primary experience which has been relived. Although the difference between knowing and being is a common dilemma, the training of parent educators should not contribute to an increasing intellectualizing or rationalizing which can be easily used against any emotional involvement. It is well known that children do not react to words which they do not understand during their early childhood but, rather, to attitudes, emotional expressions, symbols, and moods of their environment. Without convincing parents that their own inner level of affects transmits itself directly to the child (even more than to a dog or other animal which picks them up instinctively) parent education would have only a small chance to change parental behavior. Thus, in ideal terms, whoever teaches parenting methods should begin with a self-experience that enables him or her to get directly in touch with those repressed feelings which are part of his or her own experiences with his or her own parents in the past.

Success or failure of a systematic approach to teach better parenting skills might depend on an appropriate application of this insight which is the result of seventy years of documented research in child development and parenting.

PARENTS HELP PARENTS (EXPERIENCES IN GROUPS 1953–1975)

While everybody at this time was concerned with children or parents in a one-to-one therapeutic approach, we were guided by the impression that we did not know very much about groups of parents. We also assumed that parents could teach each other much more than we could, and we felt they could accomplish much more as a *group* by sharing their problems and trying to help each other with their different previous experiences. We thought parents would have much more credibility than anybody else if they could communicate their individual problems. We also considered the way they interacted with each other as an unconscious repetition of the past, a reliving of sibling rivalry as well as of different types of parent relationships. In other words, we considered the members of this parent group as a mirror of their past parent-child relations repeated in their actual, individual family dynamics.

We gave some thought to the fact that many parents have acquired remarkable theoretical and intellectual knowledge about child development, but nevertheless feel as if the emotional involvement and its affect have removed their objectivity and blocked their skills in coping with the task at hand. They are quite aware that they react irrationally but they cannot control their behavior. Many parents, when they face a situation or interaction with their children which relates to repressed conflicts of their own childhood, cannot deal with it. On a deeper level they try to solve their own conflicts by assigning a specific role to their children. We have seen children who had to act on behalf of one or the other parent, for instance, in the role of a loved or hated sibling, or in place of a mother or father. Also, very often the children had to act in a narcissistic role, overcompensating for their parents' hidden shortcomings or weaknesses. We can hardly assume that healthy ego development can take place under such conditions.

Our concepts of socialization, education, and adaptation are highly obsessional and perfectionistic, and much more aggressive than we suppose. We tend very early to impose a primitive superego structure which subsequently inhibits further autonomous ego development. I have been told by many children and adolescents that it makes it easier for them if parents are willing to expose their own weaknesses and failures. Being able to forgive the parent gives the child strength and enables him to accept the reality that all people make mistakes.

Many parents have the feeling that they are doing their best, and although this may not be fully true, they can hardly become aware of the unconscious side of their interaction with their children if we accuse them of doing wrong. Therefore, it is not helpful to tell them how much hostility may be present in a certain kind of overprotectiveness, how much envy they may be concealing in patterns of strict control, or how much unconscious aggressiveness may be the reason for their trying to bridge the generation gap by behaving as if they were as young and understanding as an adolescent. There is no emotional learning without the direct experience of repeating the past within a peer group, followed by a period of new cognitive-intellectual awareness. For a long time we have neglected the fact that the parents themselves are in a stage of development and that parenthood is really another developmental phase. How much parents are able to mature depends on what they can learn from their children. If it were true that age brings maturity, we would probably never find situations in which we cannot distinguish from their behavior whether it is the father or the son who is the adolescent: Which one, for example, is behaving in a more adolescent fashion if a father pretends to be educating his son when he is arguing with the angry adolescent without even listening?

We may believe that we understand much more about our children than our parents did, but is this true? What would happen if our children were to fulfill our dreams of being more free, more liberal, more capable of completing the task where we failed? The generation gap is real. We ought not to deny the distance which exists between generations. It is important not to try, for reasons of nostalgic self-deception, to appear younger than we are. Commercialized culture has irritating repercussions when the ideals of success and youthful strength are overemphasized despite the contradictory reality of an increasing median age.

Parents are often very lonely because their own needs for being accepted and loved have been denied and repressed, and they are tempted to expect to get from their children what they missed from their parents or even their spouses. This is a vicious circle we can break up in working with parents as a dynamic group, following a new concept of "unlearning" stereotyped patterns. If parents really hope to get back from their children what they did not get from their parents, they will not be able to give very much. The child then repeats the same pattern when he becomes a parent himself. It is easy to see how frustration, tension, and traumatization can accumulate within three or four generations, until a child breaks down under the burden, because everybody has passed the buck. The other side of the coin is that nobody can give anything that he did not receive and experience himself. The completely unexpected result of our study was that most parents not only were more satisfied with their roles, but expressed how grateful they were at receiving so much from other parents who cared and tried to help them. But the most intense confirmation came from the children. We have had piles of letters and postcards from children, also phone calls and visits. The general content of these letters, no matter what the age of the child, was: "Please keep our parents in your school; it is great. We are feeling much better now. We are a happier family. How did you do it? Can they learn a bit more? We had been very suspicious of your school, but now we think it is doing them good and us too," and so forth.

After fifteen years of experience in working with parent groups, we would conclude that this method allows individual parents to become aware of how much they still see themselves as being a son or daughter rather than a father or mother. In the School for Parents, which requires a commitment of only one year, many family and marriage problems can be solved if the parents have enough opportunity to reexperience their own childhood and to experiment with their own perceptions. By learning to understand what has happened to them, they become aware of what happens to their children in their own interaction.

This awareness could never have developed without using the group model. Although we did not consider this technique as group psychotherapy, it has had obvious therapeutic results. The continued application of this group method in Pittsburgh (1966–1970) and, since 1970, at the Menninger Foundation in Topeka, has shown quite convincingly that in spite of cultural differences, the basic problems are the same.

CURRICULUM

Since the beginning year (1953), the content and length of the curriculum has changed somewhat, according to the various cultural and subcultural conditions which also include economic considerations of funding, social environment, availability and endurance of parents in different cultures, and so forth. While under rather conservative and stable social conditions most parents are willing and able to invest time and energy for six to ten months, it is difficult for parents in metropolitan areas of high mobility and social uncertainty to make a serious commitment for more than six to ten sessions, that is, six to ten weeks, or in a condensed form with two evenings per week for more than ten sessions (five consecutive weeks). The following curriculum describes the original experimental stage.

FIRST PHASE–ONE TO SIX YEARS

Play Evenings 1 and 2

1 Playing must be learned.
2. Painting and molding can be learned with the fingers.

In the beginning there are simple finger games which are related to the child's need to explore, specifically, to sensually explore the properties of objects. Also, the play material of the first year is discussed. Finger painting, smearing, playing with clay all lead back to the earliest needs of the child to smear. (This is an attempt to reconcile the parent with the behavior of the baby when being fed and his playing with food and with feces.) After initial reluctance, parents have great fun and this can help to reconcile the parent to the infant and his needs, and to provide outlet rather than repression.

DISCUSSION EVENING 1

This evening attempts to cover the education and aspiration of the child in his first year and the significance of the very early development of the child for his later life. Unlike regular courses on infancy, the discussion explores how far the parents themselves feel the need to act against the theoretical rules. Anxieties of the mother, patience or impatience of the father, overanxieties and parental fantasies about the still very small child are reported by the parents themselves and discussed.

PLAY EVENING 3 AND 4

A play evening covers children's books, children's songs, cartoons, and prints made with potatoes. Another evening explores how it is to be small and face a tall person.

DISCUSSION EVENING 2

Discussion covers important tasks in the overall development of the two-year-old; for example, when the child learns to walk. Nongrowth promoting psychological attitudes of youngsters due to early childhood experiences will be another focus for discussion and interchange.

PLAY EVENINGS 4 AND 5

A play evening covers the making of Christmas decorations and toys out of simple things: straw, cork, corrugated cardboard or matches; dolls from remnants; vegetable theater, that is, potatoes, carrots, cucumbers as acting figures and animals.

DISCUSSION EVENING 3

Then the discussion evening is—the wonder of Christmas, the fear of excitement at the coming of Santa Claus. (In Germany, Santa Claus comes on December 6 with a huge sack of candy and nuts for the good children, and a whip for the children who have misbehaved. The Christ Child is the one who brings the gifts on December 24.) Ways of perceiving and the relationships between perceiving and emotion form the contents of this segment. In the practical evenings, the materials available are those which the child can use to form very simple things while they are being experienced. Simultaneously, discussions deal with the possibilities of relieving the mother, and reinforcing the interest of the child in the other parent: that is, illustrating what father can do with his children. Many parents are amazed with how many things one can do with completely inexpensive materials. An understanding of the collecting urge of the child and his attraction by "junk" will grow in the parent. This prepares for a sensible understanding of the collecting phase. The dangers and needs of the age where friendships are learned is also a focus here.

PLAY EVENING 6

The beginning of a musical education, painting on fabric, clay work, scratching in plaster, and simple wood carving or construction forms the subject matter for this evening.

PLAY EVENING 7

Next we cover tales and children's dreams, tales (folk), and symbols.

DISCUSSION EVENINGS 4 AND 5

Is it fantasy or lie? How does a child learn to renounce? (In self-denial, instead of gratification of an urge you renounce it.) Does the renounced need show up anyway? Father is portrayed as a comrade and as a rival; mother as a witch and as a good fairy. Curiosity and the child's urge to discover are discussed.

In the center, we find aggression, destruction, and an amorphous desire to form on the part of the child—a yet unformed desire to be creative. The parents begin to understand the difference in the relationship of the child to his reality, and his inability to understand the reality of the grown-up. This will help to prevent injuries, screaming, and crying, which understanding and communication can replace. The tendency of the child to work with sand, water, and dirt; his urge to smear and to spread dirt around or to scratch wood, furniture, and other materials—in order to channel his as yet not fully controlled active aggressive needs—can be rechanneled into less dangerous and more positive channels. The parents become aware of different possibilities that are expected to arise from the child's natural urge to expansion and discovery, and in particular, how they might be able to channel these urges into areas which do not endanger the child, but nevertheless permit him freedom to experiment. Here emerges the way to answer children's questions, by giving them the right explanations. All answers are related to the child himself; he will want to know how that which is being said to him relates to him and his world. Then he will settle for the answer. He does not understand objective answers because he does not know his parents' world. He will learn this world through his questions.

PLAY EVENING 8

Discussion and illustration of children's drawings—smoke, waves, sun, stars, flowers—things and their significance to the child—the symbolism of his drawings, the forming of trays, and flower pots are this evening's focus.

PLAY EVENING 9

Next we treat siblings as they appear in folk and fairy tales.

DISCUSSION EVENINGS 6 AND 7

Contact with and relations to other persons of his environment—the urge of the child for shared activities. Experience with pegs and blocks will help parents to understand how children perceive different dimensions of a person or object. This leads to curiosity about differences, including sexual differences. There are links from exploring form, to understanding dimensions, to forming sex identities. Parents begin to understand why children ask the first questions relatively early. They must be well prepared so as not to confuse the child with confused answers. The child's drawing is understood in terms of a question as well as a statement on the part of the child, on the basis of an understanding of symbols that have been derived from studying folk tales. In other words, the interpretation of children's drawings through symbols he uses is important. Instead of the uninformed discontent that some parents have with the lack of central form in the child's drawing, a new view is gained through understanding the significance which the child's drawings have to him. Through looking at the symbolic representation of sibling rivalry and of friendship and feud, the parent arrives at an understanding of the child's need for community, for an order in the hierarchy of things, and for contact.

PLAY EVENING 10

The question arises: to win, to lose, to cheat? Parents play children's games.

PLAY EVENING 11

The use of bamboo, straw for braiding, paper of all kinds, scissors, glue, mosaics, and balls is the topic for this evening.

DISCUSSION EVENING 8

Children encounter new communities and new relationships. Fear, anger, revenge, and reconciliation are also being discussed. The attempts to form relationships with new people are focused upon as central. New child acquaintances and new grown-ups within the gradually expanding environment bring wishes for freedom and for socializing; for freedom and individuality on the one hand, and for support and cooperative relations on the other. Self-confidence and satisfaction are important subjects. In the parents, the readiness to develop love for small things can grow. When the child is encouraged, he and his parents can become constructively creative together. Instead of the disappointment about the destruction of quickly bought mechanical toys comes the shared attempt to build a personal, individual world filled with loved objects—a world that he will feel familiar with and close to. Fantasy can lead to individualized creativity. On the other hand, perfect and prefabricated objects given to the child can sometimes paralyze the productivity of his own ideas.

DISCUSSION EVENING 9

Fathers, games, education, rivalry, and difficult children is the topic for this evening. Creative possibilities with materials are differentiated—the bending, tearing, cutting, gluing, and braiding create a connection between aggressive destruction—the urge to aggressively destroy—and rejoining. In other words, you tear apart and then find new form; you destroy and put back together. In this phase of playing, the foundation for later work processes are being laid. The experience with materials is a precondition for later similar processes of combining, disconnecting, and recombining. Existing connections are being severed, the separate individual units are collected and assembled in a new way. This will be continuous in all later processes—in the school, with a machine, in the office, or in intellectual activities. At all times, something that exists is being separated and things that are separated are newly assembled. The feelings can obtain order only slowly. Jealousy, sibling rivalry, and rivalry toward one or the other parent create difficulties. In the discussions, the insight is slowly revealed that difficult children generally have difficult parents. If the parents progress toward resolving their own problems regarding different views of life, different opinions regarding education and competition for the affection of the children, as well as toward reducing the remaining fears and hang-ups regarding their own parents, then the difficulties with their own children tend to decrease as well.

PLAY EVENING 12

Tonight's meeting involves playing theatre with old things; hand puppets.

DISCUSSION EVENING 10

Fear, mother love, marriage, and education are the topics for this evening's discussion. Role playing means trying out how it feels to be something or someone else —a hero, a princess, a magician, a crocodile, a monkey, a dog, a tree, a statue, and so forth. Everything that the child encounters in the realm of fantasy and reality will be played out, imitated, and explored. But, play is reality. Children never wholly pretend. They are a little bit convinced that they are whoever they pretend they are. Parents improvise their own role-playing without direction; they give themselves their own themes. Suddenly they might imitate their own children, or other mothers and fathers. There is lots of laughter, and then without realizing it, they begin to take things seriously. Old memories reemerge. Most parents are now ready to give their children old clothes, coats, hats, pants, remnants of fabric, and other objects that might serve theatrical purposes—to create puppets like Punch and Judy, for example.

If often happens that a couple takes on two different puppets. It then becomes laughable how many differences of opinion are being lived out quite openly. After all, it is between these two puppets and not between Mr. and Mrs. X, so these two puppets are permitted to say anything they please to one another. At home everything goes better because through the voices of their puppets the children can communicate much that they would like to unburden themselves of. The parents begin to understand the game and become capable of participating. Suddenly the parents know more about themselves as they see themselves in the mirror of their children's fantasies. Laughing and amazed, one accepts many a critique on the part of the child, for after all, it is aimed only at a puppet. But in some instances, one is rather touched and decides to reexamine these things in his or herself so as to avoid or better control in the future the impatience or violence which is mirrored back. Children are more contented because the parents know better how to deal with them and because they now have more new ideas. Separation anxieties can be reduced. Some children have even requested that the parents go to parents' school saying: "You'll learn how to play with us."

We must not avoid questions of marriage in the discussion meetings. When we have reached the point where we have sufficient confidence in each other, as opposed to feeling like strangers as we did at the beginning of the sessions, it becomes apparent that understanding the child has an educational influence upon the partners in the marriage. We are no longer so discontented by the fact that children have it so good and are permitted to play, because now we play with them when we have time: on the carpet, in the sand box; mostly on the floor because there is more room. We now realize they are working when they play. We realize too that love is a substance, not an idea. Even with the best nutrition, without love children starve. Love is not only an emotion, it is also an everyday, practical thing which shows itself in how we

guidance clinics and social agencies in the areas where the parents took the initiative and responsibility for further application. But here the principal question arises: Who needs whom for what? If parents are capable of understanding and learning new parenting skills without being taught academic jargonese and scientific hair-splitting, they can share their struggle for development in plain language understandable to other parents. Instead of investing tax money in increasing specialization, which may lead to further alienation between parent and child through contact with a candid expert who considers herself or himself as being the better parent without becoming aware of the primary need to help the parents in their own developmental struggle, we should, perhaps, consider another option.

At this point in history, it has become necessary to support and strengthen the nuclear family primarily economically and psychologically in a way that permits the rebuilding of an extended family which offers the growing child a much wider support system and multiple object choices. Therefore, parent-education methods should not be narrowed down to coping solely with the small nuclear family, thereby leaving the individual parent even more isolated and desperate in his or her search for help. The implication of the method is its political and social effect, in addition to the mutual support of parents in neighborhood groups—the basic nucleus of democratic societies. Thus, the school-for-parents approach intends to achieve more than standardization of parent effectiveness—a tendency which could possibly lead to a destructive "bottom line" approach of "parent success" through neglecting the highly loaded, emotional conflicts between parent and child, which cannot be solved through the application of any scheme or temporary fad. As described by Erikson (1959), it is always the whole person who has to go through a process of lifelong learning by mastering the crucial tasks of each developmental stage of the life cycle. These stages are not very different in the distinguishable civilized cultures and social subcultures which assume the potential for reaching intellectual and emotional maturity within or above the specific social group or subculture to which any individual originally belongs.

It is our hope that further application, studies, and evaluation may prove the importance of group-involvement methods in parent education. The basic concept is predicated on the assumption that we have to provide new opportunities for lifelong learning experiences using varied group methods within the community. The important distinction lies in the first step of "unlearning" and giving up stereotyped educational attitudes which have been used heretofore. The parent group as a group of peers increases this opportunity because it reveals why different traditional approaches to educational goals have failed in the past with the majority of parents.

SUMMARY

The School-for-Parents method described is based on a principle change in parent education. Groups of parents share their experiences in becoming and being a parent during various stages of child development. Because of their underlying repressed memories most parents unconsciously transfer attitudes, beliefs, behavior, and interactions to their own children which they have previously experienced in their interactions with their own parents. Because parents never "learn" how to be parents, although civilization demands preparation for most other professions, children can become victims of their parents' uncertainty, ignorance, and lack of experience with all the concomitant consequences for the socialization and adaptation of the vulnerable and easily impressionable child. The method enables parents to relive their childhood experiences on an emotional level by temporarily replaying special sequences and phases of childhood development in empathy workshops. The change in parental attitudes occurs through reidentification with repressed and forgotten childhood recollections, thereby enabling them to empathize with the child's perspective of parental impact. In addition, the parents as a peer group share the experience of their own developmental problems, emotional hang-ups, and prejudices stemming from their own family of origin. The comparison of parenting methods and the sharing of success and failure between parents lead to the development of supporting neighborhood groups (in urban areas up to 6,000).

The role of the parent educator shifts from that of a teaching expert (who may have difficulties with his own children or has no children at all) to a facilitator who offers direct experiences in play, working with various materials and providing experiential situations which promote direct emotional learning opportunities which can become self-evident in spontaneous happenings and verbal exchanges between parents. Instead of expanding the role of expert agencies, the method is based on economic and psychological support of neighborhood parent groups which accept responsibility and relative autonomy for mutual support and problem-solving among parents, with decreasing supervision or influence of "child experts."

Since the early 1950's, the School for Parents has become a basic movement in various European countries which, although using varied approaches of different lengths of time is always based on the same principle of parents supporting and teaching parents. Application of this method in the United States has been successful in various communities through the development of a new training method for parent-school ficilitators.

The method shifts the focus from the child as the main object toward the parents and their impact on the child's development.

BIBLIOGRAPHY

Benedek, T. Parenthood as a Developmental Phase: A Contribution to the Libido Theory. *Journal of the American Psychoanalytic Association,* 1959, 7, 389–417.

Bloom, B. S. *Stability and Change in Human Characteristics.* New York: Wiley, 1964.

Bronfenbrenner, U. The Next Generation of Americans: Family Policy in the Context of a Changing Society. Paper presented at Lilly Endowment, Inc. Forum, Washington, D.C., January 1977.

Erikson, E. Identity and the Life Cycle. *Psychological Issues.* 1:1, Monograph 1, International Universities Press, 1959.

Freud, A. et al. *The Psychoanalytic Study of the Child.* 1–30, New Haven and London: Yale University Press, 1945-1976.

Piaget, J. *The Child and Reality: Problems of Genetic Psychology.* New York: Grossman, 1973.

Piaget, J. and Inhelder, B. *Memory and Intelligence.* New York: Basic Books, Inc., 1973.

Toman, W. Birth Order Rules All: Never Mind Your Horoscope. *Psychology Today.* 4:7, pp. 45–49, 68–69, December 1970.

Tyler, R. W. Tomorrow's Education. In *200 Years of Children.* Edith H. Groteberg (Ed.). United States Department of Health, Education and Welfare, p. 212. 1976.

West, Mrs. Max. *Prenatal Care.* United States Department of Health, Education and Welfare, 1913.

Wolfenstein, Martha. *Infant Care.* United States Department of Health, Education and Welfare report, 1953.

Part Six

19

Parenting in a Pluralistic Society: Toward a Policy of Options and Choices

MARIO D. FANTINI
University of Massachusetts
Amherst, Massachusetts

JOHN RUSSO
St. Francis College
Loretto, Pennsylvania

Many volumes have been written which focus upon the parenting process as the internal experience of individual families; from its very inception this anthology has been committed to a broader view: responsibility for parenting—its goals and its consequences, its successes and its failures—must be claimed by society as a whole. The central question to which each of the contributors was asked to respond was not *whether* society should intervene in this crucial process (since every facet of a child's life in the United States—economic, legal, psychological, geographic, educational, and cultural—is influenced in some way by the attitudes and institutions outside the home), but rather, *how* society might intervene in a more intelligent and supportive way. The principle of promoting human potential in all citizens has been a long-standing ideal of American society which must find expression in child-rearing, or be lost in the modern disintegration of other social values. In this concern, we are not alone. An increasing number of government officials, foundations, and individual scholars including Urie Bronfenbrenner, Amitai Etzioni, and Kenneth Kenniston, have stressed the urgency of developing a comprehensive national policy on youth and the family. Effective parenting is obviously a pivotal issue in the development of any such social policy.

A workable national policy on this issue can only emerge out of an understanding of the many pressures that cause family structures to collapse, children to be neglected or abused, and communities to lose their organic nature. The available research would seem to indicate that the most important factors in determining the quality of child care and family stability are income and social class. Given this basic social and economic reality, the Carnegie Council study on the American family, *All Our Children* (1977), has grounded its recommendations of full employment, national health insurance, flexible working conditions, and family assistance in the form of financial support and services. The basic needs of the child for physical and psychological protection have been repeatedly emphasized in most of the contributions to this anthology; indeed, the necessity of providing food, shelter, health care, and guidance towards social and physical self-sufficiency has been one of the few unproblematical areas of most discussions of parental responsibility. Even at the most fundamental level of physical nourishment and protection, however, the children of the poor have been provided for unevenly or not at all.

Obviously, no national policy which ignores the hard economic facts of family life as it is experienced by millions of children in deprived circumstances can be formulated in good faith. *Prominent, therefore, in the guidelines which we will offer is the emphasis on the economic support of children through the economic support of their families, including a vigorous policy of antidiscrimination toward minorities and toward women who are increasingly the partial or sole sources of family support.*

This emphasis on providing a decent level of economic support should not, however, obscure the investigation and development of other levels of parenting. As Professor Etzioni (1977) has insisted in a recent paper, current data may only suggest an order of importance rather than a definitive statement on problems such as juvenile delinquency. Reviewing the data on the topic, he carefully distinguishes the implications of recent provisional conclusions:

> Proper economic conditions, housing, and employment may well be more important for the proper upbringing of a child than a lasting positive relation between the parents, and between the parents and the child. At the same time, I am not convinced it has been shown that family stability is irrelevant; it may just be a less important factor than social class. Less important is not the same as unimportant. (p.7)

Every section of this collection has contained some word of caution concerning the state of current research: Hess, Carew, and Lamb have especially emphasized the difficulties in determining what constitutes effective parenting from the researcher's point of view. Although research can locate the symptoms of dysfunctional parenting, both the content and methodology of present evaluations of parent effectiveness, and parent-effectiveness programs are inadequate for the formulation of definitive policy in this area. In addition, those authors who have analyzed the special problems of minority children (Burgess, Suzuki, Comer, Ramirez, and Cox) have also alerted us to the dangers of prematurely judging the state of their families by imposing one (perhaps outdated) normative model of child-rearing which might assume that differing cultural patterns of a particular group were less effective or even pathological. Furthermore, even those families who are able to provide very high standards of material comfort are subject to the stresses of social change and are not always able to provide either the emotional support or the preparation for adulthood which their offspring may require. The casualties of ineffective parenting through neglect, physical abuse, or psychological alienation are not exclusive to the lower classes. *A second guideline for policy recommendation, therefore, is that research should be promoted which works towards a comprehensive understanding of both universal material and psychological factors in parenting (as discussed by Levine and Jordan) and in the further delineation of the specific sociocultural factors which affect the process.*

The guidelines offered thus far have been associated in a general way with the efforts of fellow scholars and professionals in formulating a comprehensive social policy on the family. This collection, however, has maintained a more distinctive emphasis in two directions: First, the contributions have addressed themselves predominantly to the questions of the family in a *pluralistic* society, and second, the question of improving parenting has been approached from the educational point of view, that is, in relation to both the pedagogical and institutional possibilities of parenting as teaching, and teaching as a supportive service for parenting. Since both these areas figure prominently in the next guidelines to be proposed, and in the recommendations which conclude this chapter, it may be appropriate to review the considerations which have made these two particular areas especially relevant to our discussions.

REDEFINITIONS: THE "FAMILY" AND THE "NEW PLURALISM"

It is still true that 98 percent of all children are raised in a family setting. It is also true that the definition of what constitutes that family has now radically changed. The trend away from the extended family of grandparents, aunts, uncles, cousins, and parents has continued. Very few children now grow up in households which include three or more generations of relatives to offer adult assistance, companionship, or alternative role models. The assumption that relatives are no longer important in child care is, however, a false one: The statistics on child-care arrangements made by working mothers (as reported by Carew) indicate that relatives contribute over one-third of the total child care required (18.9 percent of the caregivers in the home are relatives in place of the mother, slightly more than care given by fathers; additionally 15 percent of the arrangements made for care outside the home are made with relatives). Undoubtedly, the participation of the extended family is more common in some cultural settings than in others, but this form of family cooperation in child care must not be discounted in discussions of family policy.

More highly publicized, at this point, is the instability of the modern nuclear family as evidenced in the growing rate of separation, divorce, and illegitimate births. The one-parent family, most often with a female head of the household who must be supported through her own work outside the home, or by welfare payments (the Carnegie report indicates that only 3 percent of divorced women receive child support or alimony payments sufficient for them to live on without an additional income) is no longer an oddity. "Blended or reconstituted" families through remarriage may establish new kinship systems, but the full emotional effects of these new relationships have not been evaluated adequately. The numbers of unmarried couples living together and of single people living alone are also increasing. The effects of these new domestic arrangements on the child, either as he experiences them directly in the various child-care settings, both institutional and home-centered, or in his psychological awareness of the transitoriness of adult relationships and living situations, have not been entirely understood. Whether they turn out to be harmful or relatively insignificant in child development, we can no longer go on assuming the existence of one model of family and social identification; the functions formerly carried out by the traditional nuclear family are no longer exclusive to that particular form of social organization. The changing patterns of employment, sex roles, cultural values, and the individual expectations for personal growth and family support must be acknowledged and not merely subsumed in an outdated or rigidly ideological model of the family.

Similarly, the old notions of cultural assimilation must be reassessed. Formerly, the concept of pluralism in America was contained in the metaphor of the "melting pot" with each new group losing itself in the mélange of a new society. In practice, the process was less accomodating to non-Anglo-Saxon Protestants than the image had suggested. In his contribution on the black family, Comer has insisted that the study of that group has been often prone to misinterpretation by comparisons with white families who have not undergone the same adaptive changes in dealing with discrimination and exploitation. Comer, for one, argues that any supportive intervention must respect the social organization and coping skills which are appropriate to the exigencies of black life. This suggests an increased sensitivity to the present situations of black families and to their separate historical experience.

In an analogous way, Suzuki laments the deculturalization of Asian-American life. He argues that the institutions of education and mental health have mistakenly failed to realize the successes of Asian-American child-rearing in inculcating family values which may run counter to the accepted norm in terms of individualism and aggressiveness. Ramirez and Cox offer the model of Mexican-American child-rearing as a replacement for the old conflict-replacement model in which ethnic diversity is seen as a problem for society which can only be solved through an assimilative process. According to the authors, the Mexican-American model of a vigorous biculturalism is more flexible, and ultimately enhances the strengths of both the individual and the greater society. Burgess, in his study of native-American communities, concludes in much the same vein, that values which are weak or entirely lacking in the dominant culture are present in native-American parenting: Respect for the elderly, cooperative behavior, and collective organization as opposed to self-assertion are suggested as examples that contribute to a new sense of the American family; he urges, as well, an increased awareness of the very harsh conditions under which the native American must carry out child-rearing.

What all of these viewpoints have in common is a realization that neither the outdated model of the white, middle-class family nor the myth of the old pluralism can provide a workable frame for understanding and assisting human development of minority children. While it is undoubtedly true that some versions of ethnic pride result in idealized or nostalgic versions of a social cohesiveness which is long gone or has never existed, still this sense of worth from cultural difference has communicated a new respect for pluralism which recognizes the value of separate and diverse experience and acknowledges both the responsibilities of groups which have suffered acute hardships in our society and alternatives which they offer for the enrichment of the total society. The third guideline, therefore, is that any social policy recommendation, whether concerned with research or intervention, must be respectful of a new pluralistic concept of the family, and of the diverse cultural models of parenting.

A CURRICULUM FOR CARING:
PARENTS, PROFESSIONALS, AND INSTITUTIONS

Urie Bronfenbrenner (1977), in a recently published interview on the state of the family, has suggested that every child from elementary school onward should become acquainted with human development, including child care and care for the elderly, as a means of fostering the concern and involvement which is expressed in the continued cycle of need and nurture throughout life; he calls this educational course of learning a "curriculum for caring." In many ways, Bronfenbrenner's suggestion is unfashionable: criticism of professional intervention in family life and in particular, of the school system as an instrument of social reform has been severe following what has been for many a disappointing performance in the last decade. Although we would argue that the schools simply mediate the complex relations between the social and political goals of a society and the individuals who must negotiate those aims, and that the overall record of the educational sector in providing access and choice for self-development has been relatively encouraging with regard to the progress of society as a whole, it may nonetheless prove useful to review the assumptions underlying school-reform policy which have been proven faulty, as an introduction to the guidelines on professional and institutional involvement in parenting.

The primary assumption of urban school policy in the 1960's was that there were problem schools and problem learners who needed to be rehabilitated; that is to say, many of our federal policies dealt with identifying the families and students who were not succeeding and concentrating efforts on them. Subsequently, teachers were charged with remedying the situation. The solution recommended was that of *compensatory* services. Thus, if a child was behind in reading, more reading teachers were hired who could offer compensatory instruction; if a child were too disruptive, then we would hire more counselors; if a child had experiential gaps, we would take more field trips. In short, the assumption was that the problem was with the learner and efforts had to be directed at the learner so that he or she would be more able to fit in and therefore succeed in the school. This theory envisioned the learner and family as a type of *pathology* needing corrective intervention. We asked professionals to design programs, and these took the form of more-of-the same, more concentrated remediation. Today, and billions of dollars later, we have reached the uncomfortable verdict that there was "little payoff." That is to say, our compensatory efforts have not had the effects hoped for—poor children are still behind scholastically.

Based on this experience, the assumption has been modified in more recent views of schooling: The problem is now viewed as the institution, not the learner. The task would seem to be to reform the school to fit the learner and not the other way around; the learner and his family are no longer viewed as sick, needing treatment. Rather, the mission is to develop a responsive educational institution—one capable of responding to diversity.

Similarly, the policies being considered for parent strengthening may view the family as "sick" needing special treatment; certainly there are experts who would agree with such a diagnosis. The current opinion is not, however, unanimous; there are those who view the family as pathological, those who view the family as simply changing, and others somewhere between the two. At the level of individual families, any of the possibilities may indeed hold true. The point in developing family policy, as opposed to school policy which has been the case in the past, is to avoid a narrowly rehabilitative approach or one which focuses on the failings of children and their parents at the expense of a more comprehensive evaluation of the social contexts of those "failures."

Professors Cárdenas and Zamora have attacked a related assumption in the school-reform policies of the 1960's: Education was correctly identified as being crucial to the advancement of minorities and this was translated into many programs following upon the passage of the historic Elementary and Secondary Education Act including Head Start, Right to Read, and Follow Through; the success of these programs has been limited; minority children still show poor performance records in school. Cárdenas and Zamora cite many factors which have contributed to this ineffectiveness, but the major factor was that minority children were seen as being not only different "but inferiorly different." In turn, this perception generated a "deficit" educational model which assumed that the middle-class behavioral and learning attitudes would correct this lack in minority children.

Again, there is a lesson to be learned. Many of the more visible problems in the modern family are associated with poor or minority families. In the past, they have been subjected to teachers, social workers, and bureaucrats who have generalized from what is perceived as a curative norm. Experience would seem to indicate that respect for differences and the possibility of community-based choices for any support services is paramount for a workable program.

Reviewing the failures of school reform with regard to black students, Professors Carney and Bowen have insisted that any future planning with regard to social support or change must avoid the "fragmentation" of resources in the short-sighted or narrowly conceived programs of the past. In the first guideline for policy, we emphasized the interconnectedness of social, economic, and psychological factors in parenting. Here we are in agreement as to another application of the principle of comprehensive planning: Any policy on the family not only must be inclusive of the external factors *around* the experience of parenting, but must be comprehensive with regard to the inclusion of people of all classes, ages, and locations. A family policy should not be defined as only a program for the poor or for helpless infants. As Bronfenbrenner has stressed, the needs of adolescents and adults of all ages, particularly the disabled and the aged, continue; a society committed to caring for its young, and offering effective models to them for concerned parenting, cannot afford to be callous with regard to the needs of other dependent citizens. Dr. Brocher has emphasized the cyclical nature of the caring process; we recall the models of our parents in approaching our own children. Good parenting, to the extent that it can be taught well (and it is always *taught*, whether in a formalized setting, at home, through media influence, or by grandparents) must be taught well at every developmental stage.

The preceding observations on the relevance of the experience of school-reform policy for the recommendations for a comprehensive family policy, is by way of preparation for *the fourth guideline, namely, that the schools must be considered central to parenting: first, pedagogically, since parenting is in very essential ways a teaching process, and second, institutionally, since the educational system is closely identified with community participation and offers the personnel, facilities, and capability to provide choices and access to information for all citizens.*

In formulating this guideline, we began with the most obvious fact (offered statistically by Hess): Parents seek advice on their children mainly at school. The school is already the major support service to parents, and in addition, many of the functions of parents are duplicated by teachers in the school setting. Teachers are already involved in parenting. Students take from them, in addition to specialized subject matter, a model of teaching and in a general sense, parenting. The quality of and organization of materials relating to caring for others and the expectations of human developmental processes must, however, be more closely evaluated in developing curricula.

The education of adults who are already parents has up to now encountered some philosophical opposition; we have previously indicated our opposition to any narrow ideological or sociological model for parent education. The information, however, which is not available, concerning nutrition, health, social services, cognitive development, and affective behavior could be more easily disseminated through the schools in optional adult classes, workshops featuring other extended family members, community advocates, paraprofessionals and professionals, and through resource centers to coordinate the social, legal, political, and psychological support services available to parents within the greater community. *The emphasis in the involvement of schools is on alternatives and options which respect the cultural values of parents—freely accessible choices for members of families of all ages and circumstances.*

In conclusion, the following recommendations for a comprehensive national policy on youth and parenting are offered in the framework of the guidelines elaborated above.

I. Economic support of children through the economic support of their families, including a vigorous policy of antidiscrimination toward minorities and toward women who are increasingly the partial or sole sources of family support. Recommendations:
   A. Employment
      1. To protect children and their families there must be an economic policy of full employment which guarantees a job for every willing worker at a minimum wage adequate for the maintenance of a decent standard of living.
      2. There must be an end to wage and job discrimination for women and minorities so that they can adequately support their families.
   B. Organization of Work and Working Conditions
      1. As increasing numbers of women are required to work and increasing numbers of men choose to devote themselves to child care and supervision, more flexible work schedules must be developed to accomodate these needs and give parents more time to spend with their children.
      2. Maternity leaves must be protected in the negotiation of health care insurance at a national level.
      3. Leaves of absence for fathers must be optional.
      4. Day-care facilities must be made available at the place of work or nearby within the community.
      5. Business, labor, and government should cooperate in developing these programs through a national commission on the family and child care.
   C. Housing
      1. More and better low-income housing must be made available so that a minimum level of comfort is possible for every family.
      2. Housing projects should be integrated with regard to class, race, and age.
   D. Welfare and Tax Reform
      1. The welfare system must be reformed so that fathers are not encouraged to leave their homes in order to entitle their families to higher benefits.
      2. The tax structure must be restructured so as to remove the disparity between married and unmarried persons in the rate of taxation.
   E. Health Care
      1. A national health-care program, guaranteeing the right to adequate medical attention, including psychological services, to every citizen from birth onward.

2. Health-care centers should be located in every community or in close proximity by public transportation.
3. Information concerning the physical development of children and their nutritional and psychological needs should be available at health-care centers or in a resource center at a local school.

II. Research should be promoted which works toward a comprehensive understanding of both universals—material and psychological—in parenting in the further delineation of the specific sociocultural factors which affect the process.

   A. A systematic review of research and research methodologies on parenting and family life should be given institutional or governmental support.
   B. A systematic review of the existing parent-education programs should be supported.
   C. The adequacy of present child-care facilities should be evaluated to establish standards for community management.
   D. Research into the impact of current legislation on families and children should be initiated at the national level and be made available for public debate.
   E. Information regarding the present state of research into effective parenting should be made available to the public, including information concerning the limitations of such research for immediate application.
   F. Parents should be given an opportunity to formulate the questions of research interest which seem more crucial to their particular cultural or individual experience.
   G. Parents and other family members should have the opportunity to react in public forums to the programs and proposals which directly effect their lives.

III. Any social-policy recommendations whether concerned with research or intervention, must be respectful of a new pluralistic concept of the family and of the diverse cultural models of parenting.

   A. The special needs of the single-parent family must be determined and met by support services if necessary.
   B. The role of foster parents should be supported by funding and information services, so that as many children as possible can grow up outside an institutional setting.
   C. Minority groups should have a strong role in planning and evaluating programs which effect their families.
   D. Community day-care centers should be available at a subsidized or reduced fee for parents who must work.
   E. Child care within the home should be subsidized in order to provide for the payment of neighbors or extended-family members who provide this service.
   F. Age segregation should be discouraged by the maintenance of paid or volunteer positions for aging and retired persons in schools and child-care facilities.
   G. Coordination of social services should be administered within the community, respecting the various forms of family life, language, and cultural values.
   H. Greater commitment must be made to those structures which constitute the primary supports of the family—neighborhoods, and community programs centered around school, church, or recreational facilities.

I. Every effort must be made to respect multicultural and multisocial models of family life in policy statements, textbooks, and television programming.

IV. Schools must be considered central to parenting: First, pedagogically, since parenting is, in very essential ways, a teaching process; and second, institutionally, since the educational system is closely identified with community participation and offers the personnel, facilities, and capabilities to provide choices in support services and access to information. (See Hess, table 10.2, p. 155, indicating parents most likely to seek advice from children's teachers.)

A. Every child should be involved from elementary school in a "curriculum for caring" which would include information on human development at every level and encourage a sensitivity to the needs of others. Obviously, at higher levels of schooling, this would include more advanced information on child care, family life in its various forms, and psychological, social, and economic facts to prepare students realistically for the job of supporting and nurturing other family members.

B. Parent-education courses which include the available information concerning effective parenting should be offered in every community.

C. Family workshops organized to discuss the problems of child care and family life with professionals from the areas of social work, law, medicine, mental health, education, labor, industry, and government should be offered regularly.

D. Schools should develop information and referral systems to facilitate access to support services and inform parents as to the choices available.

E. Textbooks, tapes, and educational television should continue to address the problems of changing and diverse patterns of child-rearing.

F. Parent-teacher organizations should be regularly organized so as to include public debate on legislation or program proposals which may affect family life in the community.

G. In the institutions of higher education, research, and programs to study the state of the art of parenting with a view to informed recommendations concerning curricula or pedagogy should be encouraged.

Finally, the recommendations offered must include a mechanism for the evaluation of governmental policy on the issues related to the family. Therefore, a presidential advisory board should be organized to regularly report directly to the President, on those issues affecting family policy. This board, comprised of professionals, paraprofessionals, and concerned citizens would act as advocates for American children and their families in the review and formulation of all relevant government policy.

The preceding recommendations have been developed in good faith from our present understanding of the parenting process and deserve serious consideration. We believe, if implemented, that they will improve parenting and family life and consequently provide the framework for a just society.

BIBLIOGRAPHY

Bronfenbrenner, U. "Nobody Home: The Erosion of the American Family," *Psychology Today,* May 1977, Vol. 10, No. 12.

Etzioni, A. "The Family: Is It Obsolete?" *Journal of CurrentSocial Issues,* Winter 1977, Vol. 14.

Keniston, K. *All Our Children.* Report of the Carnegie Council on Children, New York: Harcourt Brace Jovanovich, 1977.

Appendix A
Selected Bibliography

Ames, Louise B. *Child Care and Development.* Philadelphia: Lippincott, 1970.

Anchor, K. and Anchor, F. "School Failure and Parental Involvement in an Ethnically Mixed School: A Survey." *Journal of Community Psychology,* 1974, *2,* 265–267.

Auerbach, S. (ed.). *Child Care: A Comprehensive Guide Vol. II: Model Programs and Their Components.* New York: Human Sciences Press, 1976.

Bane, Mary Jo. *Here to Stay: American Families in the Twentieth Century.* New York: Basic Books, Inc., 1976.

Beck, Helen L. *Don't Push Me, I'm No Computer—How Pressures to "Achieve" Harm Pre-School Children.* New York: McGraw Hill, 1973.

Bell, T. H. *An Educator Looks at Parenting.* Speech given at a Joint Regional Parenting Conference sponsored by the National Conference of Parents and Teachers and the National Foundation-March of Dimes. Washington, D.C., 1976.

Benson, J. and Ross, L. "Teaching Parents to Teach Their Children." *Teaching Exceptional Children,* 1972, *5,* 30–35.

Breiling, A. "Using Parents as Teaching Partners." *Educational Digest,* 1977, *42,* 50–52.

Brodsky, I. *The World's Newest Profession.* Philadelphia: The Profession of Parenting Institute, 1975.

Bronfenbrenner, U. "Nobody Home: The Erosion of the American Family." *Psychology Today,* May 1977, Vol. 10, No. 12.

Brown, Susan and Kornhauser, Pat. *Working Parents: How to Be Happy with Your Children.* Atlanta: Humanics Press, 1977.

Cahir, Stephen. *Selected Bibliography on Mexican American and Native American Bilingual Education in the Southwest.* Las Cruces: ERIC/CRESS, 1975.

Callahan, Sidney Cornelia. *Parenting: Principles and Politics of Parenthood.* New York: Doubleday and Co., 1973.

Children and the Public Responsibility. Washington, D.C.: Day Care and Child Development Council of America, 1972.

Chrisman, Robert (ed.). "The Black Family," *The Black Scholar,* 1974, *5,* (9), 66p.

Christenberry, Mary Anne and Wirtz, Paul J. *A Strategy for Locating and Building Support Systems for the Expectant and the New Parent.* Paper presented at "Toward the Competent Parent: An Interdisciplinary Conference on Parenting." Atlanta, 1977.

Coletta, Anthony. *Working Together: A Guide to Parent Involvement.* Atlanta: Humanistics Limited, 1977.

Collins, Alice H. and Watson, Eunice L. *Family Day Care: A Practical Guide for Parents, Caregivers, and Professionals.* Boston: Beacon Press, 1976.

Commentaries on Family and Society Films. Newton: Education Development Center, 1974.

Daniel, J. H. and Hyde, J. N. "Working with High-Risk Families: Family Advocacy and the Parent Education Program." *Children Today,* 1975, *5,* 23–25.

Datta, L. E. *Parent Involvement in Early Childhood Education: A Perspective From the U. S.* Washington, D.C.: National Institute of Education, 1973.

Davies, D. (ed.). *Schools Where Parents Make a Difference.* Boston: Institute for Responsive Education, 1976.

Day Care Today. Minnesota: Polymorth Films, 1976. (Film)

de Lone, Richard H. *Small Futures: Inequality, Children and the Failure of Liberal Reform.* New York: Harcourt Brace Jovanovich or Academic Press, 1979.

Directory for the Child Care Advocate. Washington, D.C.: Day Care and Child Development Council of America, 1974.

Dunmore, Charlotte J. *Black Children and Their Families: A Bibliography.* San Francisco: R & E Research Associates, 1976.

Dunn, Lynne P. *American Indians: A Study Guide and Sourcebook.* San Francisco: R & E Research Associates, 1975.

Dunn, Lynne P. *Black Americans: A Study Guide and Sourcebook.* San Francisco: R & E Research Associates, 1975.

Durrett, Mary Ellen et. al. "Child-Rearing Reports of White, Black and Mexican-American Families." *Developmental Psychology,* 1975, 11 (6), 871–872.

The Economy and the Child: Parenthood in America. New York: Parents' Magazine Films 1976. (5 filmstrips w/cassettes or records.)

Elardo, Richard and Pagan, Betty (eds.). *Perspectives on Infant Day Care.* Orangeburg, S. C.: Southern Association of Children Under Six, 1976.

Etzioni, A. "The Family: Is It Obsolete?" *Journal of Current Social Issues,* Winter 1977, Vol. 14.

Fedder, Ruth and Gabaldon, Jacqueline. *No Longer Deprived: Use of Minority Cultures and Language in Education of Disadvantaged Children.* New York: Teachers College Press, 1970.

Ferguson, D. H. "Can Your School Survive a Parent Evaluation?" *National Elementary Principal.* 1977, *56,* 71–73.

Fisher, Seymour and Fisher, Rhoda L. *What We Really Know about Child Rearing: Science in Support of Effective Parenting.* New York: Basic Books, 1976.

Gesell, Arnold; Ilg, Frances L.; and Ames, Louise B. *Infant and Child in the Culture of Today.* New York: Harper and Row, rev. ed., 1974.

Gilberg, Arnold L. *"The Stress of Parenting." Child Psychiatry and Human Development,* 1975, *6,* (2), 59–67.

Gliedman, John and Roth, William. *Handicapped Children in America.* New York: Harcourt Brace Jovanovich or Academic Press, 1979.

Goad, Marcine. *Every Parent's Guide to Day Care Centers.* Chatsworth, Ca.: Books for Better Living, 1975.

Gordon, I. J. "What Do We Know About Parents as Teachers?" *Theory Into Practice,* 1972, *11,* 146–149.

Grando, Roy and Ginsberg, Barry G. "Communication in the Father-Son Relationship: The Parent-Adolescent Relationship Development Program." *Family Coordinator,* 1976, *25* (4), 465–473.

Greenberg, Kenneth R. *A Tiger by the Tail; Parenting in a Troubled Society.* Chicago: Nelson Hall, 1974.

Grumbaum, E. "Parental Involvement." *Instructor,* 1975, *84,* 72.

Harrison-Ross, Phyllis, and Wyden, Barbara. *The Black Child: A Parent's Guide.* New York: Peter Wyden, Inc., 1973.

Hess, R. D. *Effectiveness of Home-Based Early Education Programs.* Paper presented at the annual convention of the American Psychological Association, Washington, D.C. 1976.

Hiemstra, R. "Educating Parents in the Use of the Community." *Adult Leadership,* 1974, *23,* 85–88.

The Home School New Educational Partnership. Washington, D. C.: Home and School Institute, Inc., 1974.

Implementing Child Development Programs: Report of an August 1974 Symposium. Denver: Education Commission of the States, 1974.

Inglis, Ruth Langdon. *A Time to Learn: A Guide for Parents to the New Theories in Early Childhood Education.* New York: Dial Press, 1973.

James, Shirley M. *Living with Children in Transition: Resources for Parents of Pre and Early Adolescents.* Paper presented at "Toward the Competent Parent: An Interdisciplinary Conference on Parenting," Atlanta, 1977.

Jeffers, Camille. "Child Rearing Among Low Income Families in the District of Columbia," a project sponsored by the Health and Welfare Council of the National Capital Area, National Institute of Mental Health Grant 5-R11-Mh278-5.

Johnson, D. L. *Parent Education and the Educationally Disadvantaged Child.* Paper presented at the annual meeting of the American Psychological Association, Washington, D.C., 1976.

Johnson, E. "The Home-School Partnership Model For Follow Through." *Theory Into Practice,* 1977, *16,* (1), 35–40.

Kaplan, L. "Survival Talk for Educators-Parent Involvement." *Journal of Teacher Education,* 1976, *27,* 167–168.

Kappelman, Murray and Ackerman, Paul. *Between Parent and School.* New York: Dial Press, 1977.

Keniston, K. *All Our Children.* Report of the Carnegie Council on Children, New York: Harcourt Brace Jovanovich, 1977.

Kimmel, C. "Parent Power: A Plus for Education." *Educational Leadership,* 1976, *34,* 24–25.

Kruger, W. Stanley. "Education for Parenthood and School-Age Parents." *Journal of School Health,* 1975, *45,* (5), 292–295.

Lane, M. B. *Education for Parenting,* Urbana: ERIC Clearinghouse on Early Childhood Education, 1974.

Leichter, Hope (ed.). *The Family as Educator.* New York: Teachers College Press, 1974.

Levine, Milton I. and Seligmann, Jean H. *The Parent's Encyclopedia of Infancy, Childhood and Adolescence.* New York: Crowell, 1973.

Lillie, David and Trohanis, Pascal (ed.). *Teaching Parents to Teach.* New York: Walker and Company, 1976.

Masse, N. and Deschamps, J. P. "Child Development Indicators and Public Health." *Carnets de l'Enfance,* 1975, (32), 18–32.

Massoglia, Elinor T. *Early Childhood Education in the Home.* Albany: Delmar Publishers, 1977.

Mattox, B. and Rich, D. "Community Involvement Activities: Research Into Action." *Theory Into Practice.* 1977, *16* (1), 29–34.

Maynard, Fredelle. *Guiding Your Child to a More Creative Life.* New York: Doubleday, 1973.

McDowell, R. L. "Parent Counseling: The State of the Art," *Journal of Learning Disabilities,* 1976, *9,* 614–619.

Mead, Margaret. The Heritage of Children in the United States." *Journal of Current Social Issues,* 1975, *12* (3), 4–8.

Meijer, J. *Current Status and Future Prospects for the Nation's Children and their Families.* Paper presented at the annual convention of the National Association for the Education of Young Children, Anaheim, California, 1976.

Melton, D. H. *Career Education and Your Child: A Guide for Parents.* Bradenton, Fla: Florida Career Education Consortium, 1976.

Mondale, Walter F. "Anticipating the Needs of Families and Children." *Journal of Current Social Issues,* 1975, *12* (3), 20–23.

Morrow, L. A. and Worth, Richard. *The Future of the Family.* New York: Guidance Associates, 1972. (Filmstrip w/cassettes.)

Mussen, Paul Henry; Conger, John Jay and Kagan, Jerome. *Child Development and Personality.* 3rd edition. New York: Harper, 1969, p. 16.

Nuttall, Ena V. and Nuttall, Ronald L. *Parent-Child Relationships and Effective Academic Motivation.* Paper presented at the annual meeting of the American Educational Research Association. San Francisco, 1976.

O'Connell, Christine Y. "Helping Parents with Their Children." *Today's Education,* 1976, *65* (4), 43–44.

Ogbu, John U. *Minority Education and Caste: The American System in Cross-Cultural Perspective.* New York: Academic Press, 1978.

Ogg, Elizabeth. *Preparing Tomorrow's Parents.* New York: Public Affairs Committee, Inc., 1975.

Ogletree, Earl J. and Garcia, David. *Education of the Spanish-Speaking Urban Child.* Springfield: Charles C. Thomas, 1975.

Otto, Herbert A. (ed.). *The Family in Search of a Future: Alternate Models for Moderns.* Englewood Cliffs, N. J., Prentice-Hall, 1970.

Parent Education: A Teacher's Guide. Los Angeles: Los Angeles City Schools/Division of Career and Continuing Education, 1975.

Parenthood Today and Tomorrow: Parenthood in America. New York: Parents' Magazine Films, 1976. (Film)

Parenting in 1976: A Listing from PMIC. Austin: Southwest Educational Development Laboratory, 1976.

Perrone, V. "Parents as Partners." *Urban Review,* 1971, *5,* 35–40.

Platt, Marguerite Beer. *The Economics of Parenthood: Understanding Parenthood.* New York: Parents' Magazine Press, 1974. (5 filmstrips w/cassette or records.)

Prescott, Elizabeth, et. al. *The Politics of Day Care.* Washington, D.C.: NAEYC, 1972.

Report of the Committee on Labor and Public Welfare, *U. S. Senate Special Sub-Committee on Indian Education.* "Indian Education: A National Tragedy—A National Challenge," U.S. Government Printing Office, Washington, D.C., 1969.

Rich, D. and Jones, C. *A Family Affair: Education.* Washington, D.C.: The Home and School Institute, 1977.

The Role of the Family in Child Development: Implications for State Policies and Programs. Denver: Education Commission of the States, 1975.

The Role of Parents as Teachers. Philadelphia: Recruitment Leadership and Training Institute, 1975.

The Role of Parents as Teachers. Pueblo, Co.: Public Documents Distribution Center, 1975.

Rosser, Pearl L. *Mental Health of Black Children.* Paper presented at the annual meeting of the American Psychological Association, Washington, D.C., 1976.

Satir, Virginia, et. al. *Helping Families to Change.* New York: Jason Aronson, Inc., 1975.

Schwartz, J. L. Social and Emotional Effects of Day Care: A Review of Recent Research. Paper presented to the Society for Research in Child Development Study Group on the Family, Ann Arbor, Michigan, October, 1975.

Schwartz, J. L.; Strickland, R. G. and Krolick, G. Infant Day Care: Behavioral Effects at Preschool Age. *Developmental Psychology,* 1974, *10,* 502–506.

Schulz, David A. *The Changing Family: Its Function and Future.* Englewood Cliffs, N. J., Prentice-Hall, 1972.

Seligman, M. E. P. *Helplessness.* San Francisco: W. H. Freeman & Co., 1975.

Steinmetz, Suzanne K. and Straus, Murray A. *Violence in the Family.* New York: Dodd Mead & Co., 1974.

Stern, Carolyn. *Increasing the Effectiveness of Parents As Teachers.* Arlington: ERIC Document Reproduction Service, 1971.

Toward Comprehensive Child Care. Washington D.C.: Day Care and Child Development Council of America, 1974.

Unger, Steven (ed.). *The Destruction of American Indian Families.* New York: Association on American Indian Affairs, 1977.

Wenar, Charles. *Personality Development from Infancy to Adulthood.* Boston: Houghton Mifflin, 1971.

Appendix B
For Further Information

A selected and by no means all-inclusive list of agencies, which may be consulted by professionals and laymen alike for more information about various aspects of parenting follows.

East Coast

Appalachia Educational Laboratory, Inc.
P. O. Box 1348
Charleston, West Virginia 25325

Association for Childhood Education
3615 Wisconsin Avenue, N. W.
Washington, D.C. 20016

Center for Parenting Studies
Wheelock College
45 Pilgrim Road
Boston, Massachusetts 02215

Citizen Involvement Network
1216 Connecticut Avenue, N. W.
Washington, D.C. 20036

Citizens Alliance for Public Education
P. O. Box 41
Wilmington, Delaware 19899

Coalition for Children and Youth
1910 K Street, N. W.
Washington, D.C. 20036

Day Care and Child Development Council of America, Inc.
1012 14th Street, N. W.
Washington, D. C. 20005

Federal Community Education Clearinghouse
6000 Executive Boulevard
Rockville, Maryland 20852

Home and School Institute
Trinity College
Washington, D.C. 20017

Institute for Responsive Education
704 Commonwealth Avenue
Boston, Massachusetts 02215

Massachusetts Education Center
101 Mill Road
Chelmsford, Massachusetts 01824

National Association for the Education of Young Children
1834 Connecticut Avenue, N. W.
Washington, D.C. 20009

National Clearinghouse for Volunteers
1735 I Street, N. W.
Washington, D.C. 20006

National Coalition of ESEA Title I Parents
1010 Vermont Avenue, N. W.
Washington, D.C. 20005

National Coalition of ESEA Title I Parents
414 West Sixth Street
Wilmington, Delaware 19801

National Committee for Citizens in Education
Suite 410
Wilde Lake Village Green
Columbia, Maryland 21044

National School Volunteer Program, Inc.
300 North Washington Street
Alexandria, Virginia 22314

New England Center for Community Education
University of Connecticut
U – 142
Storrs, Connecticut 06268

Research for Better Schools, Inc.
1700 Market Street, Suite 1700
Philadelphia, Pennsylvania 19103

Schoolwatch
104 North Broad Street
Trenton, New Jersey 08608

Southeastern Public Education Program
American Friends Service
52 Fairlie Street, N. W.
Atlanta, Georgia 30344

Midwest

CEMREL, Inc.
3120 59th Street
St. Louis, Missouri 63139

Citizens Council for Ohio Schools
517 The Arcade
Cleveland, Ohio 44114

Home/School/Community Relations Project
Room 562
Wisconsin Research and Development Project
1025 West Johnson Street
Madison, Wisconsin 53706

Mid-Continent Regional Educational Laboratory
7302 Pennsylvania Avenue
Kansas City, Missouri 64114

Minnesota Early Learning Design
123 East Grant Street
Minneapolis, Minnesota 55403

National Congress of Parents and Teachers
700 North Rush Street
Chicago, Illinois 60611

National Information Center on Volunteerism
P. O. Box 4179
Boulder, Colorado 80203

Parents As A Resource
464 Central Avenue
Northfield, Illinois 60093

Pendell Books
P. O. Box 1666R
Midland, Michigan 48640

Southwest

Southwest Educational Development Laboratory
Parenting Materials Information Center
211 East Seventh Street
Austin, Texas 78701

West Coast

Center for Educational Research
School of Education
Stanford University
Stanford, California 94305

Center for the Study of Parent Involvement
5420 Boyd Street
Oakland, California 94618

Far West Lab for Educational Research and Development
1855 Folsom Street
San Francisco, California 94103

National School Volunteer Program
450 North Grand Avenue
Los Angeles, California 90051

Northwest Regional Education Laboratory
710 S. W. Second Avenue
Lindsay Building
Portland, Oregon 97204

Index